W9-BJE-193

HANDBOOKS

ACADIA
NATIONAL PARK

HILARY NANGLE

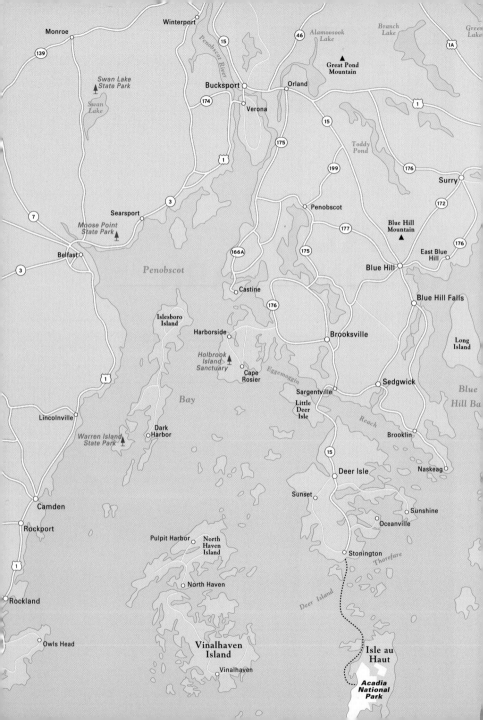

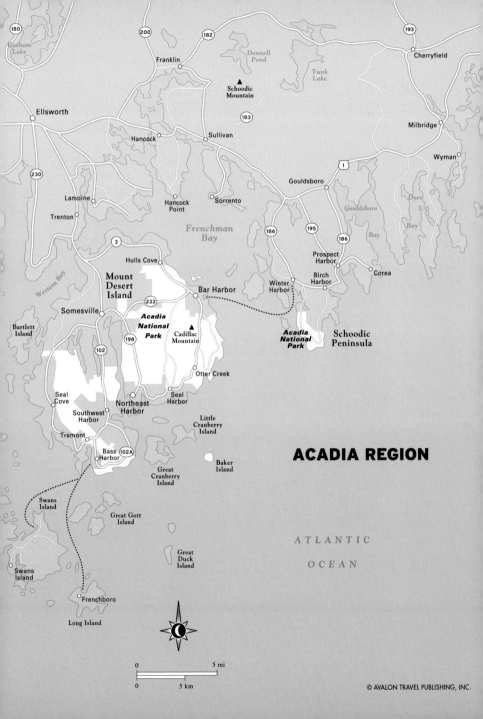

ACADIA REGION

DISCOVER
ACADIA NATIONAL PARK

Acadia National Park is a miniature masterpiece, a gem of a natural and cultural resource that dangles like a pendant just south of the mainland. Some 30,000 of its 46,000 or so acres fit into a Maine island that's only 15 miles from north to south and 12 miles from west to east.

If stretched taut, Hancock County – with Acadia as its center-piece – would have more than 1,000 miles of coastline. No saltwater locale on the entire eastern seaboard can compete with the variety of scenery on Mount Desert Island. The vistas from the park's 26 mostly open summits look out onto ocean, lighthouses, boats, and dozens of islands near and far.

Within and beyond the park's boundaries, you can hike and bike, paddle and picnic, swim and stroll, camp and climb. With Acadia's

carriage road, Mount Desert Island

© TOM NANGLE

130 miles of hiking trails and 57 miles of car-free carriage roads (created between 1913 and 1940 by John D. Rockefeller, Jr.) you'll never run out of ways to play. Best of all, you can temper your choices to your abilities, desires, and fitness level.

Of course you're going to travel the Park Loop Road, which takes in many of the park's Must See sights, including Sieur de Monts Spring, Sand Beach, Thunder Hole, and Cadillac Mountain—but how you do so is up to you. Pedal it on a bicycle, drive through in a car, or enjoy a narrated tour. Stop for tea and popovers at the Jordan Pond House, before walking or bicycling the famed carriage roads or after a hike.

Take a leisurely walk along the Jesup Path or Ocean Train. Ratchet up the difficulty a bit with a hike up Great Head or Gorham

Sand Beach, Mount Desert Island

Mountain. Serious hikers can challenge themselves on the park's famed ladder trails. Then there's the Carriage Trail network – another must, whether on foot, on a bicycle, or in a horse-drawn carriage.

While it's easy to stay and play in the east side of the park, the quiet west side awaits, with more hiking trails, ponds for boating, a much-photographed lighthouse, and a lovely picnic spot with a put-in for kayakers and other boaters.

If you're at all nervous about exploring the park on your own, you don't have to. Acadia's rangers lead a variety of fun programs that immerse you in the park and let you learn a bit about its cultural and natural elements. Consider an early morning birding walk, a guided bike ride on the carriage roads, or an easy, kid-oriented family hike.

Fringing the island is the park's support network – the towns and villages where you'll find beds, bars, food, shops, boat cruises, and a handful of small museums. The contrast with Acadia's lakes

Great Head

and woodlands is astonishing, as the park struggles to maintain its image and character.

Bar Harbor, the largest and best-known of the island's communities, is the source of just about anything you could want (if not need), from T-shirts to tacos, books to bike and kayak rentals. You can go lobster fishing, whale-watching, or sailing, and many of these adventures have tours narrated by park rangers – a real plus.

Elsewhere on the island are Southwest Harbor, Tremont (including Bass Harbor and Bernard), and the town of Mount Desert, encompassing the villages of Northeast Harbor, Seal Harbor, Otter Creek, Somesville, Pretty Marsh, Beech Hill, and Hall Quarry. From Bass, Northeast, and Southwest Harbors, private and state ferries shuttle bike and foot traffic to offshore Swans Island, Frenchboro (Long Island), and the Cranberry Isles, and cars to Swans Island. Each town and island has its calling cards: small museums, roads for

Isle au Haut Light

mountain biking, boat-filled harbors, and of course, lobster shacks or, in some cases, palaces.

Beyond Mount Desert, don't miss the park's splendid acreage on the mainland Schoodic Peninsula and offshore Isle au Haut. Schoodic has its own look, with pink granite shores at the peninsula's tip the biggest reward. Like the mainland, you can either drive or hike to Schoodic Head's summit for gull's eye views up and down the coast. Isle au Haut, accessible only by boat, is magical. It's well off the beaten path, with good hiking and primitive lean-to camping or, for a real treat, stay in the lighthouse keeper's house, now a bed-and-breakfast. Wend your way to Isle au Haut through the Blue Hill Peninsula and Deer Isle, and to Schoodic through Hancock and Sullivan, all areas prized by artists and artisans and dotted with studios and galleries.

A recent quote put this area in its proper contemporary perspective: "Maine is so lovely," a British visitor to Acadia sighed nostalgically, "I do wish England had fought harder to keep it."

Sieur du Monts Spring

Contents

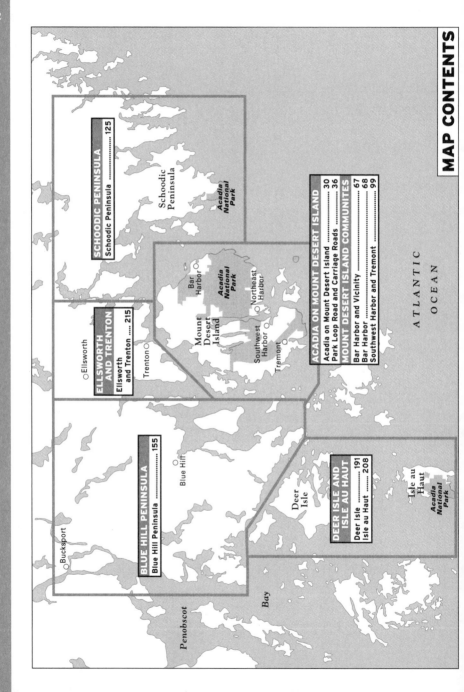

MAP CONTENTS

Schoodic
Peninsula

Acadia National Park

Bar Harbor

Acadia National Park

Northeast Harbor

Mount Desert Island

Southwest Harbor

Tremont

ATLANTIC OCEAN

Ellsworth

Trenton

Blue Hill

Deer Isle

Isle au Haut

Acadia National Park

Bucksport

Penobscot Bay

The Lay of the Land

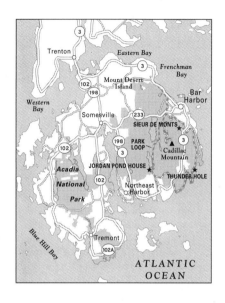

ACADIA ON MOUNT DESERT ISLAND

When most folks think of Acadia, this is the section of the park they're contemplating. The images are iconic: mountains tumbling to the sea, ocean waves crashing upon granite ledges, serene ponds and wildflower-filled meadowlands. Best of all, it's accessible. Get a taste of the park by pedaling or driving the **Park Loop,** taking in sights such as **Sieur de Monts Spring, Sand Beach, Thunder Hole,** and **Cadillac Mountain.** Venture a bit by walking or riding the famed **carriage roads,** hiking an easy trail, or canoeing across a quiet pond. Or kayak along undeveloped coastline and scale soaring cliffs. No matter which way you choose to explore, make time for one of its most civilized institutions: Tea and popovers at the **Jordan Pond House.**

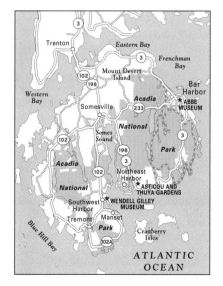

MOUNT DESERT ISLAND COMMUNITIES

While the park is what attracts most people to Mount Desert Island, there is much more to see and do in the surrounding communities than just eat and sleep. **Somes Sound** is a rare fjord; the **Abbe Museum** traces Maine's Native American history; the **Wendell Gilley Museum** is a testament to one man's craftsmanship and a must for bird-watchers; the **Oceanarium** educates visitors about Maine's lobster industry; **Asticou** and **Thuya** gardens show that the wilds of Acadia can be tamed. It's also easy to see the region by boat, perhaps on a **whale-watching** excursion or with **Diver Ed,** who exposes the mysteries of the deep; on a nature-oriented cruise with Island Cruises; or simply by taking a passenger ferry to the **Cranberry Isles** for a taste of island life.

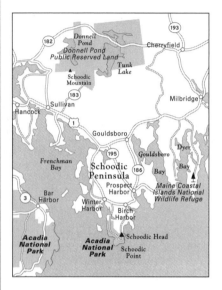

SCHOODIC PENINSULA

Everything changes when you continue north on Route 1. This is a region where independence reigns. If you think you've fully experienced Acadia on Mount Desert—you haven't. The pink-granite shores of **Schoodic Point** are undoubtedly the highlight of the park's **Schoodic Loop,** which skirts around the point. Still, the hike up **Schoodic Head** is well worth the effort for the outstanding views. More outdoor pleasures await at the **Donnell Pond Public Reserved Land,** a 15,000-plus acre preserve which offers hiking, canoeing, fishing, and camping, plus the **Maine Coastal Islands National Wildlife Refuge,** a bonanza for bird-watchers. Art lovers can easily while away a day **gallery hopping** in Hancock and Sullivan.

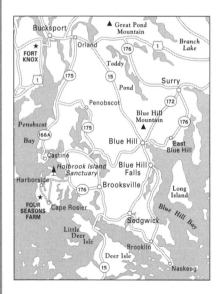

BLUE HILL PENINSULA

While the Blue Hill peninsula isn't part of the park, it shares many qualities that make the park special. It's home to back-to-the-land movement pioneers Helen and Scott Nearing, whose **Good Life Center** continues to espouse their values. The **Four Season Farm,** renowned among organic gardeners, continues the tradition. History is palpable in **Castine,** where signs throughout the beautifully preserved town explain its turbulent past. Another sign of that past is **Fort Knox,** which protected the all-important Penobscot River from invaders. Shaking up the relative quiet of the peninsula is the **Flash in the Pans Community Steel Band. Sea kayaking** is excellent from Castine; trails lace the **Holbrook Island Sanctuary,** which is also popular with bird-watchers; and hikers can summit **Blue Hill Mountain** for a 360-degree view.

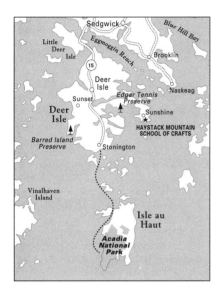

DEER ISLE AND ISLE AU HAUT

Cross the bridge over Eggemoggin Reach to Deer Isle, a community presided over by fisherfolk. **Arts and crafts galleries** are abundant, thanks to talented artists lured here by the **Haystack Mountain School of Crafts.** Preserves such as the **Edgar Tennis Preserve** and the **Barred Island Preserve** dot the island. Walk the easy trails, watch for eagles and osprey, and plan a picnic on the rocky shorefronts. **Sea kayaking** is one of the best ways to explore or book a tour with Capt. Walter Reid's **Guided Island tours.** From Stonington, it's a short boat ride to Isle au Haut, where the most remote and rugged piece of Acadia National Park awaits hikers and those for whom even Deer Isle is a bit too crowded.

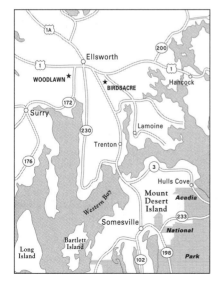

ELLSWORTH AND TRENTON

If you're going to visit Acadia, you must pass through Ellsworth. While the small city is best known for its traffic-clogged, curse-inducing strip, there are a few gems here. Fans of historic homes shouldn't miss **Woodlawn,** a Georgian mansion with carriage houses, gardens, and walking trails. More trails await at **Birdsacre,** the former home of ornithologist Cornelia Stanwood, now a preserve, with nature and bird rehab centers. At the **Great Maine Lumberjack Show,** Tina Scheer and her crew amaze the children and adults with their ax- and log-rolling skills and other timber-cutter's traditions. And if you want a better understanding of the Acadia region's convoluted coastline, get an eagle's-eye view with an **aerial tour** in a glider, bi-plane, or small plane.

Planning Your Trip

When most folks refer to Acadia National Park, they're thinking of Mount Desert Island (MDI). Indeed, MDI is home to the largest and most dramatic section of the park, but two key outposts also beckon—Isle au Haut and the Schoodic Peninsula—and each has its own siren song. While the park is the reason for your visit, once here, you'll probably want time to explore the regions that connect the sections of the park. Which is all to say, if you want to do it all, you need to do your homework. And if your time is limited, you need to determine your priorities.

What's the best way to get to Acadia National Park, you ask? Drop in by parachute. Next best choice? Probably fly from Boston to the Bar Harbor Airport and take a bus or taxi from there to your lodging site. Most popular choices? Flying into Bangor or Portland, renting a car, and driving. But much depends on where you're starting, when you're coming, how long you plan to stay, and what else you plan to do while you're here.

How long should you stay at Acadia? Well, you can get a feel for the park on a daylong visit to Mount Desert Island, but an ideal minimum stay would be three or four days. Enough time to take a hike or two, visit a museum, bike a stretch of the carriage roads, go whale-watching or sailing, and sample some appealing restaurants.

Staying a week allows you to explore the park's major outlying sections—the Schoodic Peninsula and offshore Isle au Haut. You'll have no trouble filling the days with hikes, picnics, shopping, sea kayaking, and gallery hopping.

If time and budget allow, plan one to two weeks on MDI: four days to a week for the Blue Hill region—including the Isle au Haut section of the park—and another three days for Schoodic. If the fog rolls in, settle in with a book or hit the galleries, museums, and shops. And when the sun shines, opt for more hikes, more bike rides, a horse-drawn carriage ride, a few more museums, and a beach day.

WHEN TO GO

Realistically, Acadia National Park is a three-season park (spring, summer, and fall), even though it's open in winter for cross-country skiing, snowshoeing, snowmobiling (with some restrictions), and even camping. Peak travel time for Acadia is July Fourth to Labor Day, with the absolute peak around the first week in August, when it's insane to show up without a room or campsite reservation. (Why spend valuable vacation time hanging out at information centers or making the rounds of lodgings to find a vacant room or site? Plan ahead.)

Spring tends to be something of a blip in Maine; the park starts reawakening only around mid- to late April, when the entire Park Loop Road has reopened (including the Cadillac Mountain road). Even then, some of the carriage roads tend to be fragile and open only for foot traffic, not for bicycles. Trails can be muddy, and ice still coats some of the rocks, but you'll be rewarded by hardy wildflowers poking up here and there. Until about mid-May, you'll also be spared from annoying black flies. In May, the weather can be unpredictable—cold and rainy one day, dramatically clear and sunny the next—and some lodgings still haven't opened for the season.

Summer kicks off with a Memorial Day burst in late May, but June is relatively quiet until the end of the month, when schools release their captives. If you yearn to be car-free on Mount Desert, plan to be here in summer, particularly between late June and mid-October, when Acadia's Island Explorer shuttle service operates. (If you're arriving by RV, without a car in tow, the Island Explorer buses are a major asset.) Summer means lots of festivals and fairs, nightlife in Bar Harbor, nature tours, concerts (jazz, classical, pops), carriage rides, hiking, and whale-watching trips.

Fall is fantastic in the park and on the island—it's my favorite season here. Nights are cool (mid-40s to mid-50s), days are (often) brilliant, and the fall-foliage vistas are dramatic (visit www.mainefoliage.com). The grapevine has spread the word, though, so you won't be alone—but the visitor headcount is still far lower than in July and August.

The **Atlantic hurricane season** runs from June 1 to November, and even though Maine is almost literally at the end of the tracks, tropical storms and hurricanes can affect Maine's weather, particularly in September and October. As with any other weather situation in Maine, it's a crapshoot, so always stay on top of weather information when hurricanes start moving northward along the Atlantic coast.

WHAT TO TAKE

The adage "If you don't like the weather, wait a minute," certainly applies to Maine. I've seen June days that begin in the 70s and finish in the 30s. Similarly, it can be 80°F and sunny a mile or so inland and damp and foggy on the coast. A coastal breeze can make it feel much cooler than the temperature indicates. Layering clothing is the best option.

In the peak of summer, temperatures can range from the 60s to the 80s, with usually a handful of hot, muggy days that might reach into the 90s. Pack shorts, swimwear, rain gear, jeans and other long pants, a sweater or fleece or two, nightwear, and a warm jacket. I've found that pants that convert to shorts take me through a long day of touring, from foggy morning through hot afternoon to cool evening. Unless you're dining at one of the island's fancier or rooted-in-tradition restaurants (the Claremont or the Asticou, for example, both request tie and jacket), leave the fancy clothes behind. Resort casual is acceptable pretty much everywhere.

In spring and fall, skip the shorts, swimwear, and water shoes, double up on all the rest, and add a pair of gloves or mittens, a wool hat, and rubber-bottomed shoes or boots. In winter, add winter-weight clothing and expedition gear, but always make sure to pack clothing you can don or doff in layers. It's far easier to peel off layers than to freeze from lack of them.

For hiking, you'll want sturdy shoes, a brimmed hat, and a waterproof daypack. If you have a yen for freshwater swimming, throw in a pair of water shoes for navigating wet grass and slippery rocks.

If you're planning on going out on a windjammer sail, whale-watching cruise, puffin excursion, or kayak tour, check with the outfitter about appropriate gear for the outing. Many of these boats venture well offshore, where it can be significantly colder. Extra fleece, wool sweaters, gloves, and a hat can be worth their weight in gold, even in summer. If you're prone to motion sickness, pack appropriate precautions.

Explore Acadia National Park

THE 15-DAY BEST OF ACADIA

Spend 15 days here, and you'll have enough time to visit all sections of Acadia National Park, browse the studios of mega-talented artisans, go whale-watching, hike magnificent trails, kayak along undeveloped coastline, and view working lobstering villages and lighthouses. This tour begins in the Schoodic Region, then heads to Mount Desert Island before heading to the Blue Hill Peninsula via Ellsworth, with Isle au Haut as the grand finale.

Best air access is via Bangor International Airport. Book your first two nights lodging in the Schoodic Region, nights three through 10 on Mount Desert Island (perhaps the first four on the east side of the island and the rest on the west side), nights 11 and 12 on the Blue Hill Peninsula, and nights 13 and 14 on Deer Isle.

DAY 1

Begin with a drive or bicycle loop around the **Schoodic section of Acadia National Park.** Depending on your interests, day hike the Schoodic Head Loop or spend the rest of the day sea kayaking.

DAY 2

Head to either **Maine Islands National Wildlife Refuge,** on Petit Manan, for bird-watching and easy hiking or to the **Donnell Pond Public Reserved Lands** for a day hike followed by a swim. Don't forget a picnic lunch.

DAY 3

Browse the numerous artisans' **galleries** tucked in all corners of the region as you make your way to Mount Desert Island. Begin at Lee Art Glass and move on to Luna Form, Barter Family Gallery, Spring Woods Gallery, and Hog Bay.

DAY 4

Spend the day in **Acadia National Park.** Begin by driving or bicycling the **Park Loop**

to take in the park's highlights. Stop for a hike along the way – perhaps an easy stroll along the Ocean Trail, a moderate hike up Great Head or Gorham Mountain, a challenging one up one of the trails that leave from Sieur de Monts Spring, or a strenuous climb up a ladder trail. Reward your efforts with tea and popovers at the **Jordan Pond House.**

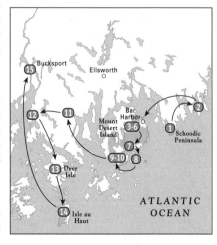

DAY 5

Another day in the park. Get up early and catch sunrise from atop **Cadillac Mountain,** then indulge your passions: hiking, sea kayaking, or bicycling. Check the *Beaver Log* to see what Naturalist Programs are scheduled, and make it a point to take part in one that intrigues you.

DAY 6

Spend the day in Bar Harbor. Reserve a spot on a whale-watching trip. Bookend that with visits to the Whale Museum and **Abbe Museum,** shopping the downtown shops, and strolling the **Shore Path.** End the day with a sunset carriage tour in the park.

DAY 7

Explore Northeast Harbor. Visit the **Asticou** and **Thuya** gardens, and perhaps wander out the back gate of Thuya and up Eliot Mountain. Shop downtown and gawk at the yachts in the harbor. Bicycle or drive Sargent Drive along the shores of **Somes Sound.**

DAY 8

Choices, choices: Pack a picnic lunch and either take to the carriage roads on foot or bike or hop aboard a passenger ferry to the **Cranberry Isles.** If you want to have a sunset dinner on Islesford, make advance reservations and either go on a day when there's a late boat or arrange for a water taxi.

DAY 9

Head for the western side of the island and visit pretty **Somesville** and Southwest Harbor, allowing time to tour the **Wendell Gilley Museum.** In the afternoon, hike Acadia, St. Saviour, or Flying Mountain, then refresh yourself with a dip in Echo Lake, followed by dinner at Thurston's Lobster Pound.

DAY 10

Drive out to **Bass Harbor Lighthouse,** then continue to the village and take the luncheon nature cruise to **Frenchboro** with Island Cruises (be sure to make advance reservations). Or if you're an experienced cyclist, take a bike aboard the state ferry to **Swan's Island** for the day.

DAY 11

Depart Mount Desert for the Blue Hill Peninsula. En route, visit **Birdsacre,** a peaceful preserve and bird refuge. You could also put the region in perspective with a plane or glider flight. Spend the afternoon in Blue Hill, beginning with a tour of the **Parson Fisher House.** Afterward, if time permits, visit some of the many **galleries** in town. Do ask locally to see if the **Flash in the Pans** are performing during your days on the peninsula, and make it a point to hear them.

DAY 12

Your choice: Hike **Blue Hill Mountain,** followed by more time for visiting galleries; hike **Great Pond Mountain,** followed by a visit to the **Craig Brook National Fish Hatchery;** or mosey over to **Castine** and pick up a brochure for a self-guided walking or bicycling tour followed by a guided sea kayaking tour.

DAY 13

Explore **Deer Isle** and **Stonington,** allowing plenty of time to browse the galleries along the way. Hike the **Edgar Tennis** or **Barred Island** preserves, and, if your timing's right, visit the **Haystack Mountain School of Crafts.**

DAY 14

Another day in the park, this time the **Isle au Haut** section. Plan in advance and book a seat on the mail boat's morning trip, then spend the day hiking. Don't forget a picnic lunch or water; supplies are limited on the island.

DAY 15

Visit **Fort Knox** in the morning, before heading home. If you're flying out of Bangor, you can either mosey up Route 15 or connect via Route 174 to Route 1A north.

A STUDIO TOUR: ARTISTS AND ARTISANS

Given the inspiring scenery, it's no surprise that the Acadia region is home to dozens of immensely talented artists and artisans. Visiting them in their studios allows you to view the region through their eyes. Galleries are abundant on the Blue Hill Peninsula and Deer Isle, the Schoodic Region, and more and more artists and artisans are calling Mount Desert Island home. You'll find detailed information on galleries and studios in the appropriate chapters.

BLUE HILL AND DEER ISLE

Pottery and sculpture are abundant throughout the Blue Hill peninsula and Deer Isle, and you can often catch nationally renowned artists such as Jud Hartman, Laura Balombini, Mark Bell, and Melissa Green at work in their studio-galleries. Woodworkers and blacksmiths are also plentiful, especially on Deer Isle. You'll also have the opportunity to visit with fiber artists – weavers, papermakers, knitters, and the like. If you really want to do it all, allow a minimum of five days to tour galleries and studios in these two regions, and be sure to check the schedule at **Haystack Mountain School of Crafts** to take advantage of lectures, tours, and auctions. You might want to split your lodging, with two or three nights on the peninsula and the balance on the island.

Begin in downtown Blue Hill, and spend the better part of a day there, with a side trip to East Blue Hill, if you desire. Consider visiting the **Parson Fisher House,** as he was a painter, photographer, and furniture maker, among his many other talents. Next day, loop around Brooksville, visiting the galleries along the way and perhaps heading over to Cape Rosier to stretch your legs in the **Holbrook Preserve.** Day three, weave your way down Route 175 through Blue Hill Falls, Brooklin, Sedgwick, and Sargentville and over the bridge and onto Little Deer Isle. After visiting the galleries on Little Deer, cross the causeway and make your way south on Route 15, detouring on the side roads so as not to miss any must-see galleries.

SCHOODIC REGION

The artwork created and exhibited in small home studios and galleries in this region is diverse: furniture, pottery, weavings, paintings, quilts, even bells. If it all rings true for you, plan a minimum of two full days, ideally three, to meander the main roads and byways in Hancock, Franklin, Sullivan, and on the Schoodic Peninsula seeking out the perfect souvenir or gift.

To cover the region, you'll make three loops, with a few side road detours. This suggested itinerary, meant to be split among two or three days, takes it all in. For loop one, begin in Hancock, and loop off Route 1 on Route 182, connecting to Route 200 in Franklin to return to Route 1. The roads circle Egypt, Taunton, and Hog Bays, allowing visits to **Glista Jewelry, Hog Bay Pottery,** and **Spring Woods Gallery** among others. Then continue north on Route 1 to Route 186. Loop two circles the Schoodic Peninsula taking in **U.S. Bells, Lee Art Glass, Stave Island Gallery, Gypsy Moose Glass Studio,** and **Maine Kiln Works.** Return south on Route 1 to West Sullivan, heading north on the Hog Bay Road, just before the bridge. After visiting **Lunaform, Wildfire Run Quilt Gallery, Arts and Africana,** and the **Barter Family Gallery** on this road and its offshoots, retrace your steps to Route 1, and cross the bridge. Loop three circles around Hancock

Point on the Hancock Point Road. Along the way, visit **Raven Tree Gallery, Ragna Bruno Torkanowsky Studio,** and **Gull Rock Pottery.** You'll reconnect with Route 1 to complete your tour.

MOUNT DESERT ISLAND

Studios and galleries are scattered throughout the island. The good news is that in 2005, an Artists Directory was created that lists nearly 50 artists along with nine galleries and information on locations with arts shows. Best of all, it includes a map noting studio and gallery locations. Look for it in info centers and galleries. It's a great resource, and it's free. Plan on three days of touring, if you want to cover all of the island.

You can easily spend a full day or longer visiting galleries in Bar Harbor and Hull's Cove. Be sure to make time to visit the **Abbe Museum,** to see Native American arts, and **St. Saviour's Church,** for its Tiffany windows. Two sculpture gardens add a bit of whimsy: the **Davistown Museum Sculpture Garden,** in Hull's Cove, and the informal display of works by Melitta Westerlund outside the Ullikana B&B, in downtown Bar Harbor.

Plan on a half day in Northeast Harbor, where top-quality galleries line Main Street. Then head over to Southwest Harbor. Before touring the galleries, visit the **Wendell Gilley Museum,** which exhibits the master bird carver's works.

Spend yet another day looping around the rest of the west side. Galleries dot the roadsides of Route 102, 102A, and side roads throughout the area.

PUFFINS AND EAGLES AND WOODCOCK, OH MY!

If you're looking to add a few species to your life list, the Acadia region is a great place to do so. Throughout the region, the birding is fine. Here is a small selection of some of the best places and activities for bird-watchers. An excellent resource to explore before your trip is www.mainebirding.com; of special interest are the sighting notes.

PETIT MANAN

This section of the **Maine Coastal Islands National Wildlife Reserve** is a must for bird-watchers. The refuge's primary focus is colonial seaboard restoration and management, but its varied habitats – rocky shore line, fresh- and saltwater marshes, coastal raised peatlands, old hayfields, blueberry barrens, alder thickets, ponds with jack pine stands, and forested lands – provide homes for numerous birds. Neotropical migratory songbirds thrive in the woodlands. Waterfowl, wading birds, and shorebirds hang out in the salt marshes and mudflats. Joining them in the salt marshes are black ducks, great blue herons, and American bitterns, while semipalmated sandpipers, dowitchers, and dunlins prefer the mudflats. Grassland birds, including bobolinks and savannah sparrows, prefer the old hayfields and the blueberry barrens.

Waterfowl migration usually begins by late March. Come in spring to see American woodcock. Shorebird migration peaks in September, followed by raptor, waterfowl, and songbird migrations. Oldsquaw, surf and white-winged scoters, common goldeneyes, and common eiders winter here, and you might also sight common and red-throated loons, sea docks, a dovekie, king eider, harlequin duck, boreal chickadees, spruce and ruffled grouse, and perhaps even a snowy owl. You also have a good chance of sighting puffins, but for the best opportunities, take one of the commercial excursion boats to **Petit Manan Island** or **Machias Seal Island.**

MOUNT DESERT ISLAND

Various eagles, hawks, and peregrine falcons are among the more than 320 bird species that have been sighted on Mount Desert Island. This includes more than 20 species of warblers. Each spring, the island hosts a Warblers and Wildflowers weekend filled with events and tours.

Especially good spots for birding include the sandbar connecting the Bar Harbor to Bar Island at low tide, **Sieur de Monts Spring, the Precipice Trail** for peregrine falcons, and **Cadillac Mountain,** for migrating hawks (the park offers programs for the latter two). On the west side, be sure to take Route 102 A and visit **Seawall Bog,** a raised coastal peatland; the **Ship Harbor** and **Wonderland** park trails; **Bass Harbor Head Light;** and **Bass Harbor Marsh.** And don't miss the **Wendell Gilley Museum,** in Southwest Harbor.

MDI offers so much that perhaps the best solution is to arrange a tour with Michael Good of **Down East Nature Tours.** He knows where to sight native and migrating birds, including bald eagles, osprey, peregrine falcons, shorebirds, and warblers as well as rare birds, including the Nelson's sharptailed sparrow.

SCHOODIC POINT AND ISLE AU HAUT

Both of these sections of Acadia National Park are well worth visiting for their birding opportunities. The mix of headlands, rocky coastline, jack pine stands, and spruce forest on Schoodic Point provide for diversity of bird species, including pelagic birds, spruce grouse, and warblers. Isle au Haut mixes spruce forest with rocky oceanfront, a freshwater pond, marshlands, and headlands. It's renowned for wintering harlequin ducks and in both locations, you'll see migrating birds and bald eagles. The loop roads circle through varied habitats, so they're good options for multiple sightings – to view specific birds, choose a trail that passes through the appropriate habitat.

LOBSTER, LIGHTHOUSES, AND L.L. BEAN

Yes, you can hit the three Ls in the Acadia region. Book your first three nights on Mount Desert, nights four and five in the Blue Hill region (perhaps the First Light B&B in East Blue Hill, a faux lighthouse), nights six and seven on Deer Isle. If time and your budget permit, consider adding on a three-night package (nights 7–10) at the Keeper's House on Isle au Haut, a bona fide lighthouse keeper's home (all packages start on Monday).

DAY 1

Make your first stop on **Mount Desert Island** the Acadia National Park Visitor Center to purchase your park pass, pick up a copy of the *Beaver Log,* and chat with a ranger. Tonight, head to **Thurston's Lobster Pound** for the Real Thing, a lobster dinner with all the fixings.

DAY 2

Rise early and beat the crowds on the **Park Loop Road.** In the afternoon, take a trip on *LuLu,* and learn everything there is to know about lobsters. Afterwards, stroll up Main Street to **Ben & Bill's** for a lobster ice cream cone (it's a good idea to ask for a taste first). Still want more? Head to **Maggie's** for lobster crepes.

DAY 3

Take a spin out to **Bass Harbor** to see the lighthouse, then board Island Cruises' *R.L. Gott* for the luncheon tour to **Frenchboro**. There's no finer place for a lobster or lobster roll than **Lunt's**.

DAY 4

Book a morning whale- and puffin-watching cruise that includes **Petit Manan Light** on its itinerary. Afterwards, leave MDI for the Blue Hill Peninsula, stopping at **L.L. Bean's factory store** in Ellsworth. It's nowhere near as big or complete as the mother ship in Freeport, but it will provide a taste of what the gigunda outdoor-oriented retailer offers. After your shopping spree, it's on to the Blue Hill region.

DAY 5

Head to **Castine,** pick up a walking-tour brochure at a local business, and take a leisurely stroll around town, making sure to see **Dyce's Head Lighthouse.** For lunch, order a lobster roll at **The Breeze,** a waterfront takeout stand. Spend the afternoon pursuing your interests: perhaps a hike up Blue Hill Mountain, a sea kayaking tour, gallery browsing throughout the peninsula, or visiting the Wooden Boat School in Brooklin.

DAY 6

On to **Deer Isle.** When you cross the bridge onto Little Deer Isle, bear right at the info

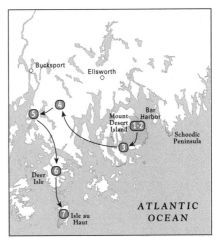

booth and head to the end of the road for views of **Pumpkin Island Light.** Then mosey on down the peninsula to **Stonington,** a bona fide lobstering community. Spend the afternoon with Capt. Walter Reed's **Guided Island Tours** (be sure to book in advance and tell him what you want to see – lighthouses and lobster fishing). Finding a lobster dinner in these parts is easy.

DAY 7

Pack a picnic lunch and take the ferry to **Isle au Haut,** which passes by a couple of lighthouses, and spend the day hiking in **Acadia National Park.** Go for one last lobster dinner in Stonington or Deer Isle before heading home tomorrow.

MOUNT DESERT ISLAND WITH KIDS

Acadia National Park is a great place to introduce kids to the great outdoors. Begin at park headquarters, where you can sign them up as junior rangers. Check out the programs offered, and pick a few to join that appeal to your kids. Be sure to ask about ranger-led hikes that appeal to your family's interests and abilities, and pick up any guides available. Good choices for easy family hikes include the Ocean Trail, Jordan Pond Nature Trail, Ship Harbor Nature Trail, and Wonderland. In between park visits, you'll find plenty of other activities with real kid appeal. Here are a few sure bets.

SLIMY SEA CREATURES

You can't beat the wow appeal of **Diver Ed's Dive-In Theater Boat Cruise.** Ed dives to the depths with an underwater camera, while you wait onboard and watch the action. When he resurfaces, he brings along with him a variety of creatures from the depths for passengers to see, feel, and learn about. Great stuff.

OLYMPICS OF THE FOREST

Expert lumberjack Tina Scheer and her crew perform the most amazing skills at **The Great Maine Lumberjack Show.** During the 75-minute performance, two teams compete in 14 events, including ax throwing and log rolling. You can participate in some activities and even arrange for your youngster to learn how to log roll. Talk about a great story for that "What I did on my summer vacation" assignment.

I SCREAM, YOU SCREAM

The ultimate kid-in-a-candy-store experience, at **Ben & Bill's** in Bar Harbor, you can buy not only chocolates made on-site but also to-die-for ice cream in both adult- and kid-pleasing flavors. Be sure to ask for a taste of the lobster ice cream.

CRAFT CRAZY

Need a new teddy bear? Want to make a mug or create a mosaic piece? It's easy for your kids (and you) to express creativity at **All Fired Up!** in Bar Harbor. This rainy day godsend is worth visiting even when sunny, especially if your kids are craft oriented. There are no specific class times — just walk in and start making your own souvenir. Although you might want to call in advance on rainy days to find out when it's least crowded.

HANDS-ON NATURE

Please touch is the philosophy at the **George B. Dorr Natural History Museum** (207/288-5015), a small museum on the College of the Atlantic campus in Bar Harbor. Kids have the opportunity to touch fur, sculls, and even whale baleen. Call to find out what's being highlighted and when in the daily interpretive program.

A WHALE OF A TIME

Skeletons, a model of a prehistoric walking whale, and a video of whales in their habitat all enthrall kids at the **Bar Harbor Whale Museum.** If the kids can't get enough (and if they're good on boats and able to handle a three-hour trip), consider following the museum visit with a **whale-watching** tour.

FERRY HOPPING

Spend the better part of a day on the **Cranberry Isles,** visiting both Big and Little Cranberry and either walking or biking around, or take the passenger ferry to **Winter Harbor,** and hop on the Island Explorer bus to visit the Schoodic section of Acadia

National Park. While on the ferries, watch for seals, seabirds, and for lobstermen and women pulling their traps.

NATIVE AMERICAN CULTURE

Check with the **Abbe Museum** in Bar Harbor about special kids' programs on the schedule, and try to time your visit to take advantage of them. There's a resource room for children downstairs and a few other kid-friendly exhibits at this Native American history museum, but the events bring it all alive.

If you're in the area while the **Native American Festival** is taking place (the first Saturday after July 4), go. There's dancing and drumming, storytelling, craft demonstrations, food, and more.

STARRY, STARRY NIGHT

Rent a telescope from the **Island Astronomic Institute** in Bernard and spend an evening trying to identify star formations and planets. Rental includes basic instruction, and if you get hooked, half the rental price can be applied to a purchase.

SPECIAL PLACES FOR SPECIAL INTERESTS

Of course you're going to take in Acadia's big picture, but part of the fun of traveling is finding places that match your interests. History buffs, gardeners, and those with eclectic tastes ranging from organic gardens to offbeat museums will want to seek out these spots.

GARDENS

The **Wild Gardens of Acadia** at Sieur de Monts Spring contains more than 400 species of wildflowers. At College of the Atlantic in Bar Harbor, an original **Beatrix Farrand Garden** is undergoing restoration. Two Northeast Harbor gardens, both designed by Charles K. Savage, are mustsees for garden buffs. **Asticou** is a Japanese-influenced garden where about 70 varieties of azaleas, rhododendrons, and laurels bloom in spring. **Thuya Gardens** is a formal garden inspired by Beatrix Farrand. Thuya Lodge has an extensive botanical library.

Although tiny, the heirloom garden at the **Mount Desert Island Historical Society Museum** in Somesville is a treat. Ditto for the **Charlotte Rhoades Park and Butterfly Garden** in Southwest Harbor. Fans of organic farming must also visit **Four Seasons Farm** in Cape Rosier on the Blue Hill peninsula. If you're seeking garden pottery, be sure to visit **Lunaform** in Sullivan.

HISTORY BUFFS

Without question, anyone intrigued by American History must visit **Castine,** a small village on the Blue Hill Peninsula, where you're immersed in the past. Dozens of historical plaques detail the town's turbulent history as the French, Dutch, and English fought over its strategic location. Not only that, but the town is loaded with well-preserved, Georgian and Federalist architectural gems; the **John Perkins House** is open for tours. Next door to it is the eclectic and wonderful **Wilson Museum.** The **Parson Fisher House,** in Blue Hill, is filled with creations and inventions and artwork by Blue Hill's Renaissance man. Yet another historical house filled with treasures is **Woodlawn,** in Ellsworth.

In Bucksport **Fort Knox** is a well-preserved,

sprawling granite fort that dates from 1844. For a real understanding of Bar Harbor's history, spend some time at the **Bar Harbor Historical Society Museum,** where photos detail the great fire. Fans of Native American history can follow a timeline of Maine's four tribes at the **Abbe Museum,** in Bar Harbor.

OFFBEAT

There's really no way to categorize these special places. Each appeals to a niche audience, and that may include you. Anyone with an interest in sustainable living will appreciate the **Good Life Center,** a way-off-the-beaten-path spot in Cape Rosier on the Blue Hill peninsula, where back-to-the-landers Helen and Scott Nearing had their last home.

Whimsy is the word at **Nervous Nellie's,** a combination jam kitchen, tea room, and recycled-item sculpture garden in Deer Isle that delights folk art fans, foodies, and really, anyone. In Bar Harbor, take either a guided or self-guided tour of **St. Saviour's,** home to 11 original Tiffany windows. Over in Northeast Harbor, fans of author Marguerite Yourcenar can tour her home, **Petite Plaisance,** and even visit her gravesite. The **Wendell Gilley Museum,** in Southwest Harbor, is filled with exquisite sculptures by the noted bird carver. Fans of antique autos especially will appreciate the **Seal Cove Auto Museum,** which houses some extremely rare vehicles from the Brass Age. For a taste of a true island community, make a day trip to **Frenchboro.**

ACADIA ON
MOUNT DESERT ISLAND

Rather like an octopus, or perhaps an amoeba, Acadia National Park extends its reach here and there and everywhere on Mount Desert Island. The park was created from donated parcels—a big chunk here, a tiny chunk there—and slowly but surely fused into its present-day size of more than 46,000 acres. Permanent boundaries do exist (Congress certified them as permanent in 1986), but they can be confusing to visitors. One minute you're in the park, the next you've stepped into one of the island's towns. This symbiotic relationship reminds us that Acadia National Park, covering a third of the island, is indeed the major presence here on Mount Desert. It affects traffic, indoor and outdoor pursuits, and, in a way, even the climate.

Acadia's history is unique among national parks and indeed fascinating. Several books have been written about some of the high-minded (in the positive sense) and high-profile personalities who provided the impetus and wherewithal for the park's inception and never flagged in their interest and support. Just to spotlight a few, we can thank George B. Dorr, Charles W. Eliot, and John D. Rockefeller Jr. for what we have today.

© TOM NANGLE

HIGHLIGHTS

◖ Park Ranger Programs: Make it a point to join in one of the numerous programs, from hikes and photography tours to natural history programs and children's activities, offered daily by park rangers (page 32).

◖ Park Loop Road: If you do nothing else on Mount Desert, drive this magnificent road that takes in many of Acadia National Park's highlights (page 35).

◖ Sieur de Monts Spring: This lovely oasis is home to the Wild Gardens of Acadia, a Nature Center, the Sweet Waters of Acadia spring, and the original Abbe Museum, as well as the base for hiking Dorr Mountain (page 37).

◖ Sand Beach: Enjoy one of the few rare beaches in this region of Maine (page 38).

◖ Thunder Hole: Time your visit right to see the tide surge and explode through this geological formation (page 39).

◖ Jordan Pond House: Come for tea and popovers and ice cream on the lawn, but allow time to walk or ride the Carriage Trails or explore the nature trail (page 39).

◖ Cadillac Mountain: Acadia's prime feature is the tallest point on the eastern seaboard, allegedly where the sun's first rays land. You can drive, bike, or hike to the 1,530-foot summit for stunning views (page 39).

◖ Carriage Roads: On the eastern side of Mount Desert Island, 57 miles of meandering, crushed-stone paths, crossing 17 handsome stone bridges, welcome walkers, bikers, horseback riders, snowshoers, and cross-country skiers (page 41).

◖ Eagle Lake: A mountain backdrop and undeveloped shores contribute to Eagle's popularity. A small-boat launch and carriage road make it easy to explore (page 41).

◖ Gorham Mountain Trail: This trail requires a minimum amount of effort to produce maximum rewards, and it's an excellent family hike – kids love the Cadillac Cliffs (page 50).

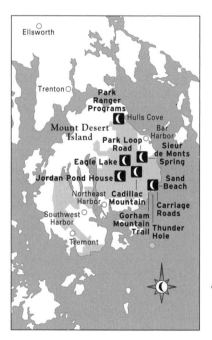

LOOK FOR **◖** TO FIND RECOMMENDED SIGHTS, ACTIVITIES, DINING, AND LODGING.

Exploring the Park

INFORMATION CENTERS

There are two major centers on Mount Desert Island for Acadia National Park information. Some Acadia information is also available from the Bar Harbor Chamber of Commerce's two offices (one on Rte. 3 in Trenton, as you approach the island), the Southwest Harbor Chamber of Commerce, and the Mount Desert Chamber in Northeast Harbor.

Thompson Island Visitor Center

As you cross the bridge from Trenton toward Mount Desert Island, you might not even notice that you arrive first on tiny Thompson Island, site of a visitor center established jointly by the chambers of commerce of Mount Desert Island's towns and Acadia National Park.

The rustic building (on your right) has walls lined with brochures for accommodations, restaurants, and activities. There are also restrooms. Across Route 3 is a picnic area overlooking Mount Desert Narrows.

If you've arrived without a place to stay (particularly in July and August), the welcoming staffers here are incredibly helpful—they keep track of lodging vacancies throughout Mount Desert Island and will go to great lengths to funnel you somewhere. In high season, don't expect to be overly choosy, though—room rates are high, vacancies are few, and you take your chances.

The center opens for the season in mid-May and is open 8 A.M.–6 P.M. daily. Everything wraps up soon after Columbus Day, when the center closes for the season.

In season, a park ranger usually is posted

PARK RULES

All parks have rules, and Acadia is no exception. Most are just common sense; some are specific to Acadia's situation and needs.

- It's forbidden to disturb or remove any public property – plants, minerals, artifacts, animals, etc. This extends to the rocks on the beach, and you'll see signs here and there reminding you of that.

- Pets are allowed in Acadia, with some exceptions, but they must be leashed or physically restrained. Voice control is not acceptable. They must not be left unattended. Pets are not allowed on Sand Beach, the beach at Echo Lake, or in the Duck Harbor campground on Isle au Haut. They are also banned from the park's ladder trails and from the visitors centers and other public buildings. Pets should not be taken on Park Ranger tours. (Service dogs, of course, are always exempted from the rules.)

- In-line skating and skateboarding are not allowed in the park.

- Bicycles are not allowed on any hiking trails. They're allowed on 45 miles of park carriage trails, but *not* on 12 miles of signposted (Green Rock Company) private carriage roads.

- Motorcycles and motorbikes are not allowed on park trails and carriage roads; ATVs are not allowed anywhere in the park. Electric wheelchairs *are* allowed on the carriage roads.

- Camping is allowed only at the park's two campgrounds on Mount Desert Island and one on Isle au Haut. There is no backcountry camping in the park or anywhere else on Mount Desert Island, but the island has a dozen commercial campgrounds.

- Camp stoves and grills are allowed only in designated campgrounds and picnic areas; fires are allowed only in fire rings and fireplaces at these sites.

- Alcohol use is not allowed at Sand Beach or Echo Lake beach.

- Hunting is not allowed in the park.

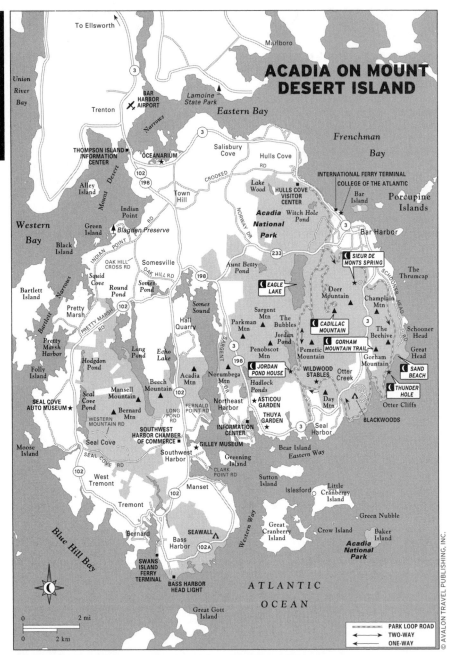

on Thompson Island to answer questions and provide basic advice on hiking trails and other park activities, but consider this a stopgap—be sure also to continue on to the park's main visitors center. You can purchase your Acadia pass here, too ($20 per vehicle, late June to mid-October—when the Island Explorer bus is running, $10 mid-October to late June, valid for seven days).

Hulls Cove Visitor Center

The modern Hulls Cove Visitor Center (Rte. 3, Hulls Cove, 207/288-3338) is eight miles southeast of the head of Mount Desert Island, and well signposted. Here you can buy your park pass, rendezvous with pals, make reservations for ranger-guided natural and cultural history programs, watch a 15-minute film about Acadia, study a relief map of the park, buy books and park souvenirs, buy cassette guides, and use the restrooms. Pick up a copy of the *Beaver Log,* the tabloid-format park newspaper that lists the schedule of park activities, plus tide calendars and the entire schedule for the excellent **Island Explorer** shuttle bus system, which operates from late June to Columbus Day. The Island Explorer is supported by entrance fees, as well as by Friends of Acadia and L.L. Bean. If you have children, enroll them for $1.95 in the park's **Junior Ranger Program.** They'll receive a booklet. To earn a Junior Ranger Patch, they must complete the activities and join one or two Ranger-led programs or walks.

Parking usually is ample at the visitors center, although the lot gets mighty full in midsummer, when as many as 9,000 people a day visit the center. Day-trippers also use the lot to leave their cars and hop on the Island Explorer bus. The bus stops at the base of the winding stairway from the parking lot to the center, which is open 8 A.M.–4:30 P.M. mid-April through October and 8 A.M.–6 P.M. July and August.

Acadia Park Headquarters

From November to April, information is available at **Acadia National Park Headquarters** on Eagle Lake Road (Route 233), about 3.5 miles west of downtown Bar Harbor. These months, the headquarters office is open 8 A.M.– 4:30 P.M. daily except Thanksgiving, December 24 and 25, and New Year's Day. During the summer, park publications are also available here, but the office is open only weekdays.

Park Headquarters is also the meeting point for the three-times-weekly volunteer work projects organized by the park and Friends of Acadia.

PARK ENTRANCE FEES

A single glance at the map of Mount Desert Island immediately raises the question: How do you sell passes and count heads in a park that has patches of land here and there and everywhere—even on a section of the mainland and offshore islands? The answer: Not easily.

So… let's look at the picture another way. Thanks to action by Congress, about 80 percent of the fees Acadia collects are now returned to the park for much-needed maintenance and educational projects. The private Friends of Acadia organization and other donors often match these funds to make the money even more effective. Thus, consider just a few of the projects your pass helps fund:

- Trail and carriage road reconstruction and rehabilitation
- The Island Explorer bus system
- New and improved restroom facilities
- Repairs to historic stone bridges
- New and improved informational exhibits
- Rock wall reconstruction
- Campground rehabilitation

At many of the project sites, you'll see brown Park Service signs—This Project Funded by Your Park User Fee—think of it as Acadia's thank-you note for your support.

Where to Buy Your Park Pass

- **The Hulls Cove Visitor Center,** the park's visitor information center from May through October. (No entrance fees are collected November through April.)

- The Acadia National Park information office opposite the **Village Green** in downtown Bar Harbor. It also faces the hub for the propane-powered Island Explorer bus system.
- The **Sand Beach Park Entrance Station,** on the Park Loop Road, between the Schooner Head Overlook and Sand Beach.
- The **Blackwoods and Seawall Campgrounds,** the park's only camping areas.
- **Thompson Island Information Center** (Route 3, Trenton).
- **Acadia Park Headquarters** (Eagle Lake Rd., Rte. 233, Bar Harbor), open weekdays in summer.

Within the park, you can also purchase your pass at the **Jordan Pond House** and at the summit of **Cadillac Mountain.**

Park Fees and Passes

- **Entrance fee:** $20 per vehicle (car or RV), late June to mid-October (when the Island Explorer is running). It covers everyone in the vehicle and valid for seven days. Mid-October to late June, the fee is $10. The motorbike fee is $10, also is valid for seven days.
- **Acadia Annual Passport:** $40, valid for one year from the day you buy it. If you're hoping to be in Acadia more than a week in any given year, you'll easily amortize this fee.
- **National Parks Pass:** $50, allowing unlimited entrance for one year to all national parks with entrance or vehicle fees. You can buy this online anytime after mid-April at http://buy.nationalparks.org, or call toll-free, 888/467-2757. For an additional $15, you can get a **Golden Eagle** hologram to apply to the National Parks Pass, thus allowing you to enter—besides all the national parks—all sites managed by Fish and Wildlife, the Forest Service, and the Bureau of Land Management (BLM).
- **Golden Age Passport:** $10, for U.S. citizens and permanent residents who are 62 or older, allowing lifetime entrance to the more than 300 national parks, historic sites, and monuments. It also entitles you to half-price camp-

ing. This is an incredible bargain. Purchase has to be made in person, with proof of age (driver's license, passport, etc.). The pass covers everyone in the passholder's vehicle.

- **Golden Access Passport:** free for any U.S. citizen or permanent resident who is blind or permanently disabled (a temporary disability, such as a broken arm or leg, does not qualify). It allows lifetime entrance to all national parks, as well as Fish and Wildlife, Forest Service, and BLM sites. It also allows half-price camping. The pass covers everyone in the vehicle accompanying the passholder.

GUIDED TOURS

The variety of guided activities in the park and nearby is astonishing—park ranger walks and talks and cruises, bus tours, bicycling tours, sea kayaking tours, birding expeditions, guided hikes, horse-drawn carriage rides, and even deluxe camping outfitters.

🄲 Park Ranger Programs

When you stop at the Hulls Cove Visitor Center and pick up the current issue of the park's *Beaver Log* newspaper (or download it ahead of time at www.nps.gov/acad/), you'll find a whole raft of possibilities for learning more about the park's natural and cultural history.

The Park Ranger programs, lasting one to three hours, are great—and most are free. During July and August, there are about 100 programs each week, all listed in the *Log.* Included are early-morning (7 A.M.) birding walks; mountain hikes (moderate level); tours of the historic Carroll Homestead, a 19th-century farm; Cadillac summit natural-history tours; children's expeditions to learn about tidepools and geology (an adult must accompany kids); trips for the wheelchair-borne; and even a couple of tours a week in French. Some tours require reservations, while some do not. (Reservations can be made up to three days in advance.) Reservations and fees are required for several different boat cruises with park rangers

THE CAR-FREE PARK

Every way you look at it, the **Island Explorer** bus system seems to be a success. Since 1999, when the fare-free propane-fueled buses began running on an experimental basis throughout Mount Desert Island, ridership has more than doubled, more than 316,000 car and RV visits were eliminated, and pollutants were reduced by an estimated 24.4 tons.

Each year since the service began, expansion has occurred, with increased stops and routes, and 2003 saw a six-week extension in the fall schedule, thanks to a million-dollar grant from L.L. Bean. Service now begins in late June and lasts until Columbus Day (the Schoodic Peninsula route, established on a trial basis in 2003, stops on Labor Day).

"The little bus system that could," as Friends of Acadia president Ken Olson calls it, transports passengers to ferry landings, saves hikers and bikers from backtracking, gets commuters to work, and generally has revolutionized the summertime traffic patterns on Mount Desert Island.

Why spend valuable vacation time looking for a place to park your car? Why be disappointed when you reach a hiking trailhead and find the parking lot full? Take the bus. Feeling unsteady and unable to hike or bike? Tour the park and the island on the bus. Each bus can handle two bikes and a wheelchair.

The fleet is operated by the nonprofit Downeast Transportation (www.exploreacadia .com), with support from your park entrance fees, Friends of Acadia, and area towns and businesses.

The Island Explorer hub is the Bar Harbor Village Green, where all of the routes (except Schoodic) begin or end. Between late June and Labor Day, service begins at 6:45 A.M., although not every route starts that early. But, like the Energizer bunny, the buses keep going and going and going... until late into the summer evening (last bus leaves downtown Bar Harbor about 11 P.M. for the campgrounds in the northern end of the island). A geolocator system provides tracking information at the Village Green and at the Hulls Cove Visitor Center.

Specific stops are listed on the schedule, but drivers will pull over and pick you up or drop you off anywhere they feel it's safe. Don't hesitate to request a stop or flag down a bus.

So pick up a schedule — copies are everywhere on Mount Desert — and use the Island Explorer to explore the island!

© TOM NANGLE

The free Island Explorer bus service makes it easy to explore the park without your car.

who provide natural-history narration (the specific cruises vary from year to year).

Park rangers also give the evening lectures during the summer in the amphitheaters at Blackwoods and Seawall Campgrounds. And the good news is that between late June and mid-October, you can join almost every ranger program via an Island Explorer bus.

Bus and Trolley Tours

The veteran of the Bar Harbor–based bus tours is **Acadia National Park Tours** (tickets at Testa's Restaurant, Bayside Landing, 53 Main St., P.O. Box 52, Bar Harbor 04609, 207/288-3327, www.acadiatours.com), operating May through October. A 2.5-hour, naturalist-led tour of Bar Harbor and Acadia departs at 10 A.M. and 2 P.M. daily from downtown Bar Harbor (Testa's is across from Agamont Park, near the Bar Harbor Inn). Reservations are wise in midsummer and during fall-foliage season (late September and early October); pick up reserved tickets 30 minutes before departure. Cost is $25 adults, $10 children under 12.

If there's a time crunch, take the one-hour trolley-bus tour operated by **Oli's Trolley** (P.O. Box 794, Bar Harbor 04609, 207/288-9899, www.acadiaislandtours.com), which departs downtown Bar Harbor five times daily (between 10 A.M. and 6 P.M.) in July and August, including Bar Harbor mansion drive-bys and the Cadillac summit. Starting point is the Oli's Trolley Ice Cream Shop, 58 Cottage Street, across from the post office. (Tickets are also available at Harbor Place, the waterfront marketplace near the Bar Harbor Inn.) Dress warmly if the air is at all cool; it's an open-air trolley. Cost is $15 adults, $10 children under 12. Reservations are advisable. The trolley also does 2.5-hour park tours at 10 A.M. and 2 P.M. May through October. Tickets are $20 adults, $10 children under 12. The bus and trolley routes both include potty stops.

While the Island Explorer buses do reach a number of key park sights, they are not tour buses. There is no narration, and the bus cuts off the Park Loop at Otter Cliffs; it excludes the summit of Cadillac Mountain.

Birding and Nature Tours

For private tours of the park and other parts of the island, contact Michael Good at **Down East Nature Tours** (P.O. Box 521, Bar Harbor, 207/288-8128, www.mainebirding.net/downeast/). A biologist with a special interest in birds, he'll take neophyte or advanced birders on two-hour, four-hour, or all-day tours they won't forget. Good gives special attention to native and migrating birds, including bald eagles, osprey, peregrine falcons, shorebirds, and warblers. He'll even take serious birders to spot the Nelson's sharptailed sparrow and other life-list birds. Prices begin at $50 pp for two hours and include transportation from your lodging; family rates are available. Camping trips, photography tours, and sunrise or sunset trips also are available. What better place to begin a life list than Acadia National Park? Bring your own binoculars, but Michael supplies a spotting scope.

For a sea-based birding tour, ask **Wanderbirdcruises** (866/732-2473, www.wanderbirdcruises.com), about any cruises that include Acadia National Park.

Hiking Itineraries

If you're happy to hike on your own but you'd like to have someone suggest and plan routes geared to your abilities (especially if you have a group), contact Earl Brechlin at **Base Camp Outfitters** (207/288-4859, www.justmaine.com/brechlin/basecamp.html). He's the author of several books on Acadia, Bar Harbor, and Mount Desert (see *Suggested Reading*), a newspaper editor, and a Registered Maine Guide. He'll suggest hikes and provide insider advice. Cost depends on the many possible variables—group size, number of hikes, amount of help needed.

Carriage Tours

A fabulous way to recapture Acadia's early carriage-roads era is to take one of the horse-drawn open-carriage tours run by Ed Winterberg's **Carriages in the Park,** departing from Wildwood Stables, 0.5 mile south of the Jordan Pond House, on the Park Loop Road (P.O. Box 241, Seal Harbor 04675, 207/276-3622, www.acadia.net/wildwood). Don't pooh-pooh this as too touristy—on a gorgeous day, the vistas are everything, and you won't be disappointed. Half a dozen one- and two-hour trips start daily at 9:30 A.M., mid-June to Columbus Day. Reservations are encouraged, especially at the height of summer. The best outing is the two-hour **Sunset at the Summit** to the top of Day Mountain; call for departure times; cost is $22 adults, $9 children 6–12, and $6 for kids 2–5. Other routes are $16–18 per adult. If you take the two-hour carriage ride to Jordan Pond House, departing daily at 1:15 P.M. ($18 adults, not counting food and beverage), you're guaranteed a reserved lawn chair for tea and popovers.

You also can arrange for a private carriage-road tour of 1–4 hours. A one-hour trip is $150 for up to four passengers, plus $35 for each additional passenger; two hours is $200 plus $50; three hours is $300 plus $75; and four hours is $400 plus $100. Wildwood has no trail rides, but you can bring your own horse and stable it here at $20 a night for a box stall. (A basic campground has sites for stall renters for $10 a night; parking for a two-horse trailer is $6 or a four-horse trailer is $10.)

DRIVING TOUR

The ideal way to fully appreciate Acadia is to hike the miles of trails, bike the carriage roads, canoe the ponds, swim in Echo Lake, and camp overnight. It seems rather a shame to treat Acadia as a drive-through park, but circumstances—time, health, and other factors—sometimes dictate that.

◖ Park Loop Road

Logically, then, a driving tour in Acadia would follow the 27-mile Park Loop Road. It begins at the visitors center, winds past several of the park's scenic highlights (with parking areas),

PEREGRINE FALCONS

One of Acadia's great success stories is that of a seasonal mountain dweller, the peregrine falcon. DDT and other pollutants caused a decline in the falcons until the last breeding pair in Acadia was observed in 1956. (Before DDT, peregrines were depleted by trappers, hunters, and nest robbers.) The peregrine was listed as a federal endangered species in the early 1970s and removed from that list in 1999; it remains an endangered species in Maine. In the 1980s, biologists worked to reintroduce the falcons to Acadia. Their efforts proved successful when, in 1991, a breeding pair of falcons settled on the east-facing cliffs of Champlain Mountain and produced young. Since then, there have been up to three breeding pairs of falcons nesting in Acadia (at Champlain, Jordan Cliff, and Beech Cliff).

Their nests, or scrapes, are but shallow ledges on cliffsides, which provide them with an unimpeded view of potential prey (other birds) below. Their high-speed pursuits of prey thrill those who are lucky enough to witness them.

During the spring and summer, park staff are stationed at the Precipice Trail Parking Area each morning (weather permitting), 9 A.M.–noon, with spotting scopes to help anyone who stops by to view the peregrines and their scrapes, and to provide information about their habits. Check the park newspaper, the *Beaver Log*, for the latest information.

During breeding and fledging season (April to mid-August), the trailhead for the **Precipice Trail** is gated, with an informational sign explaining the history and status of peregrines in the park. (When you arrive, other trails may be closed for the same reason; check at the Hulls Cove Visitor Center.)

(Contributed by Kristen Britain)

ascends to the summit of Cadillac Mountain, and provides overlooks to magnificent vistas. Allow a couple of hours so you can stop along the way. You can rent an audio tour on cassette or CD for $12.95 (including directions,

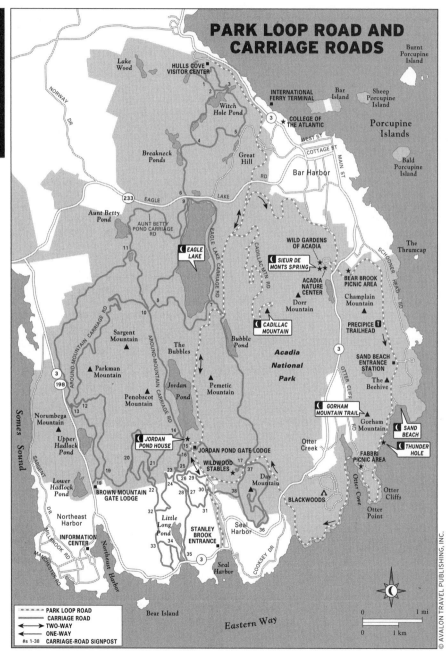

PARK LOOP ROAD AND CARRIAGE ROADS

Burnt Porcupine Island

Lake Wood

HULLS COVE VISITOR CENTER

Witch Hole Pond

INTERNATIONAL FERRY TERMINAL

Bar Island

Sheep Porcupine Island

Porcupine Islands

COLLEGE OF THE ATLANTIC

WEST ST

COTTAGE ST

MAIN ST

Breakneck Ponds

Great Hill

Great Hill

RD

LAKE

Bar Harbor

Bald Porcupine Island

NORWAY DR

EAGLE

233

Aunt Betty Pond

AUNT BETTY POND CARRIAGE RD

EAGLE LAKE CARRIAGE RD

EAGLE LAKE

WILD GARDENS OF ACADIA

SIEUR DE MONTS SPRING

ACADIA NATURE CENTER

BEAR BROOK PICNIC AREA

Champlain Mountain

The Thrumcap

SCHOONER HEAD RD

CADILLAC MTN RD

Dorr Mountain

CADILLAC MOUNTAIN

AROUND-MOUNTAIN CARRIAGE RD

Sargent Mountain

The Bubbles

Bubble Pond

Acadia National Park

PRECIPICE TRAILHEAD

SAND BEACH ENTRANCE STATION

The Beehive

Parkman Mountain

AROUND-MOUNTAIN CARRIAGE RD

Jordan Pond

Pemetic Mountain

3

OTTER CLIFF

Penobscot Mountain

198

3

Norumbega Mountain

GORHAM MOUNTAIN TRAIL

Gorham Mountain

SAND BEACH

THUNDER HOLE

Upper Hadlock Pond

JORDAN POND HOUSE

JORDAN POND GATE LODGE

WILDWOOD STABLES

Day Mountain

Otter Creek

FABBRI PICNIC AREA

Lower Hadlock Pond

BROWN MOUNTAIN GATE LODGE

BLACKWOODS

Otter Cove

Otter Cliffs

Northeast Harbor

Little Long Pond

STANLEY BROOK ENTRANCE

Seal Harbor

Otter Point

INFORMATION CENTER

MANCHESTER RD

MILLBROOK RD

SARGENT DR

Northeast Harbor

3

Seal Harbor

COOKSEY DR

Somes Sound

Bear Island

Eastern Way

PARK LOOP ROAD
CARRIAGE ROAD
TWO-WAY
ONE-WAY
#s 1-38 CARRIAGE-ROAD SIGNPOST

0   1 mi
0   1 km

© AVALON TRAVEL PUBLISHING, INC.

instruction sheet, and map) at the Hull's Cove Visitor Center. Another option is to pick up the drive-it-yourself tour booklet, **Motorist Guide: Park Loop Road** ($1.50), available at the Thompson Island and Hulls Cove Visitor Centers.

Start at the parking lot below the Hulls Cove Visitor Center and follow the signs; part of the loop is one-way, so you'll be doing the loop clockwise. Traffic gets heavy at midday in midsummer, so aim for an early morning start if you can. Maximum speed is 35 mph, but be alert for gawkers and photographers stopping without warning and pedestrians dashing across the road from stopped cars or tour buses. If you're out here at midday in midsummer, don't be surprised to see cars and RVs parked in the right lane in the one-way sections; it's allowed when the designated parking lots are filled (and even when they aren't).

Along the route are trailheads and overlooks, as well as **Sieur de Monts Spring** (Acadia Nature Center, Wild Gardens of Acadia, Abbe Museum summer site, and the convergence of several spectacular trails), **Sand Beach, Thunder Hole, Otter Cliffs, Fabbri picnic area** (there's one wheelchair-accessible picnic table), **Jordan Pond House, Bubble Pond, Eagle Lake,** and the summit of **Cadillac Mountain.** Just before you get to Sand Beach, you'll see the Park Entrance Station, where you'll need to purchase a pass if you haven't already done so. (If you're here

during nesting/fledging season—April to mid-August—be sure to stop in the Precipice Trailhead Parking Area; see the *Peregrine Falcons* sidebar.)

Island Tour

If you still have time for and/or interest in more driving after you've done the loop, take a spin around the rest of the island. Exit the Park Loop Road (near Bar Harbor) onto Route 233, heading west. Continue to Route 198 and go left (south). In just over a mile, watch for a smallish sign for **Sargent Drive.** (Only cars are allowed on this road—no RVs.) Take Sargent Drive, skirting gorgeous **Somes Sound,** into Northeast Harbor.

Leave Northeast Harbor via Route 198, northward, until you reach the head of Somes Sound. Go left around the head of the sound, to **Somesville,** a gem of a historic hamlet, then continue southward on Route 102 to Southwest Harbor. If you have time, take the Route 102A loop, with a chance to see **Bass Harbor Head Light**—you'll want to walk from the parking lot to get the best view. Otherwise, continue on Route 102 to Tremont (maybe detour into Bernard for great lobster on the wharf), then clockwise around to West Tremont, Seal Cove, Pretty Marsh, and back to Somesville. From there, you can go directly north to leave the island via Route 102/198, or go to Bar Harbor by heading eastward (follow signs).

Sights

The **Park Loop Road** will lead you to the major sights on the east side of the park—Sieur de Monts Spring, Sand Beach, Thunder Hole, Otter Cliffs, and the summit of Cadillac Mountain—but then there's also the fantastic carriage-road system. As you explore the rest of the park acreage on Mount Desert, particularly its west side, you'll come upon still more surprising spots.

◖ SIEUR DE MONTS SPRING

About two miles from Bar Harbor and close to the often-busy Park Loop Road, Sieur de Monts Spring is an oasis in a tranquil woodland setting. Named after 17th-century French explorer Pierre du Gua, Sieur de Monts, the spring is the centerpiece of a 10-acre parcel donated in 1916 for a future national park by George Bucknam Dorr, the Father of Acadia.

It was Dorr who erected the pretty Italianate Spring House and dubbed this "The Sweet Waters of Acadia"—after the Sweet Waters of Europe and the Sweet Waters of Asia, two springs that had deeply impressed him on a visit to Constantinople. (The water here, incidentally, is not safe to drink—nor, for that matter, is the water in those Istanbul springs.)

Also here is the Acadia **Nature Center,** containing exhibits on flora and fauna and explanations of the ongoing efforts to preserve the park's natural resources. The center is open mid-May through mid-October (9 A.M.–5 P.M. daily in July and August). Admission is free.

Below the Nature Center, take time to walk through the **Wild Gardens of Acadia,** touted as "an outdoor field guide" to the island's plantlife. Maintained by the Bar Harbor Garden Club, the Wild Gardens are divided into a dozen different habitats containing more than 400 species of wildflowers. The gardens are open mid-May to mid-October: 9 A.M.–5 P.M.

© TOM NANGLE

Spring House, Sweet Waters of Acadia, Sieur de Monts Spring

in July and August, shorter hours early and late in the season.

An important feature of this lovely area is the privately run **Abbe Museum** (207/288-3519, www.abbemuseum.org), the original home of Dr. Robert Abbe's extensive personal collection of prehistoric and historic archaeological artifacts, some dating back 11,000 years. Built in 1928, the museum outgrew this National Historic Register building and now has a handsome year-round structure in downtown Bar Harbor. The Sieur de Monts Spring site, with exhibits on Maine archaeology and the history of the museum, is open Memorial Day Weekend to mid-October: 9 A.M.–5 P.M. July and August, 10 A.M.–4 P.M. in spring and fall. Admission is $2 adults, $1 children 6–15; free admission for Native Americans and children under six; admission to this site is included with tickets to the Bar Harbor museum.

The Sieur de Monts Spring area provides access to several Acadia trails. To the west of the Spring House are strenuous trails leading up **Dorr Mountain** (originally Dry Mountain, then Flying Squadron Mountain). To the north is the easy **Jesup Path**—two to three miles in this valley between Dorr Mountain and Huguenot Head. The Jesup Path (also called the Jesup Trail) is particularly spectacular during the fall foliage season. You can also access the Tarn and Hemlock Trails at Sieur de Monts.

Sieur de Monts Spring is accessible on the Island Explorer via either Route 3/Sand Beach or Route 4/Blackwoods.

◖ SAND BEACH

Below the Park Loop Road and the newly spiffed-up Park Entrance Station, Sand Beach is the park's only large sandy beach on saltwater—*cold* saltwater. Well, it's not really sand, as a sign posted here will tell you—it's composed of zillions of crushed shells, pulverized so they look like sand. If you haven't purchased your park entrance pass by this point, you'll need to do it here. Via the Island Explorer bus (Route 3/Sand Beach), Sand Beach is about

© TOM NANGLE

Time your visit to the tide to see Thunder Hole at its most thunderous.

25 minutes from Bar Harbor (a bit less than that by car before and after the bus season). You can access the **Great Head** trail from here.

◖ THUNDER HOLE

Thunder Hole gets pumped up as a spectacular attraction, and it is—but only if your timing is right. When the wind is coming from the south or southeast, when a storm has churned up the sea, or when the tide is rushing inward—then you'll hear (and feel) how Thunder Hole got its name. As the water rushes into a narrow slot in the rocks, it creates a powerful roar, shoots into the air, and often showers the closest bystanders.

If your schedule can be flexible, check the tide tables in the local paper (or in the park's *Beaver Log* newspaper) and try to be here for the incoming tide, preferably about midtide.

Because of the sea spray, the steps leading down toward Thunder Hole often are very slippery. Take particular care with small children and anyone who tends to be unsteady.

◖ JORDAN POND HOUSE

Afternoon tea on the lawn at the rustic Jordan Pond House (207/276-3316, 11:30 A.M.–9 P.M.) was a summer tradition in the late 19th century, and it's still on everyone's list of Acadia highlights. You can even arrive by carriage and re-create the car-free era. While tea (with hot-from-the-oven popovers and strawberry jam and homemade ice cream) is the most popular choice here, the restaurant—now in a modern building—also serves lunch and dinner between mid-May and mid-October. From late June to Columbus Day, the Island Explorer bus (Route 5/Jordan Pond) will get you here in 20 minutes from Bar Harbor. (In summer, the last bus for Bar Harbor leaves the restaurant at 8:50 P.M.)

The Jordan Pond House is a great base for using the area's carriage roads. Also here is a short nature path.

◖ CADILLAC MOUNTAIN

As the highest point (1,530 feet) in Acadia, the Cadillac summit receives the day's first ray of sunlight between early October and early March. A couple of trails will get you to the Cadillac summit (including one from Blackwoods Campground), and you can get a good mountain-bike workout on the road (bikes aren't allowed on trails), but in the end, most summiteers tend to get there by car—a seven-mile round-trip via paved road. (The Island Explorer bus does not go to the Cadillac summit.)

Formerly named Green Mountain, Cadillac was topped by the wooden Summit Hotel, built by an ambitious developer who eventually fell on hard times and went into bankruptcy. Some might say he deserved it for blighting the landscape. Before his decline in the late 19th century, however, his 6,000-foot Green Mountain Cog Railway transported guests to the summit, where the view was just as spectacular as it is today. (Photos of the Cog Railway era are part of the collection at the Bar Harbor Historical Society, on Ledgelawn Street.) The summit road was built in 1931.

JORDAN POND HOUSE

In the late 19th century, when Bar Harbor was in the throes of becoming "the great new place" to escape the heat of Washington, New York, Philadelphia, and the Midwest, gentle ladies and men patronized an unassuming farmhouse/teahouse on the shores of Jordan Pond. By 1895 or 1896, under the stewardship of Thomas McIntire, it became Jordan Pond House – a determinedly rustic establishment, with massive fieldstone fireplaces, serving afternoon tea and leisurely luncheons during the summer and fall.

And rustic it remained, well into the late 20th century – until leveled by a disastrous fire in the summer of 1979. At that point, it was owned by Acadia. John D. Rockefeller Jr. had bought it in the 1930s and donated it to the park in the early 1940s. Since then, it's been managed on behalf of the park by concessionaires – currently the Acadia Corporation (which also operates gift shops in several locations).

Today, Jordan Pond House, the only restaurant within Acadia National Park, must rely on its framed antique photos to conjure up a bit of nostalgia for the bygone era. The building is modern and open, the pace in summer is frenetic, and the food is average. But the view from the lawn over Jordan Pond and the astounding Bubbles is incredible. Surely *it* hasn't changed.

So, at least once, brave the crowds and have afternoon tea on the lawn at Jordan Pond House. Order tea or Oregon Chai or even cappuccino and fresh popovers (two) with extraordinary strawberry jam. That package will set you back $7.50-8.75, but how much would you pay for the view?

Lunch (salads, sandwiches, and entrées include a popover) and afternoon tea are served 11:30 A.M.-5:30 P.M. daily, inside or on the lawn. Dinner (entrées $15-20) begins at 5:30 P.M. – inside or on the porch. The reservation system is unique: call 207/276-3316, any time from 9:15 A.M., which puts you "on the list." You'll probably have to wait when you arrive, so stop in the gift shop for a jar of jam to take home.

Perhaps because of all the sweet drinks and jam served outdoors, patrons at the lawn tables sometimes find themselves pestered by bees. They don't usually sting unless you pester them back, but if you're hyperallergic to bee stings, or are with anyone who is, be alert.

Jordan Pond House, on the Park Loop Road, is open 11:30 A.M.-8 P.M. mid-May to mid-October (until 9 P.M. July and August). From late June to Columbus Day, it's easy to reach via the Island Explorer bus, and several park hiking trails originate or pass near here.

If you need a popover fix when you return home, you can always buy a package of the mix along with the jam in the gift shop, but if you don't, here's the Jordan Pond House recipe:

JORDAN POND HOUSE POPOVERS

2 large eggs
1 cup whole milk
1 cup all-purpose flour (presifted)
1/2 teaspoon salt
1/8 teaspoon baking soda

Preheat oven to 425°F. Beat eggs with electric mixer at high speed three minutes. Reduce mixer speed to lowest setting and very gradually pour in half the milk. In separate bowl, combine sifted flour, salt, and baking soda and sift again.

With mixer still running at slowest speed, add dry ingredients to egg-and-milk mixture. Turn off mixer and use rubber spatula to blend mixture thoroughly.

Set mixer to medium speed and very gradually pour in remaining milk, blending one minute. Raise mixer speed to highest setting and beat 10 minutes.

Strain batter through fine-mesh strainer to remove lumps, then pour into well-buttered popover or custard cups. Bake 15 minutes. Without opening oven, reduce heat to 350° and bake 15 more minutes (20 minutes if oven door has a window).

Serve immediately, with fresh jam and room-temperature butter. Recipe makes two popovers. Increase as desired, but be sure to measure carefully. Popovers turn out significantly better if baked in ovenproof cups rather than in metal or glass.

At the height of summer, sunrise, midday, and sunset are the busiest times on the summit; if you're not looking for bragging rights about sunrise or sunset, try to be here an hour or two after sunrise or an hour or two before sunset.

At the top are head-swiveling vistas and a gift shop and restrooms. Be sure to walk the paved, 0.3-mile Summit Trail loop for the full effect, but *please stay on the trail* to preserve the summit's fragile plants and soil.

From late August to mid-October, the park runs the **Hawkwatch** program near the Cadillac summit. (The observation site is on the Cadillac North Ridge Trail, about 600 feet from the summit parking lot.) Each day during the Hawkwatch, 9 A.M.–2 P.M., weather permitting, park interpreters are on hand to help you identify the various species of hawks, falcons, eagles, and ospreys that migrate through Acadia each fall. More than 3,000 visitors participated in 2004. Since the Hawkwatch project began in 1995, the annual raptor count here during the migration season has averaged about 2,500.

◖ CARRIAGE ROADS

Bare summits, woodlands, gemlike ponds, 17 handsome stone bridges, and dazzling vistas—you'll see them all as you walk or bike the fantastic 57-mile carriage-road network that makes Acadia unique among America's national parks.

Forty-five miles of the broken-stone roads—all on the east side of the island, between the Hulls Cove Visitor Center in the north and Seal Harbor in the south—are open for walking, bicycling, and horseback riding (and in winter for cross-country skiing and snowshoeing). Twelve additional miles, on private land owned by the Green Rock Company, are open for walking and horseback riding but not biking (be alert for the No Bikes signs when you're cycling; all of the private roads are south of the Jordan Pond House).

◖ EAGLE LAKE

The largest lake on the eastern half of the island, Eagle Lake is entirely within the park, so its shoreline is undeveloped. Cadillac, Pemetic, Sargent Mountains, and the Bubbles surround it. You can pedal or walk around Eagle on a carriage road or launch a canoe or kayak here and paddle its waters. Or just find a rock to sit upon and enjoy the scenery. You might spot osprey, eagles, great blue heron, loons, and other wildlife here. Two parking lots off Route 233 make access easy (one by the boat launch and a larger one on the other side of the road).

BASS HARBOR HEAD LIGHT

At the southern end of Mount Desert's western "claw," follow Route 102A to the turnoff toward Bass Harbor Head. Drive or bike to the end of Lighthouse Road, walk down a steep wooden stairway, and look up and to the right. Voilà! Bass Harbor Head Light—its red glow automated since 1974—stands sentinel at the eastern entrance to Blue Hill Bay. Built in 1858, the 26-foot tower and lightkeeper's house are privately owned, but the dramatic setting is a photographer's dream. Winter access to the parking lot may be limited, but otherwise the area is open all year. Not far from the light (east along Route 102A) are the trailheads for the easy Ship Harbor and Wonderland nature trails, part of Acadia National Park (see Recreation).

PRETTY MARSH PICNIC AREA

Picnic spots are everywhere on Mount Desert, but an Acadia National Park site that many people miss is the Pretty Marsh Picnic Area, overlooking Pretty Marsh Harbor, on the opposite side of the island from Bar Harbor. Dense woods shelter grills and tables, and you can walk down to the shoreline and even launch a sea kayak. Kids love this place, but be prepared with insect repellent. The picnic area is just west of Route 102 (Pretty Marsh Rd.), on the westernmost shore. Pretty Marsh is not on an Island Explorer bus route; you'll need a car or bike to get there.

MR. ROCKEFELLER'S ROADS

Imagine being able to build your own network of pathways where you could step into a horse-drawn carriage and meander through matchless terrain. Petroleum heir John D. Rockefeller Jr. did just that on Mount Desert Island – and, thanks to him, we can all walk and bike these roadways, and even go for our own horse-drawn carriage rides.

The story of Acadia's car-free carriage roads has been told and retold, but Rockefeller's granddaughter, Ann R. Roberts, had the inside track when she wrote *Mr. Rockefeller's Roads: The Untold Story of Acadia's Carriage Roads & Their Creator* (see *Suggested Reading*). Her book relates a fascinating saga of benevolence and sensitivity and talent and organization. The carriage-road system is one of Acadia's most valued cultural resources – listed since 1979 on the National Register of Historic Places.

Between 1913 and 1940, Rockefeller was involved in the purchase of acreage and the design and construction of more than 57 miles of carriage roads on Mount Desert. (Forty-five miles of these roads are now within Acadia National Park boundaries and 12 are on private land but open to the public.) And "involved" is the operative word here. Not only did he conceptualize the project, finance it, and consult on every aspect of the road and bridge designs, he was on hand during the construction and landscaping phases. No detail escaped his scrutiny.

Rockefeller's passion for road engineering and landscaping came from watching and working with his father, John D. Rockefeller Sr. who planned carriage roads and rustic stone bridges for the family's estate near Cleveland. Later, father and son created carriage roads through Pocantico Hills, their vast Hudson River estate. Lessons learned from those undertakings laid the groundwork (literally and figuratively) for the even more ambitious project on Mount Desert.

Rockefeller Jr. first visited Mount Desert as a Brown University student in 1893, but it was his 1908 trip to Seal Harbor – with his wife Abby – that shaped his lifelong love for the island. In 1910, they bought "The Eyrie," a Seal Harbor estate that still remains in the family, and he soon began the other land acquisitions that continued until 1940. Around 1913, he began laying out his astonishing network of carriage roads, stepping up the pace in 1916 when he

Hiking

It would take weeks of nonstop all-day hiking to cover every trail in the Mount Desert Island acreage of Acadia National Park. And it would consume most of this book to write about them. Not a bad idea—but few of us have enough free time to manage such a feat. (Island resident Tom St. Germain, author of *A Walk in the Park,* somehow finds time to hike each of the trails at least once a year. More power to him!) Best to do as much as you can when you're here—and return as often as possible to do more!

What follows, therefore, is a selection of choice hikes, ranging from very easy to strenuous. Evaluate your schedule, your skills and/or limitations (especially the capabilities of your least-sturdy hiking partners), gather your gear, pack a picnic and plenty of water, and head out.

As you take your first step on your first park trail, however, keep in mind the Leave No Trace philosophy that governs all recreation in the park—but especially hiking. Stick to it for yourself, your family, and the generations to come.

Until the establishment of the **Island Explorer** bus system, hikers had to do loop trails in Acadia in order to return to their cars

hired Charles P. Simpson as his chief engineer. In 1922, Simpson turned over the task to his son Paul ("Chip"), who remained chief engineer until 1940. Renowned landscape architect Beatrix Farrand worked with Rockefeller on roadside plantings, and dozens of other people – noted and not-so-noted – became part of the team at some point during the nearly three-decade-long project.

Distinctive features of the roads are 17 handsome rough-stone bridges (with single, double, and triple arches; no two alike), 16-foot-wide broken-stone roadbeds that required more man-hours than anyone could count, and tasteful carved trail markers. A holdover from Rockefeller's previous carriage-road experience was the use of roadside borders of squared-off granite coping stones – known at Acadia as "Mr. Rockefeller's teeth."

And then there are the two stone gate lodges (or gate houses) – Brown Mountain Gate Lodge and Jordan Pond Gate Lodge – heralding entrances to the original carriage-road system. (Many more access points exist today.) Designed by Grosvenor Atterbury in a whimsical French Romanesque style, the handsome structures are startling, to say the least. It's hard not to smile when you come upon them (near Northeast Harbor, and near Jordan Pond, respectively). During the carriage road building, engineer Paul Simpson and his family occupied the Jordan Pond Gate Lodge.

Until his death in 1960 (when Acadia assumed responsibility for 45 miles of the carriage road system), John D. Rockefeller Jr. continued his magnanimity by financing the maintenance of the carriage road network. By the early 1990s, however, the roads, bridges, and drainage systems had seriously deteriorated, and the fabulous vistas had become overgrown. Enter Friends of Acadia, an amazing nonprofit organization that helped the park obtain federal funding and then maximized the grant with matching private funds – generating enough to cover the $6 million face-lift and begin a carriage-road endowment. Thanks also to the impetus of Friends of Acadia, work began in 2003 to repair more than two dozen bridges and nearby sections of historic hiking trails – an estimated $3 million project.

As one carriage road admirer put it: "The roads are just the way God would have made them if he only had the money."

or bikes, or they had to make elaborate arrangements for pickup or shuttling. The bus schedule now has created all kinds of other options. It allows you to skip the backtracking—and in some cases lets you pick up transport along the way if you (or the kids) wear out earlier than expected. (Of course, this holds true only for the bus season—late June to Columbus Day, and the schedule is reduced between Labor Day and Columbus Day.) Even if your destination/locale isn't on the bus schedule, you can request a stop or flag down a bus anywhere that's safe for the driver to pull over. The bus schedules vary slightly each year. Pick up the latest schedule at the Hulls Cove Visitor Center or download it before you leave home (www.exploreacadia.com). Then take advantage of the system while you're on Mount Desert Island.

All of the hikes described here follow Acadia National Park hiking trails. (See the *Mount Desert Island Communities* chapter for info on the in-town Shore Path, which is not part of the park.) The separate but sometimes interconnected carriage roads, which also are open to hiking (more like strolling, in many cases)—as well as horseback riding and bicycling—are described later, under *Biking*.

The hikes that follow are divided into two sections—the east side of Mount Desert Island and the west side. Because Somes Sound almost bisects the island, none of the trails cross from one side of the island to the other, and almost every one of the peaks' ridgelines runs in a north-south (or south-north) direction. The hikes are described below in the order of difficulty, from very easy to strenuous; lengths of hikes vary within each category (length, of course, doesn't always determine the difficulty). Ratings are based on park advisories and personal experience.

While you plan, bear in mind that most visitors tend to spend more time on the east side of the island, for a variety of reasons—more trails, a range of easy-to-moderate trails, the carriage-road network, the auto road to Cadillac's summit, the Park Loop Road, the park's only restaurant (Jordan Pond House), and so on. So heading for the west-side trails, even at the height of summer, can provide you with quieter spaces and some truly great hikes. The 2002 trails census (taken on the first weekend in August, arguably the busiest time of the summer) counted 5,225 hikers on east-side trails and 2,717 hikers on west-side trails. The numbers tell the story.

Acadia's trails are in the midst of a 10-year rehabilitation project destined to repair the 120-mile system and establish the first trails endowment in national park history. The project is funded with $4 million in user fees and appropriates and $9 million in private donations from the Friends of Acadia. The result: the trail system will be maintained in perpetuity. In the meantime, you may come across construction workers and areas undergoing restoration as you hike.

You'll find a number of commercial maps available. I like the *Acadia National Park Trails, Carriage Roads, Hiking, Biking* map ($4.95), published by Map Adventures L.L.C. (www.mapadventures.com), because it's easy to read. The only drawback is it doesn't include the entire island, making it a bit difficult to easily figure out locations if you're not familiar with the area.

EAST-SIDE TRAILS
Jordan Pond Nature Trail
- Distance: 1 mile loop
- Duration: 30–45 minutes round-trip

- Elevation gain: Minimal
- Effort: Very easy
- Trailhead: Jordan Pond Parking Area (Island Explorer Route 5/Jordan Pond)

This oh-so-easy trail is perfect for little ones. You can pick up a brochure detailing 10 numbered sites at the trailhead ($0.50 donation), so you can pepper the walk with fun info and quiz the kids along the way. Reward them afterward with ice cream at the Jordan Pond House.

The trail loops from the Jordan Pond overflow/hikers' parking lot through the woods and down to the pond, following its shore for a bit before looping back to starting point.

Ocean Trail
- Distance: 4 miles round-trip
- Duration: 1–1.5 hours
- Elevation gain: Level
- Effort: Very easy
- Trailhead: Take the Park Loop Road to either the Sand Beach or the Otter Point parking lot. The Island Explorer bus (Route 3/Sand Beach) stops at Sand Beach and Otter Cliffs Parking Areas, so you can begin the walk at either end. If you want to do the trail once, rather than backtracking, get off the bus at one end or the other, then pick up another bus when you're ready to continue onward—mix and match, if you will.

Because this trail is so easy, and easy to reach, it's extremely popular. In fact, lovely as it is, you'd have to be crazy to be on it between 10 A.M. and 3 P.M. at the height of summer. At the risk of divulging the solution, the last time I walked it, at 7 A.M. on a bright June day, I had the path all to myself—a minor miracle, actually—and the tide was at just the right height for Thunder Hole to live up to its name.

The first bus doesn't arrive at Sand Beach until 9:25 A.M., so if that's your mode of transport, consider doing this trail later in the day at the height of summer.

The trail runs close to the shore for about half of its length and takes in several of the

Park Loop Road's highlights—Sand Beach, Thunder Hole, Otter Cliffs, and the giant sea stack in Monument Cove—not to mention gorgeous sea-level views of Frenchman Bay.

Along here, it's especially tempting to "liberate" rocks from the shore—resist the urge. Remember the slogan, "Leave the rocks for the next glacier." If you forget, a few judiciously placed national park signs will remind you.

Compass Harbor

• Distance: 1 mile round-trip
• Duration: 30 minutes
• Elevation gain: Level
• Effort: Very easy
• Trailhead: Compass Harbor section of the park, off Main Street, approximately one mile south of intersection with Mount Desert Street.

This is an easy stroll through an oft-ignored section of the park. You can easily walk from downtown, if you want to lengthen the hike

without adding any difficulty. The path loops through old-growth forest to a point on Compass Harbor and by the ruins of George B. Dorr's summer cottage. There are plenty of nice spots for a picnic here.

Great Head Trail

• Distance: 1.4 miles round-trip
• Duration: 1 hour
• Elevation gain: 145 feet
• Effort: Moderate
• Trailhead: Take the Park Loop Road to the Sand Beach Parking Area (Island Explorer Route 3/Sand Beach)—the lower one is closer to the beach, but it fills up first. Walk down the steps to the beach and across it to the far (eastern) side, where you'll see the trailhead marker. You'll need to cross a rivulet here to reach the trailhead. If you're not here at low tide, and you don't have waterproof shoes, remove your shoes so you won't be hiking with wet feet.

© TOM NANGLE

The easy 3.3-mile Jordan Pond Shore Path circles the pond.

TIPS FOR DAY HIKING

Since Acadia has no backcountry camping, all the hikes in the park are day hikes – guaranteeing, at least, a load off your back! You'll need far less gear for a half-day or daylong hike, but don't be complacent or stupid – use common sense and be prepared for emergencies. That way, they probably won't happen.

Experienced hikers and backcountry campers won't need my advice here, but a few reminders never hurt, and it's worth noting the "maps and guides" information, specific to Acadia.

In general, the gear you carry (and the size of your day pack) depends on your plans for the day – following a short nature trail then calling it quits; hiking for a few hours then stopping for a swim; hiking all day with a noontime picnic – lots of options. Here's a checklist that should help you get organized (divvy up the items if you're hiking with friends or family):

- **Identification,** such as a driver's license. Even if you don't carry your regular wallet, be sure you have your health-insurance card.

- **Maps and guides.** Purchase a trail map at the park's visitors center. The National Park Service map of Acadia that's available free at the visitors center will give you the lay of the land and useful general info, and it's serviceable if you're planning only to drive or bike the Park Loop Road, but *do not* rely on it for hiking. The map published by Jim Witherell is particularly good (contour interval 20 feet), as is the Parkman Publications map, published in conjunction with Friends of Acadia (contour interval 50 feet). On the east side of the island, even if you are planning to stick to the hiking trails, *be sure* also to carry a map of the park's carriage roads to avoid confusion where carriage and hiking trails meet and cross.

- Purchase and use a trail guide as well. I recommend *A Walk in the Park* by Tom St. Germain ($11.95) and/or *Hiking Acadia National Park* by Dolores Kong and Dan Ring ($16.95). Both provide useful detailed maps and elevations for each hike. Also valuable is the Appalachian Mountain Club's *Discover Acadia National Park,* by Jerry and Marcy Monkman ($16.95), which comes with a fold-out map (contour interval 100 feet). Besides hikes, the Appalachian Mountain Club guide includes information on bike and paddling routes as well as other recreational activities in the park.

- Between late June and Columbus Day, carry a copy of the **Island Explorer bus schedule,** which you can find almost anywhere on the island (or download it before you leave home: www.exploreacadia.com). Stuff it in your day pack, even if you're getting to your trailhead by car. If someone in your hiking party wants to quit early, you'll want to know the nearest spot (and time) to catch a bus.

- **Water and food.** Even though some ponds in the park are used as drinking-water sources for surrounding towns, it's treated before they get it. Don't risk intestinal problems; carry your own water. If you're worried about carrying weight, include iodine tablets if you can stand the taste. To avoid excessive thirst, don't bring salty snacks – carry gorp or energy bars (without chocolate, so you don't have to deal with a melting mush). If you're carrying picnic fare, don't be overambitious (or greedy) if you're planning a strenuous hike. Be sure to pack any mayo-based food in a flexible insulated bag; peanut-butter-and-jam (jelly for the kids) sandwiches are a safer bet.

- A couple of wastebasket-size **trash bags** – carry in, carry out. A spare bag can also come in handy for protecting maps, camera, binoculars, etc., in the event of a sudden squall (not unheard of during a Maine summer).

- A **compass or GPS,** particularly if you're directionally challenged or are planning a lengthy hike (or both). If you own a cell phone, carry it, but *turn it off* and use it *only* in an emergency. Wireless service can be iffy in some parts of Acadia; check when you arrive.

- A small **first-aid kit** (in a waterproof or zip-top bag) containing a few basic items: adhesive bandages, aspirin or acetaminophen, ibuprofen, perhaps an Ace bandage. Even though bees don't tend to be a problem in Acadia (except perhaps on the lawn at Jordan Pond House), be sure you're carrying a prefilled epinephrine syringe to prevent anaphylaxis if you're allergic to bee stings (or, for that matter, shellfish). Include a few wooden matches and a whistle in case of emergency.

- **Moist towelettes** for various cleanup tasks, or for cleansing minor scrapes.

- **Swiss Army knife.** Carry the kind with a corkscrew if you're planning on having wine with a picnic. Or you could decant white wine into a plastic water bottle to save weight – but go easy on the alcohol. Not only will it dehydrate you, but you're more prone to tripping and falling.

- A full-brimmed **hat** and decent **hiking shoes** (not sandals, which provide no ankle support).

- **Sunblock, lip balm** (the kind with UV protection), and **insect repellent.** Buzz-Off, a new natural repellent, is a good choice, especially for children. Ben's and Cutter's tend to be widely available.

- **Camera** (and a spare battery) and **binoculars.** Take plenty of film or memory cards if you're planning to be out all day. Most of the island's summits are bare, allowing fabulous views – photo ops are everywhere in Acadia.

- A **mini-flashlight** and spare batteries (just in case).

- Depending on your plans for the day, carry a change of socks, a rain jacket and/or windbreaker, maybe a fleece vest, perhaps a swimsuit for a hike such as Penobscot and Sargent Mountains, where you can pause for a swim in Sargent Pond.

- Most importantly, don't hike alone, or if you do, tell someone – a friend, a relative, your lodging manager, a campground ranger, your shrink, anyone – or leave a note to say where you are headed. If for any reason you don't return, the park rangers at least will know where to start looking.

- Remember, bikes are banned from *all* hiking trails. Dogs must be leashed (not always convenient on strenuous scrambles), and they are banned from Sand Beach and hiking trails with ladders ("ladder trails"). Best advice: Don't bring a dog. If you do, hike only the shorter, easier trails – and *do* come equipped to clean up after your pet.

- And a health note: Lyme disease has been reported here, so when you return from hiking, check for ticks.

First take the trail to the right, which climbs a few dozen steps (the "moderate" part), then continue right toward the headland ("head"), from which you can see the beach and the prominent mound of The Beehive. Out in Frenchman Bay is Egg Rock Light and beyond is Schoodic Point. Continue on the trail counterclockwise, following the perimeter of the head, perhaps pausing for a picnic near the ruins of a mid-19th-century stone teahouse. Continue the loop around the head, then return back to Sand Beach.

You can reach Sand Beach (and therefore the Great Head Trail) via the Island Explorer bus, but since the Park Loop Road is one-way at this point, you won't be able to return to Bar Harbor the way you came. You'll need to grab a bus and continue its loop back to Bar Harbor, but the time is the same: 25 minutes from Bar Harbor to Sand Beach, 25 minutes back to the Village Green from Sand Beach. If you're staying in Bar Harbor, consider bicycling to the trail via the relatively quiet Schooner Head Road, off Route 3, just south of town.

Option: Another way (easier) to hike Great Head is to begin on the north side of the head and go in a clockwise direction. Take Main Street (Route 3) southward out of Bar Harbor, and at about 0.8 mile after the athletic field, bear left onto Schooner Head Road, which roughly parallels the Park Loop Road. Continue just beyond the turn for the Schooner Head Overlook, park at the dead end, and begin your hike from this end of Great Head. There are actually two loops, which could end up taking you 1.8–2 miles. Keep bearing left (clockwise) so you'll skirt the perimeter of Great Head.

Jordan Pond Shore Path

- Distance: 3.3 miles round-trip
- Duration: 1 hour minimum
- Elevation gain: Level
- Effort: Easy to moderate
- Trailhead: Jordan Pond

This mostly level counterclockwise circuit of Jordan Pond is a great way to walk off a Jordan Pond House lunch (including those popovers). Or do the hike first and reward yourself with afternoon tea. Start on the east side, the easiest; the west side has the only moderate section—rocky and rooty and, depending on recent weather, possibly a bit squishy. Log bridges have been installed in a number of spots.

Jordan Pond is part of the island's drinking-water supply, so no swimming (or even wading) here.

As if the summer setting here weren't enough, this trail is even more beautiful in the fall, when stands of birches add gold to the palette. Plus the trail is far less crowded in late September and early October (except perhaps for Columbus Day weekend).

Option: The giant glacial erratic known as **Bubble Rock** is enough of a phenomenon that you may want to detour from the shore trail to see it, via the Bubble Rock Trail (at the northeast corner of the pond). It's a slightly steep 0.8-mile round-trip, up and back on the trail. At the risk of perpetuating a cliché, I'll add that the classic photo here is a Sisyphus imitation—the mythological fellow relentlessly pushing the boulder up a mountain, only to have it roll back. Fortunately, this one doesn't move, since it's the size of an SUV. There must be thousands of photo albums (and probably CDs) all over the world containing this image. Needless to say, kids love it.

In the summer of 2003, trail areas around Jordan Pond House and Jordan Pond were upgraded for wheelchair access, part of a major public-private collaborative effort to increase accessibility in the park. The improved access is on the east side of Jordan Pond.

By car from Bar Harbor, take the Park Loop Road (the two-way west side of the loop) to the Jordan Pond parking lot. An Island Explorer bus follows the same route. (In midsummer, another auto option is to take Route 3 south from Bar Harbor to Seal Harbor, then take the Stanley Brook entrance to the park, going north toward Jordan Pond.) Park and head toward the boat-launching ramp; you'll see the trailhead to the right.

WITH A LITTLE HELP FROM OUR FRIENDS...

As we watch federal funding for national parks lose headway year after year, every park in America needs a safety net like **Friends of Acadia (FOA),** a dynamic organization headquartered in Bar Harbor. Historic stone bridges need repairs? FOA raises the funds. Propane-powered shuttle-bus service needs expanding? FOA finds a million-dollar donor. Well-used trails need maintenance? FOA organizes volunteer work parties. New connector trails needed? FOA gets them done. No need seems to go unfilled.

FOA – one of Acadia National Park's greatest assets – is both reactive and proactive. It's an amazingly symbiotic relationship. When informed of a need, the Friends stand ready to help; when they themselves perceive a need, they propose solutions to park management and jointly figure out ways to make them happen. It's hard to avoid sounding like a media flack when describing this organization.

Friends of Acadia was founded in 1986 to preserve and protect the park for resource-sensitive tourism and myriad recreational uses. Since 1995, FOA has contributed more than $4.6 million to the park and surrounding communities for trail upkeep, carriage-road maintenance, and other conservation projects. Plus FOA cofounded the Island Explorer bus system and instigated the Acadia Trails Forever program, a joint park-FOA partnership for trail rehabilitation. In 2003, for instance, FOA and the park announced the reopening (after considerable planning and rebuilding) of the Homans Path, on the east side of Dorr Mountain. The trail, built around 1916 and named after Eliza Homans, a generous benefactor, fell into disuse in the 1940s. It ascends via a granite stairway to a ledge with a commanding view of the Great Meadow and Frenchman Bay. More recently, it reconstructed the East Cliffs Trail on Sargent Mountain and reopened the abandoned Penobscot Mountain Trail. As part of its Tranquility Project to reduce traffic congestion on the island, FOA purchased an option to buy land in Trenton for an off-island transportation center.

Friends of Schoodic (www.friendsofschoodic.org), an FOA committee, does much of the same type of work to preserve and protect the Schoodic section of the park. It also assists in staffing the park's information center, maintaining the Schoodic Education and Research Center buildings, and inventorying natural resources and counting visitors.

You can join FOA and its 3,000 members and support this worthy cause for $35 a year, or $100 for a family (43 Cottage St., P.O. Box 45, Bar Harbor 04609, 207/288-3340 or 800/625-0321, www.friendsofacadia.org). You can also lend a hand (or two) while you're here. FOA and the park organize volunteer work parties for Acadia trail, carriage road, and other outdoor maintenance three times weekly between June and Columbus Day: 8:30 A.M.-12:30 P.M. Tuesday, Thursday, and Saturday. Call the recorded information line (207/288-3934) for the work locations, or 207/288-3340 or 800/625-0321 for answers to questions. The meeting point is Park Headquarters (Eagle Lake Rd., Rte. 233, Bar Harbor), about three miles west of town. This is a terrific way to give something back to the park, and the camaraderie is contagious. Be sure to take your own water, lunch, and bug repellent. Dress in layers and wear closed-toe shoes. More than 8,000 volunteer hours a year go toward this effort.

Each summer, Friends of Acadia also sponsors a handful of **Ridge Runners,** who work under park supervision and spend their days out and about on the trails repairing cairns, watching for lost hikers, and handing out Leave No Trace information.

If you happen to be in the region on the first Saturday in November, call the FOA office to register for the annual carriage-road cleanup, which usually draws 250 or so volunteers. Bring water and gloves; there's a free hot lunch at midday for everyone who participates. It's dubbed Take Pride in Acadia Day – indeed an apt label.

Gorham Mountain Trail

- Distance: 1.8 miles round-trip
- Duration: 1.5–2 hours
- Elevation gain: 525 feet
- Effort: Moderate
- Trailhead: On the one-way section of the Park Loop Road, continue past Sand Beach and Thunder Hole to the Gorham Mountain Parking Area. (The Island Explorer bus (Route 3/Sand Beach) can drop you off here, or walk a short distance along the Ocean Trail after getting off the bus at the Thunder Hole stop.) The trailhead is at the back of the parking lot.

The round-trip distance specified here covers the trail directly to the summit, then a return the same way with a short detour via Cadillac Cliffs. (You can also continue onward from the Gorham summit, following part of the Bowl Trail down to the Park Loop Road, then walk along the Ocean Trail back to your car—if you've left it in the Gorham lot.)

Follow cairns across ledges up from the trailhead to a fork, where you'll see a plaque commemorating Waldron Bates, the ingenious pathmaker who instigated the strategic use of granite staircases and iron ladders for Acadia's trails.

Bates was a lawyer for his day job, but his summer avocation as head of the Roads and Paths Committee for the Bar Harbor Improvement Association (1900–1909) gave him the greatest pleasure. Think of him as you navigate the Cadillac Cliffs Trail, one of his projects.

For now, though, bear left (saving the Cadillac Cliffs route for the return) and head for the open-ledge summit (525 feet, third-lowest of Acadia's peaks). A signposted cairn marks the spot. From here, you'll see Sand Beach, Egg Rock Light in Frenchman Bay, the Beehive, Champlain Mountain, and lots more—a fabulous view.

Return via the same route, but make the short detour left onto the U-shaped Cadillac Cliffs Trail, featuring stairs, rocky footing, granite "tunnels," and even an ancient sea cave, now high and dry. (This sea cave once was filled with beach cobbles, but slowly, slowly it's been cleaned out by hikers—a prime example of the damage done by removing "just one.")

Beachcroft Trail

- Distance: 1.6 miles round-trip
- Duration: 1.5–2 hours
- Elevation gain: 1,100 feet
- Effort: Moderate to difficult
- Trailhead: The Tarn parking area, just north of Route 3, near Sieur de Monts Spring, and just west of the Park Loop Road, near the Jackson Laboratory (or take the Island Explorer bus, Route 4/Blackwoods).

The Beachcroft Trail on Huguenot Head leads up the west side of Champlain. Also called the Beachcroft Path, the trail is best known for its nearly 1,500 beautifully engineered granite steps, built by the Civilian Conservation Corps (CCC). It's a moderate climb via switchbacks to the granite ledges of Huguenot Head and its views to the Atlantic. Take in the views and replenish yourself with a snack to prepare for the next section. The trail descends briefly before climbing steeply over rocks to the Champlain's summit. The views are stupendous. From there, you can connect with the Bear Brook or Precipice Trails.

Penobscot and Sargent Mountains

- Distance: 6 miles round-trip
- Duration: 4 hours
- Elevation gain: 1,200 feet
- Effort: Difficult to strenuous
- Trailhead: Park your car in the overflow lot at Jordan Pond House, go left of the restaurant and look for the carved trail signpost.

You'll cross Jordan Stream and a carriage road before starting on the rough part—heading upward rather steeply with rocky, ledgy underfooting. Handholds have been installed in strategic spots. (This part is even less fun on the return route.) But the rewards are worth the effort. Continue on to the Penobscot summit (1,194 feet, fifth-highest in the park), with wide-open views. In August, you'll have wild blueberries (but leave some for others) en route to the top.

The best feature of this hike is that you get to reach one summit then go for a swim in gorgeous little Sargent Pond before tackling the next one. From Penobscot's summit, it's only 10 minutes downhill to the pond. (If you're retracing your route, you can even have a second swim on the way back.) This is a long hike, however; if you're hiking with kids, be sure they're up to the challenge. For that matter, be sure *you* are.

From Sargent Pond, head upward on the South Ridge Trail to the summit of Sargent Mountain (1,373 feet, second-highest in the park).

Don't rush the return—the vistas are superb up here—but when you're ready, go back the same way.

Dorr Mountain via Homans Path and Dorr Mountain East Face

- Distance: 2.8 miles round-trip
- Duration: 1.5–2 hours
- Elevation gain: 1,200 feet
- Effort: Difficult to strenuous
- Trailhead: Take Hemlock Trail from the beginning of the Sieur de Monts parking lot (look for the split rail fence) and follow it to the intersection with the Jesup Path. Continue on the Hemlock Trail another few yards to the trailhead on your left. You can also take the Hemlock Trail from Bar Harbor to the trailhead.

Avid hiker Tom St. Germaine, author of *A Walk in the Park,* rediscovered the Homans Path, originally built in 1915, while searching for abandoned trails in the early 1990s and wrote about it in another book, *Trails of History.* He deserves a big thanks, and Friends of Acadia and the Park Service also deserve accolades for restoring the trail, which reopened in 2004.

The Homans Path ascends rapidly via steps and switchbacks 0.3 mile to the intersection with the Dorr Mountain East Trail. It's a beautiful trail that weaves through narrow passages in the granite ledges and even under slabs of

granite. From the intersection with the East Trail, the Homans Path continues its climb over rocky terrain. Along the way, expect nice views over Frenchman Bay.

Option: On the return, follow the East Face Trail all the way down to the Sieur de Mont Spring parking lot or veer off on Kurt Diederich's Climb, which also returns to the lot.

Other Recommended East-Side Trails

For an easy hike, consider **Jesup Path,** a two- to three-mile hike through the lovely area around Sieur de Monts Spring. Also, the **Seaside Path** (or Seaside Trail) runs about two miles through the woods (use insect repellent) between Seal Harbor and the Jordan Pond House. Use the Island Explorer bus to make this a one-way hike, or retrace your route for a longer hike.

A choice moderate hike is **Conner's Nubble,** with super views down to Eagle Lake and the mountains off to the east. For

Granite steps are a distinguishing feature of a number of Acadia's trails.

© TOM NANGLE

a moderate-to-strenuous hike, try **Parkman Mountain**—not too strenuous but enough to make it worthwhile, especially with the views from the bald summit—what you might call an "all-purpose hike."

You can access the **Cadillac South Ridge Trail** from Blackwoods Campground. Start the trail at the entrance to the campground and do a 7.4-mile round-trip. The hike is moderate to strenuous (1,530-foot elevation gain), with a couple of quite easy stretches (the last part is the steepest).

Experienced, serious hikers seeking real challenges in the *strenuous* category should consider the **Beehive** and **Precipice** trails. These two "ladder trails" (where no pets are allowed) are the park's toughest routes, with sheer faces, iron ladders, and strenuous ratings. As already mentioned, Champlain Mountain's 1.6-mile round-trip Precipice Trail often is closed (usually mid-April into August) to protect nesting peregrine falcons. Avid hikers consider the 0.8-mile round-trip Beehive a "must-do." If challenges are your thing, you're not acrophobic, and these trails are open (check beforehand at the Hulls Cove Visitor Center), go ahead. Both trailheads are on the Park Loop Road (Island Explorer Route 3/Sand Beach).

WEST-SIDE TRAILS
Wonderland

- Distance: 1.4 miles round-trip
- Duration: 45 minutes
- Elevation gain: Minimal
- Effort: Easy
- Trailhead: The Wonderland trail begins on the south side of Route 102A, a mile west of the Seawall Campground. Walk from Seawall; if you're staying elsewhere, ask the Island Explorer bus driver (Route 7/Southwest Harbor) to drop you off (it's not a regular stop).

Shortest and easiest of the park's trails, Wonderland follows an old fire road and is more a walk than a hike—a great starter-upper for a family ensconced at Seawall Campground. Most of the route is wooded—trees gnarled from the wind, branches laden with moss—

with the rugged shoreline and a small cobble beach as your reward at the end.

Across Route 102A from the Wonderland trailhead is the 420-acre Big Heath, considered one of Maine's "critical areas." Because of its sensitive peatland—wet and squishy and fragile underfoot (not to mention its battalions of mosquitoes)—avoid it. (You'll be skirting its edges, though, if you walk the Hio Trail from the back of Seawall Campground.)

Ship Harbor Nature Trail

- Distance: 1.3 miles round-trip
- Duration: 45–60 minutes
- Elevation gain: Level
- Effort: Easy, some uneven ground
- Trailhead: The parking area (with restrooms) for Ship Harbor is less than half a mile west of the Wonderland Parking Area. The trail is on the south side of Route 102A. As with Wonderland, you can be dropped off by an Island Explorer bus (Route 7/Southwest Harbor) and/or flag one down after your hike.

The Ship Harbor Nature Trail isn't quite as easy as Wonderland—roots can snag you along the way, and rocks can be slippery if it has rained or the tide has receded—but it's even more educational as a family hike. At the Thompson Island Visitor Center, the Hulls Cove Visitor Center, or at Seawall Campground, pick up a copy of the park's 12-page *Ship Harbor Nature Trail* booklet and use it along the way.

Legend has it that the harbor earned its name during the Revolutionary War, when an American privateer, seeking refuge, became stranded here.

If the tide has gone out, follow the trail along the shore first (counterclockwise) so the kids can check out what's been left in the tidepools. If the tide is high, perhaps you'll want to follow the booklet's suggested clockwise route. Or you can do a "figure-eight" route. In any case, you won't get lost.

Option: Since Wonderland and Ship Harbor are so close together, consider doing both trails in a morning or afternoon. Carry a picnic and enjoy it on the shore.

Flying Mountain Trail

- Distance: 1.5 miles round-trip
- Duration: 1 hour
- Elevation gain: 200 feet
- Effort: Moderate, some steep sections
- Trailhead: The trail begins at the end of Fernald Point Road, 0.8 mile east of Route 102 (at the northern edge of Southwest Harbor). If you're driving from the Bar Harbor area, slow down after passing Echo Lake and take the next left. Drive to the end of the road, park in the Valley Cove lot, and begin at the carved signpost. Fernald Point was the site of the early 17th-century St. Sauveur mission settlement established by French Jesuits. The Island Explorer bus headed to or from Southwest Harbor can drop you off and/or pick you up at the corner of Route 102 and Fernald Point Road; from there, walk down the road to the trailhead.

At 284 feet, Flying Mountain has the lowest of Acadia's 26 summits, so theoretically it shouldn't have one of the best views—but it does. With minimum effort (some minor scrambling up and over, but level at the end), you're surveying the mouth of Somes Sound, including Northeast and Southwest Harbors and Greening Island between them. It hardly gets better than this (well, it does, but this is pretty spectacular).

From the trailhead, the rise through the trees is a bit steep, with some stepped ledges, but it's quick (why rush, though?). At the summit, relax and take photos, then descend toward Valley Cove. You'll encounter roots and rocks, and your knees may complain a bit, but again, it's really not strenuous and it doesn't last long. At the bottom, bear left onto the woods road and return to the parking area.

You can hike the Valley Cove Trail as an extension of the Flying Mountain Trail, but it may be closed April–mid-August, as peregrine falcons have been nesting there in recent years.

Beech Mountain Trail

- Distance: 1.2 miles round-trip
- Duration: 1–1.5 hours
- Elevation gain: 700 feet
- Effort: Moderate
- Trailhead: From Route 102 in Somesville, take the Pretty Marsh Road westward to Beech Hill Road. Turn left and continue to the end, climbing gradually to the parking area for Beech Cliff and Beech Mountain. (This trail is not accessible via the Island Explorer.)

Several hiking routes merge and converge in the Beech Mountain area. Some begin from a trailhead on the southern side of Beech and can be more strenuous than this one. This hike starts from the northern side. None of the Beech Mountain hikes are particularly convenient to the Island Explorer bus system.

A short distance from the beginning of the Beech Mountain Trail, you'll reach a fork—the Beech Mountain loop. Bear right to do the loop counterclockwise—the rewarding vistas over Long Pond come sooner, and it's less steep this way.

At the summit (839 feet) stands the park's only fire tower, now disused. During unseasonably hot summers, when the ranger-posted fire-danger level is high, volunteers come up to keep an eye on things, but small charter planes do most of the fire patrols these days. Besides having great views of Long Pond, from here you can see as far as Blue Hill to the northwest and the Cranberry Isles to the south. A knob near the summit is a prime viewing spot for the migration of hawks (and other raptors) in September.

From the summit, continue your counterclockwise route or backtrack the way you came, heading down to the trail junction and back to the parking area.

Option: If you're particularly fascinated by mosses and lichens (and have brought insect repellent), consider a three-mile round-trip to Beech Mountain that begins with a lovely walk-in-the-woods starting at the same trailhead. Instead of taking the Beech Mountain Trail, follow the Valley Trail on fairly level ground for just under a mile. Then bear right onto the Beech Mountain South Ridge Trail and start climbing stone steps (lots of them) toward the summit. Descend from the summit via the Beech Mountain loop route, going clockwise (left) to take advantage of the Long Pond vistas.

Acadia Mountain Trail

- Distance: 2.5 miles round-trip
- Duration: 1.5–2 hours
- Elevation gain: 1,050 feet
- Effort: Difficult
- Trailhead: From Somesville (west of Bar Harbor), take Route 102 southward for just over three miles, alongside Echo Lake, until you see the signposted Acadia Mountain parking lot. Cross the road to the trailhead. (The Island Explorer's Route 7/Southwest Harbor goes right along Route 102; request a stop to start your hike and flag down the bus when you've finished the hike.)

Climb the steps and continue to the junction with the St. Sauveur Mountain Trail. (If you're up for a much longer hike, do an Acadia and St. Sauveur loop, for a four-mile round-trip.) Continue left on the Acadia Mountain Trail, where it's briefly deceptively flat and lovely. After you cross a fire road (your eventual return route), begin the rocky, ledgy ascent, following cairns.

It's less than a mile to the open summit—with fantastic views up and down Somes Sound. (Actually, there's a sort of double summit, with the second one only slightly lower than the 641-foot maximum height.) In summer, you'll find wild blueberries. The descent toward the Sound is longer and quite steep—take it slowly. At the bottom, when you reach the spur to Man o' War Brook, detour briefly to follow the brook to Somes Sound. Allegedly, Revolutionary War vessels stocked up on water here during their exploits along the Maine coast. Return to the trailhead via an easy walk on the mile-long fire road.

Biking

Bicycling on Mount Desert Island is a joy, but you have to pedal in the right locations. The island is mountainous, and that includes the roads; many have serious ups and downs. Serious, experienced road cyclists will have a blast. Mountain bikers, casual bikers, families, and everyone else will be more than pleased with the carriage roads. These gravel roads lace through the heart of the park and are punctuated with beautiful stone bridges. They provide a variety of challenges, and you can create a ride of practically any length by linking them together.

Information about rental bikes, organized rides, and tours appears in the Bar Harbor and Southwest Harbor sections of the *Mount Desert Island Communities* chapter.

You'll find a number of commercial maps available. I prefer the *Acadia National Park Trails, Carriage Roads, Hiking, Biking* map ($4.95) published by Map Adventures L.L.C. (www.mapadventures.com), because I find it easiest to read, it details in-town roads, and it shows some of the dirt roads described below. One big drawback for cyclists is that this map doesn't include the entire island; the northern third is simply lopped off, so if you're cycling that section, you'll need another map as well.

ROAD BIKING

Road biking on Mount Desert Island is best left to the experienced. Roads are often narrow, shoulders frequently nonexistent or soft, and gawking visitors often aren't paying attention to the road while driving. Families, once-a-year pedalers, and casual bicyclists will do best on the carriage roads. That said, serious road bikers do have a few choices. Stop in at one of Bar Harbor's bike shops for recommendations or to find out about group rides. If you go by yourself, timing is critical. For the best ride with the least traffic, get up at the crack of dawn and start pedaling once it's truly light outside. It's very important to wear reflective clothing on these roads. It's also wise to drive the roads before cycling them to check conditions. If it's been a while since they've been resurfaced, you might be in for a very rough ride.

Park Loop Road

Since bikes are not allowed on hiking trails in Acadia, the **Park Loop Road** provides a good workout for mountain or road bikers, but its prime drawback is the volume of car and RV exhaust fumes you'll be inhaling if you decide to take this route in the middle of the day at the height of summer. So don't. (Park-wide ozone alerts are not common, but they do occur in Acadia.) Nor are the Park Loop's shoulders as wide as they might be to comfortably accommodate a great many bikes. Besides, on most of the one-way sections of the Park Loop, overflow auto parking is allowed in the right lane. Dodging cars ain't fun. The 27-mile route is indeed spectacular, so if you want to bike it, plan your pedaling for early in the day (around 7 A.M. in summer), later in the day (around "happy hour," when everyone else has packed it in and headed for bars and/or restaurants), or during "shoulder" months (June, September, even October).

Southeast Quarter of the Island

This route dips you in and out of the park. Begin in Bar Harbor and follow Route 3 to Schooner Head Road, then follow signs to Park Loop Road. Ride the Park Loop to the end of the one-way section in Seal Harbor, go right on Jordan Pond Road heading to Seal Harbor, then pick up Route 3 to the intersection with Route 198 in Northeast Harbor. Go left on Route 198 into Northeast Harbor, taking Harborside Road to Joy Road to Manchester Road. Go right. Manchester Road merges into Sargent Drive. Follow it until it meets Route 198, go left and continue to the intersection with Route 233. Go right, and follow Route 233 back to Bar Harbor.

You can increase the mileage by exploring some of the back roads of Seal Harbor (watch out for Martha Stewart) or Northeast Harbor. Another option is to take the Duck Brook Road off Route 233, just after the Eagle Lake parking lots. That meanders into Bar Harbor, merging onto West Street.

Routes 102/102A

Experienced riders who are accustomed to traffic might consider this loop around the western half of Mount Desert Island. It passes through Somesville, Southwest Harbor, Bass Harbor, Tremont, and Pretty Marsh. While little mileage on this route is actually in the park, there are quite a few offshoots that do venture into it, but in most cases, these are dirt roads. If you do the full loop, it's about 26 miles. Unless you're intent on getting in mileage, plan time to stop and explore along the way. Expect nonexistent or soft shoulders on much of the route and moderate to heavy traffic.

To add to the distance, venture down some of the side roads along the way, such as Ripples Road to Beech Hill Road (dead ends), Hall Quarry Road (loop), or detouring north in Pretty Marsh on the Indian Point Road, which ends at Routes 198/102.

CARRIAGE ROADS

The better alternative for most aspiring bicyclists is to bring, borrow, or rent a bike and take advantage of the spectacular carriage road system—57 miles of crushed-rock roadways with nary a car in sight (bikes are allowed on only 45 of the 57 miles; 12 miles are on private land, so be alert for signs).

At every junction in the carriage road system stands a tall wooden post with a number and directional signs. Use these numbers, together with the park's free carriage road map, to navigate the network. Also very helpful are a couple of portable books—*A Pocket Guide to the Carriage Roads of Acadia National Park,* by Diana

© TOM NANGLE

carriage road bridge

Abrell, and *A Pocket Guide to Biking on Mount Desert Island,* by Audrey Minutolo.

Periodically, carriage roads and their bridges undergo necessary repair, and since such work is possible only in decent weather, you may encounter closures. When you obtain the carriage road map at the Hulls Cove Visitor Center, ask a ranger to indicate on the map any sections that may be under repair and/or closed.

Some sections of the carriage roads are fine for wheelchairs, particularly near Eagle Lake and Bubble Pond. Since these are multiuse roadways, bicyclists in particular should remember and adhere to the rules:

- Bikes yield to everyone (pedestrians, horses, wheelchairs, strollers); pedestrians yield to horses. Horses tend to become skittish around bikes, so be particularly cautious when you're pedaling near them. Better still, pull off to the right, stop, and let them pass.
- Wear a helmet.
- Keep to the right and signal clearly when passing on the left.

- Do *not* speed; speeders are a danger to walkers, horses, children, the disabled, and sometimes themselves.
- Pets must be leashed.

As with the park's hiking trails, it would take a whole book just to focus on all the options on the carriage roads. While the carriage roads make wonderful walking paths, they are the best places in the park for bikes. So most of the route suggestions that follow are geared to cyclists.

It cannot be said often enough: *There is no off-road biking in Acadia, and bikes are not allowed on the hiking trails.*

At the end of the following section, there is one recommended carriage road loop for walking—on private land where bikes are not allowed.

Eagle Lake and Witch Hole Pond

These two loops are probably the most popular in the park—because they're not difficult (thus good for families) and they're close to Bar Harbor, where so many visitors stay. Thus, if you decide to do either of these in the middle of summer, *get an early start.* If you're planning to rent bikes, rent them the night before, so you can be on your way right after breakfast.

If you're doing this anytime between late June and Columbus Day, be sure to check the schedule for the Island Explorer bus and use it to get to and from your starting points.

For the Eagle Lake loop, the Route 6/Northeast Harbor bus makes a stop at the head of Eagle Lake on Route 233, or you can pedal or drive from downtown Bar Harbor via Mount Desert Street. At the end of the street, cross over to Route 233 (Eagle Lake Road) and follow it to the beginning of this route. (Park in the Eagle Lake Parking Area, across Rte. 233 from the beginning of the carriage road.)

To reach the Witch Hole Pond loop from downtown Bar Harbor, take West Street to its end, cross Route 3, then continue on West Street Extension. Take a right on Duck Brook Road and continue from there to the carriage road (starting at numbered signpost 5).

Option: Drive to the Hulls Cove Visitor

Center, park there, and bike (or walk your bike) up the steep trail to the first carriage-road intersection, number 1. From there, continue to 2 and then veer right to make the circuit via junctions (signposts) 4 and 5 and then to 3, making a loop back to 1. From there, it's pretty much downhill to your car.

Each of those rides is about six miles. If you'd prefer to double your biking mileage, park at the Eagle Lake Parking Area and do both loops from there.

Jordan Pond/Bubble Pond

To ride this loop, take the Island Explorer bus with your bike to the Jordan Pond Parking Area or drive there via the Park Loop Road (use the Jordan Pond area, not the Jordan Pond House area). Pedal back along the Park Loop Road (follow bike rules and stay with the traffic; it's two-way here) to the handsome stone Jordan Pond Gate Lodge. Now you have two choices—a clockwise route or a counterclockwise one.

The counterclockwise route allows you a downhill coast along Jordan Pond near the end of your 8.5-mile circuit. Enter the carriage road next to the gatehouse and continue to signpost (junction) 17. Head north, passing Bubble Pond along its west shore—practically in the water—to signpost 7. Bear left around the bottom of Eagle Lake, to signpost 8, continue to 10, then turn south, skirting Jordan Pond, to signpost 14. Continue south to 15 and 16, exiting onto the Park Loop Road across from where you entered.

After these warm-up rides, you'll have a good sense of this amazing network. And now how about a walk on private carriage roads, where you won't be dodging bikes. (Bikes are banned from the 12 miles of private Green Rock Company carriage roads; you're free to walk there, however.)

Amphitheatre Loop

This is a fabulous 5.5-mile loop that takes you into the heart of the park, far from the noises of traffic and civilization. You'll pass over two bridges—the gently curving Amphitheatre

The Amphitheatre Trail is a lovely walk in the woods that parallels and often crosses Harbor Brook.

Bridge, at 236 feet one of the longest in the system, and Little Harbor Brook Bridge, which must be one of the smallest. The route has some steady climbs, but the rewards are panoramic views to the Cranberry Islands. Follow a clockwise route beginning at the Brown Mountain Gatehouse parking lot on Route 198 (one mile north of Northeast Harbor). Enter the system and bear right at signposts 18 and 19 and keep straight or left at signpost 20. Keep right again at signposts 21 and 22. When you return to signpost 20, go left and keep left until you're back at the parking area.

Option: Hikers can enjoy the 0.8-mile Amphitheatre Trail connecting the two bridges. It's a lovely walk in the woods paralleling and often crossing Harbor Brook as it babbles and descends over waterfalls in into small pools—perfect for cooling hot, tired feet. Don't take this trail during spring run-off periods or after heavy rains, when that sweet brook might be a raging torrent.

Around the Mountain

This 11-mile loop is an outstanding ride for experienced mountain bikers. It circumnavigates several of the park's major peaks, including Sargent, Penobscot, Cedar Swamp, Parkman, and Gilmore, and it passes by numerous bridges and waterfalls. The views are glorious. It's not an easy ride, however, as it climbs numerous hills. Begin at the Parkman Mountain parking lot on Route 198. Begin by heading right. At signpost 13, go left and then left at signpost 12.

You're now on the Around the Mountain road. At signpost 10, turn right and then keep right, staying on the Around the Mountain road, at signposts 14, 21, 20, and 19. At signpost 12, turn left, then right at signpost 13 to return to the parking lot. You can also access this route from the Jordan Pond area.

FIRE ROADS
Hio Trail

This old Acadia fire road begins at the back of the Seawall campground (behind Loop C) and goes over to Route 102. It's an easy four-mile round-trip. The path is mostly wooded, passing near the Big Heath, so if you take the trail late in the day, be sure to use insect repellent. It's a great family ride, with plenty of bird- and wildlife-watching opportunities.

Long Pond Fire Road

This five-mile loop off Route 102 just south of Pretty Marsh Picnic Area (park here) follows a dirt road to Long Pond and back, with a short section on Route 102 to close the loop. The terrain is moderate, with many long hills. Spruce and fir trees line most of the route, and you'll pass by boggy areas as well as a few ponds. This is prime moose territory in the park, so be on the lookout for the gangly beasts. If you see one, observe from a distance; if it starts coming toward you, move away quietly.

Other Recreation

CALM-WATER PADDLING

Both **Eagle Lake** and **Jordan Pond** have boat ramps. The Eagle Lake put-in is off Route 233, the Jordan Pond put-in is adjacent to the hiker parking lot near the Jordan Pond House, on the Park Loop Road. No swimming is allowed in either lake.

Another fine pond for paddling is **Seal Cove Pond,** in Tremont. Route 102 skirts the western edge of the 1.5-mile-long pond, and the shoreline has plenty of houses, but most of the forested eastern shore is in the park. The primary access point is off the Western Mountain Road. To find it, take the Seal Cove Road from Seal Cove, go left on the first park road and follow it to its intersection with the Western Mountain

Road. Go right, the road ends at the put-in. You might also be able to find a spot or two to park on Route 102 with easy access.

SWIMMING

Acadia has a limited number of swimming areas; they and their parking lots are mighty crowded on hot days. Go early in the day or take your chances.

Don't assume you can swim in any freshwater pond or lake you encounter in the park or even elsewhere on the island. Six island locations—Upper and Lower Hadlock Ponds, Bubble and Jordan Ponds, Eagle Lake, and the southern half of Long Pond—are drinking-water reservoirs where swimming and windsurfing are banned (but boating is allowed). Don't let your dog swim in these ponds, either. Five of the six are within the park; Long Pond borders the park.

Also see Penobscot and Sargent Mountains under Hiking; Sargent Pond is a lovely spot to cool off midhike.

Sand Beach

Located slightly below the Park Loop Road (Take Island Explorer Route 3/Sand Beach), Sand Beach is the park's (and the island's) biggest sandy beach. Lifeguards are on duty during the summer, and even then the biggest threat can be hypothermia. The saltwater is terminally glacial—in mid-July, it still might not reach 60°F; by September, it's usually warmer, though the air will be cooler. Even though kids seem not to notice, they can become chilled quickly; keep an eye on their condition. The best solution is to walk to the far end of the beach, where a warmer, shallow stream meets the ocean. Also, if you arrive here on the incoming tide, after the sun has warmed up the cove's bottom, the water temperature is marginally higher. On a hot August day, arrive early; the parking lot fills up. Bring a picnic. There are changing rooms and restrooms. Dogs are *not* allowed on Sand Beach.

After hiking nearby Great Head on a hot day, go for a swim at Sand Beach—you'll be surprisingly grateful for the chilly water.

Echo Lake

The park's most popular freshwater swimming site, staffed with a lifeguard and inevitably crowded on hot days, is **Echo Lake,** south of Somesville on Route 102 and well signposted (take Island Explorer Route 7/Southwest Harbor). Pets are not allowed on the beach.

Swimming Holes

If you have a canoe, kayak, or rowboat, you can reach swimming holes in **Seal Cove Pond** and **Round Pond,** both on the western side of Mount Desert. Both have shorelines bordering the park. The eastern shore of **Hodgdon Pond** (also on the western side of the island) is accessible by car (via Hodgdon Road and Long Pond Fire Road).

Another popular swimming hole is **Lake Wood,** at the northern end of Mount Desert. It has a small beach and auto access. To get to Lake Wood from Route 3, head west on Crooked Road to unpaved Park Road. Turn left and continue to the parking area, which will be crowded on a hot day, so arrive early.

After hiking Great Head, cool your tootsies – or more if you dare – in the ocean at Sand Beach.

ROCK CLIMBING

Acadia has a number of splendid sites prized by climbers: the sea cliffs at Otter Cliffs and Great Head; South Bubble Mountain; Canada Cliff (on the island's western side); and the South Wall and the Central Slabs on Champlain Mountain. The climbing season usually runs May–October. Occasionally, it can be extended at either end, but you'd have to be on or near the island to be able to catch the decent weather before it deteriorated. (Heck, that can happen even in summer.)

Some park regulations you need to know for Acadia climbing:

- Don't leave your dog tied up or on the loose while you're climbing.
- The park's bridges are off-limits for climbing or bouldering.
- From April to mid-August, while peregrine falcons are nesting, the Central Slabs area on The Precipice is almost always closed.
- Sign in at the registration box at climbing sites—registration is required at Otter Cliffs, the South Wall, and Canada Cliff.

If you've forgotten any climbing gear or need replacements, the best source is **Cadillac Mountain Sports** (26 Cottage St., Bar Harbor 04609, 207/288-4532, www.cadillac-sports.com), on the ground floor next to Atlantic Climbing School (ACS).

Climbing Schools and Guides

If you haven't tried climbing, *never* do it yourself, without instruction. Best advice is to contact one of Bar Harbor's two climbing operations. **Acadia Mountain Guides Climbing School** (198 Main St., Bar Harbor, 207/288-8186 or 888/232-9559, www.acadiamountain-guides.com) offers all levels of instruction and guided climbs for individuals and families from mid-May to October. The American Mountain Guides Association–accredited school is directed by AMGA-certified rock and alpine guide Jon Tierney. A private full-day guided climb is $210; a half-day is $120. Beginning and intermediate group courses are $145 for two days, $75 for one day; student rates are

available. Family rates ($190 half day; $290 full day for up to four people) are available for families with kids younger than 10.

Atlantic Climbing School (ACS) (24 Cottage St., 2nd floor, P.O. Box 514, Bar Harbor 04609, 207/288-2521) provides basic half-day courses (3.5 and 4.5 hours), including a "family climbing experience," all by reservation (minimum age is eight). You'll learn just enough to introduce you to the sport and do an initial basic climb—with guides and in line with park rules. ACS also offers a series of courses for intermediate climbers. A half- or full-day guided course for experienced climbers also is available. Half-day courses are $60 each for three people, $80 each for two people, and $100 for a private course. The family course is $179 for up to four related students. Full-day guided courses are $105 per person for three, $125 per person for two, or $180 for a private outing. All gear is provided by both firms.

Jeff Butterfield, ACS's founder, has written the "must-have" book for experienced climbers: *Acadia: A Climber's Guide,* which covers all the best-known routes as well as some lesser-known crags. Routes are described and rated (with maps and symbols), and there's all kinds of other essential information. For instance, the book recommends that South Bubble climbers wear helmets for protection from rocks dropped ("by yahoos," as he puts it) from hiking trails overhead. At $25 for a 160-page book, it's expensive—but it may save your life. How valuable is that? (It's even entertaining just reading the route names: Selfless Bastard, Homosexual Armadillo, Fear of Flying, Arms Race, Pickled Amnesiac, and dozens more.)

WINTER SPORTS

As mentioned earlier, these miles of car-free carriage roads are fantastic for cross-country skiing and snowshoeing. The only problem is that even though Acadia gets about five feet of snow during an average winter, it's not like a ski resort, where there's a base and more snow keeps piling on top of it. Here, it might snow one day and rain or thaw the next. But now and then, a bumper crop of snow creates a winter wonderland for days and even weeks. Acadia's proximity to the ocean and its Gulf Stream current means that you take your chances with snow. January and February can be good bets… but then again, you never know. The park publishes a very handy *Winter Activities Guide,* a foldout map/brochure that explains what you can and cannot do, where you can and cannot go.

Cross-country skis and snowshoes are available for rent from **Cadillac Mountain Sports** (26 Cottage St., Bar Harbor 04609, 207/288-4532, www.cadillacsports.com), which is open all year.

For carriage road information and other visitor information about Acadia during the winter, when the Hulls Cove Visitor Center is closed, contact Park Headquarters (Eagle Lake Rd., Rte. 233, P.O. Box 177, Bar Harbor 04609, 207/288-3338, www.nps.gov/acad/), which is open all year. In winter, it's open 8 A.M.–4:30 P.M. daily except Thanksgiving, December 24 and 25, and January 1; in summer, it's closed on weekends.

Snowmobilers can ride the 27-mile Park Loop Road, two miles of the carriage roads, and the road to Cadillac's summit.

Any hardy souls up for experiencing Acadia in winter can stay at the **Blackwoods Campground** (Rte. 3, Otter Creek, five miles south of Bar Harbor), the park's only year-round campground.

Practicalities

CAMPING

Mount Desert Island has at least a dozen private (commercial) campgrounds, but there are only two—**Blackwoods** and **Seawall**—within park boundaries on the island. (A third park campground is on Isle au Haut.)

Blackwoods and Seawall have *no* hookups. Most sites at both are for tents, but some do accommodate pop-ups, vehicle campers, and RVs up to 35 feet in length. Both campgrounds have seasonal restrooms (no showers) and dumping stations. Less than half a mile from Blackwoods, and even closer to Seawall, are coin-operated hot showers and small markets for buying incidental supplies.

Both campgrounds are wooded, with no sea views but not far from the water. In June, be prepared for black flies; in July and August, bring insect repellent for mosquitoes. Maximum capacity at each site is six persons, one vehicle, and one large tent (or two small ones). Quiet time in both campgrounds is 10 P.M.–6 A.M.

Both campgrounds also have **amphitheaters,** where park rangers present free, hourlong evening programs (various starting times) during the summer on a variety of natural- and cultural-history topics. Non-campers are also welcome at these events, and there's wheelchair access. Some of the programs have included "Forces of Nature," "Avian Mysteries," "Acadia's Treasures," "The French in Acadia," and "All Things Furry." Even sing-alongs are sometimes on the schedule. Blackwoods has programs several nights a week; Seawall programs tend to be on weekend evenings.

Firewood collection is no longer allowed within Seawall's grounds. Rather than scrounge for what little duff remains around the campgrounds in order to build a campfire, stop on your way to Acadia and pick up a stash of firewood. All along Route 3 in Trenton, and along Route 3 on Mount Desert (near the clusters of commercial campgrounds), you'll see signs for firewood for sale (usually around $2, sometimes less). Bring your own to Blackwoods and Seawall and do your part to preserve the environment.

The propane-powered Island Explorer buses serve both Blackwoods (Route 4/Blackwoods) and Seawall (Route 7/Southwest Harbor) between late June and Columbus Day. Leave your vehicle at your campsite and do your park and island exploring by bus.

Blackwoods Campground

With more than 300 campsites, Blackwoods Campground, just off Route 3, five miles south of Bar Harbor, is open all year. Because of its location on the east side of the island, it's also the more popular of the two campgrounds. Reservations are suggested May 1–October 31. Call 800/365-2267; have your credit card handy. Or register online at http://reservations.nps.gov. Cost is $20 per site per night; you cannot reserve specific sites or adjoining sites. Reservations are taken on a floating system: For reservations May 1–June 4, call beginning January 5; for reservations June 5–July 4, call beginning Feb. 5; for July 5–Aug. 4, call beginning March 5; for August 5–September 4, call beginning April 5; for September 5–October 4, call beginning May 5; and for October 5–31, call beginning June 5. Mail-in reservations requests will be accepted no earlier than two weeks before the call dates and are randomly processed on those dates. (These dates and regulations are subject to change, so call to check so as to not be disappointed.) Camping is free December–March, and no reservations are necessary. For the winter of 2006-2007, no facilities will be available. This means you'll have to carry in and carry out everything, including human waste. There will be no water or bathrooms, nor will the area be plowed. Off-season, when the bathrooms are still open, there is a minimal camping fee.

If you're staying at Blackwoods, consider adding the **Cadillac South Ridge Trail** to your hiking list. Of course, you can drive to the Cadillac summit and get the same fabulous 360-degree views, but this hike makes you feel you earned it.

Seawall Campground

Reservations are not accepted at Seawall Campground, on Route 102A in the Seawall district, four miles south of Southwest Harbor—it's first-come, first-served. But in midsummer, you'll need to arrive as early as 8:30 A.M. (when the ranger station opens) to secure one of the 200 or so sites. Seawall is open Memorial Day weekend through September. Cost is $20 per night for drive-up sites and $14 per night for walk-in sites.

RV length at Seawall is limited to 35 feet, with the width limited to an awning extended no more than 12 feet. Generators are not allowed in the campground.

INFORMATION AND SERVICES
Emergencies

If you have an emergency while in the park, call **911**. The park's general information number is 207/288-3338. If you're in a remote location, it helps if you're carrying a cell phone, but *please* keep it turned off while hiking or biking; save it for an emergency. The nearest hospital, in downtown Bar Harbor, is Mount Desert Island Hospital, with a 24-hour emergency room. The nearest major medical center is in Bangor (Eastern Maine Medical Center), via a congested route that can take an hour or longer at the height of summer. (Bangor, however, is one of the state's bases for a LifeFlight medevac helicopter.)

Best advice for averting emergencies: Be cautious and sensible in everything you undertake in the park. Wear a helmet while biking. Don't hike alone or go off the trails—nearly every year, someone is seriously injured or killed falling from the cliffs. Keep a sharp eye on children.

Accessibility

The park publishes an *Access Guide* that provides accessibility information about general facilities, programs, and services. If you have other questions, call 207/288-3338, 8 A.M.–4:30 P.M. Monday–Friday.

MOUNT DESERT ISLAND COMMUNITIES

Perhaps no national park has as symbiotic a relationship with its "feeder towns" as Acadia National Park. Is it a chicken-and-egg situation? Not really. Whereas other national parks have served as magnets for the creation of clusters of new towns, the towns that surround Acadia are long-termers—island communities that made do and eked out a living from fishing and boatbuilding long before the first 19th-century "rusticators" unloaded their families and steamer trunks—and long before the first chunk of pristine island real estate was donated to the nation.

Mount Desert Island's official towns (tax-collecting entities with all the bureaucracy that ensues) are **Bar Harbor, Mount Desert, Southwest Harbor,** and **Tremont.** Within each of these towns are villages—some with post offices and zip codes, some without. Bar Harbor, for instance, includes the villages of Hulls Cove, Salisbury Cove, Town Hill, and Eden (all in the northern sector of the island), and part of the village of Otter Creek.

The town of Mount Desert can be the most confusing, since it includes the villages of Seal Harbor, Hall Quarry, Pretty Marsh, Beech Hill, Somesville, Northeast Harbor, and part of Otter Creek.

Be sure to drive or bike (or take the Island Explorer bus between late June and Columbus Day) around the smaller villages, especially Somesville, Bass Harbor, and Bernard. Views are fabulous, the pace is slow, and you'll feel you've stumbled upon "the real Maine."

© TOM NANGLE

COMMUNITIES

HIGHLIGHTS

◖ Abbe Museum: The downtown Abbe Museum and its seasonal museum at Sieur de Monts Spring are fascinating places to while away a few hours and learn about Maine's Native American heritage (page 66).

◖ Oceanarium: Visit a lobster hatchery and learn about ocean ecology on this fascinating tour (page 66).

◖ Dive-In Theater Boat Cruise: Got kids? Don't miss this tour, where Diver Ed brings the undersea world aboard (page 75).

◖ Whale-Watching Excursions: Board a high-speed catamaran and cruise well offshore to view whales and the puffin colony at Petit Manan Light (page 75).

◖ Somes Sound: It's worth the journey to the quiet side of the island to see the only fjord on the East Coast (page 91).

◖ Asticou and Thuya Gardens: Magical and enchanting best describe these two peaceful gardens. While Zen-like Asticou is best seen in spring, Thuya delivers color through summer and also has hiking paths (page 91).

◖ Wendell Gilley Museum: Gilley's intricately carved birds, from miniature shorebirds to life-size birds of prey, are a marvel to behold (page 97).

◖ Seal Cove Auto Museum: A must for fans of antique automobiles, the museum hosts one of the largest collections of Brass Era vehicles in the country, including a few extremely rare models (page 110).

◖ Island Cruises: Adults and kids alike enjoy Capt. Kim Strauss's extremely informative and fun nature cruises (page 111).

◖ Cranberry Isles: Do make it a point to cruise to at least Islesford for a taste of island life (page 115).

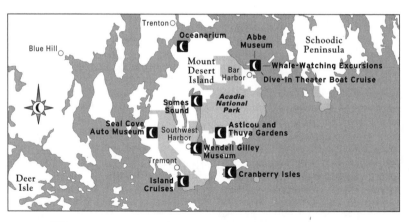

LOOK FOR ◖ TO FIND RECOMMENDED SIGHTS, ACTIVITIES, DINING, AND LODGING.

PLANNING YOUR TIME

Arrive in **Bar Harbor** in mid-July these days, and you'll find it tough to believe that the year-round population is just shy of 5,000. Bar Harbor is liveliest (in both positive and negative senses) in July and August, but the season keeps stretching. Many clued-in travelers try to take advantage of September's prime weather, relative quiet, and spectacular foliage, although even September and October activity has stepped up. Cruise ships have "discovered" Bar Harbor in recent years, many opting for September and October visits. You won't be competing with the passengers for beds, but about 80 percent of them make a perfunctory visit to Acadia, usually by chartered bus. (The cruise visits add about $10 million annually to the island's coffers.) In the dead of winter, the town is close to moribund, kept alive by devoted year-rounders, including students and faculty at the College of the Atlantic (a unique four-year liberal-arts college geared to environmental studies) and the 1,200 or so staff members at the internationally recognized Jackson Laboratory for Mammalian Research.

If you're traveling with children, Bar Harbor can be a very convenient base of operations for exploring Acadia National Park and the rest of the island. In the smallish downtown area, kids can walk around, play in the parks, hang out at the waterfront, buy ice cream, and hit the movies. It's also a source for sporting-gear rentals and the starting point for boat, bus, kayaking, and walking tours. Staying downtown can be a real plus, but the high cost of even ordinary lodging can be a minus—especially for families. Bar Harbor Chamber of Commerce staffers are particularly adept at rounding up rooms, but don't abuse their helpfulness; contact them well ahead if you're planning a peak-season holiday.

The **Southwest Harbor** also area serves as a very convenient base for exploring Acadia National Park, as well as the island's less-crowded villages and offshore Swan's Island, Frenchboro, and the **Cranberry Isles.**

Bar Harbor and Vicinity

In 1996, Bar Harbor celebrated the bicentennial of its founding (as the town of Eden). In the late 19th century and well into the 20th, the town grew to become one of the East Coast's fanciest summer watering holes.

In those days, ferries and steam yachts arrived from points south, large and small resort hotels sprang up, and exclusive mansions (quaintly dubbed "cottages") were the venues of parties thrown by summer-resident Drexels, DuPonts, Vanderbilts, and prominent academics, journalists, and lawyers. The "rusticators" came for the season, with huge entourages of servants, children, pets, and horses. The area's renown was such that by the 1890s, even the staffs of the British, Austrian, and Ottoman embassies retreated here from summers in Washington, D.C.

The establishment of the national park in 1919 and the arrival of the automobile changed the character of Bar Harbor and Mount Desert Island; two world wars and the Great Depression took an additional toll in myriad ways; but the coup de grâce for Bar Harbor's era of elegance came with the Great Fire of 1947.

Nothing in the history of Bar Harbor and Mount Desert Island stands out like the Great Fire of 1947, a wind-whipped conflagration that devastated more than 17,000 acres on the eastern half of the island and leveled gorgeous mansions, humble homes, and more trees than anyone could count. Only three people died, but property damage was estimated at $2 million. Whole books have been written about the October inferno; fascinating scrapbooks in Bar Harbor's Jesup Memorial Library dramatically relate the gripping details of the story. Even though some of the elegant cottages have survived, the fire altered life here forever.

SIGHTS

Acadia National Park comes right up to the edge of town, but the Bar Harbor area has plenty of attractions of its own.

◖ Abbe Museum

The fabulous Abbe Museum is a superb place to introduce children (and adults) to prehistoric and historic Native American tools, crafts, and other cultural artifacts, with an emphasis on Maine's Micmac, Maliseet, Passamaquoddy, and Penobscot tribes. Everything about this privately funded museum, established in 1927, is tasteful. It has two campuses. The new main campus (26 Mount Desert St., Bar Harbor, 207/288-3519, www.abbemuseum.org, open 9 A.M.–5 P.M. Apr.–Dec., call ahead off-season as hours may change, $6 adults, $2 ages 6–15), built in 2001 and incorporating the former YMCA, is home to a collection spanning nearly 12,000 years. Museum-sponsored events include craft workshops, hands-on children's programs, archaeological field schools, and the **Native American Festival** (held at the College of the Atlantic usually the first Saturday after July 4). The museum's gift shop has an especially nice selection of Native American-made baskets.

Admission to the in-town Abbe also includes admission to the museum's original site in the park, about 2.5 miles south of Bar Harbor, at Sieur de Monts Spring, where Route 3 meets the Park Loop Road (9 A.M.–4 P.M. mid-May–mid-Oct.). Everything about this small, privately funded museum is tasteful, including the park setting, a handsome National Historic Register building, and displays from a 50,000-item collection. Admission to only Sieur de Monts Spring Abbe is $2 adults, $1 children 6–15.

While you're at the summertime Abbe Museum, take the time to wander the paths in the adjacent **Wild Gardens of Acadia,** a 0.75-acre microcosm of more than 400 plant species native to Mount Desert Island. Twelve separate display areas, carefully maintained and labeled by the Bar Harbor Garden Club, represent native plant habitats; pick up the map/brochure that explains each.

St. Saviour's Episcopal Church

St. Saviour's (41 Mount Desert St., Bar Harbor, 207/288-4215, 7 A.M. to dusk), close to downtown Bar Harbor, boasts Maine's largest collection of Tiffany stained-glass windows. Ten originals are here; an 11th was stolen in 1988 and replaced by a locally made window. Of the 32 non-Tiffany windows, the most intriguing is a memorial to Clarence Little, founder of the Jackson Laboratory and a descendant of Paul Revere. Images in the window include the laboratory, DNA, and mice. In July and August, volunteers regularly conduct free tours of the Victorian-era church (completed in 1878); call for the schedule or make an appointment for an off-season tour. The church is open for self-guided tours (8 A.M.–8 P.M.)—pick up a brochure in the back. If you're intrigued by old cemeteries, spend time wandering the 18th-century town graveyard next to the church.

◖ Oceanarium

At the northern edge of Mount Desert Island, 8.5 miles northwest of downtown Bar Harbor, is this understated but fascinating spot, also called the Maine Lobster Museum and Hatchery (1351 Rte. 3, Bar Harbor, 207/288-5005, 9 A.M.–5 P.M. Mon.–Sat. mid-May to mid-Oct.), one of the island's two related oceanariums. This low-tech, high-interest operation awes the kids, and it's pretty darn interesting for adults, too. David and Audrey Mills have been at it since 1972 and are determined to educate visitors while showing them a good time. At this facility (there's also a sister site in Southwest Harbor), visitors on tour view thousands of tiny lobster hatchlings, enjoy a museum, and meander along a salt marsh walk, where you can check out tidal creatures and vegetation. All tours begin on the hour and half hour. Allow 1–2 hours to see everything. Tickets are $10 adults, $6 children 4–12 for a program with two talks; an expanded

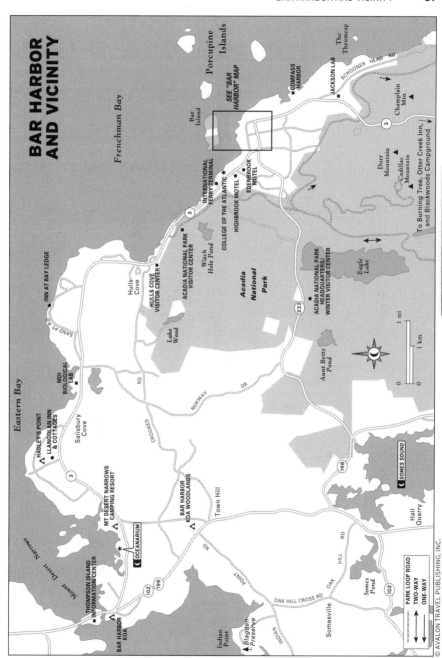

COMMUNITIES

BAR HARBOR AND VICINITY

Porcupine Islands

Frenchman Bay

The Thrumcap

COMPASS HARBOR

JACKSON LAB

SCHOONER HEAD RD

Bar Island

SEE "BAR HARBOR" MAP

Champlain Mtn

3

Dorr Mountain

INTERNATIONAL FERRY TERMINAL ★

Cadillac Mountain

HIGHBROOK MOTEL ●

COLLEGE OF THE ATLANTIC ■

EDENBROOK MOTEL ●

To Burning Tree, Otter Creek Inn, and Blackwoods Campground

INN AT BAY LEDGE ●

ACADIA NATIONAL PARK VISITOR CENTER ■

Witch Hole Pond

HULLS COVE VISITOR CENTER ■

Hulls Cove

ACADIA NATIONAL PARK HEADQUARTERS/ WINTER VISITOR CENTER ■

Eagle Lake

Acadia National Park

SAND PT RD

Lake Wood

233

Eastern Bay

MDI BIOLOGICAL LAB ■

NORWAY DR

CROOKED RD

Aunt Betty Pond

1 mi

1 km

0

0

HADLEY'S POINT ▲

LLANGOLLAN INN & COTTAGES ●

Salisbury Cove

3

MT DESERT NARROWS CAMPING RESORT ▲

198

OCEANARIUM ◀

BAR HARBOR KOA WOODLANDS ▲

Town Hill

RD

Somes Sound ◀

Hall Quarry

THOMPSON ISLAND INFORMATION CENTER ■

Mount Desert Narrows

102

198

POINT RD

OAK HILL RD

Somes Pond

102

BAR HARBOR KOA ▲

Indian Point

Blagden Preserve ▲

OAK HILL CROSS RD

INDIAN

Somesville

PARK LOOP ROAD
TWO-WAY
ONE-WAY

© AVALON TRAVEL PUBLISHING, INC.

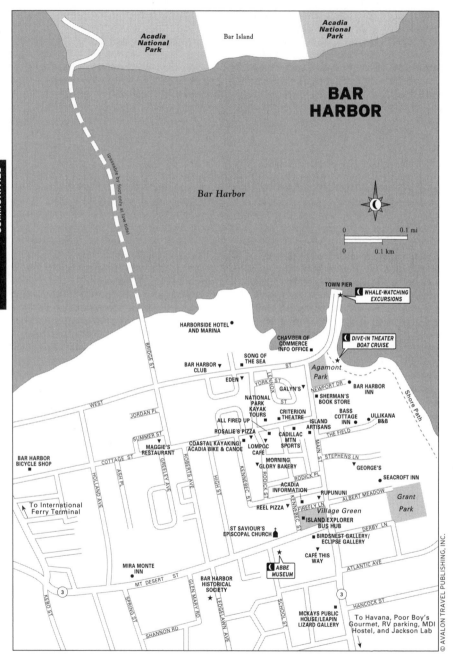

Acadia National Park

Bar Island

Acadia National Park

BAR HARBOR

Bar Harbor

(passable by foot only at low tide)

0   0.1 mi
0   0.1 km

TOWN PIER

WHALE-WATCHING EXCURSIONS

HARBORSIDE HOTEL AND MARINA

CHAMBER OF COMMERCE INFO OFFICE

DIVE-IN THEATER BOAT CRUISE

BAR HARBOR CLUB

SONG OF THE SEA

EDEN

Agamont Park

BRIDGE ST

WEST

JORDAN PL

SUMMER ST

YORK ST

KENNEBEC ST

GALYN'S

NEWPORT DR

BAR HARBOR INN

SHERMAN'S BOOK STORE

NATIONAL PARK KAYAK TOURS

CRITERION THEATRE

ISLAND ARTISANS

BASS COTTAGE INN

ULLIKANA B&B

THE FIELD

Shore Path

ALL FIRED UP

ROSALIE'S PIZZA

CADILLAC MTN SPORTS

COASTAL KAYAKING/ ACADIA BIKE & CANOE

LOMPOC CAFE

MAGGIE'S RESTAURANT

COTTAGE ST

ROBERTS AVE

GREELEY AVE

HIGH ST

RODICK ST

MORNING GLORY BAKERY

STEPHENS LN

GEORGE'S

SEACROFT INN

BAR HARBOR BICYCLE SHOP

HOLLAND AVE

ASH ST

ACADIA INFORMATION

RODICK PL

RUPUNUNI

ALBERT MEADOW

Grant Park

To International Ferry Terminal

REEL PIZZA

FIREFLY LN

Village Green

ISLAND EXPLORER BUS HUB

DERBY LN

ST SAVIOUR'S EPISCOPAL CHURCH

BIRDSNEST GALLERY/ ECLIPSE GALLERY

MIRA MONTE INN

MT DESERT ST

SPRING ST

GLEN MARY RD

LEDGELAWN AVE

BAR HARBOR HISTORICAL SOCIETY

ABBE MUSEUM

CAFÉ THIS WAY

ATLANTIC AVE

KEBO ST

SHANNON RD

SCHOOL ST

MCKAYS PUBLIC HOUSE/LEAPIN LIZARD GALLERY

HANCOCK ST

To Havana, Poor Boy's Gourmet, RV parking, MDI Hostel, and Jackson Lab

MAIN ST

program includes a 45-minute Marsh Walk for $12 adults, $7 children; an all-access pass to both sites is $15 adults and $9.75 children.

College of the Atlantic

A museum, a gallery, and a pleasant campus for walking are reasons to visit the college (105 Eden St., Rte. 3, Bar Harbor, 207/288-5395, www.coa.edu), which specializes in human ecology, or humans' interrelationship with the environment. In a handsome renovated building, the **George B. Dorr Natural History Museum** (207/288-5015) showcases regional birds and mammals in realistic dioramas made by COA students. The biggest attraction for children is the please-touch philosophy, allowing kids to feel fur, skulls, and even whale baleen.

Tickets are $3.50 adults, $2.50 seniors, $1.50 teenagers, and $1 children (3–12). The museum is open 10 A.M.–5 P.M. Monday–Saturday mid-June to Labor Day; off-season by appointment. In summer, a daily interpretive program (usually 11 A.M.) focuses on the museum collection; a Wednesday lecture series (7:30 P.M.) runs throughout July and August. The museum also sponsors an excellent and very popular **Family Nature Camp**—six one-week programs—between late June and mid-August; well-in-advance registration is essential (800/597-9500 or www.coa.edu/summer). Families are housed and fed on the campus ($655 per adult, $265 per child 5–17, $105 kids younger than 5, covers almost everything). The museum gift shop has a

CHANGING THE WORLD, ONE MIND AT A TIME

Wherever you turn on Mount Desert Island, you'll find evidence of **College of the Atlantic.** The students are highly visible; graduates have established numerous island businesses; and the college itself is a integral part of the year-round island community. In addition to its Bar Harbor campus, COA owns marine research facilities on two offshore islands with lighthouses, Mount Desert Rock and Great Duck Island. And it has an 85-acre, Maine Organic Farmers and Gardeners Association–certified organic farm in Mount Desert dedicated to sustainable agriculture that provides produce for the school's kitchen as well as for local businesses and its own farmstand.

Founded in 1969, COA is an accredited, four-year independent college with a graduate program. Despite being a small school – it has fewer than 300 students – it has a far-reaching reputation. The student body hails from 35 states and 33 foreign countries. The school and the curriculum are built around the concept of sustainability. COA awards two degrees, the bachelor of arts and the master of philosophy. Both are in human ecology, which the college defines as "the study of the interconnected relationships between people and our natural,

social, and constructed environments." That translates to programs designed for long-term results that help people and nature flourish.

Many of the innovative school's alumni remain on the island to start new businesses or take over existing ones. COA alumni are behind the Dive-In Theater Boat Cruise, Gulf of Maine Expedition Institute, Reel Pizza Cinerama, Wildwood Stables, Leapin Lizard Gallery, Criterion Theatre, and several restaurants including Burning Tree, Café This Way, Carmen Verandah, Havana, Joe's Smoke Shop, Morning Glory Bakery, and Rupununi. That's just skimming the top. Town Hill Market, Sunflower Gardens & Greenhouses, Sweet Pea's Farm Store, and more than a dozen services are COA-graduate initiatives. And that's just on the island.

The college's admission policy, like its curriculum, is geared to the individual student, and interested students are encouraged to visit the campus, take a tour, and talk with faculty and staff. Even if you're not interested in pursuing the COA's educational opportunities, the gorgeous 35-acre, oceanfront campus is well worth a visit. It houses a museum, gallery, gardens, and a shorefront path.

particularly good collection of books and gifts for budding naturalists.

Across the way is the **Ethel H. Blum Gallery** (207/288-5015 ext. 254, 10 A.M.–4 P.M. Tues.–Sat. in summer, 9 A.M.–4 P.M. Mon.–Fri. during the academic year), a small space that hosts some intriguing exhibits.

Also on campus is a **Beatrix Farrand Garden,** which is undergoing restoration, and below that an ill-maintained **shorefront nature path.** The garden, designed in 1928, contained more than 50 varieties of roses and was the prototype for the rose garden at Dumbarton Oakes in Washington, D.C. Both are known for Farrand's use of garden rooms, such as the terraces in this garden. If you choose to take the shore path, be extremely careful and don't let little ones get ahead. There are cliff sections—some without guardrails, others where the rails are rotted.

The college and its museum are a half mile northwest of downtown Bar Harbor. It's on Route 2/Eden St. of the Island Explorer.

The George B. Dorr Natural History Museum is a big hit with kids.

Bar Harbor Whale Museum

College of the Atlantic reopened the Bar Harbor Whale Museum (52 West St., Bar Harbor, 207/288-0288, 10 A.M.–9 P.M., hours may vary off-season) in collaboration with Acadian Whale Adventures. Features include a life-sized model of a prehistoric walking whale, a pilot whale skeleton, seals, marine birds, a 22-foot-long minke porpoise, and exhibits on whales. There's also a mesmerizing video of whales in their habitat. Admission is free, but donations support marine mammal research and conservation. While here, ask about COA's **Adopt A Finback Whale** program. Biologists from Allied Whale, at the college, have identified more than 1,000 finbacks. Your $30–50 contribution supports research and nets you a color photo of your whale, a brief history of it, and a book, as well as an adoption certificate and newsletter subscription.

The Bar Harbor Historical Society

The Bar Harbor Historical Society (33 Ledgelawn Ave., Bar Harbor, 207/288-0000, 1 P.M.–4 P.M. Mon.–Sat. mid-June to mid-Oct., free), in its own National Register building, has fascinating displays, stereopticon images, and a scrapbook about the 1947 fire that devastated the island. The photographs alone are worth the visit. Also here are antique maps, Victorian-era hotel registers, and other local memorabilia. In winter, it's open by appointment.

For a sample of Bar Harbor before the great fire, wander over to upper West Street, which is on the National Historic Register thanks to the remaining grand cottages that line it.

Hulls Cove Tool Barn and Sculpture Garden

Part shop, part nature center, part art gallery, the Hulls Cove Tool Barn and Sculpture Garden (17 Breakneck Rd., behind Hulls Cove General Store, Hulls Cove, 207/288-5126, www.jonesport-wood.com, 9 A.M.–5 P.M. daily June–Labor Day, Thurs.–Sun. Labor Day–Columbus Day, Sat. and Sun. in winter) is just one of creative Skip Brack's enterprises. Inside

ADOPT A FINBACK WHALE

Here's a trump card: When everyone else is flashing photos of kids or grandkids, you can whip out images of your very own adopted whale. And for that you can thank the **Adopt-a-Finback-Whale** program at the College of the Atlantic (COA) in Bar Harbor.

In 1972, COA established Allied Whale, a marine-mammal laboratory designed to collect, interpret, and use research on the world's largest mammal. Although Allied Whale's primary focus is the Gulf of Maine, its projects span the globe, involving international scientific collaboration. Since 1981, part of the research has involved assembling an enormous photo collection (more than 25,000 images) for identification of specific humpback and finback whales (with names such as Quartz and Elvis) and tracking of their migration routes. The photo catalog of finbacks already numbers more than 1,000.

And here's where the adoption program comes in – a way to support the important research being done by Allied Whale and its colleagues. If you sign up as an adoptive "parent" for a year, you'll receive a Certificate of Adoption, a large color photo and a biography of your whale, its sighting history, an informational booklet, and a subscription to Allied Whale's newsletter. It's a superb gift for budding scientists. The adoption fee is $30 for a single whale or $50 for a mother and calf.

For further information, obtain *The Finback Catalogue* from College of the Atlantic, 105 Eden Street, Bar Harbor 04609, 207/288-5644, fax 207/288-4126, www.coa.edu/alliedwhale/adopt.htm.

the barn is an extensive selection of old tools, with an emphasis on woodworking hand tools. Paths lace through perennial gardens, woods, and fields at the Davistown Museum Sculpture Garden, which surrounds the barn and continues across the street. Throughout the garden are sculptures by noted Maine artists

and found-object creations by Brack. Take the Island Explorer Route 1/Campgrounds and request a stop at the Hull's Cove General Store, then walk up the road.

Research Laboratories

Some of the world's top scientists work year-round or come to Bar Harbor in summer to work at two renowned scientific laboratories.

World renowned in genetic research, **The Jackson Laboratory for Mammalian Research** (610 Main St., Rte. 3, Bar Harbor, 207/288-6000, www.jacksonlaboratory.org) breeds special mice used to study cancer, diabetes, muscular dystrophy, and other diseases—with considerable success. More than two million mice are shipped from JAX (as it's called locally, or just "the lab") to more than 12,000 research labs worldwide, generating annual revenues of about $48 million. The free, hourlong "summer visitor program," held on most Wednesdays from late June to early September, begins at 3 P.M. in the lab's auditorium and includes a lively audiovisual program explaining the lab's impressive work, one of the staff scientists describing his or her work, and a Q&A session. To check on the topic, or for other information, call 207/288-6051. The lab is 1.5 miles south of downtown Bar Harbor.

No less impressive is the **Mount Desert Island Biological Laboratory** (Old Bar Harbor Rd., Salisbury Cove, 207/288-3605, www.mdibl.org), one of the few scientific research institutions in the world dedicated to studying marine animals to learn more about human health and environmental health. It is the only comprehensive effort in the country to sequence genomes. Public tours are offered Wednesdays at 10:30 A.M. and 1:30 P.M. from late June through late August, beginning at Maren Auditorium. The program begins with a presentation by a laboratory scientist about the lab's history and research, and a short video. Then a naturalist talks about animal life in Frenchman Bay and how it pertains to the lab's research. It includes a hands-on presentation at the touch tank, filled with marine animals from Frenchman Bay, a visit to a 15-foot glass tank with other marine creatures, and a stroll through the visitors center, where there are smaller tanks. The tour takes about 1.5 hours. To avoid crowds, go on a nice day. The lab also presents an evening lecture series. Most are serious scientific talks, but there's also usually a children's program. The lab is six miles north of Bar Harbor off Route 3.

Bar Harbor and Park Tours

The veteran of the Bar Harbor–based bus tours is **Acadia National Park Tours** (tickets at Testa's Restaurant, Bayside Landing, 53 Main St., Bar Harbor, 207/288-3327, www.acadiatours.com), operating May–October. A 2.5-hour, naturalist-led tour of Bar Harbor and Acadia departs at 10 A.M. and 2 P.M. daily from downtown Bar Harbor (look for the green-and-white bus across from Testa's). The bus makes three 15-minute stops in the park. Reservations are wise in midsummer and during fall-foliage season (late Sept.–early Oct.); pick up reserved tickets 30 minutes before departure. Cost is $25 adults, $10 children under 12.

If you have a time crunch, **Oli's Trolley** (1 West St., Bar Harbor, 208/288-9899 or 866/987-6553, www.acadiaislandtours.com) operates a one-hour trolley-bus tour five times daily (between 10 A.M. and 6 P.M.) in July and August, including Bar Harbor mansion drive-bys and the Cadillac summit. Cost is $15 adults, $10 children under 12. Oli's also offers 2.5-hour tours daily at 10 A.M. and 2 P.M. Purchase tickets at One Harbor Place, next to the Town Pier on the waterfront; aboard the trolley; or at Oli's Trolley Ice Cream on Cottage Street. Dress warmly; it's an open-air trolley.

Take a 90-minute walking tour of downtown Bar Harbor with **A Step Back in Time,** based at Acadia Bike and Canoe (48 Cottage St., Bar Harbor, 207/288-9605). The costumed guide leads you up one street and down the other, all the while staying in Victorian character and sharing the secrets of the rich and famous (and often outrageous) of the 19th century. Sounds kitschy, but it's most entertaining, primarily for adults. The tours occur daily at 4 P.M. mid-June through September, although that schedule may change when cruise boats are in port. Additional tours are added from time to time. Reservations aren't required, but they're wise. Cost is $12 per person.

PARKS AND PRESERVES
Shore Path

A real treat is a stroll along downtown Bar Harbor's Shore Path, a well-trodden, granite-edged byway built around 1880. Along the craggy shoreline are granite-and-wood benches, town-owned **Grant Park** (great for picnics), birch trees, and several handsome mansions that escaped the 1947 fire. Offshore are the four Porcupine Islands. The path is open 6:30 A.M.–dusk, and leashed pets are okay. Allow about 30 minutes for the mile loop, beginning next to the town pier and the Bar Harbor Inn and returning via Wayman Lane, near the Bar Harbor Hospital. There's also access to the path next to the Balance Rock Inn.

Bar Island

Check local newspapers or the Bar Harbor Chamber of Commerce visitor booklet for the times of low tide, then walk across the gravel bar (wear hiking boots or rubberized shoes) to wooded **Bar Island** (formerly Rodick's Island) from the foot of Bridge Street in downtown Bar Harbor. Archaeologists have confirmed that Native Americans enjoyed this turf in the distant past. (Part of the island now belongs to Acadia National Park.) You'll have the most time to explore the island during new-moon or full-moon low tides, but plan on no more than three hours—about 90 minutes before and 90 minutes after low tide. *Be sure* to wear a watch so you don't get trapped by the tide (for up to 10 hours). The foot of Bridge Street is also an excellent kayak-launching site.

Compass Harbor

About a mile southeast of downtown, along Main Street (Route 3), is Compass Harbor, a section of the park where you can stroll through woods to the water's edge and explore the overgrown ruins of park cofounder George Dorr's home.

Indian Point/Blagden Preserve

In the far northern corner of the island (still within the Bar Harbor town limits) is a lovely preserve owned by The Nature Conservancy. From the junction of Routes 3 and 102/198, continue 1.8 miles to Indian Point Road and turn right. Go 1.7 miles to a fork and turn right. Watch for the preserve entrance on the right, marked by a Nature Conservancy oak leaf.

Five trails wind through forested, 110-acre Indian Point/Blagden Preserve, a rectangular parcel with island, hill, and bay vistas. Seal-watching and birding are popular—harbor seals on offshore rocks and woodpeckers (plus 130 other species) in blowdown areas. To spot the seals, plan your hike around the time of low tide, when they'll be sprawled on the rocks close to shore. Wear rubberized shoes or boots. Bring binoculars or use the telescope installed here for the purpose. To keep from disturbing the seals, watch quietly and avoid jerky movements. Park near the preserve entrance and follow the Big Woods Trail, running the length of the preserve. A second parking area is farther in, but then you'll miss walking through much of the preserve. When you reach the second parking area, just past an old field, bear left along the Shore Trail to see the seals. Register at the caretakers' house (just beyond the first parking lot, where you can pick up bird and flora checklists), and respect private property on either side of the preserve. Open dawn–6 p.m. daily, all year.

RECREATION

Acadia National Park of course steals the limelight for most of Mount Desert Island's recreation, but Bar Harbor has its own pursuits—plus several outfitters for anyone headed to Acadia. (See the *Acadia on Mount Desert Island* chapter for information on rock-climbing guides in Bar Harbor.)

Great Meadow Loop

This easy walk connects downtown Bar Harbor with the park's Jesup Path, which leads to Sieur de Monts Spring. From there, you have access to the Dorr Mountain trails. To find the Great Meadow Loop, head up Mount Desert Street from the Village Green to Spring Street. Take Spring Street to the Cromwell Harbor Road and turn left. At the edge of Ledgelawn Cemetery, you'll see the trail. It meanders through the woods for a bit, before emerging on Ledgelawn Avenue. Turn right, then continue until it re-enters the woods across the road. It parallels the road for a bit before re-crossing it and paralleling the Park Loop Road; the Kebo Valley Golf Club will be on your right. Just before the trail crosses Harden Farm Road, you'll see the Jesup Path trailhead on your left, across the Park Loop Road. Take that if you want to head to Sieur de Monts Spring (0.6 miles). Otherwise, continue along the trail as it follows and crosses Harden Farm Road until its intersection with Cromwell Harbor Road. Turn right, and return to Spring Street and follow it back to Mount Desert Street and the Village Green. It's just shy of two miles round-trip.

Bicycling

With all the great biking options, including 45 miles of carriage roads (12 miles of which are off-limits to bicycles) and some of the best roadside bike routes in Maine, you'll want to bring a bike or rent one here. Two rental firms based in downtown Bar Harbor also handle repairs. Expect to pay $18–20 per day for a rental bike, including helmet, lock, and map. It's wise to make advance reservations.

The Minutolo family's **Bar Harbor Bicycle Shop** (141 Cottage St., Bar Harbor, 207-288-3886, www.barharborbike.com), on the corner with Route 3, has been in business since 1977 and has earned an excellent reputation (it's also known as Island Adventures). If you have your own bike, stop here for advice on routes—the Minutolos have cycled everywhere on the island and can suggest the perfect mountain-bike or road-bike loop based on your ability and schedule. The shop organizes free Sunday morning group road rides, usually 9 A.M.–noon, with a longer option for more experienced cyclists. Evening rides for various abilities, including a Ladies' Ride, are also organized. The shop has rentals ranging from standard mountain bikes to full-suspension models and even tandems ($39) as well as all the accessories and gear you might need. Hours in summer are 8 A.M.–8 P.M. daily, 9 A.M.–5:30 P.M. Tuesday–Saturday other months. The shop stays open March through Christmas.

Acadia Bike & Canoe (48 Cottage St., Bar Harbor, 207/288-9605 or 800/526-8615, www.acadiabike.com) also rents bikes. Reserve ahead with a credit card for a better rate. The shop opens daily at 8 A.M. in spring, summer, and fall.

For a low-key, insider bicycle tour of the region, you can't do better than **Maine Coast Bicycle Tours** (48 Cottage St., Bar Harbor, 207/288-0050 or 888/412-BIKE, www.mainecoastbicycletours.com), a division of Acadia Bike and Canoe. Locally owned and operated, Maine Coast specializes in all-inclusive bicycle tours of Mount Desert Island, with forays to Schoodic Point and Swan's Island. These folks know the island and are willing to share their insider info. The six-day tour is offered once a month from July through October and costs about $1,500. That fee covers most meals (usually in top-rated restaurants), 24-speed rental bicycle and related gear, guide and support vehicle, an afternoon guided sea kayak or hiking tour, a guided walking tour of downtown Bar Harbor, a welcome reception at an oceanfront private home, a sunset tour of Cadillac, round-trip ferry to Swan's Island, and five nights of upscale hotel lodging. This is not for super-serious cyclers; trips cover a mere 15 to 25 miles each day, allowing plenty of time to enjoy the scenery and relax.

If you're headed to Southwest Harbor, perhaps for a day trip to Swan's Island, see the information on Southwest Cycle in the *Southwest Harbor* section farther on in this chapter.

Sea Kayaking

Sea kayaking is wildly popular along the Maine coast, and Bar Harbor has become a major kayaking destination. No experience is necessary to join tours operated by any of the firms in Bar Harbor.

Bob Mensink and Robert Shaw established **National Park Kayak Tours** (39 Cottage St.,

Bar Harbor, 207/288-0342 or 800/347-0940, www.acadiakayak.com) in 1993, and they limit their Registered Maine Guide–led tours to a maximum of six tandem kayaks per trip. Four-hour morning, mid-day, afternoon, or sunset paddles are offered, including shuttle service, a paddle/safety lesson, and a brief stop, for $45 per person in July and August, $42 off-season. Most trips cover about six miles. Multi-day camping trips also are offered. It's best if you make reservations at least one day in advance. Trips are offered from Memorial Day weekend through late September.

Half-day ($45), full-day ($69; bring your own lunch), and multi-day sea-kayak tours are on the schedule organized by **Coastal Kayaking Tours** (48 Cottage St., Bar Harbor, 207/288-9605 or 800/526-8615, www.acadiafun.com). Best option for beginners is the 2.5-hour harbor tour, beginning at 9 A.M. ($36). By prearrangement, special half-day family tours, departing at 1:30 P.M., can handle kids eight and over ($47). A 2.5-hour sunset cruise begins around 5 P.M. (depending on season), at $36, and a three-day inn-to-inn tour is $599. Other kayak trips are offered mid-May through September. All trips are weather-dependent, and reservations are essential. Rental canoes ($30), ruddered kayaks ($45 solo, $55 tandem), and open cockpits ($25 single, $35 double) are available.

Three other firms in Bar Harbor do sea-kayak tours and rentals. New tour operators spring up often; opt for experience. Other companies operate elsewhere on the island; see the *Southwest Harbor and Tremont* section. Also see the guided tours in the *Acadia on Mount Desert Island* chapter.

If you've brought your own kayak, one place to launch it is **Hadley Point Beach** (Hadley Point Road, Bar Harbor). This pebbly beach on Mount Desert Narrows has a couple of picnic tables, a portable toilet, and parking. Careful, though—the currents are very strong. To find the put-in, from the Thompson Island Visitor Center continue south on Route 3 for about four miles. The Hadley Point Road will be on your left. Follow it to the end.

Golf

Duffers first teed off in 1888 at **Kebo Valley Golf Club** (100 Eagle Lake Rd., Rte. 233, Bar Harbor, 207/288-5000, www.kebovalleyclub.com, May–Oct.), Maine's oldest club and the eighth-oldest in the nation. The 17th hole became legendary when it took President William Howard Taft 27 tries to sink the ball in 1911. Kebo is very popular, with a gorgeous setting, an attractive clubhouse, and decent food service, so tee times are essential; you can reserve up to six days in advance. Greens fees ($76 peak season) are the highest on the island, but afternoon and twilight rates are available.

Mount Desert Island YMCA

Here's a lifesaver on a stormy day. The MDI YMCA (21 Park St., Bar Harbor, 207/288-3511, www.mdiymca.org) has an indoor pool, gym, track, fitness room, and recreation room. Rates are $8 adult (19–59); $5 youth, full-time student, and senior; or $10 per family. Summer hours are 5:30 A.M.– 8:30 P.M. Mon.–Fri., 8 A.M.–4 P.M. Sat., and 10 A.M.–2 P.M. Sunday. In winter, the Y stays open until 9:30 P.M. Mon.–Fri., until 6 P.M. Sat., and 5 P.M. Sunday.

EXCURSION BOATS
◖ Dive-In Theater Boat Cruise

You don't have to go diving in these frigid waters; others will do it for you. When the kids are clamoring to touch slimy sea cucumbers and starfish at various touch tanks in the area, they're likely to be primed for **Diver Ed's** Dive-In Theater Boat Cruise (55 West St., Bar Harbor, 207/288-3483, www.divered.com), operating from the Bar Harbor Inn pier. Former Bar Harbor harbormaster Ed Monat heads the crew aboard the 46-passenger *Seal,* which goes a mile or two offshore and sends down two professional divers (including Ed) with video cameras. You and the kids stay on deck, all warm and dry, and watch the action on a TV screen. There's communication back and forth, so the kids can ask questions as the divers pick up urchins, starfish, crabs, lobsters, and other sealife. When the diver surfaces, he or she brings a bag of touchable specimens—another chance to pet some slimy creatures (which go back into the water after show-and-tell). Great concept. Watch the kids' expressions—this is a big hit. The two-hour trips depart three times daily Mon.–Fri., twice daily Saturday, and once on Sunday, from early July through early September; fewer trips are made in spring and fall. Cost is $30 adults, $25 seniors, $20 children ages 5–12, $5 younger than 5; usually twice weekly there's a park ranger or naturalist on board and the tour lasts for three hours—check the park's *Beaver Log* newspaper or Diver Ed's website for the schedule and reservation information—these trips cost an additional $5.

◖ Whale-Watching Excursions

Whale-watching boats go as much as 20 miles offshore, so no matter what the weather in Bar Harbor, dress warmly and bring more clothing than you think you'll need—even gloves, if you're especially sensitive to cold. Motion-sensitive children and adults should plan in advance for appropriate medication, such as seasickness pills or patches.

Whale-watching, puffin-watching, and combo excursions are offered by **Bar Harbor Whale Watch Company** (1 West St., Bar Harbor, 207/288-2386 or 800/942-5374, www.BarHarborWhales.com), sailing from the town pier (1 West St.) in downtown Bar Harbor. The company operates under various names, including Acadian Whale Watcher, and has a number of boats. Most trips are accompanied by a naturalist (often from Allied Whale at the College of the Atlantic), who regales passengers with all sorts of interesting trivia about the whales, porpoises, seabirds, and other marinelife spotted along the way. In season, some trips go out as far as the puffin colony on Petit Manan light. Trips depart daily from late May through late October, but with so many options, it's impossible to list the schedule, so call. Tickets are $42–46 adults, $25 children 6–14, $8 children under six. A portion of the ticket price benefits Allied Whale, which researches and protects marine animals in the Gulf of Maine.

© TOM NANGLE

A catamaran is a fast and stable boat, ideal for whale-watching cruises that venture far offshore. If you go, bring lots of extra clothing, as it can be downright cold at sea.

Trips often go longer than the 2.5–3 hours advertised. Don't plan anything else too tightly around the trip. However, try to visit the Whale Museum, either before or afterward.

Scenic Nature Cruises (1.5–2 hours) and kid-friendly Lobster and Seal Watch Cruises (1.5 hours) also are offered. Rates for these are $20–22 for adults, $15 children, $5 kiddies.

Sailing

Captain Steve Pagels, under the umbrella of **Downeast Windjammer Cruises** (207/288-4585 or 207/288-2373, www.downeastwind-jammer.com), offers 1.5- to 2-hour day sails on the 151-foot steel-hulled *Margaret Todd,* a gorgeous four-masted schooner with tanbark sails that he designed and launched in 1998. Trips depart daily at 10 A.M. and 2 and 6:30 P.M. (subject to change) mid-May to mid-October (weather permitting), from the Bar Harbor Inn pier, just east of the town pier in downtown Bar Harbor. You'll get the best wildlife sightings on the morning trip; better sailing on the afternoon trip; and live music on the sunset one. Some morning sails are narrated by a park ranger. Buy tickets either at the pier or at 27 Main Street or online with a credit card; plan to arrive at least a half hour early. Cost is $29.50 adult, $27.50 senior, $19.50 ages 11 and younger. Dogs are welcome on all sails.

Sea Venture Cruise

Captain Winston Shaw's custom boat tour by Sea Venture (207/288-3355, www.svboat-tours.com) lets you design the perfect trip aboard *Reflection,* a 20-foot motor launch. Capt. Shaw, a Registered Maine Guide and committed environmentalist, specializes in nature-oriented tours. He's the founder and director of the Coastal Maine Bald Eagle Project, and he was involved in the inaugural Earth Day celebration in 1970. He's been studying coastal birds for more than 25 years. You can pick from 10 recommended cruises lasting from one to eight hours or design your own. In any case, the boat is yours. Boat charter rate is $75 per hour for one or two people, $85 for three or four; or $95 for five or six. Capt. Shaw can also arrange for picnic lunches. On longer trips, restroom stops are available.

Lobster Cruise

When you're ready to learn The Truth about lobsters, sign up for a cruise aboard Captain John Nicolai's *Lulu,* a traditional Maine lobsterboat. Operating daily May–September, *Lulu* departs from the Harborside Hotel and Marina in Bar Harbor (55 West St., 207/963-2341 or 866/235-2341, www.lululobsterboat.com), about 8 A.M., doing four or five two-hour trips each day. Captain Nicolai provides an entertaining commentary on anything and everything, but especially about lobsters and lobstering. He hauls a lobster trap and explains intimate details of the hapless critter. (Lobstering is banned on Sunday June–August; the cruises operate, but there's no hauling that day.) Reservations are required; six passengers max. Cost is $25 adults, $22 seniors and military, $15 children under 12. No credit cards. Free parking is available in the hotel's lot.

ENTERTAINMENT AND EVENTS

At the height of the summer season, plenty of live entertainment varies from pub music to films to classical concerts.

On Thursday nights from mid-July through August, **Arcady Summer Festival** (207/288-2141 or 207/288-3151, www.arcady.org) presents musical concerts, from classical to ragtime, at Holy Redeemer Church, on the corner of Ledgelawn and Mount Desert Streets, at 7:30 P.M. Tickets are $13 adult in advance or $16 at the door, $7 college student with ID, and free for anyone 18 or younger.

The **Bar Harbor Town Band** performs free Monday and Thursday evenings (8 P.M.) July to mid-August on the Village Green (Main St. and Mount Desert St., Bar Harbor).

Above Rupununi's restaurant, **Carmen Verandah** (119 Main St., Bar Harbor, 207/288-2766) is the weekend place to be and be seen. Everything gets rolling about 9:30 P.M.—blues, rock, salsa, funk, zydeco, ska, reggae, you-name-it—and there's lots of space for dancing.

Other nights, there's a DJ. Darts and billiards round out the picture. It's open all year.

You never know quite what's going to happen at **Improv Acadia** (15 Cottage St., Bar Harbor, 207/288-2503, www.improvacadia.com, $12 adults, $6 kids age 12 and younger). Every show is different, as actors use audience suggestions to create spots. Shows are staged one to three times a night, mid-June to mid-October. Dessert, snacks, and drinks are available.

The **Bar Harbor Music Festival** (207/288-5744 in July and August, 212/222-1026 off-season, www.barharbormusicfestival.org), a summer tradition since 1967, emphasizes up-and-coming musical talent in a series of classical, jazz, and pops concerts, usually Fridays and Sundays, at various island locations, including local inns and an annual outdoor concert in Acadia National Park, early July to early August. A relatively new addition to the schedule is an opera, which received rave reviews in its debut season. Advance tickets are $20–25 adult, $12 student and can be purchased at the festival office building (59 Cottage). Preconcert dinners are also sometimes available at $25. Reservations are wise.

Cinemas

In 2001, new owners assumed the reins of the beautifully refurbished National Historic Landmark **Criterion Theatre** (35 Cottage St., Bar Harbor, 207/288-3441 for films or 288-5829 for concerts, www.criteriontheatre.com), built in 1932. Now, in addition to screening films, the Criterion puts on concerts, plays, and other special events. You'll soak up the nostalgia in this art deco classic with nearly 900 seats (including an elegant floating balcony). Beer, wine, and light fare are available. Two screenings nightly in summer (usually 7 and 9:30 P.M.); Saturday and Sunday matinees at 2 P.M.

Combine pizza with your picture show at **Reel Pizza Cinerama** (33 Kennebec Pl., Bar Harbor, film 207/288-3811, food 207/288-3828). Two showings nightly on each of the two screens. All tickets are $6; pizzas are $13–20. Doors open at 4:30 P.M.; get there early for the best seats.

Create Your Own Art

Definitely worthy of the Entertainment category is **All Fired Up!** (44 Cottage St., Bar Harbor, 207/288-3130, www.acadiaallfiredup.com), the perfect answer to "What do we do in the rain?" Solution: Paint your own pottery, make mosaics, or create a critter (stuffed animal). You'll often see three generations sharing a booth as they work away at their projects in this bright, airy space. Here's the drill for pottery: Select a mug or bowl or whatever from one of the 500 or so white-bisque pottery pieces ($2 and up). Figure out a design (check out "the inspiration center"), choose your colors, and work away. If you opt for a glaze instead of paint, so you can dine off your masterpiece, you'll need to leave it for a few days so it can be kiln-fired (and shipped to your home if you prefer). Studio time (including all the supplies) is $10 per adult, $7 per child. Owner Nina Zeldin inspires even the artistically challenged, and it's all great fun. Open all year. Summer hours (late June to Labor Day) are 9 A.M.–8 P.M. daily, to 10 P.M. in July and August.

Events

Bar Harbor is home to numerous special events. Here's just a sampling. For more, call 207/288-5103 or visit www.barharbormaine.com.

In late May, the annual **Warblers & Wildflowers Festival** attracts birders and nature lovers. Events include morning birdsong walks, garden tours, art, lectures, and other events.

In late June, **Legacy of the Arts** is a weeklong celebration of music, art, theater, dance, and history, with tours, exhibits, workshops, concerts, lectures, demonstrations, and more.

The **Fourth of July** is always a big deal in Bar Harbor, celebrated with a blueberry-pancake breakfast (6 A.M.), a parade (10 A.M.), a seafood festival (11 A.M. on), a band concert, and fireworks. A highlight is the Lobster Race, a crustacean competition drawing contestants such as Lobzilla and Larry the Lobster in a four-lane saltwater tank on the Village Green. Independence Day celebrations in the island's smaller villages always evoke a bygone era.

The Abbe Museum, the College of the Atlantic, and the Maine Indian Basketmakers Alliance sponsor the annual **Native American Festival,** 10 A.M.–4 P.M. the first Saturday after July 4, featuring baskets, beadwork, and other handicrafts for sale, and Indian drumming and dancing. Free admission; held at College of the Atlantic, Bar Harbor.

In even-numbered years, the **Mount Desert Garden Club Tour** presents a rare chance to visit some of Maine's most spectacular private gardens the second or third Saturday in July (confirm the date with the Bar Harbor Chamber of Commerce).

The **Directions Craft Show** fills a weekend in late July or early August with extraordinary displays and sales of crafts by members of Directions. You'll find it at Mount Desert Island High School (Rte. 233, Eagle Lake Rd.). Hours are Friday 5 P.M.–9 P.M., Saturday and Sunday 10 A.M.–5 P.M.

SHOPPING

Bar Harbor's boutiques—running the gamut from attractive to kitschy—are indisputably visitor-oriented; many shut down for the winter, even removing or covering their signs and blanketing the windows. Fortunately, the island has enough of a year-round community to support the cluster of loyal shopkeepers determined to stay open all year, but shop-till-you-droppers will be happiest here between Memorial Day weekend and Columbus Day, and particularly in July and August. (Remember, too, that Bar Harbor isn't Mount Desert's only shopping area.)

Galleries

Downtown Bar Harbor's best craft gallery is **Island Artisans** (99 Main St., Bar Harbor, 207/288-4214, www.islandartisans.com). More than 100 Maine artists are represented here, and the quality is outstanding. Don't miss it. You'll find basketwork, handmade paper, wood carvings, blown glass, jewelry, weaving, metalwork, ceramics, and more. (Island Artisans has a summertime branch at 119 Main St. in Northeast Harbor.)

Birdsnest Gallery (12 Mount Desert St., Bar Harbor, 207/288-4054, www.birdsnest-gallery.com) has a well-earned reputation for a fine selection of paintings, sculpture, and prints. Prices match the quality.

Right next door is **Eclipse Gallery** (12 Mount Desert St., Bar Harbor, 207/288-9048), which specializes in hand-blown glass and complementary works and represents more than 100 contemporary American artists.

Colorful, creative, and fun describes the works displayed at **Leapin Lizard Gallery** (227 Main St., Bar Harbor, 207/288-2227, www.leapinlizardgallery.com). Inside—and outdoors in the sculpture garden—is a bit of everything: paintings, sculpture, ceramics, garden art, and jewelry.

A number of artists exhibit their paintings at **Cygnet Gallery** (32 Cottage St., Bar Harbor, 207/288-1200).

For more than three decades, **Alone Moose Fine Crafts** (78 West St., Bar Harbor, 207/288-4229. www.finemainecrafts.com) has lured in collectors and browsers with its selection of sculpture, pottery, jewelry, and other works.

It's worth the brief detour off the beaten path to find **Rocky Mann Studio & Gallery** (38 Breakneck Rd., Bar Harbor, 207/288-5478, www.rockymann.com) to see Mann's porcelain and raku pottery along with paintings by Carol Shutt.

Books

Toys, cards, and newspapers blend in with the new-book inventory at **Sherman's Book Store** (56 Main St., Bar Harbor, 207/288-3161). Even some fusty clutter is here, but it's all user-friendly. Sherman's is just the place to pick up maps and trail guides for fine days and puzzles for foggy days.

Souvenir Gifts

Souvenir shops are *everywhere* on Mount Desert Island, so why single out the Acadia Shops? If you need Maine-made mementos for Uncle Harry and Aunt Mary, if the kids need trinkets for friends back home, the Acadia Corporation has several shops in downtown Bar Harbor that can cover it all. Price range is broad, quality is fairly high, and clerks are especially friendly at **The Acadia Shop** (85 Main St., Bar Harbor, 207/288-5600, www.acadiashops.com). Another branch, **Acadia Outdoors** (45 Main St., Bar Harbor, 207/288-2422), features sportswear and outdoor accessories.

Musical Instruments

Most vacationers don't expect to shop for musical instruments, but everyone with an affinity for folkloric music gravitates toward **Song of the Sea** (47 West St., Bar Harbor 207/288-5653, www.songsea.com), a unique, jam-packed harborfront shop where you can find guitars, banjos, harmonicas, and tin whistles—but also such esoterica as hammered dulcimers, doumbeks, didgeridoos, psalteries, and Chilean rainsticks. Ed and Anne Damm are extremely knowledgeable and helpful, even to the point of playing instruments over the phone for call-in orders.

ACCOMMODATIONS

If you're not planning to camp in one of Acadia National Park's two campgrounds (there are no other lodgings, and there's no backcountry camping), you'll need to search elsewhere on the island for a place to sleep. Bar Harbor alone has thousands of beds in hotels, motels, inns, B&Bs, cottages, and two hostels—and the rest of the island adds to that total, with a dozen private campgrounds thrown into the mix. Nonetheless, lodgings can be scarce at the height of summer (particularly the first two weeks in August), a stretch that just happens to coincide with an outrageously high spike in room rates (sorta like gasoline hikes that "just happen" to occur just before long holiday weekends). Off-season, there's plenty of choice, even after the seasonal places shut down, and rates are always lower—often dramatically so. (The Bar Harbor Chamber of Commerce and the Thompson Island Visitor Center will give you a list of lodgings open year-round, and both offices are helpful for finding beds even at peak times.)

Hostels

The **Bar Harbor/Mount Desert Island Hostel** (321 Main St., P.O. Box 32, Bar Harbor 04609, 207/288-5587, www.barharborhostel.com, $21 HI members, $25 nonmembers and students) reopened in 2004 in its own beautifully renovated building on the edge of town. Affable manager Ron Gamble is still in charge and eager to help guests get the most out of their stays. Inside are dorms for men and women, a family room, and a well-equipped kitchen; outside is an organic garden (planted by College of the Atlantic students), where you can help yourself to the produce. No smoking, no liquor, no credit cards. Reservations (best by mail) are essential, as this is a popular location. Open April–October.

Not officially a hostel, but with a hostel-style atmosphere, only for women, the **MDI YWCA** (36 Mount Desert St., Bar Harbor, 207/288-5008) has second- and third-floor single and double rooms, as well as a seven-bed solarium (dorm). Located in a historic downtown building next to the library and across from the Island Explorer bus hub, the "Y" lodging has bathrooms on each floor, as well as a laundry room (coin-operated machines), a TV room, and shared kitchen facilities. Free parking, no pets. There's zero tolerance for smoking, alcohol, and drugs (you'll need to sign an agreement). For July and early August reservations, call way ahead, as the Y is popular with the island's young summer workers. Singles are $37.45, doubles are $32.10 pp, the solarium beds are $26.75 each (rates include tax). Open all year.

Inns and B&Bs

Few innkeepers have mastered the art of hospitality as well as Roy Kasindorf and Hélène Harton, owners of the **(Ullikana Bed & Breakfast** (16 The Field, Bar Harbor, 207/288-9552, www.ullikana.com, $165–305), a 10-room, Victorian Tudor inn, built by Alpheus Hardy, Bar Harbor's first "cottager" in 1885. They genuinely enjoy their guests. Hélène's a whiz in the kitchen; after one of her multi-course breakfasts, usually served on the water-

view patio, you won't need lunch. She's also a decorating genius, blending antiques and modern art, vibrant color with soothing hues, folk art and fine art, with a result like a finely tuned orchestra. Roy excels at helping guests select just the right hike, bike route, or other activity. Afternoon refreshments provide a time for guests to gather and share experiences. Ten comfortable rooms all have private baths; many have working fireplaces, and some have private terraces with water views. Hélène and Roy also own The Yellow House, next door, with six lovely rooms decorated in old Bar Harbor style and a huge living room filled with antique wicker. They're located in a quiet downtown location close to Bar Harbor's Shore Path. Both are open late May–late October.

Right next door is the fabulously renovated and rejuvenated **(Bass Cottage** (14 The Field, Box 242, Bar Harbor 04609, 207/288-1234 or 866/782-9224, www.basscottage.com, $225–340). Corporate refugees Teri and Jeff Anderholm purchased the 26-room 1885 cottage in 2003 and spent a year gutting it, salvaging the best of the old and blending in new to turn it into a luxurious and stylish 10-room inn. It retains its Victorian bones, yet it is most un-Victorian in style. Guest rooms are soothingly decorated with cream and pastel-colored walls and have phones and TV with DVD (a DVD library is available—a godsend on a yucky day); many rooms have fireplaces and whirlpool tubs. The spacious and elegant public rooms—expansive living rooms, cozy library, porches—flow from one to another. Teri puts her culinary degree to use preparing baked goods, fruits, and savory and sweet entrees for breakfast and evening refreshments. A guest pantry is stocked with tea, coffee, and snacks. Open May into November.

Energetic Marian Burns, a former math/science teacher and former president of the Maine Innkeepers Association, is the reason everything runs smoothly at **Mira Monte Inn** (69 Mount Desert St., Bar Harbor, 207/288-4263 or 800/553-5109, $165–230), close (but not too close) to downtown. Born and raised here, and an avid gardener, Marian's a terrific

MDI ON A BUDGET

At first glance, Mount Desert Island might seem an expensive place to visit, especially if you're not a fan of camping. Truth is, you can afford to visit the island, even if your budget is tight.

Consider this: Once you've paid for your park pass, your recreation is free. There are no further fees to hike, canoe, bicycle, or swim, unless you need to rent equipment. If so, plan ahead and ask about any deals. Some sports outfitters offer a discount for advance reservations or multi-day rentals. Some will allow you to rent a bike after a certain time, keep it for the next day, and charge you only for one day. That allows you to get in an extra evening ride – ideal at the peak of summer when daylight lasts well into the evening.

Outside of the park, many of the recommended sights detailed here are free. Perhaps you can't afford to take the family to the Oceanarium, but you certainly can visit the MDI Biological Laboratory. Most of the 100 or so Park Ranger Programs are free (check the *Beaver Log*), including evening ones presented in the park's campgrounds. Free concerts and lectures are regularly presented in many locations around the island; check local newspapers or ask at information centers.

You must eat, but you can keep prices down, even when dining out. For starters, if possible opt for lodging with an in-room refrigerator. Then, stock up on breakfast and sandwich and salad staples (milk, cereal, bread, luncheon meats and cheeses, vegetables, fresh fruit, etc.) at the supermarket. If you don't have a refrigerator, a cooler will do, but remember to keep it stocked with ice. (Collapsible coolers are available and easy to pack or carry on an airplane, or purchase an inexpensive Styrofoam one.) You can survive on this; I've done so. Even better is to have access to boiling water to make instant soups or ramen noodles, to which you can add all kinds of vegetables for a healthful meal.

If you want to dine out, lunch is almost always less expensive than dinner. For dinner, look for restaurants with early-bird specials; many places have very reasonable meals available before 6 or 6:30 P.M. Or consider combining your meal with evening entertainment at Reel Pizza. When you do dine out, take home any leftovers (assuming you have a refrigerator or cooler). Other inexpensive options are public suppers; look for notices on bulletin boards and in local newspapers.

As for lodging, in general the farther you get from the key sights or downtowns, the less it will cost. If you're staying for a week or longer, your best move is to find a cottage rental. (Hint: Prices for many rentals drop the week before Labor Day.) Another option is to consider a camping cabin. These rustic shelters generally do not have any plumbing – you'll have to walk to a shared bathhouse – but they are clean and dry, have real beds, and some even provide linens or minimal cooking facilities. Or stay in the hostel in Bar Harbor. What you sacrifice in privacy is more than offset by the folks from around the world you'll meet.

Wherever you go, whatever you do, always ask about any applicable discounts: automobile clubs, seniors, military, family rates, etc. And finally, ditch the car and use the free Island Explorer bus to get around. Not only does doing so save you money on gasoline and avoid parking hassles, but – big bonus points – it benefits the environment.

---

resource for island exploring. Try to capture her during wine and cheese (5 P.M.–7 P.M.), and ask about her experience during the 1947 Bar Harbor fire. And don't miss her collection of antique Bar Harbor hotel photos. The 13 Victorian-style rooms have air-conditioning, cable TV, and either a balcony or fireplace, and some have whirlpool tubs; two efficiency suites

and one fully equipped apartment-style unit in a separate building are ideal for families. Early and late in the season, Marian organizes special-rate theme weekends. Rates include an extensive hot-and-cold breakfast buffet. Open early May to early November (the two suites are open all year).

Much less pricey and a find for families is

the **Seacroft Inn** (18 Albert Meadow, Bar Harbor 04069, 207/288-4669 or 800/824-9694, www.seacroftinn.com, $99–139), well situated just off Main Street and near the Shore Path. All rooms in Bunny and Dave Brown's white, multi-gabled cottage have phones, TV, refrigerator, and microwave, and a breakfast basket is delivered to your room each morning (subtract $5 from the rate if you don't want breakfast). Some rooms can be joined as family suites. There's also an apartment, available by the week for $1,550. Closed mid-Nov. until April 1; no breakfast or housekeeping April 1 until mid-May.

Outside of town in a serene location with fabulous views of Frenchman Bay is Jack and Jeani Ochtera's **C Inn at Bay Ledge** (150 Sand Point Rd., Bar Harbor 04069, 207/288-4204 summer or 207/875-3262 winter, www.innatbayledge.com, $150–475), an oasis of calm tucked under towering pines and atop an 80-foot cliff. Terraced decks descend to a pool and hot tub and to the lawn, which stretches to the cliff's edge. Stairs descend to a private stone beach below. It's an elegant, casual retreat. Almost all guest rooms have water views. Beds are topped with down comforters and feather beds, some rooms have whirlpool tubs, and second-floor rooms have private decks. A sauna and steam shower are available. Open May–mid October. Also available are cottages ($375), which lack the view but have use of the inn's facilities. Newest addition is the adjacent Summer House at Bay Ledge, a shingled cottage with a deck 25 feet from the edge of Frenchman Bay. It's available late May–October ($375–475).

On a budget? Consider the pleasant but few frills **Llangolan Inn & Cottages** (865 Rte. 3, Bar Harbor 04069, 207/288-3016, www.acadia.net/llangolan), seven miles from downtown. The well-cared-for property includes a B&B and cottages. Five rooms, one with private bath and four sharing two baths, are comfortable and welcoming and go for a bargain $65–75, including a continental breakfast. Also available are basic housekeeping cottages sleeping two to five, each with kitchenette, TV, and heat ($80–115). This property is right on Route 3, so expect traffic noise. Ask for rooms facing the back or for a cottage well away from the road. Even then, you'll probably hear the passing *vroom.*

Another budget choice is the **Otter Creek Inn** (Rte. 3, Otter Creek 04660, 207/288-5151 or 800/845-5852, www.ottercreekme.com), a well-maintained complex with a small motel-like inn, an apartment, and cottages. The inn's six guest rooms, all with mini-fridge, TV, and continental breakfast, rent for $85 spring and fall and $105 in July and August. A two-bedroom apartment rents for $125 or $175; two housekeeping cabins are $95 or $125. Cottages also are available, with nightly (three-night minimum) and weekly rates available, varying by day and month. There are laundry facilities, and all accommodations are adjacent to the Otter Creek Market, which has everything from camping supplies to lobster and wine.

Hotels and Motels

One of the town's best known, most visible, and best-situated hotels is the **Bar Harbor Inn** (Newport Dr., P.O. Box 7, Bar Harbor 04609, 207/288-3351 or 800/248-3351, www.barharborinn.com, $199–369), a sprawling complex on eight acres overlooking the harbor and Bar Island. The 153 rooms and suites vary considerably in style, from traditional inn to motel, in three different buildings. Continental breakfast is included, and special packages, with meals and activities, are available—an advantage if you have children. The kids also will appreciate the heated outdoor pool. Rooms in the Oceanfront Lodge are good choices, with reasonable rates and terrific views. The Main Inn rooms have seen the most recent upgrades. Service is attentive. Open April–November. Other Bar Harbor lodgings under the same management/ownership (www.bar-harbor-hotels.com) are the upscale **Bluenose Inn** and the less expensive, family-oriented **Acadia Inn,** both on Route 3 at the edge of town (on the free Island Explorer bus route), as well as the huge new (2003) **Bar Harbor Grand Hotel,** a four-story neo-Victorian (modeled on Bar Harbor's 19th-

© TOM NANGLE

The Bar Harbor Inn is a local landmark that anchors one end of the Shore Path.

century Rodick House) looming over Lower Main Street.

The newest and fanciest hotel in town is **Harborside Hotel & Marina** (55 West St., Bar Harbor, 207/288-5033 or 800/238-5033, www.theharborsidehotel.com, $199–329), fronting the water in downtown Bar Harbor. Almost all of the 185 rooms and suites have a water view and semi-private balconies; some have whirlpool tubs; deluxe rooms have marble baths, and some have large outdoor hot tubs. Deluxe studios have one to three bedrooms, and penthouse suites have full kitchens. Rates include a continental breakfast buffet. A fine-dining restaurant is located in the beautifully restored Bar Harbor Club; a more casual one is on the pier. Future plans call for a full-service spa, saltwater pool, tennis courts, and other amenities. Open mid-May through October.

At the opposite end of the budgetary scale is the **Edenbrook Motel** (96 Eden St., Rte. 3, Bar Harbor, 207/288-4975, www.acadia.net/eden-brook, $70–95), with an excellent location 1.5 miles from Acadia's main entrance, one mile from downtown, and 500 yards from the ferry servicing Canada. Four tiers of buildings are built on a hillside; rooms on the second floor in the highest building have balconies with panoramic views over Frenchman Bay. The 47 rooms are basic motel style but spacious, and all have phones, TV, and in-room coffee. Open late May–late October.

A little fancier and right next door is the **Highbrook Motel** (94 Eden St., Rte. 3, Bar Harbor, 207/288-3591 or 800/338-9688, www.highbrookmotel.com, $78–138), with 26 rooms in two hillside buildings. Each room has air-conditioning, TV, telephone, and a cof-feemaker, and most have refrigerators. Nicest rooms are in the quiet back building. Coffee, tea, and breakfast pastry are available in the morning. Open late May–late October.

Seasonal Rentals

Contact **Lynam Real Estate** (227 Main St., P.O. Box C, Bar Harbor 04609, 207/288-3334, fax 207/288-3550, www.lynams.com) or **Maine Island Properties** (P.O. Box 1025,

Mount Desert 04660, 207/244-4308, fax 207/244-0588, www.maineislandproperties.com) for listings of houses/cottages available by the week or month. In July and August, rates run anywhere from $700–6,000 a week or more, plus tax and deposit. Both agencies handle rentals in all parts of Mount Desert. (If you decide to stay, they also have residential listings.) The Bar Harbor Chamber of Commerce's annual guide also has listings of cottages—some private, others that are part of cottage colonies.

Campgrounds

Mount Desert Island's private campgrounds are located at the northern end of the island, down the center, and in the southwest corner. Most are also on the routes of the free Island Explorer bus service, making it easy and economic—and preferable—to leave your car (or RV) at your campsite and avoid parking panic (between late June and Columbus Day). The Thompson Island and Hulls Cove Visitor Centers have a listing of private campgrounds.

Near the Thompson Island information center are two well-sited campgrounds, both large, well maintained, and on an Island Explorer bus route. Next to the causeway, and 10 miles northwest of Bar Harbor, **Bar Harbor KOA** (136 County Rd., Bar Harbor, 207/288-3520 or 888/562-5605, www.barharborkoa.net, $42–58, mid-May to mid-Oct.) occupies 32 acres with 2,500 feet of shorefront. Many of the 200 open, grassy, and wooded tent and RV sites have terrific views. Facilities include coin showers and laundry, playground, beach, game areas, on-site sea kayak and canoe rental and tour outfitter, and a small shop. Pets are allowed. Open mid-May to mid-October. A sister site, **Bar Harbor Woodlands KOA** (1453 Rte. 102, Bar Harbor), is not on the ocean and is geared more to smaller RVs and tents, but campers have full use of the other campground's facilities. Rates are slightly less expensive, $30–54.

Mount Desert Narrows Camping Resort (1219 Rte. 3, Bar Harbor, 207/288-4782, www.narrowscamping.com, $30–80 per site varying with location and hookups, May–late Oct.), 1.5 miles east of the causeway, has a fantastic view over Thomas Bay and the Narrows. The 40-acre campground has 239 wooded and open tent and RV sites (many oceanfront), heated pool, convenience store, canoe and kayak rentals, volleyball and basketball courts, playground, coin laundry, free movie nights and hay rides, and live entertainment mid-June to Labor Day. Pets are allowed.

The Baker family has operated **Hadley's Point Campground** (33 Hadley Point Rd., RFD 1, Box 170, Bar Harbor 04609, 207/288-4808, www.hadleyspoint.com, May 15–late Oct. 15) since 1969. Tent sites are $22, sites with water and electric are $28, full hookups are $32 (seventh night free on a weekly stay). Tent sites are nicely spaced in the woods and have a sense of privacy; big-rig sites, located in fields, are tight. Facilities include a laundry, heated pool, shuffleboard courts, horseshoes, and playground. A public saltwater beach with boat launch is within walking distance. The campground is eight miles from Bar Harbor.

FOOD

You won't go hungry in Bar Harbor, and you won't find chain fast-food places. The summer tourism trade and the College of the Atlantic students have created a demand for pizzerias, vegetarian bistros, brewpubs, and a handful of creative restaurants. But of course almost every restaurant has some variant of lobster. And even if you're using Bar Harbor as a base of operations, don't miss opportunities to explore restaurants elsewhere on the island.

The island's best collection of good, inexpensive restaurants, most open year-round, are along Rodick Street, from Reel Pizza down to Rosalie's, which actually fronts Cottage Street. You'll find a good ethnic mix here, from Mexican to Thai to Italian—not a lobster in sight.

Local Flavors

Only a masochist could bypass **Ben & Bill's Chocolate Emporium** (66 Main St., Bar Harbor, 207/288-3281 or 800/806-3281), a long-running taste-treat-cum-experience in downtown Bar Harbor. The homemade candies and more than 50 ice cream flavors (including a dubious lobster flavor) are nothing short of outrageous; the whole place smells like the inside of a chocolate truffle. Some of the chocolate candies find their way into the ice cream; for example, the butter crunch ice cream contains butter crunch chocolate made in the shop. The shop, a cousin of three Massachusetts ice cream parlors, is open March–December, daily 9 A.M.–10 P.M. daily in spring and fall, 9 A.M.–midnight in summer.

Probably the least-expensive lunch or ice cream option in town is the **West End Drug Co.** (105 Main St., Bar Harbor, 207/288-3318), where you can get grilled cheese sandwiches and other old-fashioned white bread basics as well as frappes (a Maineism—frappes are made with ice cream, milk shakes aren't) and sundaes at the fountain.

Bar Harbor has a super natural foods store, the **Alternative Community Market** (16 Mount Desert St., Bar Harbor, 207/288-8225), where you can purchase sandwiches, espresso, or even fruit smoothies. There's limited seating indoors and on the deck. It's open 7 A.M.–10:30 P.M. daily.

J.H. Butterfield Co. (152 Main St., Bar Harbor, 207/288-3386) is a fine place to pick up fixings for a fancy picnic.

Between Mother's Day and late October, the **Eden Farmers Market** operates out of the YMCA parking lot off Lower Main Street in Bar Harbor each Sunday, 10 A.M.–1 P.M. You'll find fresh meats and produce, local cheeses and maple syrup, bread, honey, preserves, even prepared Asian foods.

Brewpubs and Microbreweries

Bar Harbor's longest-lived brewpub is the **Lompoc Café** (36 Rodick St., Bar Harbor, 207/288-9392, www.lompoccafe.com, 11:30 A.M.–9 P.M. late April–mid-Dec.), serving creative lunches and dinners daily ($8–19). How about a lobster and avocado quesadilla? After 9 P.M., there's just beer and thin-crust pizza until about 1 A.M. The congenial cafe has a beer garden, a bocce court, open mic night

© TOM NANGLE

Even if you don't try the lobster flavor, do stop in at Ben & Bill's in downtown Bar Harbor for luscious house-made ice cream in creative flavors.

COMMUNITIES

Thursdays, and live entertainment (blues, bluegrass, and jazz) Fridays and Saturdays May–October.

Lompoc's signature Bar Harbor Real Ale and five or six others are brewed by the **Atlantic Brewing Company** (15 Knox Rd., Town Hill, in the upper section of the island, 207/288-2337 or 800/475-5417, www.atlanticbrewing.com). Free brewery tours, including tastings, are given daily at 2, 3, and 4 P.M. Memorial Day to Columbus Day. In summer, the brewery also operates a tavern/cafe serving sandwiches, burgers, and deli plates, 11:30 A.M.–5 P.M. Every Saturday **MainelyMeat Bar-B-Q** sets up an all-you-can-eat barbecue here for $15 (11:30 A.M.–8 P.M.). It's extremely popular, so go early to avoid disappointment, as it's been known to sell out.

Bar Harbor Brewing Company & Soda Works (135 Otter Creek Rd., Rte. 3, Bar Harbor, 207/288-4592, www.barharborbrewing.com), begun in 1990 by Tod and Suzi Foster as a mom-and-pop operation, remains a small, friendly, hands-on enterprise producing five kinds of beer and ale in a basement microbrewery. Start off at the log-cabin tasting room/gift shop, where kids can sample Ba-ha-buh Root Beer. Free tours begin every 20 minutes between 3:30 and 5 P.M. Tuesday–Friday late June–late August. The brewery is 4.5 miles south of downtown Bar Harbor.

Tom St. Germain founded **Maine Coast Brewing Company** (102 Eden St., Rte. 3, Bar Harbor, 207/288-5214, www.bhmaine.com) in 1994 and opened Jack Russell's Brewpub, at the same location, in 1995. Burgers are the specialty, and there's a beer garden. Lunch is served noon–4 P.M., dinner starts at 5 P.M. Free tours and tastings are offered. Tom's the guy who wrote *A Walk in the Park,* an excellent hiking guide to Mount Desert.

Casual Dining

An unscientific but reliable local survey gives the best-pizza ribbon to **Rosalie's Pizza & Italian Restaurant** (46 Cottage St., Bar Harbor, 207/288-5666), where the Wurlitzer jukebox churns out tunes from the 1950s. This family-owned standard gets high marks for consistency with its homemade pizza (in four sizes or by the slice), calzones, and subs—lots of vegetarian options. If you need something a bit heartier, try the Italian dinners—spaghetti, eggplant parmigiana, and others—all around $7, including a garlic roll. Beer and wine are available. Rosalie's opens daily at 11:30 A.M. all year.

Combine a pizza with a first-run or art flick at **Reel Pizza Cinerama** (33 Kennebec Pl., Bar Harbor, film 207/288-3811, food 207/288-3828), where you order your pizza, grab an easy chair, and watch for your number to come up on the bingo board. Screenings usually begin at 6 and 8:30 or 9 P.M. Pizzas ($12–20) have cinematic names—Zorba the Greek, The Godfather, Manchurian Candidate. Then there's Mussel Beach Party—broccoli, tomatoes, goat cheese, and smoked mussels. You get the idea. Reel Pizza opens daily at 4:30 P.M. and has occasional Saturday matinees; closed Monday in winter. Be sure to arrive early; the best chairs go quickly.

Efficient, friendly, cafeteria-style service makes **EPI Sub and Pizza Shop** (8 Cottage St., Bar Harbor, 207/288-5853, 10 A.M.–8 P.M., to 8:30 P.M. July and Aug.) an excellent choice for picnics or a quick break from sightseeing. The dozen-plus sub-sandwich choices at EPI's (short for epicurean) are bargains (try the Cadillac); also available are salads, pizza, and Italian dinners. If the weather closes in, there are always the pinball machines in the back room. No credit cards. Closed Sunday in November, December, and from February to mid-May.

For a light, inexpensive breakfast or lunch, you can't go wrong at **Morning Glory Bakery** (39 Rodick St., Bar Harbor, 207/288-3041, 7 A.M.–4 P.M. Mon.–Fri., 8 A.M.–1 P.M. Sat.). Espresso and other fancy coffees, fresh-squeezed juices, smoothies, fresh-baked goodies ($1–2), and sandwiches (most are about $6) are all made from scratch. Planning a day in the park? Call ahead for a boxed lunch (add $2.50 to sandwich price), with drink and choice of two: chips, fruit, salad of the day, or cookie.

Adeena and Chris Fisher, owners of the

very popular George's Restaurant, added a new entry to Bar Harbor's grab-and-go lunch spots in 2005. **Not Quite the Corner Cafe** (65 Main St., Bar Harbor, 207/288-1006, 10:30 A.M.–4 P.M.). The tiny shop, that's—you guessed it—one store up from the intersection with Cottage Street, is an excellent source for takeout hot or cold sandwiches, wraps, soups, side salads, and treats, all a tad above the ordinary in creative flair. The homemade hummus wrap with minted cucumber and tomato salad and fresh sprouts and the herb-marinated grilled chicken breast, with local goat cheese, sun-dried tomato tapenade, and baby greens on focaccia, are both winners.

Far less fancy is **Adelmann's Deli** (224 Main St., Bar Harbor, 207/288-0455, 6 A.M.–3 P.M.). Build-your-own egg sandwiches are $3.49; build-your-own lunch sandwiches are $5.99. Choose from a variety of breads, Boar's Head brand meats and cheeses, veggies, condiments, and more.

If you happen to be on Route 102 in the Town Hill area around lunchtime, plan to pick up picnic fare at **Mother's Kitchen** (Rte. 102, Town Hill, Bar Harbor, 207/288-4403). The plain, minuscule building next to Salsbury's Organic Garden Center (look for the Real Good Food sign) is deceiving—it's been operating since 1995 and turns out 20 different sandwiches, as well as deli salads, scones, breakfast sandwiches, great cookies, and pies. They'll even pack up box lunches. Calling ahead would save time, but the whimsically named sandwich combos are tough to describe over the phone. (How about Charlie Noble—homemade chicken salad with walnuts and tarragon, cranberry sauce, and lettuce on onion walnut dill bread) If you're desperately hungry, there are a few picnic tables outside, but you can find better picnic settings elsewhere. Mother's Kitchen is open 8 A.M.–2 P.M. Mon.–Sat., mid-April through October.

Family Friendly

Once a Victorian boarding house and later a 1920s speakeasy, **Galyn's Galley** (17 Main St., Bar Harbor, 207/288-9706, www.galynsbar-harbor.com, 11:30 A.M.–10 P.M., March–Nov.) has been a popular eatery since 1986. Lots of plants, modern decor, reliable service, a great downtown location, and several indoor and outdoor dining areas contribute to the loyal clientele. The cuisine is consistently good if not outstandingly creative (dinner entrees $15–18). Reservations are advisable in midsummer.

Just up the street from Galyn's, **Rupununi** (119 Main St., Bar Harbor, 207/288-2886, www.rupununi.com) gets its name from a river in Guyana—the inspiration of owner Mike Boland, a College of the Atlantic grad. Billed as "an American bar and grill," Rupununi draws a lively, fun crowd for great burgers (even ostrich burgers), veggie and meat dinner entrees ($10–23), some Caribbean and Mediterranean touches, and about two dozen beers on draft. The daily poacher's special usually means buffalo or venison. On Sunday, jazz is part of the mix; on Friday nights, acoustic guitar. Open 11 A.M.–1 A.M. daily. Upstairs is **Carmen Verandah** (see *Entertainment*), which calls itself a "contemporary dinner club." It also serves a full menu and is open the same hours. Also part of the ever-expanding Rupununi empire is **Joe's Smoke Shop,** an upscale cigar bar next door.

Set back from the road behind the Leapin Lizard Gallery's sculpture garden is the very popular **McKays Public House** (231 Main St., Bar Harbor, 207/288-2002, www.mckays-publichouse.com, 11:30 A.M.–3 P.M. and 5–10 P.M.), a comfortable pub with seating indoors in small dining rooms or at the bar or outdoors, in the garden. Classic pub fare includes Reuben sandwiches, shepherd's pie with lamb, burgers, and fish and chips ($8–10). At dinner, fancier entrees, like coq au vin and seafood risotto, are also available, most in the $16–20 range.

Fifties memorabilia and old toys fill **Route 66 Restaurant** (21 Cottage St., Bar Harbor, 207/288-3708, 7 A.M.–8 P.M. or so), a fun restaurant that's a real hit with kids (check out the train running around just below the ceiling). Nothing fancy here, but a wide-ranging menu that includes sandwiches, burgers, pizza, steak, chicken, seafood, and kids' options. Dinner choices run around $8–20, breakfast $3–7, lunch $7–12.

Good food at a fair price reels them into **Poor Boy's Gourmet** (300 Main St., Bar Harbor, 207/288-4148, www.poorboysgourmet.com, opens daily at 4:30 P.M.). Until 6 P.M. it serves an Early Bird menu with a half dozen entrees as well as another 10 all-you-cat-eat pasta choices for $8.95. The price jumps just a bit after that, with most entrees running $11–15. There's even a lobster feast for $16.95.

Eclectic Fare

In 2005, **Café This Way** (14 Mount Desert St., Bar Harbor, 207/288-4483, www.cafethisway.com) received a welcome makeover. The college-funk decor has been updated with a more sophisticated look and a wall of doors now opens to the porch, providing much-needed ventilation, but the casual friendly service and fabulous food remain the same. This might be the only place in town that doesn't serve lobster. But it *does* serve such eclectic items as artichokes stuffed with trout and crab cakes with tequila-lime sauce. The breakfast menu is a genuine wake-up call; try Green Eggs and Sam ($6). Dinner entrees are in the $14–23 range; the wine list is very selective and the desserts are outstanding. In summer and fall, Café This Way serves breakfast (7–11 A.M. Mon.–Sat. and 8 A.M.–1 P.M. Sun.) and dinner (5:30–9:30-ish P.M. daily).

For breakfast or lunch, you can't beat **2 Cats** (130 Cottage St., Bar Harbor, 207/288-2808 or 800/355-2828, www.2catsbarharbor.com, 7 A.M.–1 P.M.) Fun, funky, and fresh best describe both the restaurant and the food. Dine inside or on the patio. Two Cats also serves dinner—call for nights and hours. Three upstairs rooms are $145–175, with breakfast, of course.

Pair wines by the glass with hors d'oeuvres or cobble together a light meal from such small-plate choices as smoked mussel and mixed greens salad, bruschetta, panino, lamb meatballs, soup, even chocolate salami at **Apertivo** (21A Cottage St., Bar Harbor, 207/288-8486,

2 P.M.–close). The tiny tapas bar, opened in 2005 by a local mother-and-son team with years of experience working in local restaurants, has a couple of tall tables and a bar. Open daily, late May–late October.

Ethnic and Vegetarian Fare

For Thai food, **Siam Orchard** (30 Rodick St., Bar Harbor, 207/288-9669, 5–9 P.M. daily, until 9:30 P.M. July and Aug.) gets the local's nod. House specials run $14–16, curries and noodle dishes, such as pad Thai, run $8–14 at dinner. Plenty of choices for vegetarians. Beer and wine only. Open all year.

Sharing the same building is **Gringo's** (30 Rodick St., Bar Harbor, 207/288-2326, 11 A.M.–10 P.M.), a Mexican hole-in-the-wall specializing in takeout burritos, wraps, homemade salsas, and smoothies, with almost everything less than $7. For a real kick, don't miss the jalapeño brownies.

There's a good chance ◖ **Eden** (28 West St., Bar Harbor, 207/288-4422, 5–9:30ish P.M.) could make a vegetarian out of even the most die-hard meat lover. This small restaurant (reservations highly recommended) is dedicated to using organic ingredients from area farms and preparing vegan entrees such as soy seitan piccata with lemon caper vinaigrette, sautéed greens, and sage-mashed potatoes; Thai noodle bowl with green curry coconut broth, spring vegetables, fresh tofu, and rice noodles; and bento box with grilled tofu, seasoned edamame, baby bok choy, sesame seaweed salad, umeboshi nori roll, and citrus ponzu. Too green? Try a rigatoni pasta with crimini mushrooms, sun-dried tomatoes, and sautéed rainbow chard in a garlic wine sauce. Entrees run $12.50–16.

Havana (318 Main St., Bar Harbor, 207/288-2822, www.havanamaine.com, –10 P.M. daily May–late Oct., Wed.–Sat. the rest of the year) promises "American fine dining with Latin flair," and it delivers. The innovative cuisine, bright orange walls and white tablecloths, and a jazz duo providing the background music have made it a hit. Choices might include black bean and dijon-crusted rack of lamb or flash-seared tuna. Entree range is $16–35; for $5.50, you get a *mojito*, the Cuban national drink. Save room for the chocolate torte or the Mojito cheesecake. Reservations are essential on weekends.

Over the past few years, **Miguel's Mexican Restaurant** (51 Rodick St., Bar Harbor, 207/288-5117, 5–9 P.M.) has been a roller coaster, going from one of the island's most reliable and moderate choices to an upscale Mexican seasonal spot, before settling somewhere in the middle. Traditional Mexican fare dominates the menu, but about a half dozen or so more interesting choices are listed under the New Tastes section of the menu. Locals are cautiously optimistic.

Local favorite for Italian fare is **Mama Di Matteo's** (34 Kennebec Pl., top of Roddick St., Bar Harbor, 207/288-3666, 5–9 P.M.), thanks to its friendly attitude, wide-ranging menu (lobster picatta, anyone?), good food, and fair prices. Open year round.

Fine Dining

One of Bar Harbor's fine longtime reliables, **❮ George's** (7 Stephens Ln., Bar Harbor, 207/288-4505, www.georgesbarharbor.com, 5:30–10 P.M. late May–Oct.), occupies three attractively laid-out rooms in a restored home on a downtown side street. Specialties are wild game, seafood, Greek-inspired lamb, and outrageous desserts. Appetizers ($10 and $12) are seafood- and Mediterranean-oriented. Entrees are $25; fixed-price menus are $37 and $40. Reservations are essential in July and August. There's terrace dining when weather permits. The restaurant is behind the First National Bank, where there's free evening parking.

The view's the thing at the Bar Harbor Inn's **Reading Room Restaurant** (Newport Dr., Bar Harbor, 207/288-3351, www.barharborinn.com); request a window seat. Once the stuffy Bar Harbor Reading Room, a gentlemen's club, the dining room still has a sweeping curve of windows overlooking Bar Island and Frenchman Bay. Dinner entrees emphasize meat and seafood ($20–30), the wine list is good, and the service is excellent. Soft music

plays in the background. Unfortunately, the food doesn't match the setting. Dress is informal, and there's a children's menu. The Sunday brunch buffet ($23 adults, $11.50 kids, 11:30 A.M.–2:30 P.M.) is extremely popular; in good weather, it's also served on the terrace. Reservations are essential. Breakfast (mid-Apr.–Oct.) is 7–10:30 A.M.; lunch (on the terrace, weather permitting) begins at 11:30 A.M.; dinner is 5:30–9:30 P.M.

The stylish **Bar Harbor Club** (111 West St., 207/288-5033, 7–11 A.M. and 5–10 P.M.) was the playground of the Rockefellers, Pulitzers, Astors, Cornings, and other wealthy and famous residents during Bar Harbor's heyday. It survived the fire and hung on until 1989, then sat abandoned and deteriorating for years. In 2005, after a multimillion-dollar renovation it reopened under the same ownership as the adjacent Harborside Hotel. Once again, it's providing elegant, harbor-view dining (as long as there isn't an events tent set up on the lawn; ask before you book, if the view is important to you). Entrees, such as braised coastal halibut with Wellfleet clams and roasted rack of lamb, range $24–32. Ask for a table away from the large TV in the Vanderbilt Lounge.

Fresh, fresh, fresh seafood—that's what you'll find at **Maggie's Restaurant** (6 Summer St., Bar Harbor, 207/288-9007, www.maggiesbarharbor.com, 5–9:30 P.M. Mon. –Sat., June–Oct.). The restaurant grew out of owner Maggie O'Neil's experiences as a fishmonger, and much of the equally fresh produce comes from Maggie's own farm. Entrees, such as Maine seafood provençal or bronzed cod with Latin lime tartar sauce, run $16–25. Hint: The lobster crepes are renowned. Soft music and good service complement the dining experience.

Five miles south of Bar Harbor in the village of Otter Creek (which itself is in the town of Mount Desert) is the inauspicious-looking **❮ Burning Tree** (Rte. 3, Otter Creek, 207/288-9331, 5–10 P.M. Wed.–Mon. June–early Oct., also closed Monday after Labor Day), which is anything but nondescript inside. Chefs/owners Allison Martin and Elmer Beal Jr. have created one of Mount Desert

Island's best restaurants. Bright and airy, with about 16 tables in three areas, it's extremely popular and serves a casually chic crowd. Reservations are essential in summer. Specialties are imaginative seafood entrees—such as curry pecan flounder, cioppino, Maryland (yes!) crab cakes—and vegetarian dishes made from organic produce. Scallop kebabs have *lots* of scallops, the specialty crab cakes are 90 percent crabmeat, and edible flowers garnish the entrees ($18–25). The homemade breads and desserts are delicious. At the height of summer, service can be a bit rushed and the kitchen runs out of popular entrees. Solution: Plan to eat early; it's worth it.

INFORMATION AND SERVICES

The **Bar Harbor Chamber of Commerce** (Rte. 3, Trenton, P.O. Box 158, Bar Harbor 04609, 207/288-5103 or 888/540-9990, www.barharbormaine.com) has an especially helpful staff accustomed to a steady stream of summer walk-ins seeking beds, restaurants, activities, and more. The new visitor information center on Rte. 3 (opening in 2006 in the former Acadia Visitor Center) is scheduled to be open daily 8 A.M.–8 P.M. in summer, 8 A.M.–4:30 P.M. weekdays off-season, but hours may change as this is a big move for the chamber. From Memorial Day to Columbus Day, a "branch" chamber office is located at Harbor Place, 1 West St., next to the Town Pier. (Plenty of Bar Harbor information is also available at the Thompson Island Information Center, just after you cross the bridge from Trenton toward Mount Desert Island.) Bar Harbor's annual visitor information booklet usually is off the presses in January—a big help in making early plans for a summer vacation.

Once you're on Mount Desert, if you manage to bestir yourself early enough to catch sunrise on the Cadillac summit (you won't be alone—it's a popular activity), stop in at the Chamber of Commerce office and request an official membership card for the **Cadillac Mountain Sunrise Club** (they'll take your word for it).

Library

Jesup Memorial Library (34 Mount Desert St., Bar Harbor, 207/288-4245, www.jesup.lib.me.us) is open all year (10 A.M.–5 P.M. Tues.–Sat., until 7 P.M. Wed.). The library holds its annual book sale on the third Saturday in August.

Public Restrooms

Downtown Bar Harbor has public restrooms in the Harbor Place complex at the Town Pier, in the municipal building (fire/police station) across from the Village Green, and on the School Street side of the athletic field, where there is RV parking. Restrooms are also at the Mount Desert Island Hospital and the International Ferry Terminal.

Parking

Make it easy on yourself and help improve the air quality and reduce stress levels by leaving your car at your lodging (or if day-tripping, at the chamber's visitors center on Rte. 3 in Trenton) and taking the Island Explorer.

RVs are not allowed to park near the town pier; designated RV parking is alongside the athletic field, Lower Main and Park Streets, about eight blocks from the center of town.

Northeast and Seal Harbors

Ever since the late 19th century, the upper crust from the City of Brotherly Love has been summering in and around Northeast Harbor. Sure, they also show up in other parts of Maine, but it's hard not to notice the preponderance of Pennsylvania license plates surrounding Northeast Harbor's elegant "cottages" from mid-July to mid-August. (In the last decade or so, the Pennsylvania plates have been joined by growing numbers from Washington, D.C., New York, and Texas.)

Actually, even though Northeast Harbor is a well-known name with special cachet, it isn't even an official township; it's a zip-coded village within the town of Mount Desert, which collects the breathtaking property taxes and doles out the municipal services.

The attractive boutiques and eateries in Northeast Harbor's small downtown area cater to a casually posh clientele, while the well-protected harbor attracts a tony crowd of yachties. For their convenience, a palm-sized annual directory, *The Redbook,* discreetly lists owners' summer residences and winter addresses—but no phone numbers. The directory also includes listings for the village of Seal Harbor—an even more exclusive village a few miles east of Northeast Harbor where Princess of Perfection Martha Stewart bought Edsel Ford's palatial estate in 1997, much to the chagrin of long-timers.

Except for two spectacular public gardens and two specialized museums, not much here is geared to budget-sensitive visitors—but there's no charge for admiring the spectacular scenery.

SIGHTS
◖ Somes Sound
As you head toward Northeast Harbor on Route 198 from the northern end of Mount Desert Island, you'll begin seeing cliff-lined Somes Sound on your right. This glacier-sculpted fjord juts five miles into the interior of Mount Desert Island from its mouth, between Northeast and Southwest Harbors. Watch for the right-hand turn for Sargent Drive (no RVs allowed), and follow the lovely, granite-lined route along the east side of the sound. Halfway along, a marker explains the geology of this natural fjord, the only one on the eastern seaboard. There aren't many pullouts en route, and traffic can be fairly thick in midsummer, but don't miss it. An ideal way to appreciate Somes Sound is from the water—sign up for an excursion out of Northeast or Southwest Harbor.

◖ Asticou and Thuya Gardens
If you have the slightest interest in gardens (even if you don't, for that matter), allow time for Northeast Harbor's two marvelous public gardens. Information about both is available from the local chamber of commerce. If gardens are extra-high on your priority list, inquire locally about visiting the private Rockefeller garden, accessible on a very limited basis.

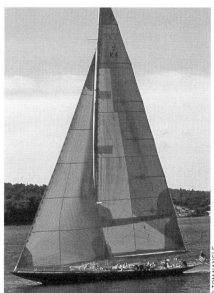

The best views of sailboats in Somes Sound are from Sargent Drive.

COMMUNITIES

One of Maine's best spring showcases is the **Asticou Azalea Garden,** a 2.3-acre pocket where about 70 varieties of azaleas, rhododendrons, and laurels—many from the classic Reef Point garden of famed landscape designer Beatrix Farrand—burst into bloom. When Charles K. Savage, beloved former innkeeper of the Asticou Inn, learned the Reef Point garden was being undone in 1956, he went into high gear to find funding and managed to rescue the azaleas and provide them with the gorgeous setting they have today, across the road and around the corner from the inn. Oriental serenity is the key—with a Japanese sand garden, stone lanterns, granite outcrops, pink-gravel paths, and a tranquil pond. Try to visit early in the season, early in the morning, to savor the effect. The garden is on Route 198, at the northern edge of Northeast Harbor, immediately north of the junction with Peabody Drive (Rte. 3). Watch for a tiny sign on the left (if you're coming from the north), marking access to the parking area. Asticou is open daily, sunrise to sunset, between May and November, and blossoming occurs here from May through August, but the prime time for azaleas is roughly mid-May to mid-June. A small pillar box suggests a $1 donation, and another box contains an attractively designed garden guide ($2). Pets are not allowed in the garden. Take Island Explorer Route 5/Jordan Pond or Route 6/Brown Mountain and request a stop.

Behind a carved wooden gate on a forested hillside not far from Asticou lies an enchanted garden also designed by Charles K. Savage, and inspired by Beatrix Farrand. Special features of **Thuya Garden** are perennial borders, sculpted shrubbery, and Oriental touches. On a misty summer day, when few visitors appear, the colors are brilliant. Adjacent to the garden is **Thuya Lodge** (207/276-5130), former summer cottage of Joseph Curtis, donor of this awesome municipal park. The lodge, with an extensive botanical library and quiet rooms for reading, is open 10 A.M.–4:30 P.M. Mon.–Sat. and noon–4:30 P.M. Sunday late June to Labor Day. The garden is open 7 A.M.–7 P.M. daily. A collection box next to the front gate requests a

If you have even the slightest interest in gardens, make it a point to visit Thuya Garden.

$5 per adult donation. To reach Thuya, continue on Route 3 beyond Asticou Azalea Garden and watch for the Asticou Terraces parking area (no RVs, two-hour limit) on the right. Cross the road and climb the Asticou Terraces Trail (0.4 mile) to the garden. Or drive 0.2 mile beyond the Route 3 parking area, watching for a minuscule Thuya Garden sign on the left. Go half a mile up the steep, narrow and curving driveway to the parking area. Take Island Explorer Route 5/Jordan Pond and request a stop.

After you've visited Thuya Garden, open the back gate, where you'll see a sign for the **Eliot Mountain Trail,** a moderately difficult (lots of exposed roots), 1.4-mile round-trip trail. Near the summit, Northeast Harbor spreads out before you. If you're here in August, sample the wild blueberries. Much of the Eliot Mountain Trail is on private land, so stay on the path and be respectful of private property.

Petite Plaisance

On Northeast Harbor's quiet South Shore

Road, Petite Plaisance is a special-interest museum commemorating noted Belgian-born author and college professor Marguerite Yourcenar (pen name of Marguerite de Crayencour), the first woman elected to the prestigious Académie Française. From the early 1950s to 1987, Petite Plaisance was her home, and it's hard to believe she's no longer here; her intriguing possessions and presence fill the two-story house—of particular interest to Yourcenar devotees. Free, hourlong tours of the first floor are given in French or English, depending on visitors' preferences. (French-speaking visitors often make pilgrimages here.) The house is open for tours daily, June 15–August 31. No children under 12 are allowed. Call 207/276-3940 at least a day ahead, between 9 A.M.–4 P.M., for an appointment and directions, or write: Petite Plaisance Trust, P.O. Box 403, Northeast Harbor 04662. Yourcenar admirers should request directions to Brookside Cemetery in Somesville, seven miles away, where she is buried.

Great Harbor Maritime Museum

Annual exhibits focusing on the maritime heritage of the Mount Desert Island area are held in the small, eclectic Great Harbor Maritime Museum (125 Main St., Northeast Harbor, 207/276-5262, 10 A.M.–5 P.M. Tues.–Sat. late June to Labor Day, plus weekends Sept.–Oct., $3), housed in the old village fire station and municipal building. ("Great Harbor" refers to the Somes Sound area—Northeast, Southwest, and Seal Harbors, as well as the Cranberry Isles.) Yachting, coastal trade, and fishing receive special emphasis. Special programs and exhibits are held during the summer.

RECREATION

Hardy folks can test the cold Atlantic waters at the small saltwater beach at the head of the harbor in **Seal Harbor** (Island Explorer Route 5/Jordan Pond). Bicycle rentals are available at **Shirt Off Your Back** (207/266-3217 or 276-5611), a laundry service tucked down a stairway in an alley at the head of Main Street. Bikes are $15 for a half day or $20 for a full day. Shirt Off Your Back is located next door to the National Bank of Bar Harbor.

Long Pond Carriage Road Trail

- Distance: 3.4 miles round-trip
- Duration: 1.5–2 hours
- Elevation gain: Minimal
- Effort: Easy
- Trailhead: South end of Long Pond, west of Seal Harbor. From Bar Harbor, take the Island Explorer Route 5/Jordan Pond bus and get off at Seal Harbor Beach, then walk west a very short distance to Little Long Pond and enter the carriage roads there. Or drive from Bar Harbor either on the Park Loop Road (the two-way section) or on Route 3, via Otter Creek and park in a small lot on the north side of Route 3 at the bottom of Little Long Pond.

This loop—part of the 12 miles of carriage roads on private land (but open to the public)—is easy, a "walk-in-the-woods" kind of experience. (If you do this late in the day, use insect repellent.) It's officially Long Pond, but it's known as Little Long Pond to distinguish it from the far larger Long Pond on the west side of the island. Head north, on the east shore of the pond, passing signpost 35 and continuing to signpost 28. Bear left toward signpost 24 (and the lovely Cobblestone Bridge), then start heading west and south, meandering to signpost 32. Turn south (left) to signpost 33, where you'll bear left toward 34 and back to Route 3. (You can also do the loop in a clockwise direction, but counterclockwise gets you near the pond right at the start.) If you're using the bus, flag it down or walk back to the Seal Harbor Beach stop.

This section of the carriage roads is not open to bicyclists.

EXCURSION BOATS

Northeast Harbor is the starting point for a couple of boat services headed for the **Cranberry Isles.** (Other boats depart from Southwest Harbor; see below.) The vessels leave from the commercial floats at the end of the concrete

Municipal Pier on Sea Street. See the Cranberry Isles section for information on the regular ferry/mailboat service between Northeast Harbor and the Cranberries. (The ferries are slightly less expensive, but there's no narration.)

Sea Princess

The 75-foot *Sea Princess* (207/276-5352, www.acadiainfo.com/seaprincess.htm) carries visitors as well as an Acadia National Park naturalist on a 2.5-hour morning trip around the mouth of Somes Sound and out to Little Cranberry Island (Islesford) for a 50-minute stopover. The boat leaves Northeast Harbor daily at 10 A.M. mid-May to mid-October. Cost is $24 adults, $15 children 5–12, $5 for children under five. A narrated afternoon trip departs at 1 P.M. on the same route. Adult tickets for the afternoon trip are $20; children's rates are the same as for the morning trip. The *Sea Princess* also does a scenic 1.5-hour Somes Sound cruise, departing daily at 3:45 P.M., late June to early September. Cost is $20 adults, $15 children 5–12, $5 for children under five. The same months, two sunset cruises are offered. The three-hour sunset/dinner cruise departs for the Islesford Dock Restaurant on Little Cranberry (Islesford) at 5:15 P.M. Dinner is on your own at the restaurant. A 1.5-hour sunset cruise of Somes Sounds departs at 7 P.M. Cost for either is $20 adults, $15 children 5–12, $5 for children under five. Reservations are advisable for all trips, although even that provides no guarantee, since the cruises require a rather hefty 15-passenger minimum. Arrive at least a half hour before departure to purchase tickets at the booth next to the harbormaster's office, at the head of the Municipal Pier.

Sailing

Sail aboard an original Friendship sloop. Captain Wilson Fletcher's *Blackjack* (207/288-3056, http://w2.downeast.net/blackjack) has been sailing since 1900. Four 90-minute cruises are offered daily, Monday through Saturday, sailing from the Town Dock in Northeast Harbor. Cost is $35 per person, and the 33-foot sloop takes a maximum of six passengers.

ENTERTAINMENT

Since 1964, the **Mount Desert Festival of Chamber Music** (207/276-3988, www.mtdesertfestival.org) has presented concerts. Concerts are staged in the century-old Neighborhood House on Main Street, on Tuesdays 8:15 P.M. from mid-July through Mid August. Past musicians have included the Borromeo String Quartet and the Miami String Quartet. Tickets ($20 general admission; $10 student section) are available at the Neighborhood House box office on Mondays and Tuesdays during the concert season or by advance phone reservation.

SHOPPING

Upscale shops, galleries, and boutiques, with clothing, artworks, housewares, antiques, and antiquarian books, line both sides of Main Street, making for intriguing browsing and expensive buying. The season is short, though, with some shops open only in July and August.

Galleries

You'll enter another world at **Shaw Contemporary Jewelry** (100 Main St., 207/276-5000 or 877/276-5001, www.shawjewelry.com). Besides the spectacular silver and gold beachstone jewelry created by Rhode Island School of Design alumnus Sam Shaw, the work of more than 100 other jewelers is displayed exquisitely. Plus there are sculptures, Asian art, and rotating art exhibits. It all leads back toward a lovely, light-filled garden. Prices are in the stratosphere, but appropriately so. As one well-dressed customer was overhead saying to her companion: "If I had only one jewelry store to go to in my entire life, this would be it." The gallery is open all year, with a varying schedule depending on the season.

A seasonal branch of Bar Harbor's **Island Artisans** (119 Main St., 207/276-4045, www.islandartisans.com) carries an exceptional selection of locally made fine crafts.

For more than a quarter century, **Redfield Artisans Gallery** (125 Main St., 207/276-3609) has been selling high-end art and crafts to the area's discriminating buyers.

Next door, at **Christopher Smith Galleries** (125B Main St., 207/276-3343, www.smith-bronze.com), browse through an array of bronze wildlife sculptures and fountains. Smith was featured in 2005 on the cover of *Wildlife Art Magazine.*

Gifts and Clothing

The tony shops here are worth a visit and maybe even a major splurge. You'll find plenty of pink and lime green; Lilly Pulitzer is big here.

Early and late in the season, the summer crowd shops at **The Kimball Shop & Boutique** (Main St., Northeast Harbor, 207/276-3300) to stock up on wedding and Christmas gifts. It's all very tasteful.

At **Local Color** (147 Main St., Northeast Harbor, 207/276-5544 or 888/582-2250), you'll find—just for a start—stunning silk and chenille sweaters and jackets and exquisite jewelry. Owner Jayn Thomas has impeccable taste. Quality is high, and so are prices.

Antiques and Antiquarian Books

A small but select inventory of pre-owned hardcover books lines the walls at the **Wikhegan Old Books** (117 Main St., Northeast Harbor; P.O. Box 370, Mount Desert 04660, 207/276-5079 or 244-7060). Specialties include nautical books, Native American lore, women's studies, poetry, and antiques. The shop doubles as **Pine Bough,** with a small but well chosen selection of antiques and decorative arts.

ACCOMMODATIONS
Inn

Unless you're celebrating a landmark occasion, Northeast Harbor's lodgings may be a little too pricey, but if money's no object and a haute ambience appeals, spring for the **Asticou Inn** (Rte. 3, P.O. Box 337, Northeast Harbor 04662, 207/276-3344 or 800/258-3373, www.asticou.com). Built in 1883 and refurbished periodically, the classic harbor-view inn has 31 second-, third-, and fourth-floor rooms and suites in the main building, plus 16 rooms and suites in several more modern cottages. Facilities include clay tennis courts, outdoor pool,

and access to the Northeast Harbor Golf Club. The elegant, mural-lined dining room, open to the public for Sunday brunch (11:30 A.M.–2:30 P.M.) and dinner (6–10 P.M.) by reservation, has fabulous views of the harbor. Jackets and ties are advised for dinner. Lunch is also open to the public, served 11:30 A.M.–5 P.M.; reservations aren't needed, but you may have to wait on a gorgeous July or August day. The inn is open mid-May to late October. July and August rates are $302–362 d, modified American plan (MAP), $225–285 without meals. Early and late in the season, rates are B&B. Try to plan a late-May or early-June visit; you're practically on top of the Asticou Azalea Garden, and Thuya Garden is a short walk away, and the rates are lowest ($130–180 d). The Asticou is a popular wedding venue, so if you're looking for a quiet weekend, check the inn's wedding schedule before you book a room.

Bed-and-Breakfasts

Less pricey and far less formal, **The Maison Suisse Inn** (144 Main St., Northeast Harbor, 207/276-5223 or 800/624-7668, www.maison-suisse.com, $165–285) is a lovely shingle-style inn set off the street behind a rustic garden. Ten rooms are in the main inn, another five in the guest cottage behind it. All have private baths, TV, and phone; some have a fireplace. Breakfast is provided at a restaurant across the street.

The casual elegance of a bygone era still exists at **Grey Rock Inn** (Rte. 3/198, Northeast Harbor, 207/276-9360 summer, 207/244-4437 winter, www.greyrockinn.com, $185–375, mid-May–late Oct.), an antiques-filled mansion with to-die-for views over Northeast Harbor to the outer islands. Guest rooms are comfortable and large; many have fireplaces. Common rooms, most with fireplaces, flow from one to another. Trails lace the property's seven acres, which are bordered by Acadia National Park on two sides. Head out for a hike, perhaps to the summit of Norumbega Mountain, or stroll down the street to downtown Northeast Harbor. Rates include a full breakfast. (Note: The owners can be eccentric.)

In 1888, architect Fred Savage designed the two shingle-style buildings that make up the three-story **Harbourside Inn** (Main St., P.O. Box 178, Northeast Harbor, 207/276-3272, www.harboursideinn.com, $125–225, mid-June–mid-Sept.). The Sweet family has preserved the old-fashioned feel by decorating the 17 spacious rooms and three suites with antiques, yet modern amenities include some kitchenettes and phones. Most rooms have working fireplaces. A continental breakfast is served. Trails to Norumbega Mountain and Upper Hadlock Pond leave from the back of the property. Do note, over the years the waterfront property has been sold, so despite the inn's name, only glimpses of the harbor can be seen.

Motel

Although it's a bit dated—every room has two double beds—and the decor is uninspired, you can't beat the location of the **Kimball Terrace Inn** (10 Huntington Rd., P.O. Box 1030, Northeast Harbor, 207/276-3383 or 800/454-6225, www.kimballterraceinn.com, $166–184, open April–late Oct.). The three-story motel faces the harbor, and every room has a patio or private balcony (ask for a harbor-facing room). Do bring binoculars for yacht-spotting. The motel has a pool, a restaurant serving three meals daily, and a lounge, and it is a short walk to Northeast Harbor's downtown. It is a popular wedding venue, so ask if there are any groups in-house before you book, if that's a concern. Early and late season, rates plummet, and there are some wallet-friendly packages.

FOOD
Local Flavors

In the **Pine Tree Market** (121 Main St., Northeast Harbor, 207/276-3335, 7 A.M.–7 P.M. Mon.–Sat., 8 A.M.–6 P.M. Sun.) you'll find gourmet goodies, a huge wine selection, resident butcher, fresh fish, deli, homemade breads, pastries, sandwiches, and salads. Free delivery to homes and boats. Also on premises is a 24-hour, coin-operated laundry.

Pop into **Full Belli Deli** (Sea St., Northeast Harbor, 207/276-4299, 8 A.M.–4 P.M. Mon.–Sat., to 2 P.M. Sun.) for soups, fat sandwiches, and breakfast fare.

From June well into October, the **Northeast Harbor Farmers Market** is set up each Thursday, 9 A.M.–noon across from the Kimball Terrace Inn on Huntington Road. Look for the usuals, as well as cheeses, cider, maple syrup, breads, cookies, yarns and related fiber products, and prepared Asian foods.

Casual Dining

Real local color and crab cakes and crab sandwiches are *the best* at the **Docksider** (14 Sea St., Northeast Harbor, 207/276-3965, 11 A.M.–9 P.M., summer only), a low-key, family-friendly, unassuming, hole-in-the-wall place inevitably jammed with devoted locals and summer folk. Just up the hill from the chamber office, the Docksider has an outside deck, plus a couple of veteran (since forever) waitresses, no view, and a reputation far and wide. Prices reflect market rates, with choices beginning around $10, and more popular options in the $20–28 range. (Early-bird specials and a 10 percent discount are offered 4:30–6 P.M.) If you're smitten, buy one of the T-shirts, featuring an upright lobster announcing, "Frankly, I don't give a clam."

Tucked in a shady corner of a parking lot behind Shaw's Jewelry is a gem. **C La Matta Cena** (5 Old Firehouse Ln., Northeast Harbor, 207/276-3305, noon–9:30 P.M.) serves "spirited Tuscan cuisine" in a rustic garden setting warmed by heat lamps (there are also tables inside). The Mediterranean-inspired food is fabulous; much is sourced locally, and pastas and gelato are made on the premises. Most entrees run $18–27. Lunch is served until 4 P.M., wine and cheese 4–5:30 P.M.

Expect to wait in line for a table at **151 Main St.** (151 Main St., Northeast Harbor, 207/276-9898, opens at 5:30 P.M. Tues.–Sat.), because no reservations are accepted. The setting is unpretentious and the food sophisticated, with choices ranging from thin-crust pizzas to gussied-up meatloaf to bouillabaisse. Entrees run $10–26. Locally grown organic produce appears in many dishes. The ambience is casual, not especially elegant, with booths and tables (and a small bar waiting area). But the food is the thing here—chef/owner Emily Pascal has a sophisticated touch in the kitchen.

Fine Dining

The elegant, mural-lined dining room at the **Asticou Inn** (Rte. 3, 207/276-3344 or 800/258-3373) is open to the public for Sunday brunch (11:30 A.M.–2:30 P.M.) and dinner by candlelight (6–9 P.M., entrees $26–33) by reservation. Jackets and ties are advised for dinner. Lunch is also open to the public, served on the harborside deck, with serene views over Northeast Harbor, 11:30 A.M.–2 P.M.

INFORMATION AND SERVICES

The harborfront Chamber Information Bureau (also called the Yachtsmen's Building) of the **Mount Desert Chamber of Commerce** (18 Harbor Rd., P.O. Box 675, Northeast Harbor 04662, 207/276-5040, 8 A.M.–5 P.M. mid-June

to mid-Oct.) covers the villages of Somesville, Northeast Harbor, Seal Harbor, Otter Creek, Pretty Marsh, Hall Quarry, and Beech Hill. The extremely cordial staff can provide information on Northeast Harbor's gardens, museums, and trails, in addition to food and lodging. They even rent tennis rackets (reserve court time here, too). Coin-operated ($1.50, quarters only) hot showers, designed primarily but not exclusively for the boating crowd, are available here around the clock. You can even rent a hair dryer. The coffee and tea are free. Request a free copy of the annual *Mount Desert Chamber of Commerce Village/Island Guide & Northeast Harbor Port Directory.*

Public Restrooms

Restrooms are at the end of the building housing the Great Harbor Maritime Museum, in the town office on Sea Street, and at the harbor.

Getting Around

Northeast Harbor is serviced by Route 5/Jordan Pond and Route 6/Brown Mountain of the Island Explorer bus system.

Southwest Harbor and Vicinity

Southwest Harbor considers itself the hub of Mount Desert Island's "quiet side." In summer, its tiny downtown district is probably the busiest spot on the whole western side of the island (west of Somes Sound), but that's not saying a great deal. "Southwest" has the feel of a settled community, a year-round flavor that Bar Harbor sometimes lacks. And it competes with the best in the scenery department.

The quirky nature of the island's four town boundaries creates complications in trying to categorize various island segments. Officially, the town of Southwest Harbor includes only the villages of Manset and Seawall, but nearby is the precious (really!) hamlet of Somesville. The Somesville National Historic District, with its distinctive arched white footbridge, is especially appealing, but traffic gets congested

here along Route 102, so rather than just rubbernecking, plan to stop and walk around.

Be sure to drive or bike around the smaller villages, especially Somesville, Bass Harbor, and Bernard to take advantage of the gorgeous views and slower pace of life.

SIGHTS
◖ Wendell Gilley Museum

In the center of Southwest Harbor, the Gilley Museum (Herrick Rd., corner of Rte. 102, Southwest Harbor, 207/244-7555, www.wendellgilleymuseum.org, 10 A.M.–4 P.M. Tues.–Sun. June–Oct., to 5 P.M. in July and Aug., Fri.–Sun. in May, Nov., and Dec., $5 adults, $2 kids 5–12) was established in 1981 to display the life work of local woodcarver Wendell Gilley (1904–1983), a one-time plumber who had

COMMUNITIES

© TOM NANGLE

The Gilley Museum, in Southwest Harbor, displays more than 200 birds carved and painted by Wendell Gilley.

gained a national reputation for his carvings by the time of his death. The modern, energy-efficient museum houses more than 200 of his astonishingly realistic bird specimens carved over more than 50 years. He was pretty much self-taught, but he benefited from tips and instruction provided by local artists. Before he began carving, he practiced taxidermy, so he had a special understanding of birds' structure and musculature. Summer exhibits also feature other wildlife artists. Many days, a local artist gives woodcarving demonstrations, and members of the local carving club often can be seen whittling away. The gift shop carries an ornithological potpourri—books to binoculars to carving tools. Kids over eight appreciate this more than younger ones. If you're caught by the carving bug, workshops are available ranging from 90-minute introductory lessons for adults and children ($25) offered most weekdays during the summer to multi-day classes on specific birds ($70).

Southwest Harbor Oceanarium

Touching a sea cucumber or a starfish may not be every adult's idea of fun, but kids sure enjoy the hands-on experience at the Oceanarium (Clark Point Rd., Southwest Harbor, 207/244-7330, http://theoceanarium.com/), sister site to the Bar Harbor Oceanarium. A knowledgeable naturalist introduces creatures from a watery touch tank during a tour of the oceanarium. Twenty tanks hold a range of sea creatures. In addition, exhibits line the walls of the intriguing, low-tech museum. It's located next to the Coast Guard station. Tickets are $8 adults, $6 children 4–12; an all-access pass to both sites is $15 adults and $9.75 children.

Mount Desert Island Historical Society Museum

This tiny museum (Rte. 102, Somesville, 207/276-9323, 1–4 P.M. Tues.–Sat., seasonal) is adjacent to the gently curving white bridge in Somesville, so there's a good chance you're going to stop, if just for a photo. In season, the heirloom garden, filled with flowering plants and herbs of the 19th and early 20th centuries, is worth a photo or two in and of itself. The

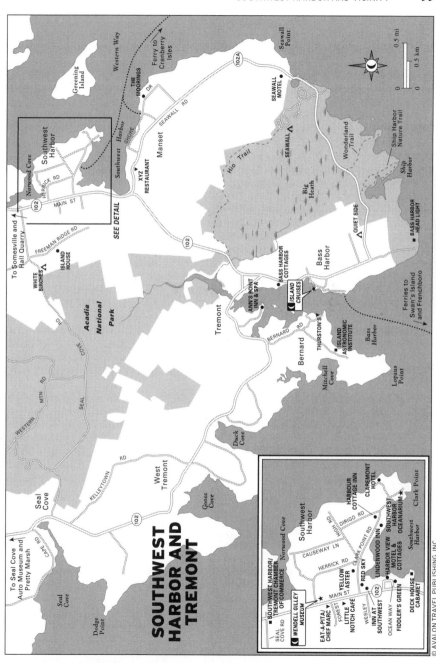

COMMUNITIES

SOUTHWEST HARBOR AND TREMONT

© AVALON TRAVEL PUBLISHING, INC.

tiny one-room museum has local artifacts and memorabilia displayed in a themed exhibit that changes annually. You can purchase a walking tour guide to Somesville in the museum. If you're especially interested in history, ask about the museum's programs, which include speakers, demonstrations, and workshops.

Charlotte Rhoades Park and Butterfly Garden

It's easy to miss the Charlotte Rhoades Park and Butterfly Garden (Route 102, Southwest Harbor), but that would be a mistake. This tiny seaside park was donated to the town in 1973 and is maintained entirely by volunteers. It's seldom busy, and it's a delightful place for a picnic. A kiosk is stocked with butterfly observation sheets. It's located on the water side of Route 102 between the Causeway Golf Club and the Seal Cove Road.

RECREATION

Acadia National Park, of course, is the recreational focus throughout Mount Desert Island;

on the island's western side, the main nonpark recreational activities are bike-, boat-, and picnic-related.

A broad swath of Acadia National Park cuts right through the center of this side of the island, and many of its hiking trails are far less congested than elsewhere in the park. A recently cleared "connector trail" from Southwest Harbor has made access to park trails even easier. Seawall Campground, as well as the Wonderland and Ship Harbor Trails, lie within the town limits of Southwest Harbor.

At the Southwest Harbor/Tremont Chamber of Commerce office, or at any of the area's stores, lodgings, and restaurants, pick up a free copy of the *Trail Map/Hiking Guide,* a very handy foldout map showing more than 20 hikes on the west side of Mount Desert Island. Trail descriptions include distance, time required, and skill levels (easy to strenuous). In 2001, thanks to a group effort spearheaded by Friends of Acadia, the half-mile-long Western Mountain Connector was opened a few miles north of downtown Southwest Harbor to provide easier access to several Acadia trails on this side of the island.

Bicycling

A veteran business with a first-rate reputation, **Southwest Cycle** (Main St., Southwest Harbor, 207/244-5856 or 800/649-5856) rents bikes by the day and week and is open all year (June–Sept., hours are 8:30 A.M.–5:30 P.M. Mon.–Sat. and 10 A.M.–4 P.M. Sun.). The staff at Southwest Cycle will fix you up with maps and lots of good advice for three loops (10–30 miles) on the western side of Mount Desert. (See *Islands near Mount Desert* for planning biking day trips to Swan's Island or the Cranberry Isles.) Rentals are $19. The shop also rents every imaginable accessory, from baby seats to jogging strollers.

Sea Kayaking

On the outskirts of Southwest Harbor's downtown, close to the chamber of commerce, is **Maine State Kayak** (254 Main St., South-

© TOM NANGLE

Charlotte Rhoades Butterfly Garden

west Harbor, 207/244-9500 or 877/481-9500, www.mainestatekayak.com). Staffed with experienced, environmentally sensitive kayakers (several are Registered Maine Guides), the company offers four-hour trips (8:30 A.M.–12:30 P.M., 10 A.M.–2 P.M., 2 P.M.–6 P.M. and a sunset tour) with a choice of half a dozen routes (depending on tide, visibility, and wind conditions). The trip is $46 pp ($42 late May through June and September) and it includes shuttle transportation, paddling equipment, and a guide. Most trips also include island or beach breaks. Maximum group is six tandems; minimum age is 12. Neophytes are welcome.

Calm-Water Paddling

Just west of Somesville (take the Pretty Marsh Rd.), and across the road from Long Pond, the largest lake on Mount Desert Island, **National Park Canoe & Kayak Rental** (145 Pretty Marsh Rd., Rte. 102, Mount Desert, 207/244-5854 or 877/378-6907, www.acadia .net/canoe) makes canoeing and kayaking a snap. Just rent the boat, carry it across the road to Pond's End, and launch it. Be sure to pack a picnic. Half-day rate (8:30 A.M.–12:30 P.M. or 1 P.M.–5 P.M.) for a canoe is $25, full-day rate is $37, weekly rate is $135; solo kayak is $24 half day, $35 full day, $135 per week; tandem kayak is $25 half day, $48 full day, $180 per week. A do-it-yourself sunset canoe or kayak tour (from 5 P.M. to sunset) is $15 pp. Reservations are advisable, and essential in July and August. Open mid-May to mid-October.

If you've brought your own canoe (or kayak), launch it here at Pond's End and head off. It's four miles to the southern end of the lake. If the wind kicks up, skirt the shore; if it *really* kicks up from the north, don't paddle too far down the lake, as you'll have a devil of a time getting back.

Another option is to launch your canoe on the quieter, cliff-lined southern end of the lake, much of which is in the park. To find the put-in, take the Seal Cove Road (on the east end of downtown Southwest Harbor). Go right on Long Cove Road to the small parking area at the end near the pumping station. You can also put in from the Long Pond Fire Road, off Route 102, in Pretty Marsh.

Almost the entire west side of Long Pond is Acadia National Park property, so plan to picnic and swim along there; tuck into the sheltered area west of Southern Neck, a crooked finger of land that points northward from the western shore. Stay clear of private property on the east side of the lake.

Deep Sea Fishing

Go fishing with the **Masako Queen Fishing Company** (Beal's Wharf, Clark Point Road, Southwest Harbor, 207/244-5385, www .masakoqueen.com) aboard *The Vagabond* and you might return with a lobster. The boat goes 8–20 miles offshore for mackerel, bluefish, codfish, and more, but on each trip every passenger is assigned a lobster trap. When that trap is hauled, any legal-sized lobster in your trap is yours. Trips last 5–7 hours, and all equipment is included. Dress warmly.

Sailing

Mansell Boat Rental Co. (135 Shore Rd., Manset, next to Hinckley, 207/244-5625, www.mansellboatrentals.com) rents sail and power boats by the day or week. A keel day sailor is $180 per day. A 13.6 Boston Whaler is $175 per day. Plenty of other choices are available. Also available are sailing lessons: $195 for a three-hour sail lesson cruise for two, which includes rigging and unrigging the boat; $75 per hour for private lessons, minimum two hours.

Half-day, full-day, and longer power boat rentals are also available from **Manset Yacht Service** (113 Shore Rd., Manset, 207/244-4040). Rates begin at $165 for a half-day rental of a standard, 18-foot Horizon; $240 for a 22-foot T-top Horizon.

Golf

Play a quick nine at the **Causeway Club** (Fernald Point Rd., 207/244-3780), which edges the ocean. Be forewarned: It's more challenging than it looks.

EXCURSION BOATS

Southwest Harbor is the starting point for a couple of boat services headed for the Cranberry Isles. (Other boats depart from Northeast Harbor; see above.) See the *Cranberry Isles* section for information on the regular ferry/mailboat service between Northeast Harbor and the Cranberries. (The ferries are slightly less expensive, but there's no narration.)

Cruise around Somes Sound, the Cranberry Isles, and Baker's Island aboard the *Elizabeth T,* a 34-foot wooden lobster boat, with **Great Harbor Cruises** (207/466-5200 cell or 207/244-9160, www.greatharbortours.com). The Lunch Cruise to Little Cranberry Island departs at 11:15 A.M. and returns about 3 P.M. The fee is $25 for adults and $15 for kids 16 and younger. You can eat at the Islesford Dock restaurant or bring your own picnic. The cruise

takes in a number of sights, including Somes Sound, and a lobster trap is hauled along the way. The boat departs from the dock at Southwest Boat, near the end of Clark Point Road.

Charter a traditional Friendship sloop with **Downeast Friendship Sloop Charters** (P.O. Box 1533, Southwest Harbor 04679, 207/266-5210, www.downeastfriendshipsloop.com) for a half-day sail or longer. Private charters start at $225, including crew, appetizer, and soft drinks. Semi-private charters begin at $35 pp.

ENTERTAINMENT AND EVENTS
Life Is a Cabaret

It's not too far to drive from Southwest Harbor to Bar Harbor for evening dinner and entertainment, but Southwest has a cabaret theater that even draws customers in the

RALPH STANLEY, NATIONAL TREASURE

Wooden boatbuilding in Maine dates from the construction of the pinnace *Virginia* by English settlers in 1607. Nearly 400 years later, traditional wooden boatbuilding survives, with many boatbuilders concentrated in the Acadia region. Only one has been declared a national treasure.

Boatbuilding for Ralph W. Stanley has been a lifelong pursuit of perfection in wood. "You could say that the fiberglass boat moves on the water, while a wooden boat moves through the water," he says in *Ralph Stanley: Tales of a Maine Boatbuilder,* by Ralph Stanley and Craig Milner (Down East Books, 2004).

Stanley's excellence was recognized in 1999, when the National Endowment for the Arts awarded him $10,000 National Heritage Fellowship. The award recognizes "lifetime achievement, artistic excellence, and contributions to our nation's traditional arts heritage."

Stanley, who was born in Bar Harbor and grew up and settled in Southwest Harbor, can trace his family roots in the area to the settlement of Little Cranberry Island in 1769. No surprise that seafaring enterprises were his

family's calling. As a child, he made wooden toy boats and watched professional boatbuilders at work. After graduating from college, he began his first boat. Over his lifetime, Stanley gained a reputation as a master designer and builder of wooden lobster boats and Friendship sloops, as well as for being a fine fiddler and a good storyteller.

"I've always had strong feelings about my own models, especially the lobster boats. When I design a boat, it's unique. It's mine. There's no other like it. It has to do with the shape, the sheer, the way I put things together, and little things that I do that nobody else does, that nobody else can do," Stanley relates in the book, which is complemented by anecdotes and historical notes.

The Stanley tradition of boatbuilding will continue. Stanley is passing his knowledge on to his children, who now work with him. As he notes: "If everybody just stopped building in wood, the art of building a boat would soon be lost." That would be a national tragedy that this national treasure hopes will never happen.

reverse direction for great entertainment and so-so food: **The Deck House Restaurant and Cabaret Theater** (Great Harbor Marina, 11 Apple Lane, off Rte. 102, Southwest Harbor, 207/244-5044, www.thedeckhouse.com). Try to arrive for dinner by 6:30 P.M. to enjoy the spectacular harbor view and order your meal (entrees are $22). The cathedral-ceilinged dining room holds 140, and the table is yours for the evening for an additional $7 pp cover charge (reservations are essential in midsummer). About 8:15 P.M., the young waitstaff, chameleonlike, unveils its other talents—singing, dancing, even storytelling and puppetry. After hearing the dozen or so numbers, you won't be surprised to learn that many Deck House staff have moved on to Broadway and beyond. The performers aren't compensated, so be prepared to leave a tip. The Deck House is open mid-June to mid-September.

Repertory Theater

Somesville is home to the **Acadia Repertory Theatre** (Rte. 102, Somesville, P.O. Box 106, Mount Desert 04660, 207/244-7260 or 888/362-7480, www.acadiarep.com, $20 adults, $15 seniors, students, and military, $10 kids under 16), which has been providing first-rate professional thespian summer stock on the stage of Somesville's antique Masonic Hall since the 1970s. Classic plays by Wilde, Goldsmith, even Molière, have been staples, as has the annual Agatha Christie mystery. Performances in the 144-seat hall run late June to late August, Tuesday–Sunday at 8:15 P.M., with 2 P.M. matinees on the last Sunday of each play. Special children's plays occur Wednesday and Saturday at 10:30 A.M. in July and August. Tickets for children's theater programs are $7 adults, $5 kids. (No credit cards; pay at the box office before the performance.)

Events

In early October, Smuggler's Den Campground on Route 102 in Southwest Harbor is home to the annual **Octoberfest and Food Festival** (207/244-9264 or 800/423-9264, www.acadiachamber.com), a one-day celebration with crafts, food, games, music, and about two dozen Maine microbrewers presenting about 80 different brews.

SHOPPING

The best shopping locale on this side of the island is Southwest Harbor. Mind you, there aren't *lots* of shops, but the small selection is interesting. You'll also find a few (okay, very few) shops in Somesville.

Crafts and Gifts

In the middle of Southwest Harbor's small shopping area is **Sand Castle Ocean and Nature Store** (360 Main St., Southwest Harbor, 207/244-4118), a delightful shop with a huge range of handcrafted items, most with a marine theme. Representing the work of several dozen artisans, the shop has wind chimes, jewelry, ceramics, ship models, and lots of other surprises.

Local artisans show and sell their works at **Flying Mountain Artisans** (28 Main St., Rte. 102, Southwest Harbor, 207/244-0404). Lots of creative goods here, from quilts to blown glass.

Art and Jewelry

Fine art of the 19th and early 20th century is the specialty at **Clark Point Gallery** (46 Clark Point Rd., Southwest Harbor, 207/244-0920, www.clarkpointgallery.com). Most works depict Maine and Mount Desert Island.

Jewelry approaches fine art at **Aylen & Son Jewelers** (Main St., Rte. 102, Southwest Harbor, 207/244-7369, www.peteraylen.com). For more than 25 years, Peter and Judy Aylen have been crafting and selling jewelry in 18-karat gold and sterling silver and augmenting it with fine gemstones or intriguing beads.

Books, Charts, and Music

The two-story **Port in a Storm Bookstore** (Main St., Rte. 102, Somesville, Mount Desert, 207/244-4114 or 800/694-4114, www.portinastormbookstore.com) is one of Maine's best independent bookstores. It's totally seductive, guaranteed to lighten your wallet. High ceilings, comfortable chairs, whimsical floor

© TOM NANGLE

Southwest Harbor is a great place for yacht spotting since it's home to Hinckley Yachts, one of the country's premier boatbuilders.

sculptures, open space, and Somes Cove views all contribute to the ambience. Inventory is not huge, but it's well selected—especially nature and children's books—and the staff is very knowledgeable. Especially in summer, noted authors often visit to lecture or sign their books.

Luddites, here's your destination. Nicols Fox, author of *Against the Machine: The Hidden Luddite Tradition in Literature, Art and Individual Lives,* touches a chord in all of us who weren't brought up lashed to a laptop. Her **Rue Cottage Books** (360 Main St., Southwest Harbor, 207/244-5542), besides containing a collection of anti-tech titles, has an eclectic mix of other specialties—mythology, environment (she's an avid Green), 1960s radicals, natural history, Native Americans, and "irresistible old books." If your budget is pinched, she also has a stash of "cheap thrills"—$2 mysteries. The shop is set off Main Street, facing the new town green and memorial.

Southwest Harbor is the home of one of the nation's premier boatbuilders, **The Hinckley Company** (130 Shore Rd., Manset, 207/244-5531), a name of stellar repute since the 1930s.

There are no tours of the Hinckley complex, but most yachters can't resist the urge to look in at the yard. Plus you can stop in at the **Hinckley Ship' Store** (207/244-7100 or 800/446-2553) and pick up books, charts, and all sorts of Hinckley-logo gear.

Don Gooding's **Mainely A Cappella** (11 Seal Cove Rd., Southwest Harbor, 800/827-2936, www.acappella.com) is the largest source of a cappella music in the world, with more than 3,000 a cappella–related items. Available are CDs, sheet music, videos, songbooks, instructional materials, and more from all over the globe.

ACCOMMODATIONS

As the Asticou Inn is to Northeast Harbor, the Claremont is to Southwest Harbor. On the other end of the lodging scale, there are several commercial campgrounds in this part of the island, plus an Acadia National Park campground.

Inn

When you're ready to splurge, **The Claremont** (22 Claremont Rd., Southwest Harbor 04679,

207/244-5036 or 800/244-5036, www.the-claremonthotel.com) may well be your choice, but you'll have to plan a year ahead to land a room in July or August. Most popular time is the first week in August, during the annual Claremont Croquet Classic. An elegant grande dame, dressed in yellow clapboard, the Claremont dominates a six-acre hilltop overlooking Somes Sound and caters to honeymooners, yuppies, and gentrified folk. The views are stupendous. Guests have access to croquet courts, a clay tennis court, bikes, rowboats, and a library. Dating from 1884, the main building has 26 rooms (with bath and phones), most of them recently refurbished yet pleasantly old-fashioned and not fancy. Other accommodations are in the six-room Phillips House, one-suite Clark House, and new Cole Cottage, with two rooms and one efficiency. Rooms in these buildings are $174 to $224 modified American plan, mid-July to Labor Day, plus a hefty 15 percent service charge and Maine sales tax. (Rooms without water views can be rented in high season at a B&B rate, $180 d.) Also on the premises are 14 cottages ($195–265, mid-June to mid-Sept.); they can go as high as $3,300 a week in midsummer. No pets, no smoking, and, surprisingly, no credit cards. Children are welcome. The hotel and dining room are open early June to mid-October; cottages are open late May to mid-October.

Bed-and-Breakfasts

Many of Southwest Harbor's B&Bs are clustered downtown, along Main Street and the Clark Point Road.

Set on a corner, well back from the Clark Point Road, is **⟨ Harbour Cottage Inn** (9 Dirigo Rd., P.O. Box 258, Southwest Harbor 04679, 207/244-5738 or 888/843-3022, www.harbourcottageinn.com), appealingly revamped in 2002, when Javier Montesinos and Don Jalbert took over the reins. Built in 1870, it was the "annex" for one of the island's original hotels and housed the increasing numbers of rusticators who patronized this part of the island. It has evolved into a lovely B&B with eight rooms ($149–159) and three suites

($199–245), decorated in a colorful and fun cottage style. Most rooms have whirlpool baths or steam-sauna showers, some have fireplaces, and all have telephones, TV, Wi-Fi, and computer ports. Rates include a full breakfast and use of beach bicycles. The inn stocks a nice selection of wine and beer. Also part of Harbour Cottage is **Pier One**, which offers five weekly waterfront suites ($1,260–1,575), including a studio cottage, all with kitchens, TV, and phone. Guests have private use of 150-foot pier, and they can dock or launch canoes or kayaks or other small boats from right outside their doors.

The the linden-blossom fragrance can be intoxicating in summer at the **⟨ Lindenwood Inn** (118 Clark Point Rd., P.O. Box 1328, Southwest Harbor 04679, 207/244-5335 or 800/307-5335, www.lindenwoodinn.com, $125–295). Jim King, the Australian owner, has imaginatively decorated the inn's nine rooms and poolside bungalow with artifacts from everywhere. After hiking Acadia's trails, the heated pool and hot tub are especially welcome, and after that, perhaps the inn's full bar, serving guests only. Open all year.

At the Victorian **Inn at Southwest** (371 Main St., Rte. 102, P.O. Box 593, Southwest Harbor 04679, 207/244-3835, www.innat-southwest.com, $125–175) guests gather for games, reading, conversation, and afternoon tea in a huge living room with fireplace and comfortable couches. Built in 1884 as the Freeman Cottage, the elegant building has 13 dormers and a wraparound veranda. Seven second- and third-floor guest rooms—named for Maine lighthouses and full of character—are fitted out with wicker furniture, ceiling fans, down comforters, and lots more. Some have gas stoves or limited water views. The inn is Wi-Fi wired. Open May through October. Breakfast is a feast, with such treats as cheesecake crepes and eggs Florentine.

Across the lane **The Kingsleigh Inn 1904** (373 Main St., P.O. Box 1426, Southwest Harbor 04679, 207/244-5302, www.kingsleighinn.com, $135–165) is a very attractive Queen Anne manse with eight well-thought-out rooms (private baths) on three floors. If you're sensitive to street noise, request a back-facing (harbor-view) room, although air-conditioners and in-room sound machines muffle the sound in summer. The huge turret suite, with fireplace, TV, telescope, large bathroom, and lots of comfortable wicker furniture, is $175–260, depending on the season. Breakfast is an elegant, three-course affair, served on the waterview porch, weather permitting. Afternoon refreshments are served, and chocolate chip cookies and port wine (now there's a combo) are replenished daily in guest rooms. Guests have access to a telephone, and Wi-Fi is throughout the inn.

Peter and Bethany Nickum Tague provide a quiet, restorative retreat at **The Yellow Aster** (53 Clark Point Rd., P.O. Box 1513, Southwest Harbor 04679, 207/244-4422 or 800/724-7228, www.yellowaster.com, $115). Breakfast features natural and organic foods, whole grain breads, and fresh produce; special dietary needs can usually be met, from vegan to allergies. You can arrange for a massage therapist to ease out the kinks after a day exploring the park (ask about packages that include two nights' lodging, a sea kayak tour, and a massage). There's even an in-house gallery featuring the works of local artisans. The four upstairs guest rooms are on the smallish side, and a few have closet baths, but there's a comfy living room to relax in, and the inn is just steps from downtown.

Next door is **Central House Inn** (51 Clark Point Rd., P.O. Box 503, Southwest Harbor 04079, 207/244-0100 or 877/205-0289, www.centralhouseinn.com, $145–175), which owner Terry Prebble has meticulously remodeled (lots of sherbet colors—lemon and lime exterior, raspberry living room) and great art throughout. Three guest rooms in subdued shades have gas fireplaces, air-conditioning, and hidden cable TV/DVD. The bathrooms have huge tiled showers with three showerheads; one room also has a whirlpool tub. On the third floor a 750-square-foot loft apartment is available by the week.

In 2004, Ann and Charlie Bradford sold the family home that had housed their long-time B&B and reopened a petite version of the **Island House** (36 Freeman Ridge., P.O. Box 1006, Southwest Harbor 04679, 207/244-5180, www.islandhousebb.com) in their new custom home, built atop a ridge in a quiet neighborhood about a mile from downtown. They've downsized the guest space to just two comfy rooms available for $110, plus a guest living/dining room all on one level (a great place for anyone with mobility problems, although it's not wheelchair accessible). Anne's warm hospitality and delicious full breakfasts remain the same. Also available is a separate, two-bedroom apartment above the garage ($150) with a tiny deck offering glimpses of distant islands. The Island House is open all year. From June through September, the Bradfords also rent Wood-Sea, a comfortable two-bedroom summer cottage, near Bass Harbor Head Light, about five miles from Southwest Harbor; call for rates.

In Manset, adjacent to the Hinckley Yacht complex and with jaw-dropping views down Somes Sound, is **The Moorings** (Shore Rd., P.O. Box 744, Southwest Harbor 04679, 207/244-5523 or 207/244-3210 or 800/596-5523, www.mooringsinn.com), owned and operated by the King family for more than 40 years. The oceanfront complex is part motel, part cottage rental, and part old-fashioned B&B, and the rates are terrific. Ten rooms in the Main House are named after locally built sailing vessels. Rates ($65–120) include juice, coffee, and doughnuts. The Lighthouse View Wing ($115) has motel-style rooms with refrigerator, microwave, waterfront decks, and incredible views (spend the afternoon counting the Hinckley yachts). Also on the property are cottage units, a combination of rooms and efficiencies ($105–165). Bikes, canoes, and kayaks are available for guests, so you can paddle around the harbor. One mile distant is Eagle Watch Cottage ($165), with two bedrooms and harbor views, and King's Mark, a garden-style apartment, with two bedrooms ($150).

Motels and Cottages

Right smack on the harbor and just a

two-minute walk from downtown is the appropriately named **Harbor View Motel & Cottages** (11 Ocean Way, P.O. Box 701, Southwest Harbor 04679, 207/244-5031 or 800/538-6463, www.mainesunshine.com/harbview). The family-owned complex comprises motel rooms ($75–115) spread out in a two older one-story buildings and a newish three-story structure that fronts the harbor. A continental breakfast is served to motel guests from July 1 through Labor Day. Also on the premises are seven housekeeping cottages with kitchenettes (weekly rentals only; $665–925), ranging from studios to two-bedrooms. The property is open mid-May through mid-October.

Right across from the famed seawall and adjacent to the park is the **Seawall Motel** (566 Seawall Rd./Rte. 102A, Southwest Harbor 04679, 207/244-9250 or 800/248-9250, www.seawallmotel.com, $95–100). The no-surprises, two-story motel (upstairs rooms have the best views) has free Wi-Fi, in-room phones and cable TV. A continental breakfast is included mid-May through October. Kids 12 and under stay free. The location's excellent for bird watchers—there's a freshwater pond, pine forest, and the ocean. The motel is also home to the Acadia Workshop Center (207/244-3020 or 800/248-9250, www.acadiaworkshopcenter.com), which offers five-day art classes from May into October. Packages are available that include lodging, meals, airport transportation, workshop, and park tour.

LSRobinson Co. (337 Main St., P.O. Box 1480, Southwest Harbor, 04679, 207/244-5563, www.lsrobinson.com) has an extensive list of cottage rentals in the area. The Southwest Harbor/Tremont Chamber of Commerce also keeps a helpful listing of privately owned homes/cottages available for rent. The chamber's annual summer guide usually contains a couple of pages of ads with photos.

Sleep Aboard

For something completely different, consider chartering a private B&B trip aboard a Friendship sloop with **Downeast Friendship Sloop Charters** (P.O. Box 1533, Southwest Harbor 04679, 207/266-5210, www.downeastfriendshipsloop.com, $300). You'll sail from Great Harbor Marina in Southwest Harbor to a quiet cove, where you'll be treated to a lobster dinner with wine before retiring to your private cabin, trimmed in mahogany and teak. Sorry, no en suite bathroom, but there is a private marine head onboard. Wake to the scent of fresh coffee, and accompany that with a huge breakfast: blueberry pancakes, blueberry muffins, bagels, fruits, and juices. You'll be back at the marina by 9 A.M., where hot showers are available.

Campgrounds

On the eastern edge of Somesville, just off Route 198 at the head of Somes Sound, the **Mount Desert Campground** (516 Somes Sound Dr., Rte. 198, Somesville, Mount Desert, 207/244-3710, www.mountdesertcampground.com) is especially centrally located for visiting Bar Harbor, Acadia, and the whole western side of Mount Desert Island. The campground has 152 wooded tent sites, about 45 on the water, spread out on 58 acres. Reservations are essential in midsummer—one-week minimum for waterfront sites, three days for off-water sites in July and August. (Campers book a year ahead for waterfront sites here.) This deservedly popular and low-key campground gets high marks for maintenance, noise control, and convenient tent platforms. Another plus is The Gathering Place, where campers can relax, play games, and purchase coffee and fresh-baked treats or ice cream. Summer rates are $30–45 a night ($45 for the waterfront sites) for two adults and two children younger than 18. Electrical hookups are available for $1 per night. No pets July–Labor Day. No trailers over 20 feet. Kayak and canoe rentals are available. Open mid-June to mid-September.

Just outside of town, on a quiet road cutting through the woods and adjacent to the park is **White Birches Campground** (195 Seal Cove Rd., Southwest Harbor, 207/244-3797 or 888/716-0727, www.mainecamper.com), with sites in a field and in the woods. This is a great location if you're going to concentrate your hiking efforts on the western side of the park. Rates for two adults and two children younger than 16 are $23 tent, $27 RV with water and electric, $65 camping cabin. With the exception of camping cabins, the seventh night is free. Facilities include a heated outdoor pool, playground, and free hot showers.

If staying at a quiet, no-frills campground in an outstanding setting appeals, head for Hall Quarry, a few miles south of Somesville. **Somes Sound View Campground** (86 Hall Quarry Rd., Mount Desert, 207/244-3890 or off-season 207/244-7452, www.acadiainfo.com/ssview.htm), among the smallest campgrounds on the island, has 60 tight tent and RV (maximum 28 feet) sites on a hillside, with some on the ocean's edge. Facilities include hot showers (if you're camping on the lowest levels, it's a good hike up to the bathhouse); the nearest store is two miles. Canoe rentals are available, and you can swim in the sound (from a rocky beach). Leashed pets are allowed (vaccinations must be up to date). Sites are $25–40 in July and August, less early and late in the season. No credit cards. Open late May to mid-October. The campground is two miles south and east of Somesville and a mile east of Route 102.

Smuggler's Den Campground (Rte. 102, P.O. Box 787, Southwest Harbor 04679, 207/244-3944, www.smugglersdencampground.com) is a mid-sized campground between Echo Lake and downtown Southwest Harbor. It's also the site of the annual Oktoberfest. Trails access back roads to both Echo Lake (1.25 miles) and Long Pond (1 mile). Big rig sites are grouped in the top third; pop-ups and small campers are in the middle third; tenting sites are in the lower third and in the woods rimming the large recreation field. Summer rates covering four adults vary from $26 (tent) to $37 (full hookups) for the 96 sites, 54 of which are designated for tents. Also available are four camping cabins that rent for $475 per week. Facilities include a heated pool and kiddie pool, laundry, free hot showers, lobsters and ice cream for sale, and entertainment. Well-behaved pets are a possibility.

FOOD
Local Flavors

Lots of goodies for picnics can be found at **Sawyer's Market** (Main St., Southwest Harbor, 207/244-7061, 5:30 A.M.–7:30 P.M. Mon.–Sat.) or across the street at **Sawyer's Specialties** (Main St., Southwest Harbor, 207/244-3317), which specializes in wine and cheese.

The students at College of the Atlantic run **Beech Hill Farm** (Beech Hill Rd., Mount Desert, 207/244-5204), 8 A.M.–5 P.M. Tues., Wed., Fri., and Sat.), a five-acre, MOFGA-certified organic farm that also has acres of heirloom apple trees, and 65 acres of forestland. Visit the farmstand for fresh produce.

Casual Dining

Some of the island's most creative sandwiches and pizza toppings emerge from Arthur and Kate Jacobs's **Little Notch Cafe** (340 Main St., Southwest Harbor, 207/244-3357, 11 A.M.–8 P.M. Mon.–Sat. May–Oct., 11 A.M.–7 P.M. weekdays Nov.–April), next to the library in Southwest Harbor's downtown. How about a broccoli, sausage, and black olive pizza? Or a prosciutto sandwich with asiago cheese and roasted peppers? All this plus Little Notch Bakery's famed breads, sinful desserts, a couple of pasta choices, and homemade soups, stews, and chowders make the cafe a winner.

By day, **Eat-a-Pita** (326 Main St., Southwest Harbor, 207/244-4344, www.eatapitachefmarc.com, 8 A.M.–9 P.M.) is a casual, order-at-the-counter restaurant, serving breakfast and lunch. At night, it morphs into **Café 2,** a tad more formal with full service. The dining room is furnished with old oak tables and chairs and an eclectic collection of stuff. Start the day with a Greek or Acapulco omelette. Lunch emphasizes pita sandwiches and salads (delicious! Call in advance for take-out); dinner choices ($14–22) include a half dozen pastas and entrees such as poached Atlantic salmon and boneless lamb loin. Desserts are homemade.

Hot diggity dog! Families and hot dog lovers

rejoiced when **The Downeast House of Dogs & More** (7 Clark Point Rd., Southwest Harbor, 207/244-0011, 7 A.M.–9 P.M. daily, mid-May–mid-Oct., 11 A.M.–9 P.M. Tues.–Sat. mid-Oct.–mid-May) opened its doors in 2005. Owners Pam and Gary White welcome kids with paper-topped, crayon- and game-stocked tables and kid-pleasing basics and hot dog connoisseurs with gourmet franks, all at reasonable prices. Choose from Specialty Hot Dogs ($2.50–4), such as Schickhause, Smithfield's, Zweigles White-Hot, and Sabrett, to Just Plain Weird Dogs ($3.25.–6), which add interesting toppings. Or, create your own signature concoction, beginning with a basic dog ($1.65) and adding your choice from about 35 toppings. Soups, salads, sausages, chili, burgers, and even Mexican standards and pizza are on the menu, as are nightly dinner specials, such as fried fish or chicken, meatloaf, and chicken pot pie, with prices beginning at $6.95.

Ethnic Fare

In 2004, **XYZ Restaurant** (80 Seawall Rd., Rte. 102A, Manset, 207/244-5221, 5:30–9 P.M.) moved to a new location at the end of a dirt driveway rising slowly to a crest—look for the faux cacti marking the parking lot. There's dining inside and on the porch. No gloppy Mexican fare here, rather this popular spot (do make reservations) delivers the flavors of interior Mexico: Xalapa, Yucatán, and Zacatecas (hence XYZ). Most popular dish? *Cochinitas*—citrus-marinated pork rubbed with *achiote* paste (it's worthy of its reputation). Entrees are $21. The margaritas are classic—requiring, allegedly, 1,100 pounds of fresh limes each year. For dessert, try the exquisite XYZ pie.

From the outside, it doesn't look like much, but locals know you can count on **DeMuro's Top of the Hill** (Rte. 102, Southwest Harbor, 207/244-0033, 4:30 P.M.–close) for a really good meal at a very fair price. Dine in the country-style, pine dining room or on the weatherized patio. The Italian-influenced menu (try the excellent veal Italiano) has something in all price ranges ($9–18), but the real

steal is the Lobster Paloozah special including a cup of clam chowder, steamed mussels, a boiled lobster, pasta or potato, and vegetable, all for about $19. Early-bird specials are served 4:30–6:30 P.M.

Check your email while savoring authentic Asian foods at **The Mouse Pad** (19 Clark Point Rd., Southwest Harbor, 207/244-4113, 8 A.M.–9 P.M.), a casual Internet cafe and coffeehouse. In addition to the usual baked goods and espresso fare, Chiaolin and Ken Korona offer a daily-changing menu of sushi, sesame noodles, pad Thai, and other specialties. Everything is available to go, and with advance notice, Chiaolin will prepare a complete dinner for you to pick up and bring back to your cottage or inn or to a picnic table.

Fine Dining

Gold walls, artwork, wood floors, and a giant hearth set a chic tone for **Red Sky** (14 Clark Point Rd., 207/244-0476, http://redsky.com, 5:30–9 (sometimes 10) P.M.), which opened in 2003 and quickly gained a loyal following among area foodies. The creative fare (entrees $17–30) emphasizes fresh seafood, hand-cut meats, and local organic produce, and there's always a vegetarian choice. Bread is baked daily and the desserts are homemade. The restaurant is open Valentine's Day through New Year's Eve.

Also earning high praise for its internationally accented fare, good service, fabulous views over the harbor, and incredible martinis is **Fiddler's Green** (411 Main St., Southwest Harbor, 207/244-9416, www.fiddlersgreenrestaurant.com, 5:30 P.M. to close). Entrees, such as coq au vin, grilled beef tenderloin, and yellow-fin tuna, range from $16–26.

The dreamy views from **Claremont Dining Room** (22 Claremont Rd., 207/244-5036 or 800/244-5036, 6–9 P.M.) descend over the lawns and croquet courts, to the boathouse and dock, and beyond to the water backed by mountains. It's truly a special place for an elegant meal complemented by an old fashioned grace (jackets and ties requested for dinner, entrees $20–27). In 2005, Chef Bill Morrison, of the former and much-missed Seaweed Café, took over the kitchen with praiseworthy results. Dining-room reservations are wise in midsummer. In July and August, informal lunches and cocktails are served in the shore-front Boat House, also open to the public.

Lobster-in-the-Rough

Putting the rough in lobster-in-the-rough is **The Captain's Galley at Beals' Lobster Pier** (182 Clark Point Rd., 207/244-7178 or 207/244-3202, 9 A.M.–8 P.M., closes at 5 P.M. after Labor Day), where you eat on covered picnic tables on the working dock. In addition to lobster, steamers, and fresh fish, you'll find chowders, sandwiches, ice cream, and baked desserts. It's at the end of the road, adjacent to the Coast Guard Base. (Early morning hours are not for breakfast—they allow customers to order lobster shipped nationwide.)

INFORMATION AND SERVICES

At the corner of Route 102 and Seal Cove Road, next to the Southwest Harbor Shoppes minimall, **Southwest Harbor/Tremont**

Chamber of Commerce (Main St., P.O. Box 1143, Southwest Harbor 04679, 207/244-9264 or 800/423-9264, fax 207/244-4185, www .acadiachamber.com) is open 9 A.M.–noon and 1 P.M.–5 P.M. Monday–Friday, 9 A.M.–3 P.M. Saturday, and 10 A.M.–2 P.M. Sunday.

Library

The **Southwest Harbor Public Library** (338 Main St., Southwest Harbor, 207/244-7065, 9 A.M.–5 P.M. Mon.–Fri., to 8 P.M. Wed., and 9 A.M.–noon Sat.) recently renovated to double its size.

Public Restrooms

In downtown Southwest Harbor, public restrooms are at the southern end of the parking lot behind the Main Street park and near the fire station. Across Main Street, Harbor House also has a restroom, and there are Port-o-lets at the town docks.

Getting Around

Southwest Harbor is serviced by Route 7/Southwest Harbor of the Island Explorer bus system.

Tremont: Bass Harbor, Bernard, and Seal Cove

The "quiet side" of the island becomes even more quiet as you round the southwestern edge into Tremont, which includes the villages of Bernard, Bass Harbor, home of **Bass Harbor Head Light** and ferry services to offshore islands, and Seal Cove. Tremont occupies the southwesternmost corner of Mount Desert Island. It's about as far as you can get from Bar Harbor, but the free Island Explorer bus service, Route 7/Southwest Harbor, comes through here on a regular basis.

SIGHTS
◖ The Seal Cove Auto Museum

On the westernmost side of the island, but eas-

ily accessible from Southwest Harbor, a nondescript blue building camouflages The Seal Cove Auto Museum (Pretty Marsh Rd., Rte. 102, Seal Cove, 207/244-9242, www.sealcoveautomuseum.org, 10 A.M.–5 P.M. daily June–late Sept., $5 adults, $2 kids under 12). It houses one of the largest collections of Brass Era (1905-1917) autos in the country comprising more than 100 antique autos and 35 antique motorcycles. All are in as-found condition; this ranges from fresh-from-the-barn to meticulously restored. It's easy for kids of any age to spend an hour here, reminiscing and/or fantasizing. Among the highlights are a 1907 Chadwick Touring Car and a 1910 Chadwick

Racer, two of only three Chadwicks still in existence; a 1915 F.R.P., the fifth of only nine built and the only one still in existence; an original 1903 Ford Model A, the first car commercially produced by the Ford Motor Co., and a 1909 Ford Model T "Tin Lizzie," from the first year of production. The oldest car in the collection is an 1899 DeDion-Bouton, one of the earliest cars produced in the world. The museum is about six miles southwest of Somesville. Or, if you're coming from Southwest Harbor, take Route 102 north to Seal Cove Road (partly unpaved) west to the other side of Route 102 (it makes a giant loop) and go north about 1.5 miles. This is not on the Island Explorer route.

Island Astronomic Institute

Find out what's hidden in the night sky. Lessons, viewings, and classes, as well as telescope rentals, are available at Peter and Linda Lord's Island Astronomic Institute (Steamboat Wharf Rd., Bernard, 207/244-9477, www.islandastro.com). Workshops, lectures, and presentations ($8–20) are offered for novices and experienced viewers; call for times and topics. Telescope rentals begin at $7 per day plus a $28 setup fee. A good selection of binoculars and telescopes are available for purchase, if you get hooked. The shop's on the water near Thurston's—look for the lighthouse-shaped building; call for hours.

RECREATION
Sea Kayaking

If you have your own boat, consider putting in at either the park's Pretty Marsh Picnic Area, off Route 102, in Pretty Marsh, or at the public boat launch at the end of Bartlett's Landing Road, off the Indian Point Road near the Route 102 end. From either put-in, you can paddle around privately owned Bartlett Island. For a longer trip, head north along the shoreline past Black and Green Islands, both privately owned, to Alley Island, which is open for day access.

◖ Island Cruises

High praise goes to Capt. Kim Strauss's Island Cruises (Little Island Marine, Shore Rd.,

Bass Harbor, 207/244-5785, www.bassharborcruises.com) for its daily, narrated 3.5-hour lunch cruise to Frenchboro. The 49-passenger *R. L. Gott,* which Strauss built, departs at 11 A.M. daily during the summer. Kim has been navigating these waters for more than 55 years, and his experience shows not only in his boat handling but also in his narration. Expect to pick up lots of local heritage and lore about once-thriving and now abandoned granite-quarrying and fishing communities, the sardine industry, and lobstering, and to see seals, cormorants, guillemots, and often eagles, too. The trip allows enough time on Frenchboro for a picnic (or lunch at the summertime deli on the dock) and a short village stroll, then a return through the sprinkling of islands along the 8.3-mile route. Kim also hauls a few traps and explains lobstering. He also earns major points for maneuvering the boat around so that passengers on both sides get an up-close view of key sights. It's an excellent, enthralling tour for all ages. Round-trip cost is $30 adults, $20 children 11 and younger. Be sure to reserve, and if the weather looks iffy, call ahead to confirm. Most of the trip is in sheltered water, but rough seas can put the kibosh on it. Island Cruises also does a two-hour afternoon nature cruise among the islands that covers the same topics but spends a bit more time at seal ledges and other spots. On either trip, don't forget to bring binoculars. You'll find the Island Cruises dock by following signs to the Swan's Island Ferry and turning right at the sign shortly before the state ferry dock.

SHOPPING

Stop in at **E. L. Higgins** (Bernard Rd., Bernard, 207/244-3983, www.antiquewicker.com). In two onetime classrooms in an 1890s schoolhouse, Edward Higgins has the state's best collection of antique wicker furniture, about 400 pieces at any given time.

Right next door is **Linda Fernandez Handknits** (Bernard Rd., Bernard, 207/244-7224), with beautiful hand-knit sweaters, mittens, hats, socks, Christmas stockings, and embroidered pillowcases all handcrafted by the talented and extended Hernandez family. The kids' lobster sweaters are especially cute.

Great place to stock up on mittens for holiday gift giving.

When a psychic told A. Jones more than 30 years ago that she would move to an island, she thought: wrong. Actually, the psychic was right. Continue down the Bernard Road than hang a left on Columbia Avenue to find **A. Jones Gallery** (Columbia Ave., Bernard, 207/244-5634). Inside is a double find: artworks in a variety of media and styles and a working studio in the barn; country antiques and folk art finds in the garage.

Back on Route 102, the **JetStream Gallery** (Rte. 102, Bernard, 207/244-4026) is a real kick. Artists Cherie Magnello and Terry Emrick have turned an old Airstream camper into a showplace for Cherie's fabulous jewelry handcrafted from precious metals and gems and Terry's smile-producing spring people. Cherie is one of the founding members/owners of the Island Artisans Galleries in Bar Harbor and Northeast Harbor.

Next door is **Beez Handmade Paper Stuff** and **Acadia Design** (Rte. 102, W. Tremont, 207/244-4026). Another small working gallery, you might catch Beth Herrick and Beth Pomroy (the Bs of Beez) making their handmade papers or crafting ceramic tiles. The tiles are especially functional—soap or butter dishes, light-switch plates, tables, etc., and the papers are made into blank journals and jewelry.

Potters Lisbeth Faulkner and Edwin Davis can often be seen working in their studio at **Seal Cove Pottery & Gallery** (Kelleytown Rd., Seal Cove, 207/244-3602). In addition to their functional hand-thrown or hand-built pottery, they exhibit Davis's paintings as well as crafts from other island artisans.

ACCOMMODATIONS
Inns and Cottages

When price is no object and you *really* want to be pampered, let Phil and Lesley DiVirgilio do so at the **Ann's Point Inn & Spa** (Ann's Point Rd., P.O. Box 398, Bass Harbor 04653, 207/244-9595, www.annspointinn.com, $280–295), their oceanfront inn at the tip of Ann's Point. The DiVirgilios are experienced innkeep-

ers, and they spoil their guests with king-size beds covered in luxurious linens, gas fireplaces in all guestrooms, afternoon hors d'oeuvres, evening turndown service, and all the amenities you might expect, including robes and slippers, in-room TV/DVDs, phones, Wi-Fi, CD players, and air-conditioning. Rooms are huge, and all have ocean views. If that's not enough, there's an indoor pool, hot tub, and sauna. All this on two acres with 690 feet of shorefront. The inn is open year-round.

Far, far less fancy but also on the water is **Bass Harbor Cottages** (Rte. 102A, P.O. Box 40, Bass Harbor 04653, 207/244-3460, www.bassharborcottages.com). The sturdy white home has three guest rooms with private baths. Room 2, with an old-fashioned bath, is least expensive. Room 1 has a fireplace, TV, and deck. Room 3 has a fireplace and full kitchen. Rates range from $75 to $165. No breakfast is served. Also on the premises are a number of cottages and suites with a wide range of amenities. The Carriage House has a fireplace, sauna, full kitchen, TV, deck, and balcony; the Pine Cottage has a fireplace, full kitchen, TV, and screened porch. All the Boat House Suites have a full kitchen, TV, and deck; some have a fireplace or balcony. Rates begin at $1,400 per week; nightly rates may be available if the unit isn't rented. There's a staircase down to a rocky beach.

Campgrounds

A budget-friendly option is the nicely wooded **Quietside Campground and Cabins** (P.O. Box 20, Bass Harbor 04653, 207/244-5992, www.quietsidecampground.com, Memorial Day weekend through Labor Day), with 37 wooded sites accommodating tents ($20, platforms provided) and small RVs ($25; up to 28 feet, some with water and 30 amp electric). It also has log camping cabins ($55; with heat, electricity, small refrigerator, but no plumbing), rustic cabins ($55; propane lantern, gas grill, screened porch), and a camping cabin ($65; microwave, gas fireplace, small refrigerator, gas grill). There are two bathhouses with free hot showers, one with coin-op laundry. Lobster bakes and bean suppers are scheduled regularly. Quiet, well-behaved pets are allowed for $1 per night. The campground is off the beaten track, but the tenting sites are very private and the location ensures quiet.

Just a 10-minute walk from Bass Harbor Light is **Bass Harbor Campground** (Rte. 102A, P.O. Box 122, Southwest Harbor 04679, 207/244-5857 or 800/327-5857, www.bassharbor.com), owned and operated by the Carsey family. The 130-site campground has pull-through sites with electric, water, sewer, and cable TV for RVs as well as plenty of wooded tent sites, some with platforms. Hot showers are free. There's a heated pool, playground, free Wi-Fi, and a self-service coin-op laundry. Tent sites are $25. Sites with utilities range from $35 to $45. Also on-site are one- and two-room camping cabins (without bathrooms), with electricity, small refrigerator, and outdoor gas grill; bring your own sheets, towels, blankets, dishes, and cooking utensils. These rent for $550–675 per week.

FOOD

If you have a penchant for puns—or can tune them out—head for the family-run **Seafood Ketch Restaurant** (McMullin Ave., Bass Harbor, 207/244-7463, 11 A.M.–9 P.M. late May–mid Oct.). The corny humor begins with "Please no fishing from dining room windows or the deck," and "What foods these morsels be," and goes up or down from there (depending on your perspective). But there's nothing corny about the seafood roll, an interesting change from the usual lobster or crab roll. There are a few "landlubber delights," but mostly the menu has fresh seafood dishes—including the baked lobster-seafood casserole (a recipe requested by *Gourmet*). Most entrees run $17–20, but sandwiches and lighter fare are available. This is a prime family spot (with a kids' menu) where the best tables are on the flagstone patio overlooking Bass Harbor. Follow signs for the Swan's Island ferry terminal.

Lobster-in-the-Rough

◖ **Thurston's Lobster Pound** (Steamboat Wharf Rd., Bernard, 207/244-7600, 11 A.M.–8 P.M. early and late in the season, to 8:30 P.M. in July and Aug., Memorial Day–Columbus Day) wins the award for the island's best lobster pound, with a screened dining room that practically sits in the water. Family-oriented

© TOM NANGLE

You won't find a better place for lobster than Thurston's, in Bernard.

THE LOBSTER EXPERIENCE

No visit to Acadia National Park and the surrounding region can be considered complete without the "real Maine" experience of a "lobsta dinnah" at a lobster wharf/pound/shack. Keep an eye on the weather, pick a sunny day, and head out.

If you're in the area before Memorial Day or after Labor Day, the options are not as great – many such enterprises have a short season, although more and more are staying open at least through September.

There's nowhere to eat lobster within Acadia National Park (unless you're camping and cook it yourself over a campfire), but Mount Desert Island and the surrounding region provide plenty of opportunities. Almost every restaurant, cafe, bistro, or whatever serves lobster in some form or other. But as you drive, bus, bike, or walk around, watch for the genuine article – the "real" lobster wharf. You want to eat outdoors, at a wooden picnic table, with a knockout view of boats and the sea. (Incidentally, if you're camping, most lobster wharves will boil lobsters for you free or for a small fee. They'll wrap them in newspaper so they stay warm until you get back to your campsite. Best advice is to order them like pizza: Call ahead so they'll be ready when you show up for them.)

At whatever place you choose, the drill is much the same, and the "dinners" are served anytime from 11 A.M. or noon onward (some places close as early as 7 P.M.). First of all, dress very casually so you can manhandle the lobster without messing up decent clothes. If you want beer or wine, call ahead and ask if the place serves it; you may need to bring your own, since many such operations don't have beer/wine licenses, much less liquor licenses. In the evening, carry some insect repellent, in case mosquitoes crash the party. (Many places light citronella candles or dispense Skin-So-Soft to keep the bugs at bay; Mosquito Magnets may soon be doing the job.)

A basic one-pound lobster and go-withs (coleslaw or potato salad, potato chips, and butter for dipping) should run $15-20, based on the seasonal lobster price. Unfortunately, some places use margarine, which doesn't do lobster any favors. Depending on your hunger level – or the length of time since your last lobster – you may want to indulge in a shore dinner (lobster, steamed clams, potato chips, and maybe coleslaw or corn), for which you might have to part with $20 or $25, again depending on the lobster market price. Don't skip dessert; many lobster pounds are known for their homemade pies.

It's not unusual to see lobster-wharf devotees carting picnic baskets with hors d'oeuvres, salads, and baguettes. I've even seen candles and champagne and cloth napkins and bibs. Creativity abounds, but don't stray too far from the main attraction – the crustaceans.

Typically, you'll need to survey a chalkboard or whiteboard menu and step up to a window to order. You'll either give the person your name or get a number. A few places have staff to take your order or deliver your meal (and help you figure out how to eat it), but usually you'll head back to the window when your name or number is called. Don your plastic lobster bib and begin the attack. If you're a neophyte, watch a pro at a nearby table. Some lobster wharves have "how-to" info printed on paper placemats. If you're really concerned (you needn't be), contact the Maine Lobster Promotion Council, 382 Harlow St., Bangor 04401, www.mainelobsterpromo.com. The council produces a brochure with detailed instructions. Don't worry about doing it "wrong;" you'll eventually get what you came for, and it'll be an experience to remember.

Here (in alphabetical order) are five great places to experience lobster between the Schoodic Peninsula and Deer Isle. Each is described in more detail in the regional chapters.

Bernard (Mount Desert Island): Thurston's Lobster Pound, 207/244-7600

Hancock (between Mount Desert and Schoodic): Tidal Falls Lobster Pound, 207/422-6457

Little Deer Isle: Eaton's Lobster Pool, 207/348-2383

Southwest Harbor (Mount Desert Island): Beal's Lobster Pier, 207/244-3202

Trenton (on the access road to Mount Desert Island): Trenton Bridge Lobster Pound, 207/667-2977

Thurston's also has chowders, sandwiches, and terrific desserts. Beer and wine are available. Be sure to read the directions at the entry and order before you find a table on one of two levels.

INFORMATION AND SERVICES

At the corner of Route 103 and Seal Cove Road, in the Southwest Harbor Shoppes min-imall, **Southwest Harbor/Tremont Chamber of Commerce** (Main St., P.O. Box 1143, Southwest Harbor 04679, 207/244-9264 or 800/423-9264, fax 207/244-4185, www.aca-diachamber.com) is open 9 A.M.–noon and 1 P.M.–5 P.M. Monday–Friday, 9 A.M.–3 P.M. Saturday, and 10 A.M.–2 P.M. Sunday.

Public Restrooms

There's a public restroom at the Swan's Island ferry terminal.

Getting Around

Tremont and Bass Harbor are serviced by Route 7/Southwest Harbor of the Island Explorer bus system.

Islands near Mount Desert

The most popular island day-trip destinations from Mount Desert Island are the Cranberry Isles and Swan's Island, but Frenchboro has begun seeing a steadier stream of visitors.

Most commercial boats and mailboats for the Cranberries depart from Northeast Harbor, although one line originates in Southwest Harbor (all carry bikes but no cars); state car ferries for Swan's Island depart from Bass Harbor, south of Southwest Harbor and part of the town of Tremont.

The Maine State Ferry Service also operates the ferry to Long Island (referred to as Frenchboro, the name of the village on the island) from Bass Harbor, but the schedule requires careful planning for day trips.

◧ CRANBERRY ISLES

The Cranberry Isles, south of Northeast and Seal Harbors, comprise **Great Cranberry, Little Cranberry** (called Islesford), **Sutton, Baker,** and **Bear Islands.** Islesford and Baker include property belonging to Acadia National Park. Bring a bike and explore the narrow, mostly level roads on the two largest islands (Great Cranberry and Islesford), but remember to respect private property. Unless you've asked (and received) permission, *do not* cut across private land to reach the shore.

The Cranberry name has been attributed to 18th-century loyalist governor Francis Bernard, who received these islands (along with all of Mount Desert) as a king's grant in 1762. Cranberry bogs (now long gone, but there's still a large marsh on the eastern side of the island) on the two largest islands evidently caught his attention. Permanent European settlers were here in the 1760s, and there was even steamboat service by the 1820s.

Lobstering and other marine businesses are the commercial mainstays, boosted in summer by the various visitor-related pursuits. Artists and writers come for a week, a month, or longer; day-trippers spend time on Great Cranberry and Islesford. According to the 2000 census, the Cranberries have 128 year-rounders (primarily on Great Cranberry and Islesford).

Great Cranberry

Largest of the islands is Great Cranberry, with a year-round population of 50 souls that swells to around 300 in the summer. You can easily explore this island's highlights in a couple of hours. The Main Road extends the length of the island, about two miles, with a few pleasant viewpoints along the way. It's an easy walk or bicycle ride, with a few gentle

COMMUNITIES

hills and very little traffic; do follow the rules of the road, though. If you bring your dog, it must be kept leashed.

As soon as you get off the boat, you'll find the **Cranberry General Store** (7:30 A.M.–5 P.M. Mon.–Fri., to 3 P.M. Sat., and noon–2 P.M. Sun., 207/244-5336), along with the takeout **Seawich Café** (not open Sun.), where you can pick up picnic fixings or sandwiches, burgers, and the like. Tucked between the store and the shore are public restrooms.

It's about a 15-minute walk to the **Historical Museum** (10:30 A.M.–4 P.M., mid June–mid Sept.) located in the schoolhouse. The volunteer-operated museum is a pleasure to visit, with well-informed staff who radiate enthusiasm. A special exhibit commemorates *Hitty, Her First 100 Years,* the Newbury Award–winning novel by Rachel Field, an island summer resident, about a doll. You can purchase Hitty at the museum or the nearby **Whale's Rib Gift Shop** (207/244-5153), which also has jewelry by island artisan Lisa Hall, as well as a nice selection of other items. Take the left after the gift shop to wander down to the **Cranberry**

Island Boatyard, which repairs old boats and also builds new ones.

Unfortunately, the island's lone B&B has shut its doors.

Little Cranberry (Islesford)

The second-largest island is Little Cranberry, locally known as Islesford. (Get a feel for the place by visiting www.islesford.com.) You'll arrive at the newly refurbished Town Dock, one of three adjacent docks (the others are the Fishermen's Wharf and the Islesford Dock).

Just east of the Islesford Dock is the handsome brick **Islesford Historical Museum,** operated by the National Park Service (207/288-3338, www.nps.gov/acad, 9 A.M.–noon and 12:30–3:30 P.M. Mon.–Sat. and 10:45 A.M.–noon and 12:30–3:30 P.M. SUN., mid-June to Labor Day, free) since 1948. The original collection was established by Harvard/MIT/Haverford professor William Otis Sawtelle (1874–1939), a Bangor native who summered here on the island. He single-mindedly assembled local memorabilia and even built this brick building to hold it all.

The General Store is the only place to shop on Great Cranberry.

© TOM NANGLE

The exhibits focus on local history, much of it maritime, so displays include ship models, a full-size dory, household goods, fishing gear, and other memorabilia. (Across the museum lawn is the **The Blue Duck,** the museum's original site—now dedicated to the island's only public restrooms.)

On the wharf nearest the museum is **The Islesford Dock** (207/244-7494, www.islesford.com/idr), hanging over the water and serving lunch and dinner 11 A.M.–3 P.M. and 5–9 P.M. Tuesday–Sunday, late June through Labor Day. Sunday brunch is 10 A.M.–2 P.M. Prices are moderate, food is home-cooked and creative, and views across to Acadia's mountains are incredible. If the weather's good, eat on the small deck. Reservations are wise in midsummer. Water taxis are available for returning to Northeast Harbor after dinner, or, three times each week, the Cranberry Cove Ferry adds evening runs at 7 and 9 P.M.

Also on the dock is **Islesford Pottery** (Box 309, Islesford 04646, 207/244-9108, www.islesford.com/idcartmb.html), Marian Baker's summertime ceramic studio. A teacher at Maine College of Art in Portland, Marian makes particularly appealing functional pieces, and she carries the work of a couple of other potters. She also sells a handy map of the island ($1, with profits given to charity). Street/road signs are scarce on the island, but the map at least provides orientation. The shop is open daily 10 A.M.–4 P.M., mid-June to Labor Day.

Also sharing the dock is **Winter's Work** (www.winterswork.com) a tiny, one-room gallery with an eclectic selection of works by primarily island and Maine artists and authors.

A five-minute walk from the waterfront will bring you to **Islesford Artists** (Mosswood Rd., www.islesfordartists.com), an excellent gallery specializing in local artists' depictions of local sites (lots of landscapes/seascapes, naturally). Run by Danny and Katy Fernald, the gallery is open daily, 10 A.M.–5 P.M. in July and August; weekdays 10 A.M.–4 P.M. or by appointment the rest of the season; closed in winter. It's several blocks from the harbor, but there's a sign (and Marian Baker's map will get

you there). Or just ask—the islanders are always helpful.

Islesford's imaginative postmaster, Joy Sprague, brought the island a bit of postal fame by initiating Maine's busiest stamps-by-mail operation. Many of the other year-round islands' postmasters have now followed suit, aided by the Rockland-based Island Institute, which publishes an order form and address list in each issue of *The Working Waterfront,* its monthly tabloid newspaper. The goal is to save a dozen island post offices from extinction; so far, so good.

Working Waterfront readers feel a real kinship to the Cranberries, thanks to each issue's "Cranberry Report," written by umpteenth-generation island historian Ted Spurling Jr. (On the island, look for a copy of his charming booklet, *The Town of Cranberry Isles.*)

The post office occupies one corner inside **The Islesford Market** (Main St., 207/244-7667, www.islesford.com/islesfordmarket), three short blocks up from the Town Dock. Suzie ("Soos") Krasnow holds forth here—giving advice, baking pizza, marketing her attractive silk-screened notecards, and doing whatever else needs to be done. The market is open Monday–Saturday, mid-June to Labor Day.

And if you want to get out and explore the neighboring waters, you have two options. Lobster lore is Capt. Stefanie Alley and naturalist Rebecca Larkin's specialty. On **Working Lobster Boat Tours** (207/244-7466; lobstertours@islesford.com) you'll haul traps and learn about the critters. The one-hour tours begin at $60, and the boat carries a max of six passengers. Or rent a single or double kayak for $30 per day from Joy Sprague's **Joy of Kayaking** (207/244-4309). Joy only has a few kayaks, so make a reservation if this is something you really want to do.

Staying overnight is an option on Islesford. Frances Bartlett owns the **Braided Rugs Inn** (1892 Main St., Islesford, 207/244-5943), across from the Islesford Market. It's a comfortable, homey place that fits right in with the relaxed pace of the island. Handmade braided rugs are throughout the 1892

FRENCHBORO, LONG ISLAND

Since Maine has more Long Islands than anyone cares to count, most of them have other labels for easy distinction. Here's a case in point – a Long Island known universally as Frenchboro, the name of the village that wraps around Lunts Harbor. With a year-round population hovering at 50, Frenchboro has had ferry service only since 1960. Since then, the island has acquired phone service, electricity, and satellite TV, but don't expect to notice much of that when you get here. It's a very quiet place where islanders live as islanders always have – making a living from the sea and proud of it. In 1999, when more than half the island (914 acres, including 5.5 miles of shorefront) went up for sale by a private owner, an incredible fundraising effort collected nearly $3 million, allowing purchase of the land in January 2000 by the Maine Coast Heritage Trust. Some of the funding has been put toward restoration of the village's church and one-room schoolhouse; islanders and visitors will still have full access to all the acreage; and interested developers will have to look elsewhere.

Frenchboro is a delightful day trip. A good way to get a sense of the place is to take the 3.5-hour lunch cruise run by Capt. Kim Strauss of **Island Cruises** (Little Island Marine, Shore Rd., Bass Harbor, 207/244-5785, www.bassharborcruises.com), see *Island Cruises* under *Southwest Harbor*. For an even longer day trip to Frenchboro, plan to take the passenger ferry *R. L. Gott* during her weekly run for the Maine State Ferry Service. Each Friday from early April to late October, the *Gott* departs Bass Harbor at 8 A.M., arriving in Frenchboro at 9 A.M. The return trip to Bass Harbor is at 6 P.M., allowing nine hours on the island. Round-trip cost is $12 adults, $5.25 children (children under five are free). The Maine State Ferry Service uses the ferry *Captain Henry Lee* (same one used on the Swan's Island route) for service to Frenchboro on Wednesday, Thursday, and Sunday, but the service is only over-and-

farmhouse, but even more interesting are the photos taken by Bartlett's grandfather in the late 19th and early 20th centuries. Three second-floor rooms share one bath and go for $70 d, including a full breakfast; lunch and dinner are available with advance notice for an additional charge. Open all year. Another choice is Evelyn Boxley's **Islesford House B&B** (207/244-0988), with four rooms sharing one bath; $95 includes a full breakfast. For **cottage rentals,** see www.islesford.com.

Getting There

Decades-old, family-run **Beal & Bunker** (P.O. Box 33, Cranberry Isles 04625, 207/244-3575) provides year-round mailboat/passenger service to the Cranberries from Northeast Harbor. The ferries don't carry cars, but you can take a bike. Or just plan to explore on foot. The summer season, with more frequent trips, runs late June until Labor Day. The first boat departs Northeast Harbor's Municipal Pier at 7:30 A.M. Mon-

day–Saturday; first Sunday boat is 10 A.M. The last boat for Northeast Harbor leaves Islesford at 6:30 P.M. and leaves (Great) Cranberry at 6:45 P.M. The boats do a bit of to-ing and fro-ing on the three-island route (including Sutton in summer), so be patient as they make the circuit. It's a people-watching treat. If you just did a round-trip and stayed aboard, the loop would take about 1.5 hours. Round-trip tickets (covering the whole loop, including intraisland if you want to visit both Great Cranberry and Islesford) are $15 adults, $10 kids under 12 (free for kids under three). Bicycles are $5 round-trip. The off-season schedule operates early May through mid-June and early September through mid-October; the winter schedule runs mid-October through April. In winter, the boat company advises phoning ahead on what Mainers quaintly call "weather days."

The **Cranberry Cove Ferry** (Upper Town Dock, Clark Point Rd., Southwest Harbor, 207/244-5882 or 207/460-1981 cell,

back (50 minutes each way) – no chance to explore the island.

When you go, take a picnic with you, or stop at **Lunt's Dockside Deli** (207/334-2922), open only in July and August. It's a very casual establishment – order at the window, grab a picnic table, and wait for your name to be called. Lobster rolls and fish chowder are the specialties, but there are plenty of other choices including sandwiches, hot dogs, and even vegetable wraps; of course, you can get lobster, too. Prices are cheap, the view is wonderful, and you might even get to watch a lobsters being unloaded from a boat.

The **Frenchboro Historical Society Museum,** just up from the dock, has interesting old tools, other local artifacts, and a small gift shop. It's usually open afternoons, Memorial Day to Labor Day. The island has a network of maintained trails through the woods and along the shore, easy and not-so-easy; some can be squishy and some are along bouldery beachfront. The trails are rustic and most are unmarked, so proceed carefully. In the center of the island is a beaver pond. (You'll get a sketchy map on the boat, but you can also get one at the Historical Society.)

Frenchboro is the subject of *Hauling by Hand,* a fascinating, well-researched "biography" published in 1999 by eighth-generation islander Dean Lunt, now a journalist in Portland (see *Suggested Reading*). His website (www.islandportpress.com/frenchboro) has helpful info for visiting the island.

Extra ferries operate for the island's annual **lobster festival,** usually the second Saturday in August, when islanders and hundreds of visitors gather in the village for lobster galore, games, and more. (For info, call the Lunt & Lunt Lobster Company, 207/334-2922.)

There's a restroom above the Dockside Deli and two others near the museum. If you're captivated by the island, you can rent a harbor-front cottage for $140 per night, minimum three nights (207/334-2973 or 207/334-2991).

COMMUNITIES

www.downeastwindjammer.com), purchased by Captain Steve Pagels in 2002, operates a summertime service to the Cranberries, mid-May to mid-October, aboard the 47-passenger *Island Queen.* Pagels also owns the *Margaret Todd* in Bar Harbor and the *Bar Harbor Ferry,* connecting Bar Harbor and Winter Harbor. The ferry route begins at the Upper Town Dock (Clark Point Road) in Southwest Harbor, with stops in Manset and Great Cranberry before reaching Islesford an hour later. (Stops at Sutton can be arranged.) In summer (mid-June to mid-September), there are six daily round-trips, with two additional evening trips Tuesdays, Thursdays, and Saturdays. The first departure from Southwest Harbor is 7 A.M.; last departure from Islesford is 6 P.M. Round-trip fares are $20 adults, $12 children. Bicycles are $6 round-trip. Off-season, call to check on the schedule (207/546-2927).

The **MDI Water Taxi,** Captain Wes Shaw's converted lobsterboat, makes frequent on-demand trips to the Cranberries. Call 207/244-7312.

Captain John Dwelley (207/244-5724) also operates a water-taxi service to the Cranberries. His six-passenger *Delight* makes the run from Northeast, Southwest, or Seal Harbor for $50–60 per trip, depending upon time of day, from early June through late September. Reservations are required for trips 6–11 P.M. and 6–8 A.M. Custom cruises are available, including excursions to Baker's Island.

SWAN'S ISLAND

Six miles off Mount Desert Island lies scenic, 6,000-acre Swan's Island (pop. 327), named after Colonel James Swan, who bought it and two dozen other islands as an investment in 1786. As with the Cranberries, fishing—especially lobstering—is the year-round way of life here; summer sees the arrival of artists, writers, and other seasonal visitors. The island has no campsites, few public restrooms (ferry dock and a portable toilet outside the museum), a tiny motel, and two small, traditional-style B&Bs. Visitors who want to spend more than a day tend to rent cottages by the week.

You'll need either a bicycle or a car to get around on the island, as the ferry comes in on one side, and the village center is on the other. Should you choose to bring a car, it's wise to make reservations for the ferry, especially for the return trip. Bicycling is good way to get around, but be forewarned that the roads are narrow, lacking shoulders, and hilly in spots.

If you can be flexible, wait for a clear day, then pack a picnic and catch the first ferry (7:30 A.M.) from Bass Harbor. At the ferry office in Bass Harbor, request a Swan's Island map (and take advantage of the restroom). Keep an eye on your watch so you don't miss the last ferry (4:30 P.M.) back to Bass Harbor.

The ferry arrives in the northeast corner of the island. Head off down the main road toward Burnt Coat Harbor. (The island has three villages—Atlantic, Minturn, and Swan's Island.) First stop is the tiny **Seaside Hall Museum,** which describes itself as "The Island's Attic." It's usually open noon to 3 P.M., but it's run by volunteers, so that's not a sure thing. Admission is a $1 donation.

Pedal around to the west side of the harbor and down the peninsula to **Hockamock Head Light** (officially, Burnt Coat Harbor Light). From the ferry landing, Hockamock Head is 4.5 miles. The distinctive square lighthouse, built in 1872 and now automated, sits on a rocky promontory overlooking Burnt Coat Harbor, Harbor Island, lobsterboat traffic, and crashing surf. The keeper's house is unoccupied; the grounds are great for picnics.

If it's hot, ask for directions to one of two prime island swimming spots: **Fine Sand Beach** (saltwater) or **Quarry Pond** (freshwater). Fine Sand Beach is on the west side of Toothacher Cove; you'll have to navigate about a mile of unpaved road to get there, but it's worth the trouble. Be prepared for chilly water, however. Quarry Pond is in Minturn, on the opposite side of Burnt Coat Harbor from the lighthouse. Follow the one-way loop around,

THE MAINE SEA COAST MISSION

Remote islands and other isolated communities along Maine's rugged coastline may still have a church, but few have a full-time minister; fewer yet have a healthcare provider. Yet these communities aren't entirely shut off from either preaching or medical assistance.

Since 1905, the Maine Sea Coast Mission, a nondenominational, nonprofit organization rooted in a Christian ministry, has offered a lifeline to these communities. The mission, based in Bar Harbor (127 West St., 207/288-5097 or 888/824-7258), serves nearly 2,800 people on eight different islands, including Frenchboro, the Cranberries, Swan's, and Isle au Haut, as well as others living in remote coastal locations on the mainland. Its numerous much-needed services include a Christmas program; in-school, after-school, and summer school programs; emergency financial assistance; food assistance; a thrift shop; ministers to island and coastal communities; scholarships; and health services.

Many of these services are delivered via the mission's *Sunbeam V,* a 75-foot diesel boat that has no limitation on when it can travel and few on where it can travel. In winter, it even serves as an ice-breaker, clearing harbors and protecting boats from ice damage.

A nurse and a minister usually travel on the *Sunbeam.* The minister may conduct services on the island, or on the boat, which also functions as a gathering place for fellowship, meals, and meetings. The minister also reaches out to those in need, marginalized, or ill, and often helps with island funerals. Onboard telemedicine equipment enables the nurse to provide much-needed healthcare, including screening clinics for diabetes, cholesterol, and prostate and skin cancer; flu and pneumonia vaccines; and tetanus shots.

During your travels in the Acadia region, you might see the *Sunbeam* homeported in Northeast Harbor or on its rounds. If you want to learn more about or support this worthwhile organization, visit www.seacoastmission.org.

and you'll see it on your right as you're rounding the far side of the loop.

Shopping options are few on Swan's, but there are two worth noting. If you head left at the end of Ferry Terminal Road, you'll come to **Saturn Press** (463 Atlantic Rd., 207/526-4000), where designer Jane Goodrich and printer James Van Pernis create notecards and papers using antique letterpresses. The shop is usually open Monday through Friday, 9 A.M.–5 P.M., and the informal tours explain the letterpress process (you can usually see them in action) and visit the studios where the designs, based on the company's library of tens of thousands of graphic image ephemera, are created. Afterwards, pick up some notecards in the small shop or at least a catalog. Saturn has few retail outlets, as most of its products are carried by museums and fine paper stores.

Although Swan's Island Blankets are no longer produced on Swan's Island (the company was sold and moved to Lincolnville in 2005), you can still purchase the blankets here. The shop at 135 North Rd. (on the way to Fine Sand Beach) is usually open 2–5 P.M. in July, August, and September; call 207/526-4120 for details or directions.

A Swan's Island summer highlight is the **Sweet Chariot Music Festival,** a three-night midweek extravaganza in early August. Windjammers arrive from Camden and Rockland, enthusiasts show up on their private boats, and the island's Oddfellows Hall is standing-room-only for three evenings of folk singing, storytelling, and impromptu hijinks. In mid-afternoon of the first two days (about 3:30 P.M.), musicians go from boat to boat in Burnt Coat Harbor, entertaining with sea chanteys. Along the route from harbor to concert, enterprising local kids peddle lemonade, homemade brownies, and kitschy craft items. It's all very festive, but definitely a "boat thing," not very convenient for anyone without waterborne transport.

Accommodations

If you want to stay over, don't expect to find a bed on the island during the festival unless you know someone. Other times, there's

The Harbor Watch Motel (111 Minturn Rd., Swan's Island, 207/526-4563 or 800/532-7928, www.swansisland.com). The motel's four rooms (two with kitchen facilities) go for $95–120. Motel rooms are spacious and clean. Two have water views. Also available here are bike rentals ($20 a day) and kayak rentals (doubles are $35/half day, $55/full day; singles are $35 and $25).

Two small B&Bs are also available. **Jeannie's Place** (Box 125, Swan's Island 04685, 207/526-4116) overlooks Burnt Cove Harbor. Jeannie Joyce has three simple rooms that share one bath (actually the best view is from the bathroom). A full breakfast is included in the $55 d rate. She also rents a small, rustic cottage that sleeps four for $450 per week. On the other side of the island, in Atlantic, is **Appletree House B&B & Guesthouse** (49 Scolfield Ln., Swan's Island, 207/526-4438, www.appletreehouse.com, $80–100/night or $500–600/week), an 1850s cape on Joyce's Beach, with two guestrooms sharing one bathroom. You can rent either individually or the entire house; both rooms go for $175 per night or $1,000 per week. The pricier Jacob Reed Room has the best view. Rates include breakfast. Note that both B&Bs have very steep and narrow stairs leading to guest rooms and therefore aren't a good choice for young children or the mobility impaired.

Food

Swan's Island's grocery store burned to the ground in 2005, creating a major hardship for islanders. Rebuilding is underway, but check beforehand and go prepared. In any case, if you're renting a cottage or staying for more than a few days, you'll probably want to stock up at a bigger supermarket.

Dining choices are few, but a good stop for day-trippers is the **Island Bake Shop** (73 Ferry Terminal Rd., 207/526-4123, 7 A.M.–2 P.M. Mon. –Sat.). Reasonably priced breakfasts, delicious baked goodies, sandwiches, soups—the seafood chowder earns rave reviews—and salads are all homemade. There are two tiny dining rooms as well as a few tables on the

COMMUNITIES

front lawn with harbor views. You'll find it on your left, just after you get off the ferry. Other possibilities include **Claire's Kitchen,** operating out of a trailer near Saturn Press, and **The Boat House,** a takeout restaurant and gift shop clinging to a cliffside overlooking the harbor on the way to the lighthouse.

Getting There and Around

Swan's Island is a six-mile, 40-minute trip on the state-operated car ferry *Captain Henry Lee.* Between mid-April and late October, the ferry makes five or six round-trips a day, the first from Bass Harbor at 7:30 A.M. (Sunday 9 A.M.) and the last from Swan's Island at 4:30 P.M. Other months, the first and last runs are the same, but there are only four or five trips. For more information, contact **Maine State Ferry Service** (P.O. Box 114, Bass Harbor 04653, 207/244-3254; 303 Atlantic Rd., Swan's Island 04685, 207/526-4273 or daily recorded info at 800/491-4883, www.state.me.us/mdot/opt/ferry/ferry). Round-trip fares are $12 adults, $5.25 children 5–11. Bikes are $11.50 round-trip per adult, $5.75 per child. Round-trip ticket for vehicle and driver is $34.50 May through October. Reservations are accepted only for vehicles (be in line at least 15 minutes before departure, or you'll risk forfeiting your space).

To reach the Bass Harbor ferry terminal on Mount Desert Island, follow the distinctive blue signs, marked Swan's Island Ferry, along Routes 102 and 102A.

Southwest Cycle (Main St., Southwest Harbor, 207/244-5856 or 800/649-5856) rents bikes by the day and week and is open all year. Hours are 8:30 A.M.–5:30 P.M. Mon.–Sat. and 10 A.M.–4 P.M. Sun. June–Sept.; Mon.–Sat. 9 A.M.–5 P.M. October–May. It also has ferry schedules and Swan's Island maps. (For the early morning ferry, you'll need to pick up bikes the day before; be sure to reserve them if you're doing this in July or August.) Another option is to call the Harbor Watch Motel (207/526-4563) beforehand for bicycle reservations and arrange to be met at the ferry with them. If you choose the latter, you'll save the bicycle ferry fee, but you'll chance it that the bike is the right size.

SCHOODIC PENINSULA

Slightly more than 2,366 of Acadia National Park's acres are on the mainland Schoodic Peninsula—the rest are all on islands (including Mount Desert). World-class scenery and the relative lack of congestion, even at the height of summer, make Schoodic a special Acadia destination.

The Schoodic Peninsula is just one of several "fingers" of land that point oceanward as part of Eastern Hancock County. Sneak around to the eastern side of Frenchman Bay to see this region from a whole new perspective. One hour from Acadia National Park's visitors center, you'll find Acadia's mountains silhouetted against the sunset, the surf slamming onto Schoodic Point, and the peace of a calmer lifestyle.

As with so much of Acadia's acreage on Mount Desert Island, the Schoodic section be-came part of the park largely due to the deft diplomacy and perseverance of George B. Dorr. No obstacle ever seemed too daunting to Dorr. In 1928, when the owners objected to donating their land to a national park tagged with the Lafayette name (geopolitics being involved at the time), Dorr even managed to obtain congressional approval for the 1929 name change to Acadia National Park—and Schoodic was part of the deal.

PLANNING YOUR TIME

While most visitors still arrive by car or RV, a new option opened up in the summer of 2003. The propane-powered **Island Explorer** bus service expanded to include a route in this area between late June and Labor Day. It connects with ferry service from Bar Harbor.

© TOM NANGLE

HIGHLIGHTS

◖ **Schoodic Point:** Remote and raw best describe the tip of the Schoodic peninsula, where surf crashes against slabs of pink granite (page 127).

◖ **Schoodic Loop:** Drive if you must, but a better way to see it is on a bicycle (page 128).

◖ **Donnell Pond Public Reserved Land:** A treasure for outdoor enthusiasts, this reserve includes mountains to hike and ponds to paddle and fish, plus sandy beaches and backwoods campsites (page 130).

◖ **Maine Coastal Islands National Wildlife Refuge:** Birds, birds, birds, as well as easy hiking with great views are your rewards for visiting the Petit Manan Division (page 131).

◖ **Schoodic Head Loop:** Although you can drive almost to the summit, it's far more rewarding – and peaceful – to hike it (page 131).

◖ **Hancock and Sullivan Gallery Tour:** Mega-talented artists and artisans are plentiful, and visiting their off-the-beaten-path shops and studios is a perfect way to explore the region, not to mention come home with a great souvenir (page 140).

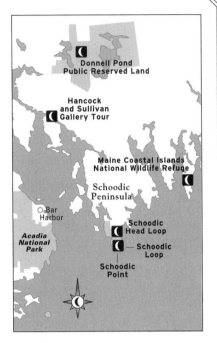

LOOK FOR ◖ TO FIND RECOMMENDED SIGHTS, ACTIVITIES, DINING, AND LODGING.

Don't limit your explorations to just the park, either. Besides the jaw-dropping scenery, the calling cards for the region are the outdoor recreation opportunities and, believe it or not, shopping. You can easily do your gift shopping for the year at the dozens of artists' and artisans' studios tucked throughout this region.

The biggest attractions in this area are the spectacular vignettes and vistas—of offshore lighthouses, distant mountains, close-in islands, and unchanged villages. Check out each small and large finger of land: Lamoine, Hancock Point, Sorrento, and Winter Harbor's Grindstone Neck. Circle the Gouldsboro Peninsula, including Prospect Harbor, and detour to Corea. Meander down the Petit Manan peninsula to the **Maine Coastal Islands National Wildlife Refuge.** If you still have enough time, head inland and follow Route 182, a designated Scenic Highway, from Hancock and on to Cherryfield, making it a point to visit the **Donnell Pond Public Reserved Lands.**

Accomplish all this and you'll have a fine sense of place. (Make sure to stock up on film, and remember that a wide-angle lens or a panoramic camera is a major asset in this area.)

LOCAL TOWNS
Winter Harbor

Winter Harbor (pop. 988) is known best as the gateway to Schoodic. It shares the area with an old-money, low-profile, Philadelphia-linked summer colony on exclusive Grindstone Neck.

Only a few clues hint at the colony's presence, strung along the western side of the harbor. Winter Harbor's summer highlight is the annual Lobster Festival, second Saturday in August. The gala daylong event includes a parade, live entertainment, games, and more crustaceans than you could ever consume.

Gouldsboro

Gouldsboro (pop. 1,941)—including the not-to-be-missed villages of Birch Harbor,

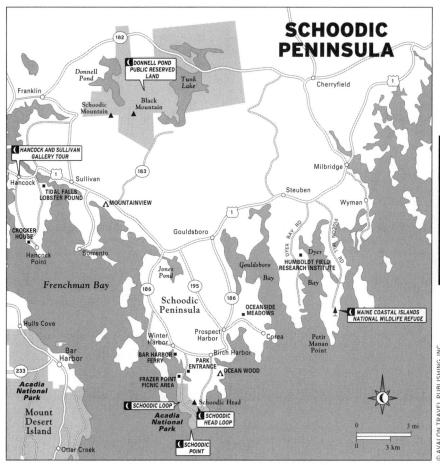

SCHOODIC PENINSULA

© AVALON TRAVEL PUBLISHING, INC.

© TOM NANGLE

Stinson Seafood's giant sardine fisherman is a can't-miss landmark.

Corea, and Prospect Harbor—earned its own minor fame from Louise Dickinson Rich's 1958 book *The Peninsula,* a tribute to her summers on Corea's Cranberry Point, "a place that has stood still in time." Since 1958, change has crept into Corea, but not so's you'd notice. It's still the same quintessential lobster-fishing community, perfect for photo ops.

Hancock and Sullivan

Between Ellsworth and Gouldsboro is Han-

cock (pop. 2,147). Venture down the oceanside back roads, and you'll discover an old-timey summer colony at Hancock Point, complete with library, post office, yacht club, and tennis courts. Meander inland, and you'll be rewarded with artisans' studios, especially in Sullivan. Route 1 ties the region together, providing just enough glimpses and vistas of Frenchman Bay.

Sorrento

Tiny Sorrento (pop. 290) isn't really much more than a classic summer colony, and that's all the reason you need for a leisurely drive down the peninsula. It has tennis courts, a yacht club, a nine-hole golf course edging the ocean, and a swimming pool, created in 1913 by damming a cove just above the village. If you fall for the place, try to find a copy of *Sorrento, A Well-Kept Secret,* by Catherin O'Clair Herson, published in 1995 for the town's centennial. It's filled with historical photos and stories.

Steuben

Continue northeast beyond the Schoodic Peninsula, and you'll arrive in Steuben, on the far side of Gouldsboro Bay. Not that you'll notice; frankly, there's little here to mark its presence on Route 1, and only a small village if you venture off it, although that's changing as the land is carved up by developers (the number of Land For Sale signs is frightening). Only a small sign indicates that the Petit Manan section of the Maine Coastal Islands National Wildlife Refuge awaits those who turn down Pigeon Hill Road.

Sights

The Schoodic section of Acadia National Park has an entirely different feel than the main part of the park on Mount Desert. It's much smaller, less busy, and provides fewer recreational opportunities, but it's still magnificent and well worth visiting. There's no official visitors center in this area, so you'll want to stop at the main Acadia Visitor Center on Mount Desert Island, or download Schoodic information before you come.

There's no camping in this section of the park, but private camping and other lodging options are available in the area. There are also no restaurants or other food sources in the park, but you won't need to go far for a bite to eat.

To reach the park boundary from Route 1 in Gouldsboro, take Route 186 south to Winter Harbor. Continue through town, heading east, then turn right and continue to the park entrance sign, just before the bridge over Mosquito Harbor.

You can also tour the park using the free **Island Explorer** bus, which circulates through Winter Harbor, around the Schoodic Loop, and on to Prospect Harbor, with stops along the way. It's an efficient and environmentally friendly way to go.

Perhaps one of the best ways to get to know the park is to become involved with the **Friends of Schoodic** (P.O. Box 194, Prospect Harbor 04669, www.friendsofschoodic.org), which supports the park with clean-up projects, trail and building maintenance, and staffing the visitor information booth at the Gatehouse.

SCHOODIC SECTION OF ACADIA NATIONAL PARK
◖ Schoodic Point

The highlight of this part of the park is Schoodic Point, with vistas that seemingly go all the way to Spain. The point is at the end of a two-way spur off the Schoodic Loop Road. Although crowds gather at the height of summer,

especially when the surf is raging, the two-tiered parking lot, amazingly, seldom fills up. (There are restrooms here, too.) Check local newspapers for the time of high tide and try to arrive here then; the word *awesome* is overused, but it sure describes Schoodic Point's surf performance on the rugged pink granite. The setting sun makes it even more brilliant. This area is open only from 6 A.M. to 10 P.M.

If you've brought children, keep them well back from the water; a rogue wave can sweep them off the rocks all too easily. It *has* happened. Picnics are great here (make sure you bring a litter bag), and so are the tidepools at mid- to low tide. Birding is spectacular during spring and fall migrations.

And on the subject of birds, you'll see a sign here: Do Not Feed Gulls or Other Wildlife. Heed it. Even if you *don't* feed the gulls, they can threaten your lunch if you're having a picnic

© TOM NANGLE

The reward for exploring a bit is finding soaring cliffs that drop to crashing surf.

LIGHTHOUSES

The best known of the Acadia region's coastal beacons is **Bass Harbor Head Light,** part of Acadia National Park. Perched high on a promontory overlooking the entrance to Bass Harbor, it flashes a distinctive red beacon (automated since 1974). To visit the light, take Route 102 to the bottom (southern end) of Mount Desert Island, then take Route 102A and watch for signs. The setting is spectacular and the grounds are accessible during the daytime. (The house is government property, occupied by the Southwest Harbor Coast Guard commander.) Be sure to descend the stairs toward the shore and view the 26-foot tower upward from there.

Roughly from north to south (strictly speaking, though, it's east to west), here are the other still-operating lighthouses in the Acadia Region. All are automated; most are accessible only by boat. None of the light towers are accessible to the public. Four lights in this area – Winter Harbor, Blue Hill, Dyce's Head, and Pumpkin Island – are no longer used as navigational beacons, although their towers still stand.

On a clear day, you can spot **Petit Manan Light** from the tip of Petit Manan Point, on the mainland Petit Manan section of the Maine Coastal Islands National Wildlife Reserve. Built in 1817 and rebuilt in 1855, it rises 119 feet from its base. It's located 3.5 miles offshore, directly south of Milbridge. Some excursion boats cruise by the island, which also is home to puffins.

Prospect Harbor Light, established in 1850,

rebuilt in 1891, and automated in 1951, sits on the tip of Prospect Point. It can be viewed across the harbor from Route 186 or you can drive to the gate for a closer look.

Clearly visible (on a clear day, that is) from Acadia's Park Loop Road, **Egg Rock Light** was built in 1875 on bleak, barren Egg Rock, protecting the entrance to Frenchman Bay. The squat, square keeper's house, topped by a square light tower, resembles no other Maine lighthouse. The light, now under the aegis of the Petit Manan National Wildlife Refuge, was automated in 1976.

The Cranberry Isles mailboat out of Northeast Harbor passes dramatically sited **Bear Island Light** on its daily rounds. Located on Acadia National Park land at the entrance to Northeast Harbor, the light tower and its keeper's house are privately leased in exchange for upkeep. (There's no public access to the island.) The automated light has been a privately maintained navigational aid since 1989. The present tower was built in 1889.

Baker Island Light, built in 1828 (during John Quincy Adams's presidency) and rebuilt in 1855, is accessible by boat, and then via a boardwalk. The brick tower rises 43 feet. Most of the 123-acre island, one of the five Cranberry Isles, is part of Acadia National Park. Charles W. Eliot, president of Harvard (1869–1909) and one of the prime movers behind the establishment of the park, shone a small spotlight on Baker Island when he published a sympathetic short memoir of a 19th-century Baker Island farmer and fisherman.

here. They'll swoop down shamelessly and snatch it away before you even realize they've spotted you. From extensive practice with unsuspecting visitors, they're adept at thievery.

【 Schoodic Loop

The major sights of Acadia's Schoodic section lie along the six-mile one-way road that meanders counterclockwise around the tip of the Schoodic Peninsula. You'll discover official and unofficial picnic areas, the hiking

trailheads, offshore lighthouses, and turnouts with scenic vistas. Also named the Park Loop Road, it's best referred to as the Schoodic Loop, to distinguish it from the one on Mount Desert.

The first landmark is **Frazer Point Picnic Area,** with lovely vistas, picnic tables, and handicapped-accessible restrooms. Other spots are fine for picnics, but this is the only official one. If you've brought bikes, leave your car here and do a counterclockwise 12.2-mile loop through

Entitled *John Gilley, One of the Forgotten Millions,* and reprinted in 1989 by Bar Harbor's Acadia Press, it's a must-read – a poignant story of a hardscrabble pioneering life.

Eleven miles out to sea from Bar Harbor, **Great Duck Island Light** stands on a 12-acre parcel owned by the College of the Atlantic (Bar Harbor). It serves as a year-round site (the solar-powered Alice Eno Biological Station) for the college's ecology researchers. The rest of the island is owned by the Nature Conservancy, which has estimated that Great Duck sustains about 20 percent of the state's nesting seabirds. In 2002, some 1,000 pairs of herring gulls nested here; others include Leach's storm petrels, black-backed gulls, and black guillemots. The 42-foot granite-and-brick light tower, built in 1890, was automated in 1986. The light is visible only from private boats, and there's no island access.

The College of the Atlantic also conducts research on the minuscule, barren, remote island surrounding **Mount Desert Rock Light,** built in 1847. The college's Allied Whale program, based in the keeper's house (the Edward Mc Blair Marine Research Station), monitors the movements of finback and humpback whales. The tower rises 68 feet; the automated light is solar-powered. Mount Desert Rock is also an automated NOAA weather station, cited daily in marine weather reports. There's no public access to the island, but whale-watching boats out of Bar Harbor frequently head this way.

Built in 1872, **Burnt Coat Harbor (or Hockamock Head) Light,** with a distinctive square white tower, protects the entrance to Burnt Coat Harbor on Swan's Island, accessible via the Maine State Ferry Service from Bass Harbor on Mount Desert Island. The town-owned light is about five miles from the ferry landing, so a bike comes in handy. Bring a picnic and enjoy it on the lighthouse grounds, with a fabulous view.

Isle au Haut Light, also known as Robinson Point Light, serves as a "night light" for guests at The Keeper's House, a unique inn on Isle au Haut. Connected by a wooden walkway to The Keeper's House, the brick light tower (built in 1907) overlooks the Isle au Haut Thorofare. Access to the island is only by ferry or private boat. The tower itself (not open to the public) is owned by the town of Isle au Haut; The Keeper's House is privately owned.

Looking rather lonely without a keeper's house, **Mark Island Light,** also known as Deer Island Thorofare Light, was built in 1857 (the lightkeeper's house burned in 1959). All that remain are the 25-foot square tower and a tiny attached shed. Deer Isle's Island Heritage Trust owns the island, which is accessible only by boat – but *not* during seabird nesting season (typically, April through August).

Another light station without a keeper's house (it was intentionally burned in 1963) is **Eagle Island Light,** in East Penobscot Bay, west of the Deer Isle village of Sunset. Built in 1858, it has a 30-foot granite tower. Plans are in the works to deactivate the light. Access is only by boat.

SCHOODIC PENINSULA

the park and back to your car via Birch Harbor and Route 186. It's a fine day trip.

From the picnic area, the road becomes one-way. Unlike the Park Loop Road on Mount Desert, no parking is allowed in the right lane. There are periodic pullouts, but not many cars can squeeze in. Despite the fact that this is far from the busiest section of Acadia, it can still be frustrating in the summer months to be unable to find a space. Best advice, therefore: Stay in the area and do this loop early in the morning or later in the afternoon, perhaps in May or June. (The late-September and early-October foliage is gorgeous, but traffic *does* increase then.) While you're driving, if you see a viewpoint you like (with room to pull off), stop; it's a long way around to return.

From this side of Frenchman Bay, the vistas of Mount Desert's summits are gorgeous, behind islands sprinkled here and there.

Drive 1.6 miles from the picnic area to Raven's Head, a Thunder Hole-type cliff with

© TOM NANGLE

Raven's Nest

SCHOODIC PENINSULA

U.S. Navy base that became part of the park in 2002. The campus is now the Schoodic Education and Research Center (locally called by its acronym, SERC); occasional lectures and programs are held here.

From Schoodic Point, return to the Loop Road. Look to your right, and you'll see Little Moose Island, which can be accessed at low tide. Be careful though, and don't get stranded here. Continue to the **Blueberry Hill** parking area (about one mile from the Schoodic Point/ Loop Road intersection), a moorlike setting where the low growth allows almost 180-degree views of the bay and islands. There are a few trails in this area—all eventually converging on **Schoodic Head,** the highest point on the peninsula. (Don't confuse this with Schoodic Mountain, which is well north of here). Across the road and up the road a bit is the trailhead for the 180-foot-high **Anvil** headland.

As you continue along this stretch of road, keep your eyes peeled for eagles, which frequently soar here. There's a nest on the northern end of Rolling Island; you can see it with binoculars from some of the roadside pullouts.

From Blueberry Hill, continue 1.2 miles to a pullout for the East Trail, the shortest and most direct route to Schoodic Head. From here, it's about another mile to the park exit, in Wonsqueak Harbor. It's another two miles to the intersection with Rte. 186 in Birch Harbor. (If you didn't bring a picnic lunch or dinner, Bunker's Wharf Restaurant is an excellent stop, with views of a working wharf).

sheer drops to the churning surf below (no fences, so not a good place for little ones) and fabulous views. The trail is unmarked, but there's a small pullout on the left side of the road opposite it. Be extremely careful here, stay on the path (the environment is very fragile and erosion is a major problem), and stay well away from the cliff's edge.

At 2.2 miles from the picnic area, watch for a narrow, unpaved road on the left, across from an "open" beach vista. It winds for a mile (keep left at the fork) up to a tiny parking circle, from which you can follow the trail (signposted "Schoodic trails") to the open ledges on 440-foot Schoodic Head. From the circle, there's already a glimpse of the view, but it gets much better. If you bear right at the fork, you'll come to a grassy parking area with access to the Alder Trail and the Schoodic Head Trail.

Continue on the Park Loop Road, and hang a right onto a short, two-way spur to **Schoodic Point.** Just before it is a small info center, staffed by volunteers and park rangers. It's located on the site of a former top-secret

◖ DONNELL POND PUBLIC RESERVED LAND

More than 15,000 acres have been preserved for public access in Donnell Pond Public Reserved Land (Maine Bureau of Parks and Lands, 207/827-1818, www.state.me.us/doc/parks), a huge mountain-and-lake area north and east of Sullivan. Developers had their eyes on this gorgeous real estate in the 1980s, but preservationists fortunately rallied to the cause. Outright purchase of 7,316 of the acres, in the Spring River Lake area, came through the foresighted

Land for Maine's Future program. Hikers can climb Schoodic, Black, and Caribou mountains; paddlers and anglers have Donnell Pond, Tunk Lake, Spring River Lake, Long Pond, Round Pond, and Little Pond, among others. Route 182, an official Scenic Highway, cuts right through the Donnell Pond preserve. The preserve encompasses lakes for boating and fishing, mountains for hiking, and primitive campsites. Do note: Hunting is permitted, so take special care during hunting season.

◖ MAINE COASTAL ISLANDS NATIONAL WILDLIFE REFUGE

Occupying a 2,166-acre peninsula in Steuben with 10 miles of rocky shoreline (and three offshore islands) is the refuge's outstandingly scenic Petit Manan Point Division (Pigeon Hill Rd., Steuben, P.O. Box 279, Milbridge 04658, 207/546-2124, www.fws.gov/northeast/mainecoastal). The remote location means it sees only about 15,000 visitors a year, most of those likely birders, as more than 250 different birds have been sighted here. The refuge's primary focus is restoring colonies of nesting seabirds. Among the other natural highlights here are stands of jack pine, coastal raised peatlands, blueberry barrens, freshwater and saltwater marshes, granite shores, and cobble beaches. When asking directions locally, you'll hear it called 'tit Manan.

The moderately easy, four-mile round-trip Birch Point Trail and easy, 1.5-mile round-trip Hollingsworth or Shore Trail provide splendid views and opportunities to spot wildlife along the shore and in the fields, forests, and marshland. The Hollingsworth Trail, leading you to the shoreline, is the best. This is foggy territory, but on clear days, you can see the 123-foot lighthouse on Petit Manan Island, 2.5 miles offshore. The Birch Point Trail heads through blueberry fields to Dyer Bay and loops by the waterfront, with much of the trail passing through woods.

From Route 1, on the east side of Steuben, take Pigeon Hill Road. Six miles down is the first parking lot, for the Birch Point Trail; another half mile takes you to the parking area for the Hollingsworth Trail; space is limited. If you arrive in August, help yourself to blueberries. The refuge is open daily all year, sunrise to sunset; cross-country skiing is permitted in winter.

Recreation

HIKING

A pleasant and short shore path begins and ends at the **Dixon Memorial Rock** and follows the water's edge, rising through the woods and passing by cottages on eastern Grindstone Neck. The views are fabulous. To find it, take Beach Street to Club House Lane, proceed across the four-way intersection, then go right on Steamboat Lane, following it to the oval at the end.

◖ Schoodic Head Loop

- Distance: 2.7 miles round-trip
- Duration: varies with route, 1.5–2 hours
- Elevation gain: 440 feet
- Effort: moderate, some steep sections

- Trailhead: Blueberry Hill parking area, Schoodic Loop

The Schoodic Head Loop comprises three connecting trails, and it can be hiked in either direction, or if time is tight, choose just one trail to hike. Clockwise begins with the easiest terrain and ends with a downhill scramble over a steep and rocky hillside. As one ranger noted, it's tough on the knees and you have to be very careful with your footing in this direction. If you hike it counterclockwise, beginning with the Anvil Trail, you'll get the toughest terrain out of the way first.

You can access the loop at various points, but the most parking is at the Blueberry Hill parking area. The easy, one-mile Alder trail departs from just south of the parking lot entrance and connects through the woods and some marshy areas to the unmarked Ranger Cabin road; head left for about 50 yards, and watch for the Schoodic Head trail marker.

The moderate Schoodic Head trail climbs for 0.7 mile, beginning in woods and emerging onto ledgy terrain as it nears the summit. The views are expansive and well worth any effort.

The one-mile Anvil Trail descends over moderate terrain with a few steep sections. A highlight here is the Anvil promontory, a rocky knoll. Whichever way you choose to hike, be extremely careful on the Anvil Trail, as the terrain is rugged, with lots of roots and loose rocks.

A fourth trail, the 0.6 mile East Trail, descends from the summit and emerges on the Park Loop Road about one mile beyond the Blueberry Hill parking area. This is the shortest and most direct route to the summit and can be hiked independently or looped in with the other trails.

You can also access this loop from the unmarked Ranger Cabin road, bearing right at the fork.

Schoodic Mountain

- Distance: 2.4 miles round-trip
- Duration: 2 hours
- Elevation gain: 800 feet
- Effort: moderately difficult
- Trailhead: off Rte. 183, Franklin

The hiking isn't easy here, but it isn't technical and the options are many. The interconnecting trail system takes in Schoodic Mountain, Black Mountain, and Caribou Mountain on Donnell Pond Public Reserved Land.

Follow the Schoodic Mountain Loop clockwise, heading westward first. To make a day of it, pack a picnic and take a swimsuit (and don't forget a camera and binoculars for the summit views). On a brilliantly clear day, you'll see Baxter State Park's Katahdin, the peaks of Acadia National Park, and the ocean beyond. And in late July/early August, blueberries are abundant on the summit. For such rewards, this is a popular hike, so don't expect to be

alone, especially on fall weekends, when the foliage colors are spectacular.

Trailheads can be accessed by either boat or vehicle. To reach the vehicle-access trailhead for Schoodic Mountain from Route 1 in East Sullivan, drive just over four miles northeast on Rte. 183 (Tunk Lake Road). Cross the Maine Central Railroad tracks and turn left at the Donnell Pond sign onto an unpaved road (marked as a Jeep track on the USGS map). Go about 0.25 mile, then turn left for the parking area and trailhead for Schoodic Mountain, Black Mountain, Caribou Mountain, and a trail to Schoodic Beach.

Black Mountain

- Distance: 5 miles round-trip
- Duration: 3 hours
- Elevation gain: 800 feet
- Effort: moderately difficult
- Trailhead: off Rte. 183, Franklin

The Black Mountain ascent begins easily enough, then climbs steadily through the woods on Donnell Pond Public Reserved Land, easing off a bit before reaching bald ledges. Continue to the true summit by taking the trail past Wizard Pond. Views take in the forested lands, nearby lakes and peaks, and out to Acadia's peaks. You can piggyback it with Schoodic Mountain, using that trailhead as a base for both climbs. Another possibility is to add Caribou Mountain. That loop exceeds seven miles, making a full day of hiking.

Follow the directions for the Schoodic Mountain trail. If you continue straight, you'll come to another trailhead for Black and Caribou Mountains. Water-access trailheads are at Schoodic Beach and Redman's Beach.

BIKING

The Maine Department of Transportation has mapped and provides info on area bicycle routes. These include the Schoodic Peninsula, with 13- and 29-mile loops, and Downeast Route/East Coast Greenway Trail, a 140-mile trail stretching from Ellsworth to Calais. PDF maps with tour details are available on www.exploremaine.org/bike/bt_downeast .html, or you can request hard copies by calling 207/624-3250. Do be extremely careful pedaling in this region, as like much of Maine, shoulders are few and traffic moves swiftly. The best choices for cycling are the **Schoodic Loop** and the quiet roads of **Grindstone Neck.**

If you have a bike, try to pedal the **Schoodic Loop Road** early or late in the day—especially if you're doing a family outing, when everyone tends to cluster together. It's a lovely bike route, but the shoulders on this peninsula are soft and sandy and not great for bikes—so you'll see Share the Road with Bicycles signs along the way. Keep to the right and use the road, not the shoulders. Leave your car at the Frazier Point Picnic Area and do a counterclockwise 12.2-mile loop through the park and back to your car via Birch Harbor and Route 186. It's a fine day trip.

SeaMyst (150 Corea Rd./Rte. 195, Prospect Harbor, 207/963-7223, www.seamyst.com or www.mooselookguideservice.com) rents bicycles on a 24-hour basis ($20); weekly rates are available.

CANOEING AND KAYAKING

Experienced sea kayakers can explore the coastline throughout this region. Canoeists can paddle the placid waters of Jones Pond, on the Schoodic Peninsula. In Donnell Pond Public Reserved Land, the major water bodies are **Donnell Pond** (big enough by most gauges to be called a lake) and **Tunk** and **Spring River Lakes;** all are accessible for boats (even, alas, powerboats).

To reach the boat-launching area for Donnell Pond from Route 1 in Sullivan, take Route 200 north to Route 182. Turn right and go about 1.5 miles to a right turn just before Swan Brook. Turn and go not quite two miles to the put-in; the road is poor in spots but adequate for a regular vehicle. The Narrows, where you'll put in, is lined with summer cottages ("camps" in the Maine vernacular); keep paddling eastward to the more open part of the lake. Continue on Rte. 182 to find the boat launches for Tunk Lake and Spring River Lake (hand-carry only). Canoeists and kayakers can access Tunk Stream from Spring River Lake.

Still within the preserve boundaries, but farther east, you can put in a canoe at the northern end of Long Pond and paddle southward into adjoining Round Pond. In early August, Round Mountain, rising a few hundred feet from Long Pond's eastern shore, is a great spot for gathering blueberries and huckleberries. The put-in for Long Pond is on the south side of Route 182 (park well off the road), about two miles east of Tunk Lake.

Outfitters and Trips

Maine Guide Jody Miller is the resident outdoor pro on the Schoodic Peninsula, and her **SeaMyst** (150 Corea Rd./Rte. 195, Prospect Harbor, 207/963-7223, www.seamyst.com or www.mooselookguideservice.com), previously known as Moose Look Guide Service, has something for everyone. She rents canoes ($30) and freshwater and sea kayaks ($30–60) on a 24-hour basis; weekly rates are available. When her schedule permits, she offers guided tours ($50), usually in late afternoon or to coincide with sunset and lasting about three to four hours. These include basic instruction and tips and paddling at a relaxed pace. Jody also will lead paddles into the sunrise from Corea or sunrise hikes. Also available with advance notification are specialty tours, including fishing, photography, and an island overnight. Jody's very flexible, and if she can't arrange what you want, she'll find others who can do it.

Antonio Blasi, a Registered Maine Sea Kayak and Recreational Guide, leads guided tours of Frenchman or Taunton Bay and hiking and camping expeditions through **Hancock Point Kayak Tours** (58 Point Rd., Hancock, 207/422-6854, www.hancockpoint-kayak.com). A three-hour paddle, including all equipment, safety and paddling demonstrations, and usually an island break, is $45. You have a choice of single or double kayak. Minimum age is 9 for a double, 12 for a single. Overnight kayak camping trips are $150 per person. Antonio also leads overnight backpacking trips for $125 pp, and cross-country skiing and snowshoe tours are available in winter.

If you prefer to do it yourself, rent a canoe

or kayak from **Water's Edge Cane & Kayak Rentals** (207/460-6350), with two locations: 108 Mud Creek Rd., Hancock, or 222 Franklin Road, Franklin. Canoe rentals are $20 for one day, $50 for three days, or $100 per week; single kayaks are $25, $65, and $125; double kayaks are $30, $80, or $150. No credit cards.

FISHING

No surprise that the Donnell Pond Public Land Reserve is a favorite among anglers. Land-locked salmon can be found in Donnell Pond, Tunk Lake, and Spring River Lake. Lake trout (togue) are fished in Tunk Lake. For brown trout, cast your line in Long Pond.

Open-water season in Hancock and adjacent Washington counties is April 1–September 30, but after August 16, you must use artificial lures in brooks, rivers and streams. Check with local wardens for information regarding catch limits and other regulations for specific bodies of water, or call the **Maine Department of Fish and Wildlife** (207/288-8000 or 207/287-8003 for 24-hour recorded information, www.state.me.us/ifw).

Fishing licenses can be purchased at many stores and most town offices. Non-resident freshwater licenses for anyone 16 or older are $53 for the season; $12 for one day (24 hours); $24 for three days (72 hours); $37 for seven days, and $41 for 15 days. Licenses for children ages 12 to 16 are $10. Licenses for saltwater fishing are not required.

SWIMMING

Best freshwater swimming in the area is at **Jones Beach,** a community-owned recreation area on Jones Pond in West Gouldsboro. Here you'll find restrooms, a nice playground, picnic facilities, boat launch, swim area with a float, and a small beach. It's located at the end of Recreation Road, off Rte. 195, which is 0.3 mile south of Rte. 1.

Two beach areas on Donnell Pond are also popular for swimming, **Schoodic Beach** and **Redman's Beach,** and both have picnic tables, fire rings, and pit toilets. It's a half-mile hike to Schoodic Beach from the parking lot. Red-

© TOM NANGLE

Local kids can often be found using the rope swing at Fox Pond.

man's Beach is only accessible by boat. Other pocket beaches are also accessible by boat, and there's a rope swing (use at your own risk) by a roadside pullout for Fox Pond.

GOLF

Play a nine-hole round at the **Grindstone Neck Golf Course** (Grindstone Ave., Winter Harbor, 207/963-7760, www.grindstonegolf.com, May–Oct.), just for the dynamite scenery and for a glimpse of this exclusive, late-19th-century summer enclave. Established in 1891, the public course attracts a tony crowd; 150-yard markers are cute little birdhouses. Tee times usually aren't needed, but call to make sure.

EXCURSION BOATS
Bird-Watching Cruise

Capt. Jaime Robertson's **Robertson Sea Tours & Adventures** (207/546-3883 or 207/461-7439 cell, www.robertsonseatours.com, May 15–Oct. 1) offers a bird-watching cruise to Petit Manan from Milbridge (about 15 minutes northeast of Gouldsboro on

PUFFINS

The chickadee is the Maine state bird, and the bald eagle is our national emblem, but probably the best-loved bird along the Maine coast is the Atlantic puffin (*Fratercula arctica*), a member of the auk (Alcidae) family. Photographs show an imposing-looking creature with a quizzical mien; amazingly, this larger-than-life seabird is only about 12 inches long. Black-backed and white-chested, the puffin has bright orange legs, "clown-makeup" eyes, and a distinctive, rather outlandish red-and-yellow beak. Its diet is fish and shellfish.

Almost nonexistent in this part of the world as recently as the 1970s, the puffin (or "sea parrot") has recovered dramatically thanks to the unstinting efforts of Cornell University ornithologist Stephen Kress and his Project Puffin. Starting with an orphan colony (of two) on remote Matinicus Rock, Kress painstakingly transferred nearly a thousand puffin chicks (also known fondly as "pufflings") from Newfoundland and used artificial nests and decoys to entice the birds to adapt to and reproduce on Eastern Egg Rock in Muscongus Bay.

In 1981, thanks to the assistance and persistence of hundreds of interns and volunteers, and despite the predations of great black-backed gulls, puffins finally were fledged on Eastern Egg, and the rest, as they say, is history. Within 20 years, more than three dozen puffin couples were nesting on Eastern Egg Rock, and still more had established nests on other islands in the area. Kress's methods have received international attention, and his proven techniques have been used to reintroduce bird populations in remote parts of the globe. In 2001, *Down East* magazine singled out Kress to receive its prestigious annual Environmental Award.

HOW AND WHERE TO SEE PUFFINS

Puffin-watching, like whale-watching, involves heading offshore (although you might get lucky and spot them at the tip of the Petit Manan division of the Maine Coast Islands National Wildlife Refuge), so be prepared with warm clothing, rubber-soled shoes, a hat, sunscreen, binoculars, and, if you're motion-sensitive, appropriate medication. Although cruises depart from Bar Harbor, on Mount Desert Island, and sometimes from Birch Harbor, on the Schoodic Peninsula, if you're willing to venture a bit afield, you'll find three companies dedicated to puffin-watching cruises. **Roberston Sea Cruises,** in Milbridge (207/546-3883 or 207/461-7439 cell, www.robertsonseatours.com, May 15–Oct. 1), heads to Petit Manan Island, and you view the birds from aboard the boat.

Two other companies provide daily up-close-and-personal opportunities for puffin-watching along the Down East Coast – specifically, on Machias Seal Island, home of the state's largest puffin colony. One boat departs from Cutler, the other from Jonesport. Weather permitting, you'll be allowed to disembark on the 20-acre island and spy on the roughly 3,000 puffins (at peak) who call it their summer home. Captain John Norton – son of the late Barna Norton, the veteran of puffin-watching trips – departs from the waterfront in Jonesport at about 7 A.M. daily, late May–August. Cost is $65. Contact **Norton of Jonesport** (888/551-4895 or 207/497-5933).

Naturalist and skilled skipper Andy Patterson of **Bold Coast Charters** (207/259-4484, www.boldcoast.com) begins his puffin tours from Cutler in mid-May, departing each morning (about 7 A.M.) aboard the 40-footer *Barbara Frost*. The season wraps up in late August. Cost is $65 pp.

ADOPT-A-PUFFIN PROGRAM

Stephen Kress's Project Puffin has devised a clever way to enlist supporters via the Adopt-a-Puffin program. For a $100 donation, you'll receive a certificate of adoption, vital statistics on your adoptee, annual updates, and a T-shirt. How's that for a special gift for the bird lover in your life? For information, visit www.projectpuffin.org.

SCHOODIC PENINSULA

Rte. 1) aboard the **Mairi Leigh,** a classic 30-foot Maine lobsterboat, built in nearby Jonesport. The three-hour Petit Manan Puffin Cruise (daily mid-May–early Oct., $55 for adults, $45 for kids 12 and younger, by reservation only) heads to Petit Manan Island, home to a section of the National Wildlife Refuge and Petit Manan Light. Puffins usually can be spotted from June through August, although there often are a few early birds in May and stragglers into early Sep-tember. Other birds sighted include com-mon, Arctic, and endangered roseate terns; razorbills, black guillemots, common eiders, and Leach's storm petrel. There's a boat mini-mum, so being flexible with your days can be helpful. Of course, you can always char-ter the entire boat for a customized cruise. Rates begin at $350 for four hours for two people. Robertson sometimes offers cruises out of Bunker's Wharf, in Birch Harbor; call for more info.

Entertainment and Events

PIERRE MONTEUX SCHOOL

The Pierre Monteux School for Conductors and Orchestra Musicians (Rte. 1, Hancock, 207/422-3931, www.monteuxschool.org), a prestigious summer program founded in 1943, has achieved international renown for training dozens of national and international classical musicians. It presents two well-attended con-cert series starting in late June and running through July. The Wednesday series (7:30 P.M., $7) features chamber music; the Sunday con-certs (5 P.M., $12 adults, $5 students) feature symphonies. An annual children's concert usu-ally is held on a Monday (1 P.M.) in early to mid-July. All concerts are held in the school's Forest Studio.

SCHOODIC ARTS FOR ALL

Concerts, art classes, coffeehouses, workshops, and related activities are presented year-round by the energetic Schoodic Arts for All (207/963-2569, www.schoodicarts.org), a volunteer or-ganization. Many activities are held at historic Hammond Hall, in downtown Winter Harbor. A summer series presents monthly concerts from May through October on Friday evenings.

The **Schoodic Arts Festival** takes place two weeks in early August and is jam-packed with daily workshops and nightly performances, for all ages. Call for a schedule, and register early for any program that you don't want to miss.

OCEANSIDE INNSTITUTE

Seeking to add more vibrancy and diversity to the peninsula's entertainment offerings and to indulge their own interests in music and the sciences, the owners of Oceanside Meadows Inn created the Innstitute for Arts and Sciences (207/963-5557, www.oceaninn.com), which presents a series of Thursday night events from late June to late September, with a break during the Schoodic Arts Festival. The wide-ranging calendar includes lectures and concerts as well as art shows. Some are free; others are $10 in advance or $12 at the door.

EAGLE HILL SUMMER LECTURES

The Humboldt Field Research Institute (59 Eagle Hill Rd., Steuben, 207/546-2821, www.eaglehill.us, 7:30 P.M. Thurs., early July to late Aug., free) sponsors three opportunities to meet and mingle with scientists and others. The institute is located four miles off Route 1. Take Dyer Bay Road off Route 1, bearing left at the fork onto Mogador Road for a total of 3.6 miles, then left on Schooner Point road, then right on Eagle Hill Road. Programs take place in the Dining Hall lecture room.

The institute began an artist-in-residence program in 2005. At least once during the sea-son, the resident artist discusses his or her ex-periences in a scheduled talk. Call for details.

The Thursday Evening Lecture Series presents guest lecturers and scholars on wide-ranging but primarily scientific topics. In past years, these have included "Between Earth and Mars," with Rick Hauck, a former NASA astronaut and Space Shuttle commander, and "Helpful and Harmful Ferns," by Robbin Moran, curator of ferns for the New York Botanical Gardens. Lectures begin at 7:30 P.M. on most Thursdays mid-July–early September. Admission is free.

Cosmos Colloquia

Listen to nationally published authors discuss the relationship between nature and culture, then dine with them afterwards. Past programs have included "The House of Ipswich Marsh: Exploring the Natural History of New England," with William Sargent, consultant for the *NOVA* science series, former director of the Baltimore Aquarium, and author of *The House on Ipswich Marsh* and *Crab Wars: A Tale of Horseshoe Crabs, Bioterrorism, and Human Health.* Another past program was "The Role of Rocks: Geology and 19th Century American Landscape Painting," by Rebecca Bedell, assistant professor of art at Wellesley College and author of a book by the same title. These occasional programs take place on Saturdays, beginning at 5 P.M., and are followed by an optional buffet dinner. The presentation is free; dinner is $20, with advance reservation required.

FARMSTEAD BARN

During July, **Hancock County Friends of the Arts** (Rte. 1, East Sullivan, 207/422-3615, www.hcfafarmsteadbarn.org) presents an entertainment series for children. The weekly shows might include jugglers, magicians, mime, comedy, or music. All are presented in a barn that Ginia Davis Wexler, a former singer, and her husband, Morris, turned into a theater more than 35 years ago for just this purpose. The funky interior is decorated with mismatched chairs, Mexican flying creatures, Chinese lanterns, posters, paintings, and other touches. Two shows are presented. Admission is free, but donations are much appreciated. The barn is three miles south of the Gouldsboro Post Office.

WINTER HARBOR LOBSTER FESTIVAL

Winter Harbor's biggest wingding is the annual Lobster Festival, the second Saturday in August. The gala daylong event includes a parade, live entertainment, lobster boat races (a serious competition in these parts), crafts fair, games, and lots and lots of crustaceans. For more information, visit www.acadia-schoodic.org.

SCHOODIC PENINSULA

Shopping

ANTIQUES

Browsers, dreamers, and collectors are welcome at **Art & Old Things** (70 Taunton Dr., Sullivan, 207/422-3551), a one-stop antiques and collectibles shop, art gallery, and sculpture garden that's just plain fun to visit. The eclectic gallery features the work of Joe Martell and other regional artists; the shop is filled with antiques, junktiques, and shabby chic furniture, decorative items, home accents, and architectural pieces; the garden is accented with granite and marble sculptures and unique functional artwork. The shop is just 500 yards off Route 1, just beyond Gazebo Park.

Winter Harbor Antiques and Works of Hand (424-426 Main St., Winter Harbor, 207/963-2547) is a double treat. Antiques fill one building and works by local craftspeople and artists fill the other. It's located across from Hammond Hall.

Antiques of a more serious sort, especially smalls, await seekers at **Whitmer-Hammond Antiques** (East Schoodic Drive, Birch Harbor, 207/963-2999, www.whitmer-hammond-antiques.com).

FOOD AND WINE

German and Italian presses, Portuguese corks, and Maine fruit all go into the creation of Bob and Kathe Bartlett's award-winning dinner and dessert wines: apple, pear, blueberry, raspberry, blackberry, strawberry, and loganberry. Founded in 1982, **Bartlett Maine Estate Winery** (175 Chicken Mill Pond Rd., Gouldsboro 04607, 207/546-2408, 10 A.M.–5 P.M. Mon.–Sat. Memorial Day to Columbus Day, or by appointment off-season) produces more than 20,000 gallons annually in a handsome wood-and-stone building designed by the Bartletts. No tours, but you're welcome to sample the wines, and you can buy single bottles and gift packages. Bartlett's is a half mile south of Route 1 in Gouldsboro.

This area boasts not one, but two excellent smokehouses. Defying its name, **Sullivan Harbor Smokehouse** (1545 Rte. 1, P.O. Box 96, Hancock, 207/422-3735 or 800/422-4014, www.sullivanharborfarm.com) has moved to spacious, modern new digs in Hancock. Big interior windows allow visitors to see into the production facility and watch the action. Among the offerings are Scottish-style smoked salmon, gravlax, smoked scallops, smoked trout, smoked Arctic char, smoked salmon pâté and more. The newer **Grindstone Neck of Maine** (311 Newman St., Rte. 186, just north of downtown Winter Harbor, 207/963-7347 or 866/831-8734, www.grindstoneneck.com) also earns high marks for its smoked salmon, shellfish, spreads, and pâtés, all made without preservatives or artificial ingredients.

Cindy and Bill Thayer's enthusiasm is contagious as they explain their prolific 150-acre certified-organic farm—home to hairy Scotch Highland cattle, turkeys, sheep, pigs, chickens, and border collies. At **Darthia Farm** (W. Bay Rd., Rte. 186, Gouldsboro, 207/963-7771, 207/963-2770, or 800/285-6234, www.darthiafarm.com), kids love feeding the pigs and riding on the hay wagon; parents can check out Hattie's Shed for Cindy's outstanding ikat weavings and work by half a dozen other craftspeople. The Farm Store (8 A.M.–5 P.M. Mon.–Fri., until noon Saturdays June–September)

sells fresh produce as well as herbal salves and vinegars, handspun hand-dyed yarn, and other products. Tours and horse-drawn wagon rides occur each Tuesday and Thursday at 2 P.M. Cost is $2 pp. The farm is 1.7 miles south of Route 1.

Chickadee Creek Stillroom (Rte. 186, West Gouldsboro, 207/963-7283 or 800/969-4372, www.chickadeecreek.com) is a toy store for herb fanciers. Jeanie and Fred Cook seem to have thought of everything—potpourri, teas, wreaths, fresh herbs for cooking. If you're being bothered by insects, request their herbal repellent; it works. The barn/shop is 1.7 miles south of Route 1. Request a copy of the mail-order catalog.

GENERAL STORE

You can find just about anything at the **Winter Harbor 5 & 10** (Main St., Winter Harbor, 207/963-7927, www.winterharbor5and10.com). It's the genuine article, an old fashioned five and dime that's somehow still surviving in the age of Wal-Mart.

ARTS AND CRAFTS GALLERIES

Art and artisan studios and galleries are numerous, and it's easy to while away a day browsing and buying. Begin by picking up copies of the *Artist Studio Tour Map,* which details and provides directions to about a dozen galleries in Franklin, Sullivan, and Hancock, and the *Schoodic Peninsula* brochure, which notes galleries and shops on the peninsula. Both are widely available and free. Hours and days of operation vary; it's best to call first if you really want to visit a gallery.

Schoodic Peninsula

Galleries dot the Schoodic Peninsula. To find these, loop down to Winter Harbor then back up on Route 186.

Architectural stoneware, with a specialty in sinks, is the drawing card at **Maine Kiln Works** (115 S. Gouldsboro Rd./Hwy. 186, Gouldsboro, 207/963-5819, www.waterstonesink.com), but you'll also find functional pottery in the shop.

© TOM NANGLE

Winter Harbor doesn't boast a lot of shops, but you can get anything you truly need at the 5 & 10.

You might also see Dan Weaver at work on the wheel in the back room. Be careful when arriving or departing, the shop is on a killer corner and traffic seems to zoom by.

Every piece handcrafted at **Gypsy Moose Glass Studio** (20 Williamsbrook Rd., South Gouldsboro, 207/963-2674, www.gypsymooseglass.com) is made from a single glass rod, which means no two are alike. You'll find glass beads, fused-glass earrings, swan weather predictors, and much more at this working studio just off Rte. 186.

If you're lucky, you might catch Susan Dickson-Smith throwing a pot at **Stave Island Gallery/Proper Clay Stoneware** (Rte. 186, South Gouldsboro, 207/963-2040, www.properclay.com). Her small gallery features her pottery as well as works by other Maine artisans.

An old post office is the new location for **Lee Art Glass** 679 S. Gouldsboro Rd./Rte. 196, Gouldsboro, 207/963-7280). Although Rod Lee has died, his works live on, thanks to Wayne Tucker and Sheldon R. Bickford, who

purchased the business after training with Lee. The fused-glass tableware is created by taking two pieces of window glass and firing them on terra cotta or bisque molds at 1,500 degrees. What makes the end result so appealing are the colors and the patterns—crocheted doilies or stencils—impressed into the glass. The almost-magical results are beautiful and delicate-looking, yet functional.

Graceful watercolors fill the **Maloue Gallery** (355 Main St., Winter Harbor, 207/963-2193). M. Louise Young Shaw's paintings depict Maine landscapes.

Visiting the **U.S. Bells Foundry & Watering Cove Pottery** (56 West Bay Rd., Rte. 186, Prospect Harbor, 207/963-7184, www.usbells.com) is a treat for the ears, as browsers try out the many varieties of cast-bronze bells made in the adjacent foundry by Richard Fisher. If you're lucky, he may have time to explain the process—particularly intriguing for children, and a distraction from their instinctive urge to test every bell in the shop. The store also carries quilts by Dick's wife, Cindy, and wood-fired stoneware and porcelain by their daughter-in-law Liza Fisher. U.S. Bells is 0.25 mile up the hill from Prospect Harbor's post office.

◖ Hancock and Sullivan Gallery Tour

Begin at **Arts & Africana** (1428 Rte. 1, Hancock, 207/422-9529), where owner Christine Covert stocks contemporary African arts and crafts and textiles, as well as local sea glass jewelry, Southeast Asian imports, Zimbabwe sculpture, beads from around the world, and even bath products.

Take the Point Road 2.5 miles to find Russell and Akemi Wray's **Raven Tree Gallery** (536 Point Rd., Hancock, 207/422-8273). Russell specializes in wood carvings, bronzes, prints, and jewelry; Akemi crafts pottery.

Continue another two miles on the Point Road to the **Ragna Bruno Torkanowsky Studio & Gallery** (983 Point Rd., Hancock, 207/422-6252). Torkanowsky's home gallery is filled with her own works as well as works by more than a dozen other artists.

Return to Rte. 1 and take Eastside Road, just before the Hancock-Sullivan Bridge, and drive 1.5 miles south to the Wray family's **Gull Rock Pottery** (325 Eastside Rd., Hancock, 207/422-3990). You'll find wheel-thrown, hand-painted, dishwasher-safe pottery decorated with blue-and-white Japanese-style motifs.

Cross the Hancock-Sullivan Bridge, then take your first left off Route 1 onto Taunton Drive to find the next three galleries. Drawing from her experiences as an oil painter and from her life in Japan, Peg McAloon creates masterful one-of-a-kind quilts at **Wildfire Run Quilt Boutique** (148 Taunton Dr., Sullivan, 207/422-3935, www.maineus.com/wildfirerun).

Nearby **Lunaform** (Cedar Ln., West Sullivan, 207/422-0923, www.lunaform.com) is in a class by itself. First there's the setting—the beautifully landscaped grounds surrounding an abandoned granite quarry. Then there's the realization that many of the wonderfully aesthetic garden ornaments created here look like

Antique shops and especially artisan's shops and galleries make a worthwhile detour.

hand-turned *pottery,* when in fact they are hand turned but made of steel-reinforced concrete. Buy an urn or pot or fountain and dazzle your friends, and even your enemies. It takes a bit of zigging and zagging to get here. Off Route 1, take the first right onto Track Road; after a half mile, go left onto Cedar Lane.

Bet you can't keep from smiling at the whimsical animal sculptures and fun furniture of talented sculptor/painter Philip Barter. His work is the cornerstone of the eclectic **Barter Family Gallery** (Shore Rd., Sullivan, 207/422-3190, www.barterfamilygallery.com). But there's more: Barter's wife and seven children have put their considerable skills to work producing hooked and braided rugs, jewelry, and other craft items. The gallery is 2.5 miles off Route 1.

Return to Route 1, then head north on Route 200 to find the next three galleries. Artist Paul Breeden, best known for the remarkable illustrations, calligraphy, and maps he's done for *National Geographic,* Time-Life Books, and other national and international publications, displays and sells his paintings at the **Spring Woods Gallery and Willowbrook Garden** (40A Willowbrook Ln., Sullivan, 207/422-3007, www.springwoodsgallery.com, www.willowbrookgarden.com). Also filling the handsome modern gallery space are paintings by Ann Breeden and metal sculptures and silk scarves by the talented Breeden offspring. Be sure to allow time to meander through the sculpture garden, where there's even a playhouse for kids.

Hand-woven textiles are the specialty at **Moosetrack Studio** (388 Bert Gray Rd./Route 200, Sullivan, 207/422-9017), where the selections range from hand-woven area rugs to shawls woven from merino wool and silk. Camilla Stege has been weaving since 1969, and her work reflects her experience and expertise. The gallery is 1.8 miles north of Rte. 1.

Overlooking Hog Bay, 3.6 miles north of Route 1, Charles and Susanne Grosjean have been the key players at **Hog Bay Pottery** (245 Hog Bay Rd., Route 200, Franklin, 207/565-2282) since 1974. Inside the casual, laid-back showroom are Charles's functional, nature-themed pottery and Susanne's stunning hand-woven rugs.

Nancy Glista's distinctive sterling silver jewelry mixes spirals and spheres accented with semiprecious stones. Her studio, **Glista Jewelry** (Shipyard Point Rd., Hancock, 207/565-3302), is a bit off the beaten path. To find it, continue north on Rte. 200 until it meets with Rte. 182, then watch for signs on the left. Do make an appointment.

Steuben

Arthur Smith (Rogers Point Rd., Steuben, 207/546-3462) is the real thing when it comes to chainsaw carvings. He's an extremely talented folk artist who looks at a piece of wood and sees an animal in it. His carvings of great blue herons, eagles, wolves, porcupines, flamingoes, and other creatures are incredibly detailed, and his wife, Marie, paints them in lifelike colors. Don't expect a fancy studio; much of the work can be viewed roadside.

Also in Steuben, but on the other end of the spectrum, is **Ray Carbone** (460 Pigeon Hill Rd., Steuben, 207/546-2170), whose masterful wood, stone, and bronze sculptures and fine furniture are definitely worth stopping to see, if not buy. Don't miss the granite sculptures and birdbaths in the garden.

SCHOODIC PENINSULA

Accommodations

There are no lodgings in the Schoodic section of the park, but within less than a half hour of the Schoodic parkland, you'll have your choice of an impressive range of places to sleep—from an elegant French-style country inn with a fantastic restaurant to a rustic campground with lovely wilderness sites.

INNS
Hancock

Buffered from the highway by a tall hedge, **Le Domaine** (Rte. 1, HC 77, Box 496, Hancock 04640, 207/422-3395 or 800/554-8498, www.ledomaine.com) has gained a five-star reputation for its restaurant, founded in 1946—

long before fine dining had cachet here. But that's only part of the story. Above the restaurant is a charming, five-room, country-French inn. The 80-acre inn property, nine miles east of Ellsworth, is virtual Provence, an oasis transplanted magically to Maine. On the garden-view balconies, or on the lawn out back, you're oblivious to the traffic whizzing by. Better yet, follow the lovely wooded trail to a quiet pond. Three guest rooms ($285 d, modified American plan (MAP), including breakfast and dinner; $200 B&B) and two suites ($370 d, MAP, $285 B&B) all are named after locales in Provence. Continental breakfast, usually including freshly made croissants and jams, can be served in your room or in the dining room. Alert the inn if you'll be arriving after 5:30 P.M., when the staff has to focus on dinner. The ultra-French restaurant is open to the public Tuesday–Sunday 6–9 P.M. Reservations are essential, especially in July and August. Le Domaine's season is early June through mid-October.

Follow Hancock Point Road 4.8 miles south of Route 1 to the three-story, gray-blue **Crocker House Country Inn** (967 Point Rd., HC 77, Box 171, Hancock 04640, 207/422-6806, www.crockerhouse.com), Rich and Liz Malaby's antidote to Bar Harbor's summer traffic. Built as a summer hotel in 1884, the inn underwent rehabbing a century later, but it retains a decidedly old-fashioned air, although Wi-Fi is now available. Eleven rooms (private baths) are $110–165. Breakfast is included. Guests can relax in the common room or reserve spa time in the carriage house. One kayak and a few bicycles are available for guests' use. Nearby are clay tennis courts, quiet walking routes past Hancock Point's elegant seaside "cottages," and a unique octagonal public library. The Malabys will pack picnic lunches (extra charge) for day trips to Campobello Island, Acadia, or Lamoine State Park. If you're arriving by boat, request a mooring. Two dining rooms are open to the public for dinner and Sunday brunch; reservations are essential. The inn is open daily May through October, then weekends in November and December.

BED-AND-BREAKFASTS
Schoodic Peninsula

Overlooking the Gouldsboro Peninsula's only sandy saltwater beach, **◖ Oceanside Meadows Innstitute** (Rte. 195, Corea Rd., P.O. Box 90, Prospect Harbor 04669, 207/963-5557, www.oceaninn.com, $128–198, May–late Oct.) is a jewel of a place on 200 acres with fabulous gardens, wildlife habitat, and walking trails. The elegant 1860s Captain's House has seven attractive rooms, and the 1820 Shaw farmhouse next door has another seven. Each room has a copy of Louise Dickinson Rich's *The Peninsula*—a thoughtful touch. Breakfast is an impressive four-course event, staged by

Oceanside Meadows Innstitute is the centerpiece of a 200-acre property with fabulous gardens, wildlife habitat, a real sand beach, and walking trails.

© TOM NANGLE

the energetic husband-and-wife team of Sonja Sundaram and Ben Walter, who seem to have thought of everything—hot drinks available all day, a guest fridge, beach toys, even detailed guides to the property's trails and habitats (great for entertaining kids). As if all that weren't enough, Sonja and Ben have totally restored the 1820 timber-frame barn out back—creating the **Oceanside Meadows *Inn*stitute for the Arts and Sciences.** Local art hangs on the walls, and from June into September, the 125-seat barn has a full schedule of classical concerts and lectures on natural history, Native American traditions, and more, usually on Thursday nights. Some are free; some require tickets; all require reservations. The inn's website is also a phenomenal resource on area activities. Oceanside Meadows is six miles off Route 1.

Watch lobsterboats unload their catch at the dock opposite **Œ Elsa's Inn on the Harbor** (179 Main St., Prospect Harbor, 207/963-7571, www.elsasinn.com, $105–155). Jeffrey and Cynthia Alley, their daughter Megan, her husband Glenn Moshier, and grandsons Andrew and Emmett have turned Jeff's mother Elsa's home into a warm and welcoming inn. The Alley family roots in the area go back more than 10 generations, so you're guaranteed to receive solid information on where to go and what to do. Every room has an ocean view, and Megan, an experienced innkeeper whose career included positions at Ritz-Carlton and luxury boutique hotels, pampers guests with luxurious linens, down duvets, terry robes, afternoon refreshments, and a hearty hot breakfast. After a day exploring, settle into a rocker on the veranda and gaze over the boat-filled harbor out to Prospect Harbor Light. And afterwards? Well, perhaps a lobster bake. Upon request, Megan's dad will bring over some fresh lobster and Megan will prepare a complete lobster dinner—corn on the cob, coleslaw, homemade rolls, and a seasonal dessert, all for about $22 pp, depending upon market rates.

Newest entry into the region's B&B scene is **Acadia View Bed & Breakfast** (175 Rte. 1, Gouldsboro, 207/963-7457 or 866/963-7457, www.acadiaview.com, $135–155), built on a bluff with views across Frenchman Bay to the peaks of Mount Desert. Pat and Jim Close built the oceanfront house as a B&B, opening it in 2005. The building may be new, but it's filled with antique treasures from the Closes' former life in Connecticut. Each of the four guest rooms has a private deck. The Rte. 1 location, while next to nothing, is convenient for everything.

Off the beaten path is Bob Travers and Barry Canner's **Black Duck Inn on Corea Harbor** (Crowley Island Rd., P.O. Box 39, Corea 04624, 207/963-2689, www.blackduck.com, $104–130, May.–mid-Oct.), literally the end of the line on the Gouldsboro Peninsula. Set on 12 acres in this timeless fishing village, the B&B has four handsomely decorated rooms and plenty of common space. Across the way, perched on the harbor's edge, are two little seasonal cottages, one rented by the day (three-night minimum) and one by the week. The inn and Corea are geared to wanderers, readers, and anyone seeking serenity (who isn't?). Rocky outcrops dot the property and a nature trail meanders to a mill pond; in early August, the blueberries are ready. If the fog socks in, the large parlor has comfortable chairs and loads of books.

Something of a categorical anomaly, **The Bluff House Inn** (Rte. 186, P.O. Box 249, Gouldsboro 04607, 207/963-7805, www.bluffinn.com, $95–135) is part motel, part hotel, part B&B—an apparently successful mix in a contemporary building overlooking Frenchman Bay on the west side of the Gouldsboro Peninsula. Verandas wrap around the first and second floors, so bring binoculars for osprey and bald eagle sightings. Pine walls and flooring give a lodge feeling to the open first floor. Settle by the stone fireplace or grab a seat by the window. Breakfast, a generous continental with excellent baked goodies, is served here. The eight second-floor rooms are decorated "country" fashion, with quilts on the very comfortable beds. (In hot weather, request a corner room.) You can walk or drive to the shore—an excellent place to launch

SCHOODIC PENINSULA

kayaks. Paddle over to Stave Island, where the first ship to round Cape Horn was built. In winter, you can cross-country ski on the owner's 400 acres across the road. Also available is a two-bedroom housekeeping apartment ($165) built above a garage. Open all year.

Hancock, Sullivan, and Sorrento

About 12 miles east of Ellsworth is the ▐ **Island View Inn** (12 Miramar Ave., Sullivan, 207/422-3031, www.maineus.com/islandview, $95–135, late May–mid-Oct.); its name is the height of understatement. Out front are the peaks of Mount Desert, a remarkable panorama. Four of the seven rooms (all private baths and decks) capture the view from this updated 1889 summer home run by Evelyn Joost and her daughter Sarah. The inn evokes the easy elegance of days gone by. The Island View has a private beach, but the water is terminally chilly. Experienced sailors can rent the inn's Rhodes 18 sloop ($45 half day, $74 for the day). Guests have free use of a canoe and a dinghy.

Sustainable living is the focus of Karen and Ed Curtis's peaceful ▐ **Three Pines Bed & Breakfast** (HC 77, Box 349AA, Hancock 04640, 207/460-7595, www.threepinesbandb.com, $85–155, year-round), fronting Sullivan Harbor, just below the Reversing Falls. The quiet, off-the-grid, oceanfront farm faces Sullivan Harbor and is home to llamas, pigs, chickens, and ducks, as well as a large organic garden, berry bushes, a developing orchard, and greenhouses. Photovoltaics provide electricity; appliances are primarily propane-powered; satellite technology operates the phone, TV, and Internet systems. Two inviting guestrooms have private entrances and water views. A full vegetarian breakfast (with fresh eggs from the farm available) is served. Bring kayaks or bikes. You can walk or pedal along an abandoned railway line down to the point or up to the lobster pound, and you can launch your kayak from the back—or is it the front?—yard.

Innkeeper Carolyn Bucklin is determined to create the perfect B&B experience at **Cottage by the Sea** (38 Kilkenny Cove, Hancock, 207/422-6783, www.cottagebytheseamaine.com, $100–125, June 1–mid-Oct.). Top-quality linens, fully equipped rooms (satellite TV, irons and ironing boards, hair dryers, telephones), evening turndown service, and air-conditioning make it hard to tear yourself away from the oceanfront inn. Three rooms are available, one with a view of Kilkenny cove. Breakfast is a multi-course affair; afternoon refreshments are served.

Sorrento is such a low-key place that lots of people don't realize it has a B&B—an ultra-casual homestay-style one at that. **Bass Cove Farm Bed & Breakfast** (312 Eastside Rd., Rte. 185, Sorrento, 207/422-3564, www.basscovefarm.com, $65–100) was opened in 1992 by spinner/weaver/gardener/editor Mary Ann Solet and her husband, Michael Tansey, a group-home supervisor whose résumé also includes the Harry S. Truman Manure Pitchoff Championship at the annual Common Ground Country Fair. The 1840s-era farmhouse uses solar-heated water; the cleaning is done with nontoxic products. Mary Ann can rattle off dozens of ideas for exploring the area, particularly in the craft department, and she raids her extensive vegetable garden daily to produce a hearty, healthful breakfast. Guest rooms have quilt-covered beds and other homey touches—some share baths. A one-bedroom apartment on the second floor rents for $350–375 a week.

MOTEL AND COTTAGES
Schoodic Peninsula

Next to their Black Duck Inn, Barry Canner and Bob Travers operate **Black Duck Properties** (Crowley Island Road, P.O. Box 39, Corea 04624, 207/963-2689 or 877/963-2689, www.blackduck.com), handling both home sales and seasonal rentals. Corea is the primary focus, with harborfront cottages a specialty, but they can suggest suitable spots in Winter Harbor, Gouldsboro, and Prospect Harbor. Most of the rentals forbid smoking. Weekly rental range is $600–1,500, with $800 being a fairly typical rate.

Roger and Pearl Barto, whose family roots in this region go back five generations, have four rental accommodations on their Henry's Cove oceanfront property, **Main Stay Cottages** (66 Sargent St., P.O. Box 459, Winter Harbor 04693, 207/963-2601, www.awaweb.com/stayinn, $90–115). Most unusual is the small, one-bedroom Boat House, which has stood since the 1880s. It hangs over the harbor, with views to Mark Island Light, and you can hear the water gurgling below you at high tide. Other options include a very comfortable efficiency cottage, a one-bedroom cottage, and a second-floor suite, with private entrance, in the main house. All have big decks and fabulous views over the lobsterboat-filled harbor; watch for the eagles that frequently soar overhead. Main Stay is on the Island Explorer bus route and just a short walk from where the Bar Harbor Ferry docks.

The rustic **Pines** (17 Main St., Rte. 186, Winter Harbor, 207/963-2296, www.ayuh.net, $55–70) comprises a mix of motel-style rooms and efficiencies and small cabins. The overall property could use some attention (it's for sale, and the snack bar hasn't been open in years), but the rooms are clean, and the location at the entrance to the Schoodic Loop road is primo, especially for those wanting to bicycle. Owner Marshall Rust runs a *very* laid-back operation: prospective guests are welcome to tour open rooms, choose one, and cross it off on a door sign that promises he'll catch up with you later; those with reservations are told how to find their room.

Also rustic and in need of serious attention, but charming in a sweet, old-fashioned way are **Albee's Cottages** (Rte. 186, Prospect Harbor, 207/963-2336 or 800/963-2336, www.theshorehouse.com, $69–106/night or $455–715/week, May–mid-Oct.), a cluster of 10 somewhat ramshackle cottages, decorated with braided rugs, fresh flowers, and other homey touches. Two things make this place special: the waterfront location—and it's truly waterfront; many of the cottages are just a couple of feet from the high tide mark—and the management. Owner Richard Rieth and manager Larry Caldwell go out of their way

to make guests feel welcome. Pick up lobsters and tell them what time you want dinner, and they'll cook them and deliver them to your cottage. Larry, a former chef, sometimes brings home-baked sweets and other treats to cottages, when he has the time and inclination. In peak season, cottages rent on a Saturday to Saturday basis, but occasionally shorter rentals are available. Dogs are allowed.

Sullivan

Set back from the highway 12 miles east of Ellsworth, **Sullivan Harbor Farm** (Rte. 1, P.O. Box 96, Sullivan 04664, 207/422-3735 or 800/422-4014, www.sullivanharborfarm.com) is a beautifully sited property with spectacular sea and mountain views. (The word "farm" is a bit misleading—it's a long way from agriculture.) Across the road from a quiet cove, the driveway curves through two giant outcrops higher than a car—great lookout points for watching the passing scene. Three whimsically named cottages are available by the week ($885–1,450, with three-night stays possible after Labor Day). The two-bedroom Cupcake cottage and three-bedroom Guzzle have phones and cable TV; one-bedroom Milo does not (bring a cell phone and you're all set, or use the phone in the main house). All are comfortably and attractively outfitted (views of Frenchman Bay from Guzzle and Cupcake). Ask owners Joel Frantzman and Leslie Harlow to steer you toward their favorite ponds and hiking trails—they'll even lend you a canoe or kayak. Or just hang out in the peaceful backyard or visit their spotless **Sullivan Harbor Smokehouse** and ship your pals some fantastic cold-smoked salmon (they also do hot-smoked salmon, not to mention fabulous salmon pâté). Sullivan Harbor's product has become the salmon *du jour* for some of the biggest-name restaurants and high-end provisioners in New England and beyond. Leslie's whimsical metal sculptures elevate the concept of "lawn art," and she accepts commissions under the name of Heezy How's Sculptures.

The closer you get to the water's edge, the

better the accommodations are at **Flander's Bay Cabins** (22 Harbor View Drive/Rte. 1, Sullivan, 207/422-6408, www.acadia.net/flandersbay). Skip the overnight cabins. Nicer are the cottages and two-bedroom cabins ($525–650 per week). Even better is a three-bedroom chalet ($895). Best is the ocean-front three- to four-bedroom house ($1,650). There's on-site access for kayaks and canoes as well as fishing and swimming. This property is adjacent to and run by the same family as Mountainview Campground.

CAMPGROUNDS
Schoodic Peninsula

On a wooded finger of land projecting eastward from the Schoodic Peninsula, **Ocean Wood Campground** (P.O. Box 111, Birch Harbor 04613, 207/963-7194, early May–late Oct.) gets kudos for eco-sensitivity, noise control, and 17 fantastic wilderness sites, most on the ocean. Don't expect frills; nature provides the entertainment. The 70 campsites (20 with hookups) are $22–33, depending on location and services. Pets (leashed) and guests are allowed at regular sites, but not at the wilderness ones. No credit cards; free hot showers. The campground is a terrific base for exploring the Schoodic section of Acadia National Park. (Note, however, that the campground is at the *end* of the one-way Schoodic Loop Road. No problem hiking back into the park area the wrong way, but if you're driving or biking, you'll need to go around, about five miles, via Route 186, to do the loop.)

Sullivan

Sites at **Mountainview Campground** (22 Harbor View Drive/Rte. 1, Sullivan, 207/422-6408, www.acadia.net/flandersbay) are spread throughout an oceanfront field, so there's not

a lot of privacy here. The best sites edge the Frenchman Bay shorefront and are reserved for tents ($23) and small campers ($27 with 20 amp service). Other sites begin at $20 and range to $30 for a full hookup with 30 amp service. Hot showers are free, and if you stay six days, your seventh day is free. There's also an antiques shop on the premises.

Donnell Pond Public Reserved Land

A handful of authorized, primitive campsites can be found on Tunk Lake (southwestern corner) and Donnell Pond (at Schoodic Beach and Redman's Beach), all accessible by foot or boat. Each has a table, fire ring, and nearby pit toilet. Many of the sites are lakefront. All are first-come, first-served (no fees or permits required) and are snapped up quickly on midsummer weekends. You can camp elsewhere within the unit, excepting Day Use areas, but fires are not permitted on unauthorized sites.

Steuben

Since 1958, the Ayr family has opened its quiet, well-off-the-beaten-path property on Joy Cove to campers. With a convenient location 15 minutes from Petit Manan National Wildlife Refuge and 20 minutes from Schoodic Point, **Mainayr Campground** (321 Village Rd., Steuben, 207/542-2690, www.mainayr.com, late May–mid-Oct.) has 35 tenting and RV sites (five with full hookups), which go for $18.25 for two people; utility connections and waterfront sites are higher. Also on the premises are a playground, laundry, beach for tidal swimming, clamming flats, grassy launch area for kayaks and canoes, camp store, berries for picking, and fresh lobsters. If that's not enough, David Ayr enjoys regaling campers with stories.

Food

LOCAL FLAVORS

There's no food in the park's Schoodic section, so if you're planning a picnic, you'll need to stock up along the way—in Winter Harbor or Prospect Harbor—if you haven't done so earlier.

Make a point to attend one of the many **public suppers** held throughout the summer in this area and so many other rural corners of Maine. Typically benefiting a worthy cause, these usually feature beans or spaghetti or the serendipity of potluck. Everyone saves room for the homemade pies. Notices of such suppers are usually posted on public bulletin boards in country stores and in libraries, on signs in front of churches, and at other places people gather. Local newspapers also often detail such events.

Hancock

Nicole Purslow, former owner of the renowned Le Domaine, opened **Mano's** (1517 Rte. 1, Hancock, 207/422-6500, 10 A.M.–6 P.M. Mon.–Sat.), a gourmet and prepared foods and wine market, shortly before selling the inn. The wine selection is extensive and well chosen, and if you have cooking facilities at your accommodations, you can't miss with the prepared foods selection. The crab cakes and chicken Provençal are both fabulous. Sandwiches and a soup usually are available, as are cheeses, crackers, baguettes, pastas, and much more.

COUNTRY STORES

By definition, old-fashioned country stores are eclectic sources of local color, last-minute items, and plenty of answers to your questions. Some good examples are right in this area.

Schoodic Peninsula

Once a true, old-fashioned country store with a classic traditional soda fountain and penny candy, **J. M. Gerrish Provisions** (352 Main St., Winter Harbor, 207/963-2727, 8 A.M.–5 P.M.), known as Gerrish's Store, has changed since coming under the new ownership. It's now an upscale specialty foods store, coffee bar with Wi-Fi, and deli that also sells prepared foods—pick up dinner and take it back to your cottage. You can still get ice cream, but the penny candy selection is tiny (and a far cry from a penny). Fresh-baked goodies, such as scones and muffins, and fancy coffees are available all day long; soups, salads, and fancy sandwiches ($4–6) are served 11 A.M.–3 P.M. All this may change, as it's for sale again (sigh).

In "downtown" Prospect Harbor is the best picnic solution in the area. The **Downeast Deli** (corner Routes 186 and 195, Prospect Harbor, 207/963-2700, 10 A.M.–8 P.M. Sun.–Thurs., to 9 P.M. Fri. and Sat.) will fix you right up with dozens of sandwich choices: hot or cold hoagies, hot dogs and burgers, Reubens, deli-style sandwiches, and good pizza with a wide array of mix-and-match choices (try a New York white or a pesto pizza). The desserts are homemade. Service is swift. Take it with you or head upstairs and grab a window table and enjoy the harbor views.

Route 1

Lots of people stop at **Dunbar's Store** (Rte. 1, Sullivan, 207/422-6844) just to admire the view—although in recent years it's become harder and harder to see above the trees. Then they go inside the old-fashioned market and almost always manage to make a purchase—maybe compensation of sorts for the scenery. Some even offer to buy the place. More of a grocery store and a gossip center than a fast-food source, Dunbar's is open 8 A.M.–9 P.M. Mon.–Sat. and 9 A.M.–6 P.M. Sunday, all year.

Farther east on Route 1, in a new building that replaced a half-century-old country store, **Young's Market** (130 Rte. 1, Gouldsboro, 207/963-7774) also has a fabulous view—along with pizza, gasoline, ATM, fishing gear and bait, auto parts, and more. It's open 5 A.M.–9 P.M. daily, all year.

SCHOODIC PENINSULA

CASUAL DINING
Schoodic Peninsula

Make it a point to find 🄲 **Bunkers Wharf** (260 E. Schoodic Dr., Birch Harbor, 207/963-2244, 11:30 A.M.–10 P.M. Mon.–Sat., brunch 10 A.M.–3 P.M. Sun.), located just one mile from the end of the Schoodic loop. The dining room overlooks a working wharf, and there's a big stone fireplace to ward off the chill on inclement days. Crisp white linens and fresh flowers add a formal touch in the dining room, yet the feeling is unpretentious. You can also dine in the pub or on a patio that's practically in the harbor. Dinner entrees are $17 and up.

You can't miss **Mama's Boy Bistro** (10 Main St., Winter Harbor, 207/963-2365, noon–2 P.M. and 5 P.M.–close Tues.–Sat. and 10 A.M.–2 P.M. and 5 P.M.–close Sun., May–mid-Oct.), which dominates the waterfront and, depending on your point of view, is either a charming New England–style building or a New York–influenced monstrosity. Whatever. The original restaurant closed, and in 2005 it came into the skilled hands of mega-successful Bar Harbor restaurateur Michael Boland, with good results. He's toned down prices (although much of the menu is à la carte; entrees are $14–26), added lunch, and is committed to working with local growers, especially organic farms. There's live music on Friday nights and a jazz brunch on Sundays. The dining area centers on a huge open kitchen, and it can be very noisy, but renovations are planned to tone down the noise and improve the overall experience.

You can also pick up veggies, meats, eggs, cheeses, and handcrafted fiber products as well as jams, preserves, and baked goods at the **Winter Harbor Farmers Market** in the Mama's Boy Bistro parking lot (corner Newman St. and Rte. 186, Winter Harbor, 9 A.M.–noon Tues., late June–early Sept.).

The Fisherman's Inn (7 Newman St., Rte. 186, Winter Harbor, 207/963-5585, www.fishermansinnrestaurant.com, open for dinner (5–9 P.M.) daily, Memorial Day to mid-October, and for lunch (11:30 A.M.–2 P.M. in summer), established in 1947, has had a roller-coaster history, with good phases and bad ones. It's now under the ownership of Kathy Johnson and her award-winning chef/husband, Carl. The only remaining tradition seems to be the "gourmet cheese spread" served to every table—but you'll also have a sample of salmon pâté from Carl's latest venture, Grindstone Neck of Maine. As is probably obvious, seafood is the specialty here, and there's a good chance that the guy at the neighboring booth caught your lobster or fish. Asian influences are evident, too. Entree range is $14–25, although some dishes can top that given seasonal market rates. One caveat: service is unpredictable.

Hancock

It's easy to miss **Chipper's** (Rte. 1, Hancock, 207/422-8238, 5–9 P.M.), a simple cape-style building hard by (close to) Route 1, but missing it would be a mistake. Chip definitely knows his way around the kitchen. The wide-ranging menu includes rack of lamb, but the emphasis is on seafood; the crab cakes get rave reviews. Entrees are in the $15–25 range.

FAMILY FRIENDLY
Schoodic Peninsula

Best place for grub and gossip in Winter Harbor is **Chase's Restaurant** (193 Main St., Winter Harbor, 207/963-7171, 6 A.M.–9 P.M.), a seasoned, no-frills booth-and-counter operation that turns out first-rate fish chowder, fries, and onion rings, a surprising vegetarian lasagna, and downright cheap breakfasts. No credit cards.

Hancock and Sullivan

Don't be put off by the lobster "sculpture" outside **Ruth & Wimpy's Kitchen** (792 Rte. 1, Hancock, 207/422-3723, 11 A.M.–9 P.M. Apr.–Dec.); you'll probably see a crowd as well. This family-fare standby serves hefty sandwiches, about two dozen lobster dishes, pizza, pasta, and steak. Prices begin at less than $3 for a cheeseburger and climb to about $25 for a twin-tail lobster dinner. Antique license plates and collections of miniature cars and trucks accent the interior. It's five miles east of Ellsworth, close to the Hancock Point turnoff.

Good food served by friendly folks is what pulls the locals into **Chester Pike's Galley** (2336 Rte. 1, Sullivan, 207/422-8200, 6 A.M.–2 P.M. Mon.–Sat., opens at 7 A.M. Sunday). The prices are low and the portions big. If you're on a diet, don't even *look* at the glass case filled with fresh-baked pies, cakes, and cookies. It's also open Friday nights for a fish fry with free seconds.

Steuben

If you're heading out to Petit Manan Wildlife Refuge, trust me on this. Ignore the exterior and venture into (**Country Charm** (336 Village Rd., Steuben, 207/546-3763, 6 A.M.–8 P.M. Tues.–Sun., until 2 P.M. Mon.). The fried fish is fabulously fresh, crispy, light, and cheap, even by local standards. You easily can get out of here for less than $10 pp, far less if you're on a tight budget. The original dining room has, well, country charm (sit here if you want to listen in on the local gossip); the newer ones (added when a real kitchen replaced the original blue trailer) are purely functional. Don't be shy about arriving early for breakfast; coffee's on by 5:30 A.M., even though the kitchen doesn't open until 6. Hungry? Order the Charm Special: two eggs, bacon, sausages, pancakes, toast, and coffee all for a whopping $4.50; omelettes begin at $2.25.

Even less fancy is **Port Side Snack Bar** (Rte. 1, Steuben, 207/546-7676, 10 A.M.–8 P.M.). Fried seafood, burgers, chowders, pizza, and subs; everything's made from scratch.

FINE DINING
Hancock

The ultra-French restaurant (**Le Domaine** (1515 Rte. 1, P.O. Box 519, Hancock, 207/422-3395 or 800/544-8498, www.ledomaine.com) has gained a five-star reputation. Although ownership changed in 2005, the same crew is in the kitchen and the menu remains trés French. The restaurant is equally renowned for its 5,000-bottle wine cellar and lovely Provençal decor. It's open to the public Tues.–Sun. 6–9 P.M., mid-June–mid-Oct. Reservations are essential, especially in July and August. The tab may dent your budget (entrees are $22–30), but stack that up against plane fare to France. Le Domaine's season is early June through November.

Crocker House Country Inn (967 Point Rd., Hancock Point, 207/422-6806, www.crockerhouse.com) has two unpretentious dining rooms open to the public for dinner (5:30–9 P.M.; entrees $22–30) and Sunday brunch (11 A.M.–2 P.M.); reservations are essential. The inn is open daily May 1–Oct. 31, then Thurs.–Sun. in April, November, and December.

LOBSTER-IN-THE-ROUGH
Schoodic Peninsula

In downtown Winter Harbor is **Suspended Fisheries** (154 Newman St./Rte. 186, Winter Harbor, 207/963-5847), a roadside trailer where Brenda Torrey cooks fresh lobsters caught by her husband, Capt. Larry Torrey (Thurs.–Tues. 10 A.M.–6 P.M., Wed. 3–6 P.M.). Price is market plus $1 per pound for cooking. There are a few picnic tables on-site, but why not take the lobstahs to the Frazier Point Picnic Area in the park or back to your cottage? If you don't want to hang around while Brenda fires up the stove and cooks the critters, call your order in about a half hour before you plan to pick them up. Cold, hard cash only; no credit cards, no checks.

Hancock

Thank the Ellsworth-based Frenchman Bay Conservancy for buying the four-acre **Tidal Falls Preserve** (off Eastside Road, Hancock), overlooking Frenchman Bay's only reversing falls (roiling water when the tide turns), and opening it to public access. When a half-century-old lobster pound went on the market a few years ago, the conservancy hastened into action, raised more than half a million dollars, and purchased the property. Today, a dozen picnic tables on the lawn overlook the falls, and seals often haul out on nearby ledges. There's also a screened-in dining pavilion and free Wi-Fi. It's an idyllic spot. In summer (**Tidal Falls Lobster Pound** (off Eastside Rd.,

Hancock, 207/422-6457, 5 p.m.–9 p.m. daily and noon–9 p.m. Thurs.–Sun. June 21–Labor Day) leases the site. Come for the lobster (market price), but landlubbers will find New York sirloin ($16.95) and kids can order hot dogs ($2.50). Skip the overpriced, embarrassingly skimpy salad ($3.95). Order at the window, then grab a seat. BYOL. Eastside Road is off Route 1 (on your right, if you're heading north) just south of the Hancock-Sullivan bridge; follow it one mile and look for a sign on your left. Follow the gravel road to the end.

Information and Services

ACADIA NATIONAL PARK

Information about Acadia National Park on the Schoodic Peninsula is available on Mount Desert Island at the park's **Hulls Cove Visitor Center** and at the **Thompson Island Visitor Center,** at the head of the island.

To plan ahead, see the Acadia website (www.nps.gov/acad/), where you can download a Schoodic map. To see the Island Explorer bus schedule for Schoodic as well as all of Mount Desert Island, log on to www.explore-acadia.com. The Bar Harbor Ferry schedule is at www.barharborferry.com.

REGIONAL INFORMATION

For advance information about Eastern Hancock County, contact the **Schoodic Peninsula Chamber of Commerce** (P.O. Box 381, Winter Harbor 04693, 207/963-7658, www .acadia-schoodic.org) and request its handy map and brochure, revised annually.

Another source for advance information is **Downeast & Acadia Regional Tourism** (394 S. Gouldsboro Rd., Gouldsboro, 207/963-7283 or 800/231-3008, www.downeastacadia.com).

The nearest convenient **information center** is run by the Ellsworth Area Chamber of Commerce (P.O. Box 267, Ellsworth 04605, 207/667-5584, www.ellsworthchamber.org), on the Route 1/3 commercial strip, close to where the highway forks toward Mount Desert Island and Eastern Hancock County. It's open daily in July and August; Mon.–Sat. from mid-June to mid-September;

and weekdays 9 a.m.–4:30 p.m. the rest of the year.

For information on the National and Maine Scenic Byways in this region, visit www.byways.org or www.exploremaine.org/byways/.

LIBRARIES

The **Dorcas Library** (Rte. 186, Prospect Harbor, 207/963-4027) is open 4–8 p.m. Monday, 1:30–4 p.m. and 6–8 p.m. Wednesday, 1:30–4 p.m. Saturday. In July and August, the library also is open 10 a.m.–noon on Saturday.

The **Winter Harbor Public Library** (18 Chapel Ln., Winter Harbor, 207/963-7556) is open 1:30–4 p.m. Wednesday, Friday, and Saturday, also 6–8 p.m. Wednesday.

The inviting octagonal **Hancock Point Library** (207/422-6400, summer only, call for hours) was formed in 1899. More than a library, it's a center for village activities. Check the bulletin boards by the entrance to find out what's happening when.

GETTING THERE AND AROUND

Although you can get here by passenger ferry from Bar Harbor or bus from Ellsworth, you'll need a car to explore beyond the Schoodic Peninsula that's served by the Island Explorer bus.

By Car

To reach the Schoodic Region from Ellsworth, continue north on Route 1 from where it splits

SCENIC BYWAYS

This region boasts not one, but two designated scenic byways, the **Schoodic National Scenic Byway,** which wraps around the peninsula, and the **State Route 182 Scenic Byway,** an inland blue highway cutting through the Donnell Pond Public Reserved Lands. If time permits, drive at least one of these two routes. Ideally, you'll do both, because the scenery differs greatly. Best idea yet: Connect the two via Route 1, creating a route that includes lakes and forests, mountains and fields, ocean and rocky coast. If you only have one day to explore this region, this takes in the best of it. In early to mid-October, when the foliage is at its peak, the vistas are especially stunning.

The 29-mile Schoodic National Scenic Byway stretches from Sullivan on Route 1 to Gouldsboro and then southward on Route 186 and around the Schoodic Peninsula, ending in Prospect Harbor. A detailed guide is available online at www.schoodicbyway.org. Other information is available at www.byways.org.

The 12.5-mile State Route 182 Scenic Byway meanders inland of Route 1, from Franklin to Cherryfield, edging lakes and passing through small villages. You'll find access to trailheads and boat launches at Donnell Pond and Tunk Lake. Although Cherryfield is beyond the Schoodic Region, it's a beautiful town to visit, filled with stately Victorian homes, and it's also the self-proclaimed Wild Blueberry Capital of the World. Maps and information are available from www.exploremaine.com or www.maine.gov/mdot/stage.

entrance sign, just before the stone-lined causeway over Mosquito Harbor.

To reach the park boundary from Bar Harbor, take Route 3 northward to the head of Mount Desert Island, then across Mount Desert Narrows to Trenton. The usual route is to continue to a congested intersection at the edge of Ellsworth, where you'll pick up Route 1 North (turn right) and continue as above. But, you can avoid some of the traffic congestion on Route 3 in Trenton by ducking east via Route 204 toward Lamoine and its state park and then back up to Route 1 via the Mud Creek Road.

By Passenger Ferry

The **Bar Harbor Ferry** (207/288-2984, www.barharborferry.com, round-trip $27.50/adult, $17.50/child, $6.50/bike), owned by Captain Steve Pagels (who also operates the four-masted schooner *Margaret Todd* and ferry service to the Cranberry Isles), runs his Bar Harbor-to-Winter Harbor passenger-only ferry throughout the year (reduced service off-season). You can board the ferry with a bike in Bar Harbor (at the Bar Harbor Inn Pier), disembark in Winter Harbor (at Winter Harbor Marine, on Sargent St.), pedal the short distance to Schoodic, then bike the Schoodic Loop Road, and return later to Bar Harbor on the ferry (last boat is 5 P.M.). The ferry departs Bar Harbor every two hours, beginning at 8 A.M., hourly in peak season 8 A.M.–6 P.M., and departs Winter Harbor every two hours, hourly in peak season, 7 A.M.–5 P.M., although a few tweaks in the schedule are planned, so it's best to call before showing up. The free **Island Explorer** bus meets the ferry, late June to mid-October on either end.

Since the ferry's summer schedule is coordinated with the Island Explorer bus's summertime Schoodic route, you can board the ferry in Bar Harbor, pick up the bus at the dock in Winter Harbor, and be shuttled along the Schoodic Loop. Stop where you like for a picnic, then board a later bus. Take the last bus back to the ferry and return to Bar Harbor. A super car-free excursion!

with Route 3. Stay on Route 1 about 16 miles (through Hancock and Sullivan) until you reach Gouldsboro. From Route 1 in Gouldsboro, the park entrance is eight miles. Take Route 186 south to Winter Harbor. Continue through town, heading east, then turn right onto Moore Road and continue to the park-

SCHOODIC PENINSULA

Hancock Point is an idyllic summer colony with its own yacht club.

© TOM NANGLE

By Bus

Vermont Transit (800/522-8737, www.vermonttransit.com) operates one round-trip daily between Bar Harbor and Bangor, via Ellsworth, and connecting with Portland, Boston, and New York City. From Bar Harbor, take the ferry to Winter Harbor. From Ellsworth, connect with **West Bus Service** (207/546-2823 or 800/596-2823, www.westbusservice.com), which provides daily service between Bangor and Calais, with a scheduled stop in Ellsworth and flag stops in Hancock, Sullivan, and Gouldsboro. You can get around Winter Harbor and through the park on the free **Island Explorer** bus, which meets the ferry late June to mid-October.

The free **Island Explorer** covers the lower part of the peninsula, from Winter Harbor through Prospect Harbor, on its hourly route.

BLUE HILL PENINSULA

The Blue Hill Peninsula, once dubbed "The Fertile Crescent," is unique. Few other Maine locales harbor such a high concentration of artisans, musicians, and on-their-feet retirees juxtaposed with top-flight wooden boat builders, lobstermen, and umpteenth-generation Mainers. Perhaps surprisingly, the mix seems to work.

Anchored by the towns of Bucksport to the west and Ellsworth to the east, the peninsula comprises several enclaves with markedly distinctive personalities. Blue Hill, Castine, Orland, Brooklin, Brooksville, and Sedgwick are stitched together by a network of narrow, winding country roads. Thanks to the mapmaker-challenging coastline and a handful of freshwater ponds and rivers, there's a view of water around nearly every bend.

You can watch the sun set from atop Blue Hill Mountain; tour the home of the fascinating Jonathan Fisher; stroll through the village of Castine (charming verging on precious), whose streets are lined with dowager-like homes; visit *WoodenBoat* magazine's world headquarters in tiny Brooklin; and browse top-notch studios and galleries throughout the peninsula. Venture a bit inland of Route 1, and you'll find lovely lakes for paddling and swimming and another hill to hike.

The peninsula is home to some of Maine's finest traditional inns and lodges and a surprising number of excellent restaurants.

PLANNING YOUR TIME

Bucksport really isn't considered part of the Blue Hill peninsula, but there are some sights here worth visiting, and you'll find reasonably

© TOM NANGLE

HIGHLIGHTS

◖ **Fort Knox:** Ongoing restoration, frequent events, and secret passages to explore make this late 19th-century fort one of Maine's best (page 156).

◖ **Parson Fisher House:** More than just another historic house, the Parson Fisher House is a remarkable testimony to one man's ingenuity (page 161).

◖ **Blue Hill Mountain Trail:** It's a relatively easy hike for fabulous 360-degree views from the summit of Blue Hill Mountain (page 162).

◖ **The Good Life Center:** Remember the back-to-the-land movement of the 1960s? Refresh that memory and learn how to live a sustainable life, as did founders Helen and Scott Nearing (page 171).

◖ **Four Season Farm:** Internationally renowned organic gardeners Eliot Coleman and

Barbara Damrosch have reopened their fabulous farmstand and farm (page 171).

◖ **Holbrook Island Sanctuary State Park:** Varied hiking trails and great birding are the rewards for finding this off-the-beaten-path preserve (page 172).

◖ **Flash in the Pans Community Steel Band:** Close your eyes, and you might think you're on a Caribbean island rather than in Maine when you hear this phenomenal steel pan band (page 174).

◖ **Castine Historic Tour:** A turbulent history detailed on signs throughout town make Castine an irresistible place to tour on foot or bike (page 180).

◖ **Sea Kayaking:** Hook up with "Kayak Karen" in Castine for a tour (page 183).

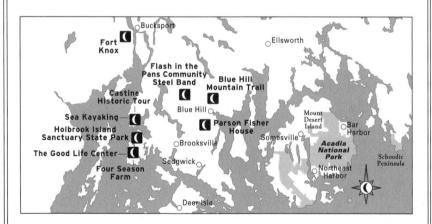

LOOK FOR ◖ TO FIND RECOMMENDED SIGHTS, ACTIVITIES, DINING, AND LODGING.

priced lodging and campsites in the area. Route 1 east of Bucksport leads to Orland, whose idyllic setting on the banks of the Narramissic River makes it a magnet for shutterbugs. It's also the site of a unique service organization called H.O.M.E. (Homeworkers Organized for More Employment). East Orland (officially part of Orland) claims the Craig Brook National Fish Hatchery and Great Pond Mountain (you can't

miss it, jutting from the landscape on the left as you drive east on Route 1).

Twelve miles south of Route 1 is the hub of the peninsula, **Blue Hill** (pop. 2,390), exuding charm from its handsome old homes to its waterfront setting to the shops, restaurants, and galleries that boost its appeal.

The towns of **Brooklin, Brooksville, and Sedgwick,** near the bottom of the Blue Hill

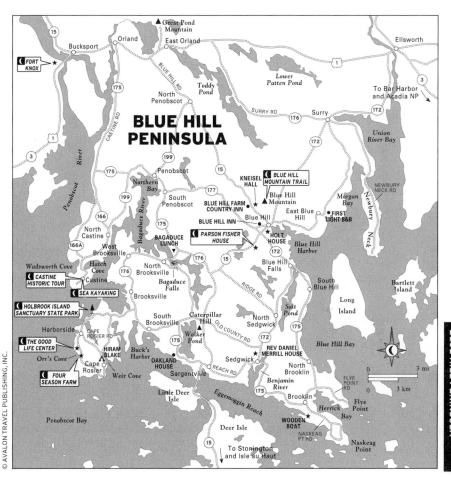

Peninsula, offer hiking, kayaking, and sailing, historic homes, unique shops and galleries, plus accommodations.

If you're staying in Blue Hill—or even Bar Harbor—spend a day in **Castine,** a National Historic Register enclave that many people never find. What visitors discover is a year-round community with a busy waterfront, an easy-to-conquer layout, a handful of traditional inns and boutiques, wooded trails on the outskirts of town, an astonishing collection of splendid Georgian and Federalist architecture, and water views from nearly every which way you turn.

Bucksport Area

Working hard and well to gentrify its longtime rough-and-ready river-port image, Bucksport changes even as you watch. Long dominated by a giant International Paper mill, Bucksport has in recent years striven to become more than a mill town—and it's succeeding. New businesses have arrived, a marina has been built, and the local newspaper has improved communications and sparked community spirit.

Bucksport is no upstart. Native Americans first gravitated to these Penobscot River shores in summers, finding here a rich source of salmon for food and grasses for basketmaking. In 1764, it was officially settled by Colonel Jonathan Buck, a Massachusetts Bay Colony surveyor who modestly named it Buckstown and organized a booming shipping business here. His remains are interred in a local cemetery, where his tombstone bears the distinct outline of a woman's leg; this is allegedly the result of a curse by a witch Buck ordered executed, but in fact it's probably a flaw in the granite. Most townsfolk prefer not to discuss the matter, but the myth refuses to die—and it has immortalized a man whose name might otherwise have been consigned to musty history books. (The monument is across Route 1 from the Hannaford supermarket, on the corner of Hinks Street; a sign tells the tale, and a new sidewalk has improved access and visibility.)

Papermaking came to Bucksport in 1930, and the International Paper mill on Indian Point still dominates the riverfront.

Just south of Bucksport, at the bend in the Penobscot River, Verona Island is best known as the mile-long link between Prospect and Bucksport. Just before you cross the bridge from Verona to Bucksport, hang a left, then a quick right to a small municipal park with a boat launch and broad views of Bucksport Harbor (and the paper mill). In the Buck Memorial Library is a scale model of Admiral Robert Peary's Arctic exploration vessel, the *Roosevelt,* built on this site.

SIGHTS
⚔ Fort Knox
Looming over Bucksport Harbor, the *other* Fort Knox (Rte. 174, Prospect, 207/469-7719, www.fortknox.maineguide.com, 9 A.M.–sunset, May 1–Nov. 1, $3 adults, $1 children 5–11) is a 125-acre state historic site, just off Route 1. Named for Major General Henry Knox, George Washington's first secretary of war, the sprawling granite fort was begun in 1844. Built to protect the upper Penobscot River from attack, it was never finished and never saw battle. Still, it was, as guide Kathy Williamson said: "very well thought out and planned, and that may have been its best defense." Begin your visit at the Visitor and Education Center, operated by the Friends of Fort Knox, a nonprofit group that has partnered with the state to preserve and interpret the fort. Guided tours are available from Memorial Day through Labor Day and are well worth it, as guides point out some of the fort's distinguishing features, including two complete Rodman canons. In 2004, restoration of the Fort Knox Officers' Quarters was completed. Wear rubberized shoes and bring a flashlight

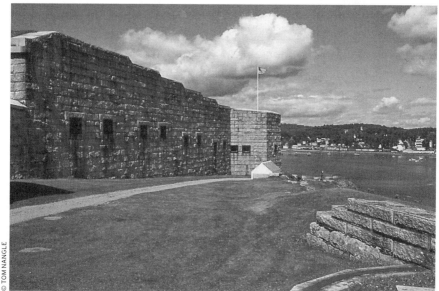

Construction on Fort Knox began in 1844, but the sprawling granite fort on the banks of the Penobscot River was never finished.

to explore the underground passages; you can set the kids loose. Bring a picnic; views over the river to Bucksport are fabulous. An observatory is planned for the top of the 420-foot high west tower of the new bridge spanning the Penobscot River. It will be open to the public via Fort Knox. Civil War reenactments occur here several times a summer (check with the chamber of commerce). The Halloween Fright at the Fort is a ghoulish event for the brave. The grounds are accessible all year.

Alamo Theatre

Phoenixlike, the 1916 Alamo Theatre (85 Main St., Bucksport, 207/469-0924 or 800/639-1636, event line 207/469-6910, www.alamo-theatre.org) has been retrofitted for a new life—focusing on films about New England produced and/or revived by the unique Northeast Historic Film (NHF), which is headquartered here. Stop in, survey the restoration, visit the displays (donation requested), and browse the Alamo Theatre Store for antique postcards, T-shirts, toys, and reasonably priced videos

on ice harvesting, lumberjacks, maple sugaring, and other traditional New England topics. One-half mile west of Route 1, it's open 9 A.M.–4 P.M. weekdays all year. The Alamo has also become an active cinema, screening classic and current films regularly in the 120-seat theater, usually weekends. Tickets are $6. Each summer there's also a silent film festival.

H.O.M.E.

Adjacent to the flashing light on Route 1 in Orland, H.O.M.E. is tough to categorize. Linked with the international Emmaus Movement founded by a French priest, H.O.M.E. (Homeworkers Organized for More Employment) was started in 1970 by Lucy Poulin, still the guiding force, and two nuns at a nearby convent. The quasi-religious organization shelters refugees and the homeless, operates a soup kitchen and a car-repair service, runs a day-care center, and teaches work skills in a variety of hands-on cooperative programs. Seventy percent of its income comes from sales of crafts, produce, and services. At the Route 1 store (corner of Upper Falls Rd.; open 9 A.M.– 4:30 P.M. daily), you can buy handmade quilts, organic produce, maple syrup, and jams—and support a worthwhile effort. You can also tour the crafts workshops on the property. To volunteer time in the workshops, store, or learning center, write P.O. Box 10, Orland 04472, or call 207/469-7961.

RECREATION
Great Pond Mountain Trail

- Distance: 1.8 miles round-trip
- Duration: 2 hours
- Elevation Gain: 500 feet
- Effort: easy to moderate
- Trailhead: 1 mile north of Craig Brook National Fish Hatchery on Hatchery Rd., East Orland

Great Pond Mountain's biggest asset is its 1,038-foot summit, with 360-degree views and lots of space for panoramic picnics. On a clear day, Baxter State Park's Katahdin is visible from Great Pond Mountain's north side. In fall, watch for migrating hawks. Access to the mountain is via gated private property beginning about a mile north of the hatchery parking area. Roadside parking is available near the trailhead, but during fall-foliage season, you may need to park at the hatchery. Pick up a brochure from the box at the trailhead, stay on the trail, and respect the surrounding private property. The **Great Pond Mountain Conservation Trust** (P.O. Box 266, Orland 04472, 207/469-6772) acts as conscientious local steward for Great Pond Mountain and surrounding wild lands. It also hosts hikes and other activities.

Craig Brook National Fish Hatchery

For a day of hiking, picnicking, swimming, canoeing, and a bit of natural history, pack a lunch and head for 135-acre Craig Brook National Fish Hatchery (306 Hatchery Rd., East Orland, 207/469-2803), on Alamoosook Lake. Turn off Route 1 six miles east of Bucksport and continue 1.4 miles north to the parking area just above the visitors center (open 8 A.M.– 3:30 P.M. weekdays and most weekends in summer, no charge), with interactive displays on Atlantic salmon (don't miss the downstairs viewing area). Maps and a restroom are available here. The grounds are accessible all year, 6 A.M. to sunset daily. Established in 1871, the U.S. Fish and Wildlife Service hatchery raises sea-run Atlantic salmon for stocking seven Maine rivers, and each river has a different strain, so they're kept separate. The birch-lined shorefront has picnic tables, a boat-launching ramp, Atlantic salmon display pool, additional parking, and a spectacular cross-lake view. Watch for eagles, osprey, and loons. Also on the premises is the small **Atlantic Salmon Museum**, operated by the Friends of Craig Brook, with salmon and fly-fishing artifacts and memorabilia. Hiking options include two to three miles of nature trails through old-growth woods between Alamoosook and Craig ponds and an easy-to-moderate two-hour (round-trip) hike up Great Pond Mountain.

Stroll the half-mile walkway along the restored Bucksport waterfront, from the Bucksport/Verona Bridge to Sprague Point. Along the way are historical markers, picnic tables, a gazebo, a restroom, and expansive views of the harbor and Fort Knox.

Canoeing

If you've brought a canoe, **Silver Lake,** just two miles north of downtown Bucksport, is beautiful place for a paddle. There's no development along its shores, and the birding is excellent. No swimming ($500 fine); this is Bucksport's reservoir. To get to the public launch, take Route 15 north off Route 1 after crossing the Verona-Bucksport Bridge. Go 0.5 mile and turn right on McDonald Road, which becomes Silver Lake Road, and follow it 2.1 miles to the launch site.

Golf

Bucksport Golf Club (Duck Cove Rd., Route 46, 1.5 miles north of Rte. 1, 207/469-7612, mid-April–Sept.) prides itself on having Maine's longest nine-hole course. Greens fees are moderate; facilities include pro shop, snack bar, driving range, and carts.

ACCOMMODATIONS
Bed-and-Breakfasts

The most attractive B&B in this area is **The Sign of the Amiable Pig** (74 Castine Rd., Rte. 175, P.O. Box 232, Orland 04472, 207/469-2561), once a hideout on the Underground Railroad. Three rooms (one with a private bath) are $60 and $75 d, including an imaginative breakfast. A separate guesthouse, sleeping five, goes for $550 a week, not including breakfast. Guests have the run of Charlotte and Wes Pipher's very comfortable home with parlor, keeping room, and lots of fireplaces. The oldest house section dates from 1765. Oriental carpets and fresh flowers are everywhere. The Amiable Pig (named for the weathervane atop the barn) is open all year, but be sure to call ahead and reserve space off-season.

Location, location, location. If only the six simple rooms at the **Alamoosook Lakeside Inn** (Off Rte. 1, P.O. Box 16, Orland 04472, 866/459-6393 or 207/469-6393, www.alamoosooklakesideinn.com, $120) actually overlooked the lake, then it would be the perfect, rustic lakeside lodge. The property is gorgeous and the location well suited for exploring the area, but the rooms are so-so, with tiny bathrooms. All have windows and doors opening onto a long sun porch overlooking the lake. A full breakfast is served. Alamoosook is great for wildlife watching and fishing, especially for bass, trout, salmon, and pickerel, and guests have access to canoes and kayaks. Paddle across the lake to the fish hatchery for a hike up Great Pond Mountain.

Motels

In downtown Bucksport, the award for best view goes to the **Jed Prouty Motor Inn** (64 Main St., P.O. Box 826, Bucksport 04416, 207/469-3113 or 800/528-1234, $99–159), a four-story Best Western motel nudged right up to the harbor's edge. Forty modern rooms have phones, air-conditioning, and cable TV. Be sure to request a water view, or you'll be facing a parking lot.

Campgrounds

The rivers, lakes, and ponds in the area between Bucksport and Ellsworth make it especially appealing for camping, and sites tend to be cheaper than in the Bar Harbor area. During July and August, especially weekends, reservations are wise.

Six miles east of Bucksport, across from Craig Pond Road, is Back Ridge Road, leading to **Balsam Cove Campground** (P.O. Box C, East Orland 04431, 207/469-7771 or 800/469-7771, www.balsamcove.com, $18–25). From Route 1, take Back Ridge Road 1.5 miles to the left turn for the campground, on the shores of 10-mile-long Toddy Pond. Facilities on the 50 acres include 60 wooded tent and RV sites, a one-room rental cabin ($50), on-site rental trailers ($65–80), dump station, store, laundry, free showers, boat rentals, and freshwater swimming. Open late May to late September. The same season holds for 10-acre **Whispering Pines Campground** (Rte. 1, East Orland 04431, 207/469-3443, www.campmaine.com/whisperingpines/, $26), also on Toddy Pond but with access directly from Route 1. Facilities include 50 tent and RV sites (request one close to the pond), canoes and rowboats, freshwater swimming, playground, free showers, and recreation hall. Whispering Pines is 6.5 miles east of Bucksport.

FOOD

MacLeod's (Main St., Bucksport, 207/469-3963, opens at 4:30 P.M. daily) is Bucksport's most popular restaurant. Slip into a booth, and choose from a varied menu. Children are welcome, it has a liquor license, and it's air-conditioned. Dinner entrees are $9–16. Reservations are wise for Saturday dinner.

On Verona Island, just before you cross the bridge to Bucksport (if you're heading north), is **Kravings Bakery and Restaurant** (42 Rte. 1, Verona, 207/469-9900, downtownme.com/kravings, Tues. –Sun. 11:30 A.M.–close), a casual restaurant with seating indoors and on an outdoor patio. The interior is pleasant, homey, and accented with knickknacks. It's also air-conditioned. Outside, you're subject to the roar of traffic on Route 1. The dinner menu varies by night, alternating between New England (Thursday), Mexican (Friday), and Italian (Saturday) fare, all at very reasonable prices. Fajitas and nachos are big hits during lunch, but the sandwiches are excellent, too.

The **Bucksport Riverfront Market** (9 A.M.–3 P.M. Sat., late May–mid-Sept.), a farmers market on the waterfront behind the Town Office, has artwork, fresh produce, baked goods, crafts, food, and more.

In what passes as downtown Orland (hint: don't blink), **Orland Market and Pizza** (Rte. 175/91 Castine Rd., Orland, 207/469-9999, 7 A.M.–9 P.M.) is a delight. Established in 1860, the old-fashioned country store has a little of this and a bit of that along with breakfast sandwiches, hot and cold sandwiches, grilled foods, salad, and all kinds of pizza. Call or drop by to find out the day's homemade specials, perhaps lasagna or spaghetti and meatballs.

INFORMATION AND SERVICES

The **Bucksport Bay Area Chamber of Commerce** (52 Main St., P.O. Box 1880, Bucksport 04416, 207/469-6818, www .bucksportchamber.org) is right next to the municipal office in downtown Bucksport. Office hours are 9 A.M.–5 P.M. Mon.–Fri., but the side door is always open for access to an extensive array of brochures, newspapers, and other publications, plus bulletin-board notices. Bucksport information is also available at the **Gateway Mobil Station,** at the traffic light on the corner of Route 1, between the bridge and the Hannaford supermarket. The local *Enterprise* newspaper and the Bucksport Chamber of Commerce produce a very helpful annual, *The Guide,* covering Bucksport, Orland, and Verona Island. Be sure to request a copy.

Public Restrooms

In Bucksport, public restrooms next to the town dock (behind the Bucksport Historical Society) are open spring, summer, and fall. Restrooms are open year-round in the Gateway Mobil gas station (at the Route 1 traffic light next to the Bucksport bridge) and in the Bucksport Municipal Office (weekdays) on Main Street.

Blue Hill

Eons back, Native American summer folk gave the name Awanadjo (Small, Hazy Mountain) to the mini-mountain that looms over the town and draws the eye for miles around. The first permanent settlers arrived after the French and Indian War, in the late 18th century, and established mills and shipyards. More than 100 ships were built here between Blue Hill's incorporation, in 1789, and 1882, bringing prosperity to the entire peninsula.

Critical to the town's early expansion was its first clergyman, Jonathan Fisher, a remarkable fellow who's been likened to Leonardo da Vinci. In 1803, Fisher founded Blue Hill Academy (predecessor of today's George Stevens Academy), then built his home (now a museum) and eventually left an immense legacy of inventions, paintings, engravings, and poetry.

Throughout the 19th century and into the 20th, Blue Hill's granite industry boomed, reaching its peak in the 1880s. Scratch the Brooklyn Bridge and the New York Stock Exchange and you'll find granite from Blue Hill's quarries. Around 1879, the discovery of gold and silver brought a flurry of interest, but little came of it. Copper was also found here, but quantities of it, too, were limited.

At the height of industrial prosperity, tourism took hold, attracting steamboat-borne summer boarders. Many succumbed to the scenery, bought land, and built waterfront summer homes. Thank these summer folk and their offspring for the fact that music has long been a big deal in Blue Hill. The Kneisel Hall Chamber Music School, established in the late 19th century, continues to rank high among the nation's summer music colonies. New York City's Blue Hill Troupe, devoted to Gilbert and Sullivan operettas, was named for the longtime summer home of the troupe's founders.

SIGHTS
◖ The Parson Fisher House
Named for a brilliant Renaissance man who arrived in Blue Hill in 1794, the Parson Fisher House (Rte. 15/176, 44 Mines Rd., Blue Hill, 207/374-2459, www.jonathanfisherhouse.org, 1 P.M.–4 P.M. Tues. and Fri. and 11 A.M.–2 P.M. Sat., July–mid-Sept., $5) immerses visitors in period furnishings and Jonathan Fisher lore. And Fisher's feats are breathtaking: he was a Harvard-educated preacher who also managed to be an accomplished painter, poet, mathematician, naturalist, linguist, inventor, cabinetmaker, farmer, architect, and printmaker. In his spare time, he fathered nine children. Fisher also pitched in to help build the yellow house on Tenney Hill, which served as the Congregational Church parsonage. Now it contains intriguing items created by Fisher, memorabilia that volunteer tour guides delight in explaining, including a camera obscura. Don't miss it.

Historic Houses
A few of Blue Hill's elegant houses have been converted to museums, inns, restaurants, even some offices and shops, so you can see them from the inside out. To appreciate the private residences, you'll want to walk, bike, or drive around town.

In downtown Blue Hill, a few steps off Main Street, stands the **Holt House** (3 Water St., Blue Hill, 207/326-8250, 1 P.M.–4 P.M. Tues. and Fri. and 11 A.M.–2 P.M. Sat. July–mid-Sept., $3 adults, free for kids 12 and under), home of the Blue Hill Historical Society. Built in 1815 by Jeremiah Holt, the Federal-style building contains restored stenciling, period

© TOM NANGLE

Jonathan Fisher's home is filled with artifacts created or collected by the mega-talented preacher, and guided tours reveal his amazing feats.

decor, and masses of memorabilia contributed by local residents. In the carriage house are even more goodies, including old tools, a sleigh, carriages, and so forth.

Walk or drive up Union Street (Route 177), past George Stevens Academy, and wander **The Old Cemetery,** established in 1794. If gnarled trees and ancient headstones intrigue you, there aren't many good-sized Maine cemeteries older than this one.

Bagaduce Music Lending Library

At the foot of Greene's Hill in Blue Hill is one of Maine's more unusual institutions, a library where you can borrow by mail or in person from a collection of 625,000 scores and sheet music (3 Music Library Ln., Rte. 172, P.O. Box 829, Blue Hill 04614, 207/374-5454, www.bagaducemusic.org, 10 A.M.–3 P.M. Mon.–Fri. or by appointment). Somehow this seems so appropriate for a community that's a magnet for music lovers. Annual membership is $10 ($5 for students). The library publishes six catalogs of its holdings; fees range from $1 to $2.50 per piece—and you can keep it for up to two months.

Scenic Routes

Parker Point Road (turn off Route 15 at the Blue Hill Library) takes you from Blue Hill to Blue Hill Falls the back way, with vistas en route toward Acadia National Park. For other great views, drive the length of **Newbury Neck,** in nearby Surry, or head west on Route 15/176 toward Sedgwick, Brooksville, and beyond.

RECREATION
◖ Blue Hill Mountain Trail

- Distance: 2 miles round-trip
- Duration: 1.5–2 hours round-trip.
- Elevation Gain: 500 feet
- Effort: easy to moderate
- Trailhead: Off Route 15 (Pleasant St., Blue Hill)

Mountain seems a fancy label for a 943-footer, yet Blue Hill stands alone, visible from Camden and even beyond. On a clear day, head

for the summit and take in the wraparound view encompassing Penobscot Bay, the hills of Mount Desert, and the Camden Hills. Climb the fire tower and you'll see even more. In mid-June, the lupines along the way are breathtaking; in fall, the colors are spectacular—with reddened blueberry barrens added to the variegated foliage. Go early in the day; it's a popular hike. A short loop on the lower slopes takes only half an hour. Take Route 15 (Pleasant Street) to Mountain Road. Turn right and go 0.8 mile to the trailhead (on the left) and the small parking area (on the right). You can also walk (uphill) the mile from the village. The trail can be squishy, especially in the wooded sections, so you'll want rubberized or waterproof shoes or boots.

Blue Hill Heritage Trust

This fine organization (101 Union St., P.O. Box 222, Blue Hill 04614, 207/374-5118, www.bhht.org, 8 A.M.–5 P.M. Mon.–Fri.) works hard at preserving the region's landscape. It also presents a Walks 'n' Talks series, with offerings such as kayaking by preservation land along Eggemoggin Reach, a full moon hike up Blue Hill Mountain, and walks through other trust properties, such as 700-acre Kingdom Woods Conservation Preserve and Cooper Farm at Caterpillar Hill. Many include talks by knowledgeable folks on complementary topics. Check the website, call, or stop by to see what's up when you're in town.

Blue Hill Town Park

At the end of Water Street is a small park with a terrific view. It has a small pebble beach, picnic tables, and a creative playground. Pick up picnic fixings at Pain de Famille or the Blue Hill Co-Op and bring it all here.

MERI Center

A great way to raise kids' environmental consciousness is to enroll them in summer activities sponsored by the **MERI Center for Marine Studies** (55 Main St., Blue Hill, 207/374-2135, www.meriresearch.org). MERI (Marine Environmental Research Institute), a nonprofit marine-ecology organization, schedules day-long island boat trips, "eco-cruises," and island walks, plus a variety of naturalist-led morning and afternoon programs, each geared to different age groups or groupings ($20–50); cruises are limited to 12 passengers. The expanding MERI Center has a touch tank, a marine lending library, and exhibit space. On Fridays at 10 A.M. it hosts a story hour for preschoolers that concludes with a craft program. During fall, winter, and spring, MERI offers a Friday evening movie night, with refreshments, during which it screens marine-related films. It's free, but a $3 donation is appreciated. MERI is open Mon.–Sat. all year.

Blue Hill Falls

A favorite spot for *experienced* kayakers and canoeists is Blue Hill Falls, which churns with white water when the tide turns. Check for times of high and low tide. Roadside parking is illegal, but the law is too often ignored. The Route 175 bridge is narrow, and cars often stop suddenly as they come over the hill, so be particularly cautious here.

Unless you own a boat or know a member of the Kollegewidgwok Yacht Club in East Blue Hill (207/374-5581), there's no sailing out of Blue Hill. If you're trailing a boat, use the public boat launch down on the harbor. *Kollegewidgwok,* incidentally, is a Penobscot Indian word meaning "blue hill on shining green water."

Rocky Coast Outfitters

Anna and Barry Snow's Rocky Coast Outfitters (Gindleville Rd., P.O. Box 351, Blue Hill 04614, 207/374-8866, rockycoastoutfitters@verizon.net) delivers rental canoes, kayaks, and bicycles, along with the necessary helmets, paddles, and life vests, to your lodging. Delivery is free. Rates vary with equipment and rental period.

ENTERTAINMENT AND EVENTS

Variety and serendipity are the keys here. Check local calendar listings and tune in to radio station **WERU** (89.9 and 102.9 FM, www.weru.org), the peninsula's own community radio; there might be announcements of concerts by local resident pianist Paul Sullivan or the Bagaduce Chorale, or maybe a contra dance or a tropical treat from Carl Chase's Atlantic Clarion Steel Band or Flash in the Pans Community Band. The George Stevens Academy also has a weekly lecture series.

Music

Since 1922, chamber-music students have been spending summers perfecting their skills and demonstrating their prowess at the **Kneisel Hall Chamber Music School** (Pleasant St., Rte. 15, Blue Hill, 207/374-2811, www.kneisel.org). Faculty concerts run Friday evenings at 8:15 P.M. and Sunday afternoons at 4 P.M. late June to late August. The concert schedule is published in the spring, and reserved-seating tickets ($30 inside, $20 on the veranda outside; nonrefundable) can be ordered by phone. There is also unreserved tent seating ($10) for the Friday evening and Sunday afternoon concerts. Other opportunities to hear the students and faculty exist, including young artist concerts, children's concerts, open rehearsals, and more. Check the website or program for details. Kneisel Hall is about a half mile from the center of town.

Chamber music continues in winter thanks to the volunteer **Blue Hill Concert Association** (P.O. Box 140, Blue Hill 04614). Five concerts are performed between January and March at the Congregational Church, a handsome, traditional New England spired edifice on Main Street.

Fairs and Festivals

The first weekend in August, the **Academy Antiques Show** draws a huge crowd to the George Stevens Academy on Union Street in Blue Hill. Admission is $7, and lunch and tea are available.

WERU's annual **Full Circle Fair** is usually held in mid-August at the Blue Hill Fairgrounds (Rte. 172, north of downtown Blue Hill).

Expect world music, good food, crafts, and socially and environmentally progressive talks.

On Labor Day weekend, the **Blue Hill Fair** (Blue Hill Fairgrounds, Rte. 172, Blue Hill, 207/374-9976) is one of the state's best agricultural fairs. Besides the food booths (good-for-you fare competes with fried dough), a carnival, fireworks, sheepdog trials, and live musical entertainment, you can check out the blue-ribbon winners for finest quilt, beefiest bull, or largest squash.

SHOPPING

Boutiques, antiques, galleries, and even two downtown bookstores make shopping a pleasure in Blue Hill, especially if you're looking for the unusual. (See the sidebar *Gallery Hopping in Blue Hill.*)

GALLERY HOPPING IN BLUE HILL

Perhaps it's Blue Hill's location near the renowned Haystack Mountain School of Crafts. Perhaps it's the way the light plays off the rolling countryside and onto the twisting coastline. Perhaps it's the inspirational landscape. Whatever the reason, numerous artists and artisans call Blue Hill home, and top-notch galleries are abundant.

Judith Leighton knows contemporary art, and her **Leighton Gallery** (24 Parker Point Rd., 207/374-5001, www.leightongallery.com) is a real treat. The airy two-story-plus-basement

When visiting Judith Leighton's gallery, don't miss the backyard sculpture garden.

space, in a converted barn on the Parker Point Road, is filled with a great selection. Be sure to visit the equally spectacular and extremely peaceful backyard sculpture garden. The **Liros Gallery** (14 Parker Point Rd., 207/374-5370 or 800/287-5370, www.lirosgallery.com) has been dealing in Russian icons since the mid-1960s. Prices are high, but the icons are fascinating. The gallery also carries Currier & Ives prints, antique maps, and 19th-century British and American paintings. From here, it's a short walk to **Blue Hill Bay Gallery** (Main St., 207/374-5773, www.bluehillbaygallery. com), which represents contemporary artists in various media.

Don't miss **Jud Hartmann** (Main St. at Rte. 15, 207/374-991, www.judhartmanngallery. com). The spacious, well-lit, in-town gallery carries Hartmann's limited edition bronze sculptures of the Woodland Tribes of the Northeast. Hartmann often can be seen working on his next model in the gallery — a real treat. He's a wealth of information about his subjects, and he loves sharing the mesmerizing stories he's uncovered during his meticulous research.

Also on Main Street are three other fun, artsy gallery-shops. **Handworks Gallery** (Main St., 207/374-5613) sells a range of fun, funky, utilitarian and fine art crafts by more than 50 Maine artists and craftspeople, including jewelry, furniture, rugs, wall hangings, and clothing. Describing the wildly whimsical figures created by Laura Balombini at **L. Balombini's** (Main St., 207/374-5142, www.lbalombini.com) is tough. Her materials are wire and polymer

Antiques

Historical and cottage goods are the specialty at **Salt Air Primitives** (5 Main St., Blue Hill, 207/374-8886). **Blue Hill Antiques** (8 Water St., Blue Hill, 207/374-2199 or 207/326-4973) specializes in 18th- and 19th-century French and American furniture—it attracts a high-end clientele. The same patrons seek out Brad Emerson's **Emerson Antiques** (Water St.,

Blue Hill, 207/374-5140), concentrating on early Americana, such as hooked rugs and ship models. Also worth a browse for antique finds is **Stephen Rowe Antiques & Mary Keeler Rowe Fine Arts** (138 Main St., Blue Hill, 207/374-3811), in front of the Blue Hill Wine Shop, which carries a mix of fine and folk art and period antiques. Just outside of town is **Belcher's Antiques** (232 Ellsworth Rd.,

© TOM NANGLE

sculpture by Jud Hartmann

clay – combined magically. The shapes are great and the colors are brilliant – each piece is a "wanna-have." Browse **North Country Textiles** (Main St., 207/374-2715, www.northcountrytextiles.com) for fine hand-woven throws, rugs, clothing, and table linens, as well as other fine crafts.

Pottery is abundant in Blue Hill. **Rowantrees Pottery** (Rte. 177, 207/374-5535) and **Rackliffe Pottery** (Rte 172, 207/374-2297 or 888/631-3321, www.rackliffe-pottery.com) both have established reputa-

tions. Rowantrees Pottery's kiln was first fired in 1934. The handmade pottery is made from local marine clay accented by rich glazes derived from local sources. Rackliffe, noted for its vivid blue wares, also makes its own glazes and has been producing lead-free pottery since 1969.

About two miles from downtown is another don't-miss. **Mark Bell Pottery** (Rte. 15, Blue Hill 04614, 207/374-5881), in a tiny building signaled only by a small roadside sign, is the home of exquisite, award-winning porcelain by the eponymous potter. It's easy to understand why his wares were displayed at the Smithsonian Institution's Craft Fair as well as other juried shows across the country. The delicacy of each vase, bowl, or other piece is astonishing, and the glazes are gorgeous. Twice each summer he has kiln openings – must-go events for collectors and fans. Call for details.

Functional porcelain pottery is Melody Lewis-Kane's specialty at **Clay Forms** (Rte. 15, 207/359-2321, www.clayformspottery.com), located four miles south of Blue Hill. The pitcher plant and hummingbird pieces are especially graceful.

Also worth a look-see are two off-the-beaten-path galleries. **Rachel Raye** (13 Schoolhouse Ln., East Blue Hill, 207/374-5944) is a master at depicting animals and capturing their personalities. **LoonSong Gallery** (232 Falls Bridge Rd./Rte. 175, Blue Hill, 207/374-5488, www.loonsonggallery.com) specializes in emerging artists and sculptors from around the world.

BLUE HILL PENINSULA

The streets of downtown Blue Hill are lined with galleries and small shops.

Rte. 172, Blue Hill, 207/374-3751). Twig furniture is a specialty, along with a broad range of eclectic collectibles, including great old signs.

Books

Blue Hill's literate population manages to support two full-service, year-round, independent bookstores. The selection is excellent at **Blue Hill Books** (2 Pleasant St., Rte. 15, Blue Hill, 207/374-5632, www.bluehillbooks.com), thanks to knowledgeable owners Nick Sichterman and Mariah Hughs. The store organizes an authors series during the summer. Around the corner, ever-helpful Bonnie Myers provides free advice on the region with a money-back guarantee at **North Light Books** (Main St., Blue Hill, 207/374-5422). It's a delight to browse, and the children's book selection is among the best in the state.

Eclectic

The Himalayas meet Blue Hill at Jeff Kaley's **Asian World Imports** (Pleasant St., Rte. 15, Blue Hill, 207/374-2284, www.asianworldimports.com). A Nepal Peace Corps veteran, Kaley seeks out eco-sensitive suppliers using fair-trade practices, bringing back custom-made Nepalese, Tibetan, Indian, and Thai clothing, jewelry, and artifacts, as well as organic Himalayan tea. The shop is loaded with treasures. Jeff also leads small-group cultural tours and treks in Nepal and Tibet; contact him for details.

In downtown Blue Hill is Peter Stremlau's **New Cargoes** (49 Main St., P.O. Box 1105, Blue Hill 04614, 207/374-3733,), following somewhat in the Pier One/Crate & Barrel tradition. Furniture, linens, notecards, candles, and on and on. The shop name is apt—new things arrive on a regular basis. Bet you can't walk out of here empty-handed.

Wine

Blue Hill Wine Shop (Main St., Blue Hill, 207/374-2161), tucked into a converted horse barn, carries more than 1,000 wines, plus teas, coffees, and blended tobaccos and unusual pipes for diehard, upscale smokers. Monthly wine tastings (2–5 P.M., last Saturday of the month) are always an adventure.

ACCOMMODATIONS
Inns and B&Bs

On a quiet side street close to town, **◖ The Blue Hill Inn** (Union St., Rte. 177, P.O. Box 403, Blue Hill 04614, 207/374-2844 or 800/826-7415, www.bluehillinn.com, $158–195, mid-May–late Oct.) has been welcoming guests since 1840. If you're trying to imagine a classic country inn, this would be it. Hosts Mary and Don Hartley do everything right. Stay here if you enjoy antiques, warm hospitality, and classic New England inns; don't stay if you're on a tight budget or have small children. Ten rooms and a suite, all with air-conditioning, boast real chandeliers, four-poster beds, down comforters, fancy linens, and braided and Oriental rugs; three have wood-burning fireplaces. The third-floor garret suite is ideal for families with well-behaved children; a first-floor room is wheelchair-accessible. Rear rooms overlook the extensive cutting garden, with chairs and a hammock. The library, dominated by a Persian chandelier, has masses of local information. Refreshments are available all day; superb hors d'oeuvres are served 6–7 P.M. in two elegant parlors or the garden. An adjacent suite in the elegant Cape House—the ground floor of a tiny dwelling—is $165–285, depending on season. Twice each year, usually May and October, the inn puts on gala wine-dinner weekends; the multicourse gourmet dinners are outstanding. The innkeepers will arrange for Kneisel Hall tickets, kayak rentals, cruises, massages, and more.

Two miles north of town, at the **Blue Hill Farm Country Inn** (Rte. 15, P.O. Box 437, Blue Hill 04614, 207/374-5126, www.blue-hillfarminn.com, $85–99), a huge refurbished barn serves as the gathering spot for guests. If the weather is lousy, you can plop down in front of the oversize woodstove and start in on cribbage or other games. Antique sleigh-runner banisters lead to the barn's seven second-floor rooms—all with private baths, skylights, hooked rugs, and quilts. A wing of the farmhouse has seven more rooms with shared baths and more quilts. Breakfast is generous continental. During the summer, visiting jazz or classical musicians sometimes entertain in the barn, but it all eases off early. On the inn's 48 acres are well-cleared nature trails, an 18th-century cellar hole, and a duck pond.

Okay, it's not a *real* lighthouse, but the waterfront **First Light B&B** (821 E. Blue Hill Rd., Blue Hill, 207/374-5879, www.firstlight-bandb.com, $110–200) is close enough to fool many folks. Huge windows frame views that, on a clear day, extend for five miles. Innkeeper Beverly Bartlett, a retired nursing professor, has three lighthouse-themed rooms. If you're a lighthouse buff, reserve the Lighthouse Suite, in the tower. Two other rooms share a bath or can be connected as a suite. Guests may climb the tower, built by an eccentric previous owner, for 360-degree views; it's the perfect place for seal-watching or birding. A comfortably cluttered common room, with fireplace, plentiful

© TOM NANGLE

Stay at the Blue Hill Inn, and you're within walking distance of downtown Blue Hill's shops, galleries, restaurants, and park.

books, and a grand piano, faces McHeard's Cove. Breakfast is served either in the dining room or on the patio. Open year-round.

Motel

Blue Hill's only motel is the **Heritage Motor Inn** (Rte. 172, P.O. Box 453, Blue Hill 04614, 207/374-5646, www.bhheritagemotorinn.com, $95–122), a clean, no-frills, 23-room, year-round place on Greene's Hill. Rooms have cable TV, air-conditioning, coffeemakers, and views of Blue Hill Bay. Also available are housekeeping-style apartments ($1,250/week), with well-equipped kitchen and living room on one floor and bedroom, bath, and laundry on the second floor. Open May 1–Nov. 30.

Seasonal Rentals

Weekly rentals (or longer) can pay off if you have a large family or are planning a group vacation. The Blue Hill Peninsula has lots of rental cottages, camps, and houses, but the trick is to plan ahead. This is a popular area in summer, and many renters sign up for the following year before they leave town. For information, contact **Peninsula Property Rentals** (Main St., P.O. Box 611, Blue Hill 04614, 207/374-2428, www.peninsula-propertyrentals.com).

FOOD
Local Flavors

Picnic fare is available at **Merrill & Hinckley** (Union St., Blue Hill, 207/374-2821, 7 A.M.–9 P.M. Mon.–Sat., 8 A.M.–9 P.M. Sun.), a quirky, 150-year-old, family-owned grocery/general store.

The **Blue Hill Co-Op and Café** (Greene's Hill, Rte. 172, Blue Hill, 207/374-2165, cafe 207/374-8999, 8 A.M.–7 P.M. Mon.–Fri., to 6 P.M. Sat., 10 A.M.–5 P.M. Sun.) sells organic and hydroponic produce and grains, cheeses, organic coffee, and more. Breads are terrific here. Sandwiches, salads, and soups—many with ethnic flavors—are available in the cafe. The staff will pack it all up for a picnic, too.

On the other side of the village, **Pain de Famille** (Main St., Blue Hill, 207/374-3839,

7 A.M.–6 P.M. Mon.–Fri., to 7 P.M. Fri., and 9 A.M.–1 P.M. Sat. and Sun.) has earned an outstanding reputation for its unusual selection of breads. You can pick up Greek pockets or ready-made sandwiches and designer juices. Obviously, bread is the thing (fantastic focaccia). It's wise to call ahead for the Friday Night Pizza Plus, when two sizes of pizza are offered with about two dozen possible toppings.

Local gardeners, farmers, and craftspeople peddle their wares at the **Blue Hill Farmers Market** (9–11:30 A.M. Sat.) It's a particularly enduring market, well worth a visit. Demonstrations by area chefs and artists are often on the agenda. The major effort is late June through September at the Blue Hill Fairgrounds (Rte. 172, just north of downtown).

Family Friendly

First choice for families or anyone looking for a casual but very good meal is **The Blue Moose** (50 Main St., Blue Hill, 207/374-3274, 10:30 A.M.–9:30 P.M. Mon.–Fri., 8 A.M.–10 P.M. Sat. and Sun.), which has a wide-ranging menu and welcomes kids. Most choices are in the $8–12 range. Kids'/small appetite menu ranges $3–5.

Very popular with local folks is **Marlintini's Grill** (The Mines Rd., Blue Hill, 207/374-2500, 11:30 A.M.–9 P.M., bar stays open until 1 A.M.), which moved to this location a couple of years ago and remains a work in progress. Inside, half is a sports bar, while the other half a restaurant. You can sit in either, but the bar side can get raucous. In 2005, a screened porch was added, with picnic table dining. Now, if only the grounds were landscaped… perhaps soon? Burgers, salads, sandwiches, fried foods, and a kids' menu are available. The portions are big, the service is good, and the food is reliable.

Fine Dining

Here's a double header: **☾ Arborvine** and **The Vinery** (Main St., Blue Hill, www.arborvine.com). For a light lunch or dinner, head to The Vinery (207/374-2441, noon–2 P.M. Wed.–Sat. and 5 P.M.–9 P.M. Wed.–Sun.), a piano and wine bar bistro in a beautifully renovated barn, where there's often evening entertainment, too. Entrees are $7–14. If you're up for something fancier, make reservations at the Arborvine (207/374-2119, 5:30–9 P.M. Tues.–Sun. summer, Fri.–Sun. winter), a conscientiously renovated two-century-old Cape-style house with four dining areas, each with a different feel and understated decor. Most entrees are in the $22–28 range; there's always at least one option for vegetarians. The wine list is small but select. Chef/owner John Hikade and his wife, Beth, operate both establishments.

Chef Daniel Sweimler and his partner Anneliese Riggall have renovated the historical old forge building that hangs over the river downtown and reopened it as **The Wescott Forge** (66 Main St., Blue Hill, 207/374-9909, www.thewescottforge.com). While one restaurant was successful here years ago, more recent ones have failed. Bets are that this one will succeed, given the partners' experience and reputations. Sweimler made his name in Bar Harbor, and his menu continues his creative and international approach with entrees such as poached halibut with a white bean cake, roasted tomatoes and salsa verde or pork tenderloin with a plum glaze, sake jus and scallion mashed potatoes. Most run $15–22. The upstairs is a casual lounge, while the downstairs has an easy elegance, all highlighted by beautiful forged accent pieces (check out the stairway railing). Request a table on the porch, and you'll be serenaded by the water rushing underneath as you dine. It's open for lunch 11:30 A.M.–2:30 P.M. Tues.–Sat. and for dinner 5:30–9 P.M. Mon.–Saturday. If you need a late-afternoon pick-me-up, a light lounge menu is served upstairs beginning at 3:30 P.M.

Seafood

For lobster, fried fish, and the area's best lobster roll, head to **The Fish Net** (Main St., Blue Hill, 207/374-5240, 11 A.M.–8 P.M. Mon.–Thurs., until 9 P.M. Fri. and Sat.). Dine outdoors on picnic tables or inside. A cheeseburger is $2.60, a lobster roll is $9.95, and a fried clam dinner is $12.95.

INFORMATION AND SERVICES

The **Blue Hill Peninsula Chamber of Commerce** (28 Water St., Box 520, Blue Hill 04614, 207/374-2281, www.bluehill-peninsula.org, 9 A.M.–4 P.M. Mon.–Fri., until 1 P.M. Sat., 11 A.M.–3 P.M. Sun.) is stocked with brochures, menus, and other information on Blue Hill and the surrounding area. You can also find information (although some is outdated) on www.bluehillme.com. One interesting feature on this site is a section on wildlife sightings.

Library

At the **Blue Hill Public Library** (Main St., 207/374-5515, 10 A.M.–6 P.M. Mon.–Fri., until 8 P.M. Thurs., 10 A.M.–2 P.M. Sat.), ask to see the suit of armor, which *may* have belonged to Magellan. The library also sponsors a summer lecture series.

Public Restrooms

In season, there's a portable toilet behind the chamber of commerce building. Public buildings that have restrooms are the Blue Hill Town Hall (Main St.), Blue Hill Public Library (Main St.), and Blue Hill Memorial Hospital (Water St.).

Brooklin, Brooksville, and Sedgwick

Nestled near the bottom of the Blue Hill Peninsula and surrounded by Castine, Blue Hill, and Deer Isle, are the often-missed towns Brooklin, Brooksville, and Sedgwick. This area offers superb hiking, kayaking, and sailing, plus historic homes and unique shops, studios, lodgings, and personalities.

The best-known town is Brooklin (pop. 841), thanks to two magazines: *The New Yorker* and *WoodenBoat.* Wordsmiths extraordinaire E. B. and Katharine White "dropped out" to Brooklin in the 1930s and forever afterward dispatched their splendid material for *The New Yorker* from here. (The Whites' former home, a handsome colonial not open to the public, is on Route 175 in North Brooklin, 6.5 miles from the Blue Hill Falls bridge.) In 1977, *WoodenBoat* magazine moved its headquarters to Brooklin, where its 60-acre shoreside estate attracts builders and dreamers from all over the globe.

Nearby Brooksville (pop. 911) drew the late Helen and Scott Nearing, whose *Living the Good Life* made them role models for back-

to-the-landers. Their compound now verges on "must-see" status. Buck's Harbor, a section of Brooksville, is the setting for *One Morning in Maine,* one of Robert McCloskey's beloved children's books. Oldest of the three towns is Sedgwick (pop. 1,175, incorporated in 1789), which once included all of Brooklin and part of Brooksville. Now wedged *between* Brooklin and Brooksville, it includes the hamlet of Sargentville, the Caterpillar Hill scenic overlook, and a well-preserved complex of historic buildings. The influx of pilgrims continues in this area—many of them artist wannabes bent on capturing the spirit that has proved so enticing to creative types.

SIGHTS
WoodenBoat Publications

On Naskeag Point Road, 1.2 miles from downtown Brooklin (Route 175), a small sign marks the turn to the world headquarters of the *WoodenBoat* empire (Naskeag Point Rd., P.O. Box 78, Brooklin 04616, 207/359-4651,

Anyone with a fondness for wooden boats should visit the campus of WoodenBoat Publications, and if you're really interested, sign up for one of the multitude of courses.

www.woodenboat.com). Buy magazines, books, clothing, and all manner of nautical merchandise at the handsome new store (www.woodenboatstore.com), stroll the grounds, or sign up for one of the dozens of one- and two-week spring, summer, and fall courses in seamanship, navigation, boatbuilding, sailmaking, marine carving, and more. Special courses are geared to kids, women, pros, and all-thumbs neophytes; the camaraderie is legendary, and so is the cuisine. One-week tuition runs $550–1,000, plus materials in some courses. Room and board is $400 per week. School visiting hours are 8 A.M.–5 P.M. Mon.–Sat. June–October.

Historical Sights

Now used as the museum/headquarters of the Sedgwick-Brooklin Historical Society, the 1795 **Reverend Daniel Merrill House** (Rte. 172, P.O. Box 171, Sedgwick 04676, 207/359-8086, 2 P.M.–4 P.M. Sun. in July and Aug., or by appointment, donations welcomed) was the parsonage for Sedgwick's first permanent minister. Inside the house are period furnishings, old photos, toys, and tools; a few steps away are a restored 1874 schoolhouse, an 1821 cattle pound (for corralling wandering bovines), and a hearse barn. Pick up a brochure during open hours and guide yourself around the buildings and grounds. The **Sedgwick Historic District,** crowning Town House Hill, comprises the Merrill House and its outbuildings, plus the imposing 1794 Town House and the 23-acre Rural Cemetery (oldest headstone dates from 1798) across Route 172.

◖ The Good Life Center

Forest Farm, home of the late Helen and Scott Nearing, is now the site of The Good Life Center (372 Harborside Rd., Box 11, Harborside, 207/326-8211, www.goodlife.org). Advocates of simple living and authors of 10 books on the subject, the Nearings created a trust to perpetuate their farm and philosophy. Resident stewards lead tours 1 P.M.–5 P.M. Thursday–Tuesday in July and August (Thurs.–Mon. the rest of the year, but call ahead). Copies of Nearing books are available for sale. From mid-June to mid-

September, Monday night meetings (7 P.M.) at the farm feature free programs by gardeners, philosophers, musicians, and other guest speakers. Occasional work parties, workshops, and conferences are also on the center's schedule. The farm is on Harborside Road, just before it turns to dirt. From Route 176 in Brooksville, take Cape Rosier Road, go 8 miles, passing Holbrook Islands Sanctuary. At the Grange Hall, turn right and follow it 1.9 miles to the end. Turn left onto Harborside Road and continue 1.8 miles to Forest Farm, across from Orrs Cove.

◖ Four Season Farm

Almost next door to the Nearing's place is Four Season Farm (609 Weir Cove Rd., Harborside, 207/326-4455, www.fourseasonfarm.com), the lush organic farm owned and operated by internationally renowned gardeners Eliot Coleman and Barbara Damrosch. Both have written numerous books and articles and starred in TV gardening shows. Coleman is a driving force behind the use of the word "authentic" to mean "beyond organic," demonstrating a

© TOM NANGLE

BLUE HILL PENINSULA

Outstanding organic produce comes from the recently reopened Four Season Farmstand.

commitment to food that is local, fresh, ripe, clean, safe, and nourishing. He's also successfully pioneered a "winter harvest," developing environmentally sound and economically viable systems for extending fresh vegetable production from October through May in cold-weather climates. After 26 years, Coleman and Damrosch reopened their farm to the public in 2005. It's a treat for the eyes as well as the tastebuds—you've never seen such gorgeous produce. It's open to visitors for self-guided tours when the farmstand is open, 1–5 P.M. Mon.–Fri. and 10 A.M.–5 P.M. Saturday, July 1–Sept. 30. To find the farm, continue past The Good Life Center and look for a sign on the left.

Scenic Routes

No one seems to know how **Caterpillar Hill** got its name, but its reputation comes from a panoramic vista of water, hills, and blueberry barrens—with a couple of convenient picnic tables where you can stop for lunch, photos, or a ringside view of sunset and fall foliage. From the 350-foot elevation, the views take in Walker Pond, Eggemoggin Reach, Deer Isle, Swan's Island, and even the Camden Hills. No wonder that a local group, the Caterpillar Hill Initiative, is striving to purchase a central, 16-acre parcel of this landscape to preserve it. In addition to preserving the view and conserving the land, CHI plans to allow the Gallery at Caterpillar Hill to remain and to add The Maine Lake Iceworks Museum in an adjacent building that was once an icehouse. Also planned is an art and education center. The signposted rest area is on Route 175/15, between Brooksville and Sargentville, next to a small gift shop; watch out for the blind curve when you pull off the road. Between Sargentville and Sedgwick, Route 175 offers nonstop views of Eggemoggin Reach, with shore access to the Benjamin River just before you reach Sedgwick village.

Two other scenic routes are **Naskeag Point,** in Brooklin, and **Cape Rosier,** westernmost arm of the town of Brooksville. Naskeag Point Road begins off Route 175 in "downtown" Brooklin, heads down the peninsula for 3.7 miles past the entrance to WoodenBoat Publications. It

also passes Amen Farm (207/359-8982, call for hours), home of the late author Roy Barrette, where the gardens and 10-acre arboretum are open for viewing; it's under restoration, but plans call for tours and serving tea and popovers. Naskeag Point Road heads finally to a small shingle beach (limited parking) on Eggemoggin Reach, where you'll find picnic tables, a boat launch, a seasonal toilet, and a marker commemorating the 1778 Battle of Naskeag, when British sailors came ashore from the sloop *Gage,* burned several buildings, and were run off by a ragtag band of local settlers. Cape Rosier's roads are poorly marked, perhaps deliberately, so keep your DeLorme atlas handy. The Cape Rosier loop takes in Holbrook Island Sanctuary, Goose Falls, the hamlet of Harborside, and plenty of water and island views.

RECREATION
◖ Holbrook Island Sanctuary State Park

In the early 1970s, foresighted benefactor Anita Harris donated to the state 1,230 acres in Brooksville that would become the Holbrook Island Sanctuary (207/326-4012, www.state.me.us/doc/parks, free). From Route 176, between West Brooksville and South Brooksville, head west on Cape Rosier Road, following brown-and-white signs for the sanctuary. Trail maps and bird checklists are available in boxes at trailheads or at park headquarters. The easy Backshore Trail (about 30 minutes) starts here, or go back a mile and climb the steepish trail to **Backwoods Mountain** for the best vistas. Other trails include one around a beaver flowage. Other attractions include shorefront picnic tables and grills, four old cemeteries, and super birding during spring and fall migrations. Leashed pets are allowed, but no bikes on the trails and no camping. Officially open May 15–Oct. 15, but the access road and parking areas are plowed for cross-country skiers.

Or you can take a picnic to the **Bagaduce Ferry Landing,** in West Brooksville off Route 176, where there are picnic tables and cross-river vistas toward Castine.

E. B. WHITE: SOME WRITER

Every child since the mid-1940s has heard of E. B. White – author of the memorable *Stuart Little, Charlotte's Web,* and *Trumpet of the Swan* – and every college kid for decades has been reminded to consult his copy of *The Elements of Style.* But how many realize that White and his wife Katharine were living not in the Big City but in the hamlet of North Brooklin, Maine? It was Brooklin that inspired Charlotte and Wilbur and Stuart, and it was Brooklin where the Whites lived very full creative lives.

Abandoning their desks at *The New Yorker* in 1938, Elwyn Brooks White and Katharine S. White bought an idyllic saltwater farm on the Blue Hill Peninsula and moved here with their young son Joel, who became a noted naval architect and yachtbuilder in Brooklin before his untimely death in 1997. Andy (as E. B. had been dubbed since his college days at Cornell) produced 20 books, countless essays and letters to editors, and hundreds (maybe thousands?) of "newsbreaks" – those wry clipping-and-commentary items sprinkled through each issue of *The New Yorker.* Katharine continued wielding her pencil as the magazine's standout children's-book editor, donating many of her review copies to Brooklin's Friend Memorial Library, one of her favorite "causes." (The library also has two original Garth Williams drawings from *Stuart Little,* courtesy of E. B., and a lovely garden dedicated to the Whites.) Katharine's book, *Onward and Upward in the Garden,* a collection of her *New Yorker* gardening pieces, was published in 1979, two years after her death.

Later in life, E. B. sagely addressed the young readers of his three award-winning children's books: "Are my stories true, you ask? No, they are imaginary tales, containing fantastic characters and events. In real life, a family doesn't have a child who looks like a mouse; in real life, a spider doesn't spin words in her web. In real life, a swan doesn't blow a trumpet. But real life is only one kind of life – there is also the life of the imagination. And although my stories are imaginary, I like to think that there is some truth in them, too – truth about the way people and animals feel and think and act."

E. B. White died on October 1, 1985, at the age of 86. He and Katharine and Joel left large footprints on this earth, but perhaps nowhere more so than in Brooklin.

A small, relatively little-known beach is Brooklin's **Pooduck Beach.** From the Brooklin General Store (Route 175), take Naskeag Point Road about half a mile, watching for the Pooduck Road sign on the right. Drive to the end. You can also launch a sea kayak into Eggemoggin Reach here.

Bicycling

Bicycling in this area is hazardous. Roads here are particularly narrow and winding, with poor shoulders. If you're determined to pedal, consider either the Naskeag scenic Route or around Cape Rosier, where traffic is light.

Canoeing

Native Trails (Miller Rd., P.O. Box 240, Waldoboro 04572, 207/832-5255), headed by Mike Krepner, is working to re-create the ancient Minnewokun Canoe Trail, a 25-mile circuit of the southeast corner of the Blue Hill Peninsula—including the Bagaduce River and Eggemoggin Reach—used by Native Americans to tap the fisheries of the Bagaduce Estuary. The name allegedly means "many-angled route," and that it is. The 15-mile section between Castine and Walker Pond is already a popular (mostly flat water) paddling route. Contact Native Trails for a map and an update on the project's status.

Sailing

Ensign class, Antares & Pegasus day sailboats are available for rental at **Buck's Harbor Marine** (on the dock, South Brooksville 04617, 207/326-8839, www.bucksharbor.com). The

BLUE HILL PENINSULA

© TOM NANGLE

Kayaking is a popular way to explore the famed sailing waters of Eggemoggin Reach, which divides the Blue Hill Peninsula from Deer Isle.

full-keel boats rent for $125 per day. Buck's Harbor also charters bareboat sail and power yachts to qualified skippers.

EXCURSION BOATS

Captain LeCain Smith sails *Perelandra* (Buck's Harbor, 207/326-4279, www.windrose-away.com), a 44-foot ketch, in the waters of Penobscot Bay. Rates begin at $35 pp for a two-hour trip and increase to $55 pp for a four-hour sail and $95 for a full day. The boat holds a maximum of six passengers.

Sail on a Maine windjammer with Capt. Bill Brown on the *Summertime* (207/326-8485 or 800/562-8290, www.schoonersummertime.com), which sails from various locations on the peninsula, including Brooksville, Sedgwick, and Stonington in spring and fall. Six-hour sails are $40 per adult, $20 per child younger than 12; three-hour sails are $18 and $9. The schooner takes a maximum of 20 guests.

ENTERTAINMENT AND EVENTS

◖ Flash in the Pans Community Steel Band

If you're a fan of Caribbean-style steel-drum music, check to see where and when Carl Chase's Flash in the Pans Community Steel Band (207/374-2172, www.peninsulapan.org) is performing. It usually performs somewhere on the peninsula on Monday nights (7:30– 9 P.M.), mid-June to early September. The musicians aren't professionals, but you'd never know it. Local papers carry the summer schedule for the nearly three-dozen-member band, which performs in various area locales and deserves its devoted following. Admission is usually a small donation to benefit a local cause. It's worth every penny to join the fun.

The Flye Point Music & Arts Festival

A relatively new event is getting excellent reviews. The Flye Point Music & Arts Festival at the Lookout (Flye Point Rd., off Rte. 175, North Brooklin, 207/359-2188, www.acadia.net/lookout) began in 2004. Held in late June, it features musicians such as Don McLean, Richie Havens, and Jonathan Edwards; check the website for details.

Eggemoggin Reach Regatta

Wooden boats are big attractions hereabouts,

so when a huge fleet sails in for this regatta (usually the first Saturday in August, but the schedule can change), crowds gather. Don't miss the parade of wooden boats. Best locale for watching the regatta itself is on or near the bridge to Deer Isle, or near the Eggemoggin Landing grounds on Little Deer Isle. Contact WoodenBoat (207/359-4651) for details.

SHOPPING

Most of these businesses are small, owner-operated shops, which means they're often catch as catch can. If you want to be sure they're open, call ahead.

Antiques

When you need a slate sink, a clawfoot tub, brass fixtures, or a Palladian window, **Architectural Antiquities** (Indian Point Ln., Harborside, 207/326-4938, www.archantiquities.com), on Cape Rosier, is just the ticket—a restorer's delight. Prices are reasonable, and they'll ship your purchases. Open all year by appointment; ask for directions when you call. Antiques dating from the Federal period through the turn of the 20th century are the specialties at **Sedgwick Antiques** (Rte. 172, Sedgwick, 207/359-8834). Early furniture, hand-made furniture, and a full range of country accessories and antiques can be found at **Thomas Hinchcliffe Antiques** (Cradle Knolls Lane, off Rte. 176, W. Sedgwick, 207/326-9411). Painted country furniture, decoys, and unusual nautical items are specialties at Peg and Olney Grindall's **Old Cove Antiques** (Rte. 15, Reach Rd., Sargentville, 207/359-2031 or 207/359-8585), a weathered-gray shop, across from the Eggemoggin Country Store.

Artists and Artisans Galleries

Small studio-galleries pepper Route 175 (Reach Road) in Sedgwick and Brooklin, most are marked only by small signs, so watch carefully. First up is **Eggemoggin Textile Studio** (off Rte. 175/Reach Rd., Sedgwick, 207/359-5083, www.chrisleithstudio.com), where the incredibly gifted Christine Leith weaves scarves, wraps, hangings, and pillows with hand-dyed silk and wool; the colors are magnificent. You might catch her at work on the big loom in her studio shop, a real treat.

Continue along the road to find for **Reach Road Gallery** (Reach Rd., Sedgwick, 207/359-8803), where Holly Meade sells her detailed woodblock prints, as well as prints from the children's books she's illustrated.

Only a few doors down is **Mermaid Woolens** (Reach Rd., Sedgwick, 207/359-2747), source of Elizabeth Coakley's wildly colorful hand-knit vests, socks, and sweaters. They're pricey but worth every nickel. She also does seascape paintings. She's a clever woman.

Continue over to Brooklin, where Virginia G. Sarsfield handcrafts paper products, including custom lampshades, calligraphy papers, books, and lamps at **Hand Papers** (Rte. 175 at Center Harbor Rd., Brooklin, 207/359-8345, www.handmadepapersonline.com).

Just a bit farther is **Naskeag Gallery** (Rte. 175, Brooklin, 207/359-4619), a small shop that makes browsing an art form, especially if you appreciate meandering about antiques and art. The eclectic selection might include antique sweetgrass baskets and 19th-century furnishings and accent pieces mixed with works by local artists and artisans. It's a fun place. Talented glass artist **Sihaya Hopkins** plans to open a studio shop in this complex in 2006.

In Brooksville, more treasures await on Route 176. You'll need to watch carefully for the sign marking the long drive to **Paul Heroux and Scott Goldberg Pottery** (2032 Coastal Rd./Rte. 176, Brooksville, 207/326-9062). The small gallery is a must for pottery fans.

Continue southwest on 176 and watch closely for signs for **Bagaduce Forge** (140 Ferry Rd., Brooksville, 207/326-9676); this isn't easy to find. Joseph Meltreder is both blacksmith and farrier, and his small forge, with big views, is the real thing. He turns out whimsical pieces. Especially fun are the nail people—you'll know them when you see them.

Wine and Gifts

Three varieties of English-style hard cider are specialties at **The Sow's Ear Winery** (Rte.

176 at Herrick Rd., Brooksville, 207/326-4649), a minuscule operation in a funky, gray-shingled building. Winemaker Tom Hoey also produces sulfite-free blueberry, chokecherry, and rhubarb wines; he'll let you sample them all. Ask to see his cellar, where everything happens. No credit cards.

Nautical books, T-shirts, gifts, food (including homemade bread and key lime pie), and boat gear line the walls and shelves of the shop at **Buck's Harbor Marine** (on the dock, South Brooksville, 207/326-8839, www.bucksharbor.com).

ACCOMMODATIONS
Inn
The Lookout (Flye Point Rd., off Rte. 175, North Brooklin, 207/359-2188, www.acadia .net/lookout/), has been owned and operated by Flye family descendants for more than 110 years (and judging from the look of the place, little has changed in that period). The inn has eight rustic rooms (with detached private and shared baths; $115–155, including breakfast) and seven rustic cottages with kitchens and wood stoves ($1,042–1,400/ week, shorter stays sometimes available). Dogs are welcome in most cottages for $40

per pet per week or $10 per day. The attached restaurant of the same name is another plus.

Bed-and-Breakfasts
A few steps up from the half-mile-long shorefront at the Oakland House Seaside Resort's cottage colony is **❰ Shore Oaks Seaside Inn** (435 Herrick Rd., Brooksville, 207/359-8521 or 800/359-7352, www.oaklandhouse.com/ inn.html), a handsome green-trimmed stone mansion carefully restored to its Arts and Crafts heritage. No in-room phones, no TV, no noise—just peaceful bliss. Hang out for too long in the common rooms or the veranda rockers and you might never leave; this place is magical and restorative. Ten first-, second-, and third-floor rooms (seven with private baths) go for $149–395 plus service charge, including breakfast and dinner (a bargain with gourmet dinners and the weekly lobster feast). Shoulder-season rates (May and late Oct.) are less expensive but still include breakfast and a five-course dinner.

In 2005, Joe Moore turned an 1874 Mansard-roofed Victorian in what passes as downtown Brooklin into the **Dragonflye Inn** (Naskeag Point Rd., P.O. Box 220, Brooklin 04616,

Views from the pier gazebo in front of the Shore Oaks Seaside Inn, in Brooksville, extend from Eggemoggin Reach to the Camden Hills.

207/359-808, www.dragonflyeinn.com, $135). It's a casual, put-your-feet-up kind of place, with a special invitation issued to WoodenBoat school students, gallery fans (lots of work by local artisans), and kayakers. Moore's goal is sustainability: towels and linens are made from organic cotton; soaps and shampoos are local and all natural; cleaning products are all natural, biodegradable, and earth friendly. Plans call for the roof to be replaced with faux slate comprising recycled auto tires, recycled-bottle insulation, and power generated on-site from the sun or the wind. Breakfast is light continental. Bicycles are available for guests. Kayak trips can be arranged, including local shuttles. A five-hour guided sea-kayaking trip off Naskeag Point is available for $100 per person.

Best known for its restaurant and pub, **The Brooklin Inn** (Rte. 175, Brooklin, 207/359-2777, www.brooklininn.com) also has five simple but comfortable bedrooms sharing two baths ($95 with breakfast; add $5 for a one-night stay). The inn also will arrange charter sails on two Brooklin-based ketches for $250 per day, including licensed captain.

Cottages

The two operations in this category feel much like informal family compounds—where you quickly become an adoptee. These are extremely popular spots, where successive generations of hosts have catered to successive generations of visitors, and reservations are usually essential for July and August. Many guests book for the following year before they leave. We're not talking fancy; the cottages are old-shoe rustic, of varying sizes and decor. Most of the cottages have cooking facilities, although both colonies include breakfast and dinner in July and August. Both have hiking trails, playgrounds, rowboats, and East Penobscot Bay on the doorstep.

Jim and Sally Littlefield are the enthusiastic fourth-generation hosts at **C Oakland House Seaside Resort** (435 Herrick Rd., Brooksville, 207/359-8521 or 800/359-7352, www.oakland-house.com), a sprawling 50-acre complex of 15 wooded and waterfront cottages, as well as Shore Oaks Seaside Inn. Much of this land, now

threaded with hiking trails, was part of the original king's grant to Jim's ancestors, way back in 1765. The Homestead, where meals are served, dates from 1767. Jim is the eighth generation on the property; his daughter, Sally, is ninth, and she and her husband, Sean McGuigan, plan to be fifth-generation hosts. Weekly rates for two people sharing a two-person cottage, mid-June to Labor Day are $1,268–2,510 plus service charge, including full breakfast and five-course dinner; lower rates for children. Thursday is lobster-picnic night, on the beach. Biggest bargains are early May to mid-June and September–October, when you can rent a whole cottage, without meals, for $475–1,375 weekly. Rowboats are free for guests' use in season, and the staff organizes other boat excursions on request. Also ask about artist workshops—what a perfect location! And wait until you see the gorgeous gardens—enough to warrant a full-time gardener. Two cottages (Lone Pine and Boathouse) are winterized and available all year; the other cottages are closed in winter. Call to ask about last-minute specials and short-term getaway packages.

The fourth generation manages the **Hiram Blake Camp** (220 Weir Cove Rd., Harborside, 207/326-4951, www.hiramblake.com, Memorial Day–late Sept.), but with a difference: the second and third generations still pitch in and help with gardening, lobstering, maintenance, and kibitzing. Thirteen cottages and a duplex line the shore of this 100-acre complex. Don't bother bringing reading matter: the dining room has ingenious ceiling niches lined with countless books. There's a one-week minimum (beginning Sat. or Sun.) July and August, when cottages go for $500–2,450 a week (including breakfast, dinner, and linens). Off-season rates (no meals or linens, but cottages have cooking facilities) are $575–775 a week. Best chances for getting a reservation are in June and September. No credit cards.

FOOD
Cooking Classes

In summer, Chef Terence Janericco (42 Fayette St. Boston, 617/426-7458, or after July 1

Box 226, Herrick Bay, Brooklin 04616, 207/359-2068, www.terencejanericcocookingclasses.com), author of a dozen cookbooks, moves his cooking school from Boston to Brooklin. The demonstration-only, three-hour classes are $60 pp, which includes dining on the foods prepared.

Local Flavors

Competition is stiff for lunchtime seats at the **Morning Moon Café** (junction of Rte. 175 and Naskeag Point Rd., Brooklin, 207/359-2373, 7 A.M.–2 P.M. Tues.–Sat.), mostly because *WoodenBoat* staffers consider it an annex to their offices. "The Moon" is a friendly hangout for coffee, pizza, or great sandwiches and salads—or order to go. It's also open 5–7 P.M. Thurs.–Sat. for takeout pizza.

In North Brooksville, where Route 175/176 crosses the Bagaduce River, stands the **Bagaduce Lunch,** a popular takeout stand (outdoor tables only) open 11 A.M.– 8 P.M. daily early May to mid-September. Check the tide calendar and go when the tide is changing; order a clam roll or a hamburger, settle in at a picnic table, and watch the reversing falls. The food is so-so, but the setting is tops.

Country Stores

Across the street from the Morning Moon Café, the **Brooklin General Store** (1 Reach Rd., junction of Rte. 175 and Naskeag Point Rd., Brooklin, 207/359-8817, 5:30 A.M.–7 P.M. Mon.–Sat. and 8 A.M.–5 P.M. Sun.), vintage 1872, carries groceries, beer and wine, newspapers, takeout sandwiches, and local chatter.

Sargentville's center (small as it is) has the well-stocked **Eggemoggin Country Store** (R.R. 1, Box 4710, Sargentville 04673, 207/359-2125), source of everything from meat and muffins to beer, wine, liquor, fresh breads, lobster pizza, spit-grilled chicken—and public restrooms. The warehousey place is open all year, 6 A.M.–9 P.M. Mon.–Sat. and 7 A.M.– 9 P.M. Sunday (7 A.M.–8 P.M. off-season).

Box lunches and boat lunches are specialties at the **Buck's Harbor Market** (Rte. 176, South

Brooksville, 207/326-8683, 7 A.M.–8 P.M. Mon.–Sat., 8 A.M.–8 P.M. Sun. all year), a low-key, marginally yuppified general store popular with yachties in summer. There's a small lunch counter in the back room. With the cafe here at the market and summertime steel-band street concerts outside, this can be a busy corner.

Casual Dining

Behind the Buck's Harbor Market is the **Bread & Water Café** (Rte. 176, South Brooksville, 207/326-8683, 5:30–9 P.M. Thurs.–Mon.), a quirky cafe with indoor and a few outdoor tables. A previous restaurant here earned rave reviews; this one has yet to hit its stride. Pizzas are served Thursday, Friday, and Sunday, $7–17; other choices range from mac and cheese ($8.50) to sesame crusted salmon ($18). Ask locally about its current reputation.

Fine Dining

Chef Woody is the whiz in the kitchen at **Oakland House Seaside Inn** (435 Herrick Rd., Brooksville, 207/359-8521), open to the public by reservation mid-June–mid-Sept. for its daily breakfast buffet, Sunday brunch, Thursday night shorefront lobster picnic, and superb five-course dinner, with seating beginning at 6 P.M. Entrees range $17–22, which includes soup or salad. The dining rooms are in the property's original farmstead, which dates from 1767. At dinner, families dine in a separate room from couples, keeping everyone happy.

Almost everything on the menu is local or organic at **The Brooklin Inn** (Rte. 175, Brooklin, 207/359-2777, www.brooklininn.com, 5:30– 9 P.M. Wed.–Mon.). The chef tries to know "who raised, grew, picked, or caught all the food," and all the fish are wild, free swimming, and locally caught. In 2005, the daily changing menu had a Mediterranean accent, with entrees ($18–24) such as *pescare l'umido,* a Mediterranean fish stew. A children's menu is available.

Renowned local chef Jonathan Chase has taken over the kitchen at **The Lookout** (Flye Point Rd., off Rte. 175, North Brooklin, 207/359-2188, www.acadia.net/lookout/, 5–8:30 P.M. Mon.–Fri.

and some Sat. evenings). The inn and restaurant, at the tip of Flye Point, has a knockout view of Herrick Bay (as long as there's no fog), and Chase continues his passion for turning local fresh foods into masterpieces. Entrees are $17.

INFORMATION AND SERVICES

The best source of information about the region is the Blue Hill Peninsula Chamber of Commerce (28 Water St., Box 520, Blue Hill 04614, 207/374-2281, www.bluehillpeninsula.org, 9 A.M.–4 P.M. Mon.–Fri., until 1 P.M. Sat., 11 A.M.–3 P.M. Sun.). Another possibility, although sorely outdated when I checked, is the website of the **East Penobscot Bay Association** (www.penobscotbay.com). Request a copy of its handy flyer/map. Once you've landed on Route 172 or 175, pop into one of the small roadside convenience stores and start asking questions. The clerks—often the owners—know it all cold, and these markets always have a fair share of local color. Of course, they won't object if you also buy something while you're there.

Libraries

The public libraries in this area are small and welcoming, but hours are limited. The award-winning **Friend Memorial Library** (Rte. 175, Brooklin, 207/359-2276) is open 10 A.M.–4 P.M. Tuesday, Friday, and Saturday, until 8 P.M. Wednesday, and until 6 P.M. Thursday in summer; closed Wednesday in winter. The library's lovely Circle of Friends Garden, with benches and brick patio, is dedicated to the memory of longtime Brooklin residents E. B. and Katharine White.

Other area libraries are the **Free Public Library** (1 Town House Rd., Rte. 176, Brooksville, 207/326-4560), open 9 A.M.–5 P.M. Monday and Wednesday, 6–8 P.M. Thursday, and 9 A.M.–noon Saturday; and **Sedgwick Village Library** (Main St., Sedgwick, 207/359-2177), open 5–7 P.M. Wednesday, 3–5 P.M. Thursday, and 10 A.M.–noon Saturday.

Castine

Castine (pop. 1,343) is a gem—a serene New England village with a tumultuous past. It's on the tip of a cape, surrounded by water on three sides, including the entrance to the Penobscot River, which made it a strategic defense point. Once beset by geopolitical squabbles, saluting the flags of three different nations (France, Britain, and Holland), its only crises now are local political skirmishes. This is an unusual community, a National Historic Register enclave that many people never find. The town celebrated its bicentennial in 1996. If you're staying in Blue Hill or even Bar Harbor, spend a day here. Or bunk here and use Castine as a base for exploring here and beyond. Either way, you won't regret it.

Originally known as Fort Pentagoet, Castine received its current name courtesy of Jean-Vincent d'Abbadie, Baron de St.-Castin. A young French nobleman manqué who married a Wabanaki princess named Pidiwamiska, d'Abbadie ran the town in the second half of the 17th century and eventually returned to France.

A century later, in 1779, occupying British troops and their reinforcements scared off potential American seaborne attackers (including Colonel Paul Revere), who turned tail up the Penobscot River and ended up scuttling their more than 40-vessel fleet—a humiliation known as the Penobscot Expedition and still regarded as one of America's worst naval defeats.

When the boundaries for Maine were finally set in 1820, with the St. Croix River marking the east rather than the Penobscot River, the last British Loyalists departed, some floating their homes north to St. Andrews, in New Brunswick, Canada, where they can still be seen today. For a while,

BLUE HILL PENINSULA

peace and prosperity became the bywords for Castine—with lively commerce in fish and salt—but it all collapsed during the California Gold Rush and the Civil War trade embargo, leaving the town down on its luck.

Today a major presence is Maine Maritime Academy, yet Castine remains the quietest imaginable college town. Students in search of a party school won't find it here; naval engineering is serious business.

Of the many historical landmarks scattered around town, one of the most intriguing must be the sign on "Wind Mill Hill," at the junction of Route 166 and State Street:

> *On Hatch's Hill there stands a mill. Old Higgins he doth tend it. And every time he grinds a grist, he has to stop and mend it.*

In smaller print, just below the rhyme, comes the drama:

> *Here two British soldiers were shot for desertion.*

Castine indeed has quite a history.

SIGHTS
◖ Castine Historic Tour

To appreciate Castine fully, you need to arm yourself with the Castine Merchants Association's visitors' brochure/map (all businesses and lodgings in town have copies) and follow the numbers on bike or on foot. With no stops, walking the route takes less than an hour, but you'll want to read dozens of historical plaques, peek into public buildings, shoot some photos, and perhaps even do some shopping.

Highlights of the tour include the late 18th-century **John Perkins House,** moved to Perkins Street from Court Street in 1969 and restored with period furnishings. It's open July and August for guided tours 2–5 P.M. Sunday and Wednesday; admission is $5.

Next door, **The Wilson Museum** (107 Perkins St., 207/326-8545, www.wilsonmuseum.org, 2–5 P.M. Tues.–Sun. late May–late Sept., free), founded in 1921, contains an intriguingly eclec-

Although no longer operating, Dyce's Head Lighthouse remains a popular attraction.

© TOM NANGLE

tic two-story collection of prehistoric artifacts, ship models, dioramas, baskets, tools, and minerals assembled over a lifetime by John Howard Wilson, a geologist/anthropologist who first visited Castine in 1891 (and died in 1936). Among the exhibits are Balinese masks, ancient oil lamps, cuneiform tablets, Zulu artifacts, pre-Inca pottery, and assorted local findings. Don't miss this, even though it's a bit musty, although that is changing thanks to a recent multi-million dollar bequest. (The only comparable Maine institutions are the Nylander Museum, in Caribou, and the L. C. Bates Museum, in Hinckley.) Open the same days and hours as the Perkins House, are the **Blacksmith Shop,** where a smith does demonstrations, and the **Hearse House,** containing Castine's 19th-century winter and summer funeral vehicles. Both are free admission. The **Castine Scientific Society** (P.O. Box 196, Castine 04421), a private foundation, operates the five-building complex (the fifth being the Doudiet House, where the administrative offices are located).

At the end of Battle Avenue stands the 19th-century **Dyce's Head Lighthouse,** no longer operating; the keeper's house is owned by the town. Alongside it is a public path (signposted) leading via a wooden staircase to a tiny patch of rocky shoreline and the beacon that has replaced the lighthouse.

Highest point in town is **Fort George State Park,** site of a 1779 British fortification. Nowadays, little remains except grassy earthworks, but there are interpretive displays and picnic tables.

Main Street, descending toward the water, is a feast for historic architecture fans. Artist Fitz Hugh Lane and author Mary McCarthy once lived in elegant houses along the elm-lined street (neither building is open to the public). On Court Street between Main and Green stands turn-of-the-20th-century **Emerson Hall,** site of Castine's municipal

MAINE MARITIME ACADEMY

The state's only merchant-marine college (and one of only seven in the nation) occupies 35 acres in the middle of Castine. Founded in 1941, the academy awards undergraduate and graduate degrees in such areas as marine engineering, ocean studies, and marina management, preparing a student body of about 750 men and women for careers as ship captains, naval architects, and marine engineers.

The academy owns a fleet of 60 vessels, including the historic research schooner *Bowdoin,* flagship of Arctic explorer Admiral Donald MacMillan, and the 499-foot training vessel TV *State of Maine,* berthed down the hill at the waterfront. In 1996-97, the *State of Maine,* formerly the U.S. Navy hydrographic survey ship *Tanner,* underwent a $12 million conversion for use by the academy. It is still subject to deployment, and, in 2005, the school had to quickly find alternative beds for students using the ship as a dormitory when it was called into service in support of rescue and rebuilding efforts after Hurricane Katrina in New Orleans. Midshipmen conduct free 30-minute tours of the vessel on weekdays in summer (about mid-July to late August). The schedule is posted at the dock, or call 207/326-4311 to check; photo ID is required.

Weekday tours of the campus can be arranged through the Admissions Office (207/326-2206 or 800/227-8465 outside Maine, www.mainemaritime.edu). Campus highlights include three-story Nutting Memorial Library, in Platz Hall (open daily during the school year, weekdays in summer and during vacations); the Henry A. Scheel Room, a cozy oasis in Leavitt Hall containing memorabilia from late naval architect Henry Scheel and his wife, Jeanne; and the well-stocked bookstore (Curtis Hall, 207/326-9333, 8 A.M.-3 P.M. Mon.-Fri.).

© TOM NANGLE

Midshipmen conduct tours of Maine Maritime Academy's training vessel, *State of Maine.*

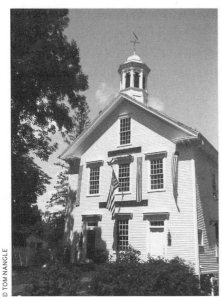

© TOM NANGLE

The Abbott School is now headquarters of the Castine Historical Society and its museum.

offices. Since Castine has no official information booth, you may need to duck in here (it's open weekdays) for answers to questions.

Across Court Street, **Witherle Memorial Library,** a handsome early 19th-century building on the site of the 18th-century town jail, looks out on the Town Common. Also facing the Common are the Adams and Abbott Schools, the former still an elementary school. The **Abbott School** (www.castinehistorical-society.org, 10 A.M.–4 P.M. Tues.–Sat. and 1–4 P.M. Sun. July–Labor Day, reduced schedule spring and fall, free but donations welcome), built in 1859, has been carefully restored for use as a museum/headquarters for the **Castine Historical Society** (P.O. Box 238, Castine 04421, 207/326-4118). A big draw at the volunteer-run museum is the 24-foot-long Bicentennial Quilt, assembled for Castine's 200th anniversary in 1996. The historical society, founded in 1966, organizes lectures, exhibits, and special events (some free) in various places around town.

On the outskirts of town, across the narrow neck between Wadsworth Cove and Hatch's Cove, stretches a rather overgrown canal (signposted British Canal) scooped out by the occupying British during the War of 1812. Effectively severing land access to the town of Castine, the Brits thus raised havoc, collected local revenues for eight months, then departed for Halifax with enough funds to establish Dalhousie College (now Dalhousie University). Wear waterproof boots to walk the canal route; best time to go is at low tide.

If a waterfront picnic sounds appealing, buy the fixings at Bah's Bakehouse and settle in on the grassy earthworks along the harborfront at **Fort Madison,** site of an 1808 garrison (then Fort Porter) near the corner of Perkins and Madockawando Streets. The views from here are fabulous, and it's accessible all year. A set of stairs leads down to the rocky waterfront.

RECREATION
Witherle Woods

This 96-acre preserve, owned by Maine Coast Heritage Trust and managed by the Conservation Trust of Brooksville, Castine, and Penobscot, is a popular walking area with a maze of trails and old woods roads leading to the water. The adjacent property is privately owned, so carry a trail map and stick to it. You'll need a map to figure out where you are in the preserve, as fallen trees sometimes block paths and there are unmarked side paths that can be confusing. Many Revolutionary War–era relics have been found here; if you see any, do *not* remove them. Access to the preserve is via a shaded old woods road on Battle Avenue, located between the water district property (at the end of the wire fence) and The Manor's exit driveway and diagonally across from La Tour Street. Several lodgings keep a supply of maps, as does the nearby Adams Gallery, or contact the **Conservation Trust of Brooksville, Castine, and Penobscot** (P.O. Box 421, Castine 04421, 207/326-9711). The Trust has been protecting the natural resources of Castine, Penobscot, and Brooksville since the early 1980s. It also offers natural history walks, canoe trips, and boat excursions. Also ask locally about the

Henderson Natural Area and other preserves, some accessible only by boat.

Bicycling

Bicycling is an easy way to see Castine. The terrain is gentle and traffic in town is light. Rental bikes are available at **Dennett's Wharf** (207/326-9045). Rates are $24 full day, $15 half day.

◖ Sea Kayaking

Also based at Dennett's Wharf is **Castine Kayak Adventures** (15 Sea St., Castine, 207/326-9045, www.castinekayak.com), spearheaded by Maine Guide Karen Francoeur. Known locally as "Kayak Karen," she's particularly adept with beginners, delivering wise advice from beginning to end. All skill levels are accommodated. Three-hour half-day trips are $55; six-hour full-day tours are around $110 including lunch. Two-hour sunset tours are $40; the sunrise tour includes breakfast for $45. Friday nights, there are special two-hour phosphorescence tours, under the stars (weather permitting), for $45 pp. Longer trips are available for $125 per day. If you have your own boats, call Karen for advice; she knows these waters.

Swimming

Backshore Beach, a crescent of sand and gravel on Wadsworth Cove Road (turn off Battle Avenue at the Castine Golf Club) is a favorite saltwater swimming spot, with views across the bay to Stockton Springs. Be forewarned, though, that ocean swimming in this part of Maine is not for the timid. Best time to try it is on the incoming tide, after the sun has had time to heat up the mud. At mid- to high tide, it's also the best place to put in a sea kayak. Park along the road.

If a pool sounds more attractive, you can swim in the **Cary W. Bok indoor pool** at Maine Maritime Academy for $4. Call 207/326-4311, ext. 451, for open- and lap-swim times.

Golf and Tennis

The **Castine Golf Club** (200 Battle Ave.,

Castine, 207/326-8844, www.castinegolf-club.com) dates to 1897, when the first tee required a drive from a 30-step-high mound. Redesigned in 1921 by Willie Park Jr., the nine-hole course is open May 15–Oct. 15. Starting times are seldom required, and greens fees are reasonable. The club also has four Har-tru tennis courts; for court reservations ($25/hour adult, $15/hour junior), call 207/326-9548.

EXCURSION BOAT

On Fridays, Capt. Melissa Terry's **Belfast Bay Cruises** (207/322-5530, www.belfast-baycruises.com, $30 adult, $22 senior, $15 ages 5–15), reverses its usual Belfast to Castine course and offers an afternoon trip to Belfast aboard the *Good Return*. Whereas Castine is all white clapboard, Belfast is red brick. Spend a few hours shopping the intriguing Main Street shops or exploring the town's three National Historical Districts on foot—pick up a walking map at the Chamber of Commerce (15 Main St.) or wander along the Museum in the Streets, a series of markers highlighting historic buildings and people.

ENTERTAINMENT

Best place for live music is **Dennett's Wharf** (15 Sea St., 207/326-9045). Some performances require a ticket. Also head to **The Reef** (tucked underneath Four Flags facing the parking area and harbor) for pizza and entertainment.

The Trinitarian Church often brings in high-caliber musical entertainment. The Castine Town Band often performs on the common. Check www.castine.org/band.htm for its schedule.

SHOPPING
Antiques and Galleries

Tucked into the back of the 1796 Parson Mason House, one of Castine's oldest residences, **Leila Day Antiques** (53 Main St., Castine, 207/326-8786, www.leiladayantiques.com) is a must for anyone in the market for folk art, period furniture, quilts, and unusual contemporary Shard pottery (from Dover-Foxcroft). Access is via a lovely, flower-lined walkway.

McGrath Dunham Gallery (9 Main St., 207/326-9175, www.mcgrathdunhamgallery .com), a well-lighted, two-story space, shows work by painter/printmaker Greg Dunham and more than two dozen other artists.

For more artwork, visit the **Adam Gallery** of local oil painters Joshua and Susan Adam (140 Battle Ave., 207/326-8272, www.adam-galleryonline.com).

Books

Driving toward Castine on Route 166, watch on your right for a small sign for **Dolphin Books and Prints** (314 Castine Rd., Castine, 207/326-0888, www.dolphin-book.com), where Pete and Liz Ballou have set up their antiquarian business with more than 10,000 books as well as framed prints and art.

In downtown Castine, a block up from the waterfront, **The Compass Rose Bookstore and Café** (3 Main St., 207/326-9366 or 800/698-9366, www.compassrosebooks.com) carries an ever-expanding selection of new books, cards, games, and prints chosen by owner Sharon Biggie. In the back of the shop is a cafe serving hot and cold drinks (espresso, too), soup, sandwiches, and tasty baked goods.

Gifts and Crafts

Water Witch (Main St., Castine, 207/326-4884, www.waterwitch-me.com) specializes in Indonesian batik and Liberty fabric, clothing, and accessories. Buy off the rack or choose a fabric and a style and Jean de Raat will have it made up flawlessly within a few days. Just down the street, close to the harbor, **Four Flags** (1 Main St., 207/326-8526) carries high-quality Maine and nautical gifts, plus an excellent card selection.

Furniture

Benchmade Windsor chairs are the specialty at **M&E Gummel Chairworks** (600 Shore Rd., P.O. Box 767, Castine 04421, 207/326-8122, www.gummelchairworks.com). The father-and-son team utilizes 18th-century methods when handcrafting the chairs, Colonial din-

ing tables, and bowls, one at a time in their late 19th-century barn workshop.

ACCOMMODATIONS
Inns

Castine is blessed with four fine traditional inns. This is not the place to come if you require in-room phones, air-conditioning, or fancy bathrooms. Rather, the pace is relaxed and the accommodations reflect the easy elegance of a bygone era.

Nicest is of the four is the three-story, Queen Anne–style **❰ Pentagöet Inn** (26 Main St., P.O. Box 4, Castine 04421, 207/326-8616 or 800/845-1701, www.pentagoet.com, May–late Oct., $99–225). It's the perfect Maine summer inn, right down to the lace curtains billowing in the breeze, the soft floral wallpapers, and the intriguing curiosities that accent—but don't clutter—the rooms. Congenial innkeepers Jack Burke, previously with the foreign service, and Julie Van de Graaf, a pastry chef, took over the century-old inn in 2000 and have given it new life, upgrading rooms and furnishing them with Victorian antiques and adding handsome gardens. Their enthusiasm for the area is contagious. The inn's 16 rooms are spread out between the main house (with Wi-Fi service) and the adjoining house. A hot buffet breakfast and afternoon refreshments are provided. Passports Pub is an adventure. It's chock-full of vintage photos and prints and exotic antiques. Borrow one of the inn's bikes and explore around town. The Main Street location is an easy walk from everything Castine offers, or just sit on the wraparound porch and take it all in. Dinner here is a treat.

The three-story **Castine Inn** (33 Main St., P.O. Box 41, Castine 04421, 207/326-4365, www.castineinn.com, May–late Oct., $105–340) earns a stellar rating for its stunning semi-formal gardens and extremely helpful staff. The 16 rooms and three suites, updated from their 1890s origins, vary in style from simple Maine to simple elegance. Interesting artwork is everywhere, and there's a very simpatico and unpretentious air, encouraged by enthusiastic

Victorian antiques fill the public and guest rooms of the Queen Anne-style Pentagöet Inn, which is open to nonguests for dinner.

innkeepers Amy and Tom Gutow. In the small, English-style pub, hikers, bicyclists, kayakers, and less energetic guests mingle with a loyal local clientele.

Once the summer "cottage" of a Arthur Fuller, a South Boston Yacht Club commodore, **The Manor Inn** (Battle Ave., P.O. Box 873, Castine 04421, 207/326-4861 or 877/626-6746, www.manor-inn.com, $110–230) overlooks town and harbor from five mostly wooded acres elevated above Battle Avenue. Though the atmosphere is informal, there are lots of elegant architectural touches. Nancy Watson and Tom Ehrman took over in 1998, upgrading beds, linens, and furniture; more renovations are ahead. The 14 second- and third-floor rooms are an eclectic mix—some with canopied beds and fireplaces, all with private baths. A separate guest building has a TV and games as well as Nancy's yoga studio; guests are welcome to join her morning Iyengear classes (Mon., Wed., Fri.; $10 drop-in fee). Wi-Fi is available. The trailhead for Witherle Woods is close by. The inn is often

the site of weddings and receptions; ask before you book unless you don't mind being the odd man out. Open mid-February through late December.

Castine's only oceanfront inn is **Castine Harbor Lodge** (147 Perkins St., P.O. Box 215, Castine 04421, 2077/326-4335, www.castine-maine.com, $85–245), an 1893 Edwardian mansion with open, screened, and glassed-in porches positioned to take in the views over Penobscot Bay to the Camden Hills. Most of the 16 rooms have private baths. Rates include a continental buffet breakfast. A separate Honeymoon Cottage ($1,250/week) is right on the water's edge. Also on premises is the Bagaduce Oyster Bar restaurant. Pets are allowed for a fee of $10 per night.

Castine's least-fancy rooms are at the **Village Inn** (P.O. Box 183, Castine 04421, 207/326-9510), set back from Main and Water Streets. Two rooms have private baths and water views ($125), while two share a bath ($95). They are above Bah's Bakehouse, but noise doesn't seem to be a huge problem.

Cabins and Cottages

Perched in a field along the edge of Hatch's Cove, with terrific views, are the six two-bedroom, pine-paneled log cabins of **Castine Cottages** (33 Snapp's Way, Rte. 166, P.O. Box 224, Castine 04421, 207/326-8003, www.castinecottages.com) operated by Alan and Diana Snapp. Weekly rate is $625 late June–late September, $500 off-season; when available, cabins are rented nightly for $75–150. Open May–October. You'll need to provide your own sheets and towels or pay an additional $10 per person.

Several Castine real estate agents have listings for summer cottage rentals; start with **Castine Realty** (5 Main St., P.O. Box 234, Castine 04421, 207/326-9392, www.castine-realty.com).

FOOD
Local Flavors

Since 1920, locals have been purchasing lunch and ice cream at **Castine Variety** (1 Main St., Castine, 207/326-8625. 5 A.M.–10 P.M. in summer, to 7 P.M. the rest of the year). Go for the vintage feeling and the reasonably priced menu ranging from sandwiches to pizza, but don't expect anything approaching friendly service unless you're a local.

Far more friendly are the folks at (**The Breeze** (Town Dock, Castine, 207/326-9200), a waterfront takeout stand with reliably good basics like burgers, fried clams, and ice cream. You can't beat the location or the view.

Casual Dining

On lower Main Street is a tiny sign for **Bah's Bakehouse** (Water St., Castine, 207/326-9510, 7 A.M.–6 P.M. Mon.–Sat., opens at 8 A.M. Sun.), a higgledy-piggledy eatery of three rooms and a deck at the end of an alleyway beneath the Village Inn. Its slogan is "creative flour arrangements," and creative it is. Stop here for morning coffee, cold juices, interesting snacks and salads, homemade soups, wine or beer, and the best sandwiches in town. The food's great, but if it's crowded,

go elsewhere—the kitchen is quickly overwhelmed and service can be slow to frustrating. Eat in the tiny dining room or on the deck, or take it to go. Bah's will pack a picnic basket for you or deliver an order dockside. Open March–Dec. (off-season hours are 7 A.M.–5 P.M. Tues.–Sun.).

Dennett's Wharf (15 Sea St., 207/326-9045, 11 A.M.–9 P.M. May–Columbus Day), next to the Town Dock, is a colorful barn of a place with outside deck and front-row windjammer-watching seats in summer. Kids are welcomed. Best sandwich is grilled crabmeat ($9.95). The crayoned kids' menu includes all the usual favorites, such as mac 'n' cheese and gummy dinosaurs for dessert. Try attaching a dollar bill to the soaring ceiling; countless others have. Service is leisurely; don't dine here if you're in a hurry.

Although closed in 2005, Chef Tom Gutrow planned to reopen the Pub at the **Castine Inn** (Main St., Castine, 207/326-4365, 5–8 P.M.) and serve a light menu, with such choices as crab cakes and fish and chips ($12–15). It would be wise to call before making a special trip.

Fine Dining

Jazz music plays softly and dinner is by candlelight at the (**Pentagöet** (26 Main St., Castine, 207/326-8616 or 800/845-1701, 5:30–8:30 P.M. Mon.–Sat. May–late Oct.). In fine weather, you can dine on the porch. Choices range from whole lobster pot pie to rack of lamb, or simply make a meal of appetizers and a salad. Don't miss the bouillabaisse, if it's available, or the chocolate budino, a scrumptious warm Italian pudding that melts in your mouth (a must for chocoholics). Entrees are in the $19–28 range.

The bilevel dining room at **The Manor Inn** (Battle Ave., Castine, 207/326-4861, 6–8:30 P.M. Tues.–Sat. in summer) overlooks the gardens and lawn. Dinner is served from an extensive menu accented with Asian flavors and Indian curries and other world flavors, accompanied by home-baked breads, and always including vegetarian choices (entrees $16–32). Reservations are essential on weekends and for the annual July Fourth pig roast. The inn's cozy pub has a smaller and less pricey menu. Open Valentine's Day to late December, but nights vary off-season.

Also worth checking out is **Bagaduce Oyster Bay** at the Castine Harbor Lodge (207/326-4335). Go for hors d'oeuvres and drinks on the extensive porches with views to the Camden Hills. The dining room has a good local reputation, but hours of operation aren't consistent, so it's best to call; reservations are essential. Most entrees are in the $20–30 range.

Chef Tom Gutrow gained a national reputation for classic and creative fare at the **Castine Inn** (Main St., Castine, 207/326-4365, 6–9 P.M. Wed.–Mon. May–late Oct.), but in 2004 he closed its doors. However, he plans to reopen seasonally in 2006 with a fixed-price, seven-course Chef's Tasting Menu three nights a week for a fee of $90 per person, plus another $40 for optional wine pairings with each course. Expect reservations to be mandatory; call for a schedule.

Lobster-in-the-Rough

At **Eaton's Boatyard** (Sea Street, P.O. Box 123, Castine 04421, 207/326-8579), a full-service marina renting moorings by the day or week, you can buy live lobsters May–Oct. and have them cooked or shipped anywhere year-round.

INFORMATION AND SERVICES

Castine has no local information office, but all businesses and lodgings in town have copies of the Castine Merchants Association's visitors' brochure/map. For additional information, go to the **Castine Town Office** (Emerson Hall, 67 Court St., Castine, 207/326-4502, www .castine.me.us, 8 A.M.–3:30 P.M. Mon.–Fri.).

Library

Witherle Memorial Library (41 School St., 207/326-4375, 4–8 P.M. Mon., 11 A.M.–5 P.M. Tues.–Fri., and 11 A.M.–2 P.M. Sat.). Also accessible to the public is the **Nutting Memorial Library** in Platz Hall on the Maine Maritime Academy campus. It's open 8 A.M.–4 P.M. Mon.–Fri. during the summer, longer hours during the school year.

Public Restrooms

Castine has public restrooms on the town dock, at the foot of Main Street.

DEER ISLE AND ISLE AU HAUT

After weaving your way down the Blue Hill Peninsula and crossing the soaring pray-as-you-go bridge to Little Deer Isle, you've entered the realm of island living. Sure, bridges and causeways connect the points, but the farther down you drive, the more removed from civilization you'll feel. The pace slows; the population dwindles. Fishing and lobstering are the mainstays, and lobster boats rest near many homes and trap fences edge properties.

Deer Isle is an artists' and artisans' colony, in equal parts due to the scenery and to the Haystack Mountain School of Crafts. But Deer Isle is also home to numerous small preserves, ideal for easy hiking and bird-watching, and its nearby islands beckon sea kayakers. While dreamers and summer rusticators are plentiful, Stonington is first and foremost a working waterfront dominated by lobster and fishing boats and the remnants of once very active granite quarrying operations.

The Isle au Haut section of Acadia is raw and rugged, beautiful, even breathtaking in parts. It's not as dramatic as the Mount Desert Island section, but it seduces visitors with its simplicity, peacefulness, and lack of cars. On the trails that hug the granite shoreline and climb the forested hills, perhaps more than in any other section of the park, you can feel truly removed from civilization.

PLANNING YOUR TIME

If your ultimate destination is the section of Acadia National Park on Isle au Haut, the drive down Deer Isle serves to help disconnect you from the mainland. To reach the park's

© TOM NANGLE

HIGHLIGHTS

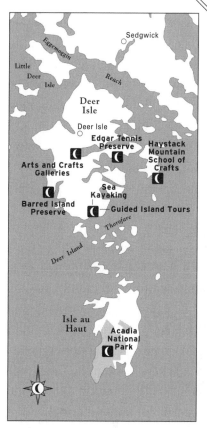

(Haystack Mountain School of Crafts: Don't miss an opportunity to visit this internationally renowned craft school with an award-winning architectural design in a stunning setting (page 192).

(Edgar Tennis Preserve: Serene views and pleasant places to picnic are reasons enough to hike the easy trails (page 195).

(Barred Island Preserve: Bring binoculars to sight nesting eagles on the island (page 196).

(Arts and Crafts Galleries: Given Haystack's presence and the inspiring scenery, it's no surprise to find dozens of fabulously talented artisans on Deer Isle (page 196).

(Sea Kayaking: Paddle between the plentiful islands off Stonington and into hidden coves (page 199).

(Guided Island Tours: Capt. Walter Reid knows these waters and is an expert on the flora and fauna (page 201).

(Acadia National Park: Isle au Haut's limited access makes this remote section of the park truly special. It's unlikely you'll have to share the trails – or the views – with more than a couple other souls (page 209).

LOOK FOR **(** TO FIND RECOMMENDED SIGHTS, ACTIVITIES, DINING, AND LODGING.

acreage on Isle au Haut, after wending your way through Little Deer Isle and Deer Isle, you'll board the Isle au Haut ferryboat for the 45-minute trip down Merchant Row to the island. In summer, you can go directly to the park's Duck Harbor landing; other months, it's a hike through the woods.

Thus, Deer Isle and Isle au Haut are inexorably linked yet distinctly separate and very different. Both seduce visitors with their rugged independence and undeveloped landscapes.

Deer Isle's main town of Stonington is a metropolis compared to Isle au Haut (about 1,200 souls versus fewer than 70). The sidewalks roll up relatively early in Stonington, but there's not much even in the way of pavement on Isle au Haut. Deer Isle has stepped tentatively into the 21st century; Isle au Haut remains pretty much in the 20th—and the early 20th at that. (Let it be said, though, that electricity came to Isle au Haut in 1970; telephone service soon followed— although cellular service is spotty at best.)

Deer Isle

"Deer Isle is like Avalon," wrote John Steinbeck in *Travels with Charley*, "it must disappear when you are not there." Deer Isle (the name of both the island and its midpoint town) has been romancing authors and artisans for decades, but it's unmistakably real to the quarrymen and fishermen who've been here for centuries. These long-timers are a sturdy lot, as even Steinbeck recognized: "I would hate to try to force them to do anything they didn't want to do."

Early-18th-century maps show no name for the island, but by the late 1800s, nearly 100 families lived here, supporting themselves first by farming, then by fishing. In 1789, when Deer Isle was incorporated, 80 local sailing vessels were scouring the Gulf of Maine in pursuit of mackerel and cod, and Deer Isle men were circling the globe as yachting skippers and merchant seamen. At the same time, in the once-quiet village of Green's Landing (now called Stonington), the shipbuilding and granite industries boomed, spurring development, prosperity, and the kinds of rough hijinks typical of commercial ports the world over.

Green's Landing became the "big city" for an international crowd of quarrymen carving out the terrain on Deer Isle and nearby Crotch Island, source of high-quality granite for Boston's Museum of Fine Arts, the Smithsonian Institution, a humongous fountain for John D. Rockefeller's New York estate, and less showy projects all along the eastern seaboard. The heyday is long past, but the industry did extend into the 20th century (including a contract for the pink granite at President John F. Kennedy's Arlington National Cemetery gravesite). Today, Crotch Island is the site of Maine's only operating island granite quarry.

Measuring about nine miles north to south (plus another three miles for Little Deer Isle), the island of Deer Isle today has a handful of hamlets (including Sunshine, Sunset, Mountainville, and Oceanville) and two towns—Stonington and Deer Isle—with a population just under 3,000. Road access is via Route 15 on the Blue Hill Peninsula. A huge suspension bridge, built in 1939 over Eggemoggin Reach, links the Sargentville section of Sedgwick with Little Deer Isle; from there, a sinuous, 0.4-mile causeway connects to the northern tip of Deer Isle.

Deer Isle is an artisans' enclave, anchored by the Haystack Mountain School of Crafts. Studios and galleries are plentiful, although many require noodling along back roads to find them. Stonington, a rough-and-tumble fishing port with an idyllic setting, is slowly being gentrified, as more and more galleries and upscale shops open for the summer each season. Long-empty downtown buildings have recently been purchased, and locals are holding their collective breath hoping that any improvements don't change the town too much (although most visitors could do without the car racing on Main Street at night). Already,

Although it's beginning to gentrify, Stonington is still a fishing town that values its heritage.

© TOM NANGLE

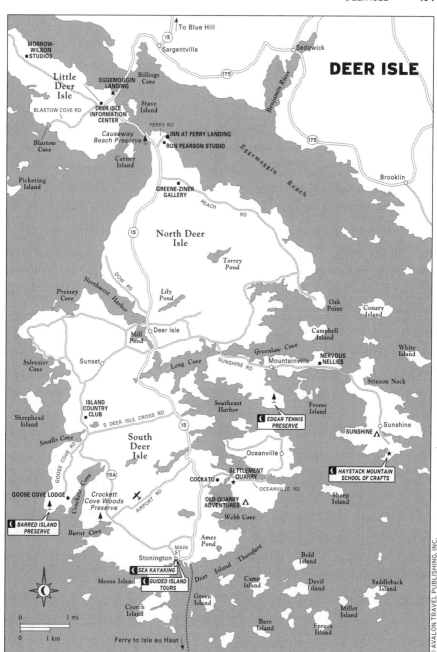

DEER ISLE

To Blue Hill

15

Sargentville

Sedgwick

175

MORROW-WILSON STUDIOS

Little Deer Isle

EGGEMOGGIN LANDING

Billings Cove

Benjamin River

DEER ISLE INFORMATION CENTER

BLASTOW COVE RD

Stave Island

FERRY RD

INN AT FERRY LANDING

RON PEARSON STUDIO

175

Causeway Beach Preserve

Blastow Cove

Carney Island

Eggemoggin Reach

Brooklin

Pickering Island

GREENE-ZINER GALLERY

REACH RD

15

North Deer Isle

Torrey Pond

DOW RD

Lily Pond

Oak Point

Conary Island

Pressey Cove

Northwest Harbor

Mill Pond

Deer Isle

Campbell Island

White Island

Sylvester Cove

Sunset

Long Cove

Greenlaw Cove

SUNSHINE RD

Mountainville

NERVOUS NELLIES

Stinson Neck

Sheephead Island

ISLAND COUNTRY CLUB

S DEER ISLE CROSS RD

South Deer Isle

Southeast Harbor

EDGAR TENNIS PRESERVE

Freese Island

SUNSHINE

Sunshine

Smalls Cove

15

GOOSE COVE RD

15A

Crockett Cove Woods Preserve

AIRPORT RD

Oceanville

SETTLEMENT QUARRY

COCKATU

OCEANVILLE RD

HAYSTACK MOUNTAIN SCHOOL OF CRAFTS

GOOSE COVE LODGE

Crockett Cove

OLD QUARRY ADVENTURES

Sheep Island

BARRED ISLAND PRESERVE

Burnt Cove

Webb Cove

Ames Pond

MAIN ST

Stonington

Deer Island Thorofare

Bold Island

Devil Island

Saddleback Island

Moose Island

SEA KAYAKING

GUIDED ISLAND TOURS

Camp Island

Green Island

Crotch Island

Millet Island

Bare Island

Spruce Island

0   1 mi

0   1 km

Ferry to Isle au Haut

© AVALON TRAVEL PUBLISHING, INC.

real estate prices and accompanying taxes have escalated way past the point where many a local fisherman can hope to purchase, and in some cases maintain, a home.

SIGHTS

Sightseeing on Deer Isle means exploring back roads, browsing the galleries, walking the trails, hanging out on the docks, and soaking in the ambience.

◖ Haystack Mountain School of Crafts

The renowned Haystack Mountain School of Crafts (Sunshine Rd., P.O. Box 518, Deer Isle 04627, 207/348-2306, www.haystack-mtn.org) in Sunshine is open to the public on a limited basis, but if it fits in your schedule, go. Tours of the campus ($5) are given every Wednesday at 1 P.M. These include a video, viewing works on display, and the opportunity to tour some studios. From early June to late August, on varying weeknights, free slide programs, lectures, demonstrations, and concerts, presented by faculty and visiting artists, start at 8 P.M. Perhaps the best opportunity is the End-of-Session auctions, held on Thursday nights every two or three weeks, when you can tour the studios free 4–6 P.M. and see the works the teachers and students have produced, then return for the auction preview at 7:30 P.M., followed by the auction at 8 P.M. It's a great opportunity to purchase craftwork at often very reasonable prices.

Historic Houses and Museums

The 1830 **Salome Sellers House** (416 Sunset Rd./Rte. 15A, Sunset Village, 207/348-2897, 1–4 P.M. Wed. and Fri. mid-June–late Sept., free), a repository of local memorabilia, is the headquarters of the **Deer Isle-Stonington Historical Society.** Volunteer guides love to provide tidbits about various items; seafarers' logs and ship models are particularly intriguing. It's just north of the Island Country Club and across from Eaton's Plumbing. Donations are appreciated.

Close to the Stonington waterfront, the

Deer Isle Granite Museum (51 Main St., Stonington, 207/367-6331) was established to commemorate the centennial of the quarrying business hereabouts. Best feature of the small museum is a 15-foot-long working model of Crotch Island, center of the industry, as it appeared at the turn of the 20th century. Flatcars roll, boats glide, and derricks move—it all looks very real. The museum is open late May through early September, but it's best to call for current days and hours of operation. Recommended donation is $5 per family.

Another downtown Stonington attraction is a Lilliputian complex known hereabouts as the **Miniature Village.** Some years ago, the late Everett Knowlton created a dozen and a half replicas of local buildings and displayed them on granite blocks in his yard. Since his death, they've been restored and put on display each summer in town—along with a donation box to support the upkeep. The village is set up on East Main Street (Route 15), below Hoy Gallery.

Pink granite from Stonington is found in buildings and monuments across the country.

© TOM NANGLE

GETTING CRAFTY

Internationally famed artisans – sculptors and papermakers, weavers and jewelers, potters and printmakers – become the faculty each summer for the unique **Haystack Mountain School of Crafts.** Founded in 1950 by Mary Beasom Bishop (1885–1972) and a group of talented Maine artisans as a studio research and study program, Haystack has grown into one of the top craft schools in the country.

Under the direction of beloved former director Francis Merritt, the school opened its first campus near Haystack Mountain, in Montville, Maine, in 1951. Ten years later, when the state unveiled plans to build a new highway (Route 3) that would bisect that campus, the school relocated to its present 40-acre oceanfront location at the end of the Sunshine Road in Deer Isle. Good move.

You would be hard-pressed to find a more artistically stimulating and architecturally stunning environment. Architect Edward Larrabee Barnes's award-winning campus perfectly complements its dramatic setting. The angular, cedar-shingled buildings are connected via walkways and teaching decks and a central staircase that cascades like a waterfall down the wooded hillside to the rocky coast below. The visual impression is one of spruce and ledge, glass and wood, islands and water.

One thing that makes Haystack work is its diverse student body. Students of all abilities, from beginners through advanced professionals come from around the globe for the two- to three-week summer sessions, taking weekday classes and enjoying round-the-clock studio access to follow their creative muses. In a recent year, students ranged in age from 18 to 75, and in professions from a retired teacher to a physicist. What brings them all here, says current director Stuart Kestenbaum, is the "direct making experience." That experience draws not only those who make but those who collect. For a collector of fine craft, he says, taking a class is a "great way to get insight into the making process; it gives a different relationship with the craft being collected." Each session also includes a range of craft. These may include blacksmithing, drawing, metals, wood, beads, clay, fiber/design, printmaking, glass, weaving, mixed media, paper, and baskets.

During a tour of the campus, you might see students at work.

Pumpkin Island Lighthouse

A fine view of Pumpkin Island Light can be had from the cul de sac at the end off the Eggemoggin Road on Little Deer Isle. If heading south on Rte. 15, bear right at the information booth after crossing the bridge and continue to the end.

Penobscot East Resource Center

A **Fisheries Museum** is planned for the new Penobscot East Resource Center, on the waterfront in Stonington (Sea Breeze Ave., 207/367-2708); fundraising is under way. The center's purpose is "to energize and facilitate responsible community-based fishery management, collaborative marine science, and sustainable economic development to benefit the fishermen and the communities of Penobscot Bay and the Eastern Gulf of Maine." Bravo to that! Plans call for educational programming, development of a kayak and small-boat launch site, and perhaps a public wharf. The enterprise is also designed to provide a space where commercial fishing men and women can interact with the public and help them understand their work and lifestyles.

Set to open in 2006 is a **Lobster Hatchery** (Stonington Lobster Co-op No. 1, 52 Indian Point Rd.). Another amazing local success story, it was constructed by volunteers from the lobster industry in donated space with $25,000 raised locally and a matching grant. The hatchery is slated to begin lobster production in 2006. Guided tours are planned; call 207/367-2708 for information.

The man behind both ventures is Ted Ames, who won a $500,000 MacArthur Fellowship Genius Grant in 2005 (see *Ted Ames, Genius* sidebar).

PARKS AND PRESERVES

Foresighted benefactors have managed to set aside precious acreage for respectful public use on Deer Isle. The Nature Conservancy owns two properties, **Crockett Cove Woods Preserve** and **Barred Island Preserve.** For information, contact the Conservancy (14 Maine St., Fort Andross, Brunswick 04011, 207/729-5181). The conscientious steward of other local properties is the **Island Heritage Trust** (3 Main St., at Rte. 15, P.O. Box 42, Deer Isle 04627, 207/348-2455). When the office is open (usually 10:30 A.M.–3 P.M. weekdays July and Aug., 10 A.M.–2 P.M. Tues. and Thurs. off-season), you can pick up notecards, photos, T-shirts, and helpful maps and information on hiking trails and nature preserves. Proceeds benefit the IHT's efforts; donations are much appreciated.

TED AMES, GENIUS

That's what Ted Ames, the man behind the Penobscot East Resource Center and the Lobster Hatchery, in Stonington, is. In 2005, he was awarded a $500,000 MacArthur Fellowship. These prestigious "genius grants" are awarded to "talented individuals who have shown extraordinary originality and dedication in their creative pursuits and a marked capacity for self-direction." The foundation credited Ames with fusing "the roles of fisherman and applied scientist in response to increasing threats to the fishery ecosystem resulting from decades of over-harvesting." Criteria for selection are: exceptional creativity, promise for important future advances based on a track record of significant accomplishment, and potential for the fellowship to facilitate subsequent creative work. No question, they found the right guy in Ted Ames.

A humble, soft-spoken man with dogged determination, Ames found little time to bask in the limelight from the award. While he certainly appreciated the money and the attention paid to his causes, the numerous interviews with TV, radio, and newspaper reporters took up valuable time, time he would rather use researching fisheries, collecting data, and devising ways to develop community-based fisheries management.

Ames is a fascinating guy, a combination of fisherman, lobsterman, and research scientist with deep Maine roots. "My family were some of the original settlers of Vinalhaven," he said. His ancestors on his father's side arrived in 1757, on the island off Rockland in Maine's mid-coast. "My mother's side came from Mount Desert." They were the original settlers on Bartlett's Island. When King George told the family to leave, they refused and stayed put. Ames grew up in a fishing family on Vinalhaven and went on to earn a master's degree in biochemistry from the University of Maine. But fishing was in his

Settlement Quarry

Here's one of the easiest, shortest walks in the area, leading to an impressive vista. From the parking lot on Oceanville Road (just under a mile off Rte. 15), marked by a carved granite sign, it's about five minutes to the top of the old quarry, where the viewing platform (a.k.a. the "throne room") takes in the panorama—all the way to the Camden Hills on a good day. In early August, wild raspberries are an additional enticement. Three short loop trails lead into the surrounding woods from here. A map is available in the trailhead box.

☪ Edgar Tennis Preserve

The 145-acre Tennis Preserve, in particular, off the Sunshine Road, has very limited parking, so don't try to squeeze in if there isn't room; schedule your visit for another hour or day. But do go, and bring at least a snack if not a full picnic to enjoy on one of the convenient rocky outcroppings (carry in, carry out, though).

Allow at least 90 minutes to enjoy the walking trails, one of which skirts Pickering Cove, providing sigh-producing views. Another trail leads to an old cemetery. Parts of the trails can be wet, so wear appropriate footwear. And do bring binoculars for bird-watching. The preserve is open sunrise to sunset. To find it, take the Sunshine Road 2.5 miles to the Tennis Road, and follow it to the preserve.

Shore Acres Preserve

The 38-acre preserve, a gift in 2000 from Judy Hill to the Island Heritage Trust, comprises old farmland, woodlands, clam flats, a salt marsh, and granite shorefront. Three walking trails connect in a 1.5-mile loop, with the Shore Trail section edging Greenlaw Cove. As you walk along the waterfront, look for the islands of Mount Desert rising in the distance and seals basking on offshore ledges. Do not walk across the salt marsh, and try to avoid stepping on beach plants. To find the

---

blood, and he eventually returned to the sea as a lobsterman and ground fisherman.

His years on the water gave him first-hand experience watching the changes in Maine's fisheries. He watched Maine's coastal economy change as fishing ports became more gentrified: Commercial piers gave way to oceanfront homes, and marine-related businesses gave way to fancy boutiques. His education combined with his experiences gave him tools and the insight needed to work toward developing new fisheries management practices and supporting fishing communities. He studied fishing patterns in the Gulf of Maine, noting spawning and habitat, and he complemented his research with listening to the stories and experiences of aging fishermen. By doing so, he was able to establish a fishing timeline beginning with historical patterns and following their evolution to current ones.

The Penobscot East Resource Center, which he founded with his wife, Robin, a former marine resources commissioner, and the Lobster Hatchery both are designed as research facilities as well as places for community members and others to learn more about fishing, meet commercial fishermen and women, and learn about their lifestyles in order to help support them and preserve the tradition and the economy. Ames, a master at gaining community support (due perhaps to his impeccable Maine credentials), managed to raise $25,000 from local fishing families and local businesses and individuals in an area not known for wealth.

Ames plans to use the unrestricted MacArthur Fellows Program money to continue his fisheries research and to develop ways for "community-based groundfishing management to make it sustainable, so coastal fishing communities can survive into the next century. That's a challenge, but we're in the midst of it." No better person to be on the forefront than Ted Ames.

preserve, take the Sunshine Road 1.2 miles, then bear left at the fork onto the Greenlaw District Road. The preserve's parking area is just shy of one mile down the road. Park only in the parking area, not on paved road.

Crockett Cove Woods Preserve

Donated to The Nature Conservancy by benevolent, eco-conscious local artist Emily Muir, 98-acre Crockett Cove Woods Preserve is Deer Isle's natural gem—a coastal fog forest laden with lichens and mosses. Four interlinked walking trails cover the whole preserve, starting with a short nature trail. Pick up the helpful map/brochure at the registration box. Wear rubberized shoes or boots and respect adjacent private property. The preserve is open sunrise to sunset daily all year. From Deer Isle Village, take Route 15A to Sunset Village. Go 2.5 miles to Whitman Road, then to Fire Lane 88. The local phone number is 207/367-2674.

◖ Barred Island Preserve

Owned by the Nature Conservancy but managed by the Island Heritage Trust, Barred Island Preserve was donated by Carolyn Olmsted, grandniece of noted landscape architect Frederick Law Olmsted, who summered nearby. A former owner of Goose Cove Lodge donated an additional 48 acres of maritime boreal fog-forest. A single walking trail, one mile in length, leads from the parking lot to the point. At low tide, and when eagles aren't nesting, you can continue out to Barred Island. Another trail skirts the shoreline of Goose Cove, before retreating inland and rejoining with the main trail. From a high point on the main trail, you can see more than a dozen islands, many of which are protected from development, as well as Saddleback Ledge Light, 14 miles distant. To get to the preserve, follow Route 15A to Goose Cove Road, then continue to the parking area on the right. If it's full, return another day.

Holt Mill Pond Preserve

The Stonington Conservation Commission administers this town-owned preserve, where more than 47 bird species have been identified

(bring binoculars). It comprises four habitats: upland spruce forest, lowland spruce/mixed forest, freshwater marsh, and saltwater marsh. A self-guiding nature trail is accessed off the Airport Road (off Rte. 15 at the intersection with Lily's Café). Look for the Nature Trail sign just beyond the Medical Center. The detailed, self-guiding trail brochure, available at the trailhead registration kiosk, is accented with drawings by noted artist Siri Beckman.

Ames Pond

Ames Pond is neither park nor preserve, but it might as well be. On a back road close to Stonington, it's a mandatory stop in July and August, when the pond wears a blanket of pink and white water lilies. From downtown Stonington, take Indian Point Road east, just under a mile, to the pond. There's no official parking, so if you're shooting photos, pull off the road as far as possible, respecting private property.

Causeway Beach

The most recent addition to the parks and preserves list is the beach along the causeway linking Little Deer Isle to Deer Isle. It's popular for swimming and is also a significant habitat for birds and other wildlife.

Reach Beach

Yet another property owned by the Island Trust, the tidal Reach Beach is at Gray's Cove. Take Reach Road, off Rte. 15, and continue past the Greenlaw District Road. The road turns to dirt, and the beach is on your left.

◖ ARTS AND CRAFTS GALLERIES

Thanks to the presence and influence of Haystack Mountain School of Crafts, supertalented artists and artisans lurk in every corner of the island. Most galleries are tucked away on back roads, so watch for roadside signs. Many have studios open to the public where you can watch the artists at work. Here's just a sampling.

Little Deer Isle

On Little Deer Isle, don't miss **Morrow Wilson**

Studios (455 Eggemoggin Rd., 207/348-6871, www.morrowwilsonstudios.com), Doug and Jennifer Morrow-Wilson's gallery. Doug has turned blacksmithing into an art form, while Jennifer makes paper by hand and uses it in three-dimensional collages that often include internal lighting. Their collaborations are especially nice. Both often open their studios to visitors.

North End of Deer Isle

Although **Ronald Hayes Pearson** has died, his innovative and beautiful jewelry lives on in his eponymous studio and gallery (29 Old Ferry Rd., 207/348-2535), where artisans continue to create his designs under the watchful eye of his wife. Do take time to visit the studio, and be sure to also visit the forge out back where Farrell Ruppert works.

The nearby **Greene-Ziner Gallery** (73 Reach Rd., 207/348-2601, www.melissagreene.com) is a double treat. Melissa Greene turns out incredible painted and incised pottery (She's represented in the Renwick) and Eric Ziner works magic in metal sculpture and furnishings. Your budget may not allow for one of Melissa's pots (in the four-digit range), but I guarantee you'll covet them. The gallery also displays the work of several other local artists.

Deer Isle Village Area

One of the island's premier galleries is Elena Kubler's **The Turtle Gallery** (61 N. Deer Isle Rd., Rte. 15, 207/348-9977, www.turtlegallery .com), in a handsome space formerly known as the Old Centennial House Barn (owned by the late Haystack director Francis Merritt) and the adjacent farmhouse. Group and solo shows of contemporary paintings, prints, and crafts are hung upstairs and down in the barn; works by gallery artists are in the farmhouse; and there's usually sculpture in the gardens both in front and in back. It's just north of Deer Isle Village—across from the Shakespeare School, oldest on the island.

Name a craft and Mary Nyburg probably has an example in her high-ceilinged barn, the **Blue Heron Gallery & Studio** (22 Church St., 207/348-2940). Formerly a Haystack board member and still an honorary trustee, she's long provided a retail outlet for the work of the school's internationally renowned faculty—printmakers, blacksmiths, potters, weavers, papermakers, glassworkers, and more. But Mary is retiring and has the property for sale. While *everyone* wants the gallery to survive, it remains to be seen whether it will and, if so, in what form.

Just a bit south is **Dockside Quilt Gallery** (33 Church St., 207/348-2531), where Nancy Knowlton, her daughter Kelly Pratt and daughter-in-law Rebekah Knowlton stitch heirloom-quality quilts. Also here are Re-Bears, one-of-a-kind teddy bears handcrafted from vintage furs and fabrics by ninth-generation islander Heather Cormier. Custom quilts and bears can be ordered.

The **Deer Isle Artists Association** (13 Dow Rd., 207/348-2330) is headquartered less than a mile northwest of the village. The co-op gallery features two-week exhibits of paintings, prints, drawings, and photos by local pros. Horse fans won't want to miss Penelope Plumb's upstairs gallery, Equine Art (207/348-6892, www.penelopeplumb.com). The entrance is in the back of the building.

Just down the street, the DOW Gallery (Dow Rd., 207/348-6498, www.dowstudiodeerisle.com) shows pottery, metalwork, jewelry, prints, and drawings by Ellen Wieske, Carole Ann Fer, and Susan Webster.

Carol Scott Wainright's hand-woven **River Horse Rugs** (Deer Isle Village, 207/348-2589, www.riverhorserugs.net) are unmistakable. Her tapestry-like designs feature organic or geometric shapes on linen warp and hand-dyed wool in deep, vivid colors. Call for an appointment.

Sunshine Road

Now for a bit of whimsy. From Route 15 in Deer Isle Village, take the Sunshine Road east 2.9 miles to **Peter Beerits Sculpture** (600 Sunshine Rd., 800/777-6845, www.nervousnellies.com). The meadows and woods surrounding the studio teem with whimsical wood and metal sculptures, including

© TOM NANGLE

Grab a cup of coffee or tea and a baked treat at Nervous Nellie's Café, then wander through the sculptures in the fields and woods.

dragons, Huns on horseback, moose, and more (all for sale). The property is also home to Beerits's other enterprise, **Nervous Nellie's Jams and Jellies,** known for outstandingly creative condiments; sample the hot pepper jelly, blackberry-peach conserve, or ginger syrup. The promotional brochures are hilarious. Best time to come is May to early October, 9 A.M.– 5 P.M., when the shop operates the ultracasual **Mountainville Café,** serving tea, coffee, and delicious scones—with, of course, Nervous Nellie's products. They're delicious—stock up, because they're sold in only a few shops.

Nearby and relatively new on the scene is the **Pitcher Masters Studio Gallery** (Good Dog Run, 45 French Camp Rd., off Sunshine Road, 207/348-2322, www.pitchermasters.com). Buzz Masters and Frank Pitcher show their paintings and pottery along with selected works by other mega-talented artists.

Stonington

Cabinetmaker **Geoffrey Warner's Studio** (431 N. Main St., 207/367-6555, www.geoffrey-warnerstudio.com) features his work as well as that of other local woodworkers in rotating shows. Warner mixes classic techniques with contemporary styles accented by Eastern, nature-based, and Arts and Crafts accents to create some unusual and rather striking pieces.

Bright and airy **Isalos Fine Art** (Main St., Stonington, 207/367-2700, www.isalosart.com) shows the work of local artists in rotating shows.

Jack and Harriet Rawle Hemenway's **Green Head Forge** (Old Quarry Rd., 207/367-2632) is a delight. Downstairs is Jack's forge and a gallery filled with his sculpted and forged metalwork; upstairs, you can watch Harriet create fabulous jewelry and small objects in gold and silver.

Debi Mortenson shows her paintings, photography, and sculptures at **D Mortenson Gallery** (10 W. Main St., 207/367-5875, www.debimortenson.com) year-round.

The **d.Watson Gallery** (68 Main St., 207/367-2900), located above the Grasshopper Shop, is a fine art gallery representing a number of artists working in varied media.

More paintings, many in bold, bright colors, can be found at Jill Hoy's **Hoy Gallery** (E. Main St., 207/367-2368).

RECREATION
Guided Walks

The Island Heritage Trust, along with the Stonington and Deer Isle Conservation Commissions, sponsors a Walks and Talks series. Guided walks cover topics such as Birds and Bird Calls for Beginners, Common Trees of Deer Isle, and Care and Culture of Your Small Woodlot. For information and reservations, call 207/348-2455.

Bicycling

As with so many other parts of Maine, the main roads on Deer Isle are narrow and winding, and hazardous for bicycling. A better bet is the 12-mile circuit of Isle au Haut. For bicycle rentals, see *Sporting Outfitters and Guided Trips.*

❰ Sea Kayaking

With lots of islets and protected coves, sea kayaking in the waters around Deer Isle, especially off Stonington, is extremely popular. Nights can be cool, but days are likely to be brilliant. Spruce-studded islands give way to granite shores, lobster buoys dot open waters

THE MAINE ISLAND TRAIL

In the early 1980s, a "trail" of coastal Maine islands was only the germ of an idea. By the end of the millennium, the **Maine Island Trail Association (MITA)** counted some 4,000 members dedicated to conscientious (i.e., low- or no-impact) recreational use of more than 100 public and private islands along 325 miles of Maine coastline between Portland and Machias.

More than a dozen of these islands (each year, new ones are added and others are subtracted) are in the Acadia region – between Isle au Haut and Schoodic Point. In fact, one of the best island clusters along the entire trail is in the waters off Stonington on Deer Isle.

Access to the trail is only by private boat, and the best choice is a sea kayak, to navigate shallow or rock-strewn coves. Sea kayak rentals are available in Bar Harbor, Southwest Harbor, Blue Hill, and Stonington, and several outfitters offer island tours. (See specific locations for details.) The best source of information is the Maine Association of Sea Kayaking Guides and Instructors (MASKGI), whose members agree to adhere to the Leave No Trace philosophy.

The trail's publicly owned islands – supervised by the state Bureau of Public Lands – are open to anyone; the private islands are restricted to MITA members, who pay $45 a year

for the privilege (and, it's important to add, the responsibility). With the fee comes the *Maine Island Trail Guidebook,* providing directions and information for each of the islands. With membership comes the expectation of care and concern. "Low impact" means different things to different people, so MITA experienced acute growing pains when enthusiasm began leading to "tent sprawl."

To cope with and reverse the overuse, MITA has created an "adopt-an-island program," in which volunteers become stewards for specific islands and keep track of their use and condition. MITA members are urged to pick up trash, use tent platforms where they exist, and continue elsewhere if an island has reached its assigned capacity (stipulated on a shoreline sign and/or in the guidebook).

A superb complement to the *Maine Island Trail Guidebook* is a copy of *Hot Showers!* by Lee Bumsted, a former MITA staff member (see *Suggested Reading*). Recognizing the need for alternating island camping and warm beds (and hot showers), she has almost single-handedly alleviated island stress and strain. Some of the B&Bs and inns listed in her guide give discounts to MITA members.

Membership information is available from **Maine Island Trail Association** (P.O. Box C, Rockland 04841, 207/596-6456, www.mita.org).

and crowd the coves, and lobstermen can be seen hauling their traps. Sailboats and wind-jammers cruise the thoroughfare. Sea birds are plentiful, and you might even spot eagles soaring overhead. It is the essence of coastal Maine, and kayaking gives you a front row seat. Beginning paddlers should book a half-day trip; experienced ones will want a full day or longer.

If you sign up with the **Maine Island Trail Association** (P.O. Box C, Rockland 04841, www.mita.org, $45 a year), you'll receive a handy manual that steers you to more than a dozen islands in the Deer Isle archipelago where you can camp, hike, and picnic—eco-sensitively, please. Boat traffic can be a bit heavy at the height of summer, so to best appreciate the tranquility of this area, try this in September, after the Labor Day holiday. Do remember this is a working harbor.

The six-mile paddle from Stonington to Isle au Haut is best left to experienced paddlers, especially since fishing folks refer to kayakers as "speed bumps."

For equipment rentals or guided trips, see *Sporting Outfitters and Guided Trips* below. Old Quarry Ocean Adventures is especially helpful and provides many services for kayakers.

Swimming
The island's only major freshwater swimming hole is the **Lily Pond,** northeast of Deer Isle Village. Just north of the Shakespeare School, turn into the Deer Run Apartments complex. Park and take the path to the pond, which has a shallow area for small children.

Golf and Tennis
About two miles south of Deer Isle Village, watch for the large sign (on the left) for the **Island Country Club** (Rte. 15A, Sunset, 207/348-2379), a nine-hole public course that's been here since 1928. Starting times are first-come, first-served, and greens fees are low; no credit cards are accepted. Open early June to late September.

Also at the club are three beautifully maintained tennis courts. Or just commandeer a rocking chair and watch the action from one of the porches. The club's cheeseburgers and salads are among the island's best bargain lunches.

Sporting Outfitters and Guided Trips
The biggest operation is **Old Quarry Ocean Adventures** (Stonington, 207/367-8977 or 877/479-8977, mobile 207/266-7778, www.oldquarry.com), with a broad range of outdoor-adventure choices. Bill Baker's ever-expanding enterprise rents canoes, kayaks, sailboats, bikes, moorings, platform tent sites, and cabins. Bicycle rentals are $18 a day or $100 a week. Canoes or rowboats are $40 half day, $50 full day, or $250 per week; sailboats are $75 or $100 half day, $100 or $150 full day. For all boat rentals, you must demonstrate competency in the vessel.

All-day guided tours in single kayaks are $105; tandems are $175. Half-day tours are $55 and $110, respectively. Plenty of other options are available, including sunset tours, family trips, and gourmet picnic paddles.

Sea kayak rental rates are $55 per day for a single, $65 for a tandem. Half-day rates (based on a four-hour rental) are $40 and $50, respectively. Overnight rates (24-hour rental) are $60.50 single and $71.50 tandem. Weekly rentals are $300 single, $380 tandem. A canoe is $50 full day, $40 half day, $55 overnight, and $250 per week. They'll deliver and pick up anywhere on the island for a fee of $20.

Overnight kayaking-camping trips on nearby islands are led by a Registered Maine Guide. Rates, including meals, begin at $275 adult, $225 children ages 12–15 for one night.

If you're bringing your own kayak, you can park your car ($6 per night up to two nights, $5 per night for three or more nights) and launch from here ($5 per boat for launching), and they'll take your trash and any trash you find. Old Quarry is off the Oceanville Road, less than a mile from Route 15, just before you reach the Settlement Quarry preserve. It's well signposted.

A smaller kayaking outfitter is in the village of Sunset—not surprisingly, on the western side of the island. **Granite Island Guide**

Service (66 Dunham Point Rd., Deer Isle, 207/348-2668, www.graniteislandguide.com) is owned by Professional Maine Guides Anne and Dana Douglass. They're avid adventurers and fascinating folks: They've bicycled around the world and trekked in Nepal's Himalayas; Doug is an ordained Congregational minister who once raced whitewater canoes on the national level. All-day guided trips, including lunch, are $90 adults, $60 children under 12. Half-day trips are $50 adults, $40 children. Island overnights are available.

Next to the restaurant of the same name and owned by the same family is **Finest Kind** (Center District Crossroad, about halfway between Routes 15 and 15A, 207/348-7714). Bicycle rentals here are $15 per day or $75 per week. Kayak or canoe rentals are $35 per day solo, $45 per day tandem, including paddles, lifejackets, spray skirts, delivery, and pickup.

EXCURSION BOATS
Isle au Haut Boat Company

If you're not up for self-propulsion, from mid-June through early September, the *Miss Lizzie* or the *Mink* departs at 9 A.M. and 2 P.M. daily from the Isle au Haut Boat Company dock in Stonington for a narrated one-hour trip among the islands; on morning tours, the crew hauls a string of lobster traps. Cost is $14 adults, $6 kids. Reservations are advisable, especially in July and August. Parking is available at the pier for $9. The *Miss Lizzie* and the *Mink* are owned by the Isle au Haut Boat Company (Seabreeze Ave., Stonington, 207/367-5193 or 207/367-6516, www.isleauhaut.com), the same company that operates the regular mailboat/passenger-ferry service to offshore Isle au Haut.

◖ Guided Island Tours

Captain Walter Reed's Guided Island Tours (207/348-6789, www.guidedislandtours.com) aboard the *Gael* are custom-designed for a maximum of four passengers. Walt is a Registered Maine Guide and professional biologist who also is a steward for Mark Island Lighthouse and several uninhabited islands in the area. He provides in-depth perspective and the

local scoop. The cost is $37.50 pp for the first hour plus $15 pp for each additional hour. Reservations required; box lunches are available for an additional fee.

Old Quarry Ocean Adventures

Yet another aspect of the Old Quarry Ocean Adventures (Stonington, 207/367-8977 or 877/479-8977, mobile 207/266-7778, www.oldquarry.com) empire are sightseeing tours on the *Nigh Duck*. The three-hour trips, one in the morning (9 A.M.–noon) and one in the afternoon (1–4 P.M.) are $35 for adults and $20 for children under 12. Both highlight the natural history of the area, as Capt. Bill navigates the boat through the archipelago. Lobster traps are hauled on both trips. The afternoon excursion features an island swimming break in a freshwater quarry. Also available is a 1.5-hour sunset cruise, departing one-half hour before sunset, for $25 adults and $10 kids under 12. And if that's not enough, Old Quarry also offers puffin, lighthouse, whale-watching, and island cruises, with rates beginning at $40 per adult, $35 for kids. Of course, if none of this floats your boat, you can also arrange for a custom charter for $175 per hour.

SHOPPING

The greatest concentration of shops is in Stonington, where galleries, clothing boutiques, and eclectic shops line Main Street.

Food

In the May 2005 issue of the *Rosengarten Report,* Hickory-Smoked Salmon, Unsliced, by **Stonington Sea Products** (100 North Main St., Stonington, 207/367-2400 or 888/402-2729, www.stoningtonseafood.com), was named one of the "25 Best Products" the noted food critic has ever recommended, describing it in terms including "Wow!" and "Bravo!" See for yourself, or try any of the company's other smoked products. If you don't visit in person, shop online.

Antiques, Books, and Gifts

Three shops are in Deer Isle Village. **Old Fire House** (12 North Deer Isle Rd./Rte. 15, Deer

Isle, 207/348-9978), just north of Main Street, is chock-full of old furniture and collectibles. Don't miss the downstairs. In "downtown" Deer Isle Village, you'll find **The Periwinkle** (8 Main St., Deer Isle 04627, 207/348-2256), where Neva Beck carries a fine inventory of Maine books, as well as crafts, notecards, and gifts. Look for Neva's hand-braided rugs and chair pads and baby quilts. Just south off Main Street you'll come to Janice Glenn's **Old Deer Isle Parish House Antiques** (7 Church St., Rte. 15, Deer Isle, 207/348-9964), a funky shop heavy into vintage clothing, antique kitchen utensils, and other collectibles, with an especially nice collection of quilts, rugs, and samplers. For browsers, this place is heaven. No credit cards.

At the bottom of the island, **The Clown** (6 Thurlow's Hill Rd., Stonington, 207/367-6348) awaits. The imaginative owners came up with this combination of art, antiques, and...food and wine. Look, it works. Part of the key is the owners' farm in Tuscany, source of extra-virgin olive oil, wines, Deruta pottery, unusual furnishings, and other "necessities." Art openings are also wine-tastings—a fine idea.

The eclectic selection at **Bayside Antiques and Gifts** (131 Main St., Stonington, 207/367-8714) includes antiques, decorative accessories, and gifts, but the specialty is quality 18th- and 19th-century furniture and accessories from the Northeast.

In downtown Stonington, below the Opera House, **Dockside Books & Gifts** (West Main St., P.O. Box 171, Stonington 04681, 207/367-2652) carries just what its name promises, with a specialty in marine and Maine books. The rustic two-room shop is open May to November. Don't miss the view from outside the shop.

Eclectic Shops

If you're looking for Maine pottery, weaving, metalwork, pewterware, imported tiles, or walking sticks, go directly to the **Harbor Farm Store** (Rte. 15, P.O. Box 64, Little Deer Isle 04650, 207/348-7755 or 800/342-8003, www.harborfarm.com), one of the state's best

© TOM NANGLE

Browse fabulous antique quilts and other vintage textiles at Parish House Antiques.

gift shops. Based in a mid-19th-century schoolhouse a mile south of the Deer Isle suspension bridge, the shop carries thousands of very unusual, high-quality items, and it's all available by mail as well. The selection of tile from around the world is beyond amazing.

Here's an interesting juxtaposition—in a pastoral island setting—**William Mor Stoneware and Oriental Rugs** (663 Reach Rd., Deer Isle, 207/348-2822, www.williamm ororientalrugs .com). Bill Mor has been throwing pottery since the 1970s, and you'll see that here, but he also imports natural-dyed Afghan and Tibetan rugs via the nonprofit Cultural Survival organization—stunning work for a worthy cause. Reach Road is a mile south of the Route 15 Little Deer Isle–Deer Isle causeway; the shop is 3.3 miles down the road.

Deer Isle may be the unlikeliest spot in all of Maine for an African gift shop, but it's here. **Deepest Africa Imports** (22A Dow Rd., Deer Isle 04627, 207/348-6624) is the creation of South African–born Jackie Pelletier, who has stocked her small shop with carvings, baskets, hand-printed fabrics, traditional jewelry, and more. Several of her sources are cottage industries supporting women and the disadvantaged, and she donates 10 percent of her profits to the Soweto Township Hospice in South Africa.

P.S. After all this browsing, you just might need a double-dip cone from **Harbor Ice Cream,** across the street from The Periwinkle. Or visit **Island Cow Ice Cream,** next to the Grasshopper Shop, in Stonington.

Clothing

Women need to be cautious going into **The Dry Dock** (24 Main St., Stonington, 207/367-5528)—the merchandise instantly sells itself. Imported women's clothing from Nigerian, Tibetan, and Indian cottage industries, unique jewelry, and unusual notecards are just some of the options in one large room and a smaller back room.

ENTERTAINMENT AND EVENTS

Stonington's National Historic Landmark, the 1912 **Opera House** (207/367-2788, www.operahousearts.org), is home to Opera House Arts, which hosts films, plays, lectures, concerts, family programs, and workshops year-round. A cafe operates during programs.

Mid-June, when lupine in various shades of pink and purple seem to be blooming everywhere, brings the **Lupine Festival** (207/348-2676 or 207/367-2420). The weekend festival includes art openings and shows, boat rides, a private-gardens tour, and entertainment, ranging from a contra dance to movies.

Seamark Community Arts (207/348-2333, www.seamarkcommunityarts.com) hosts arts workshops for children and adults in areas such as book arts, nature crafts, pottery, drawing and painting, film and video, printmaking, basketry, textile arts, and more. The summer highlight is the themed annual auction; in 2005, more than 45 local artists contributed their interpretations of that year's theme, "Box It Up."

Mid-July brings the **Stonington Lobsterboat Races** (207/348-2804), very popular competitions held in the harbor, with lots of possible vantage points. Stonington is one of the major locales in the lobsterboat race circuit.

In early October is Peninsula Potters Open Studios (207/348-5681), during which more than two dozen potters welcome visitors.

Want to meet locals and learn more about the area? **Island Heritage Trust** sponsors a series of walks, talks, and tours from mid-June through mid-September. For information and reservations, call 207/348-2455.

ACCOMMODATIONS
Inns and B&Bs

Just when you're convinced you're lost, and the paved road has turned to dirt, you arrive at **C Goose Cove Lodge** (Goose Cove Rd., P.O. Box 40, Sunset 04683, 207/348-2508 or 800/728-1963 outside Maine, www.goosecovelodge.com, $145–525), a 20-acre hillside complex of rustic and modern cottages/cabins and main-lodge rooms and suites—all with private baths, most with fireplaces, and many with stunning views of secluded Goose Cove. The environment is the primary attraction. The lodge organizes nature walks and astronomy talks and provides maps and descriptions of local trails, including the Nature Conservancy's adjacent Barred Island Preserve. Bikes, kayaks, and games are available on-site for guests; off-site tennis, horseback riding, and golf programs are offered in July and August. Artwork by local artists and artisans is displayed throughout the inn. A one-week minimum stay is requested mid-July through early September, but often you can squeeze in for shorter bookings. Rates include breakfast; modified American plan is available. Children are very welcome, and in July and August, the inn has a free children's program, 5:30–8:30 P.M. nightly that includes dinner. Additional free children's programs run Tues.–Fri., 2–4 P.M. Babysitting is available by advance reservation for $8–10 per hour. The Point dining room, open to the public by reservation for dinner, has a reputation well beyond Deer Isle. Entertainment follows dinner on Monday nights. Guests can pick up premade sandwiches for lunch at the gift shop. The inn is open mid-May to mid-October. The lodge is 4.5 miles from Route 15, via Deer Isle Village.

Pilgrim's Inn (20 Main St., P.O. Box 69, Deer Isle 04627, 207/348-6615, www.pilgrimsinn.com. $129–269) is a beautifully restored Colonial building and newer cottages overlooking the peaceful Mill Pond. The National Historic Register inn began life in 1793 as a boardinghouse named The Ark; be sure to check out the fascinating guestbook, with names dating to 1901. A bit of a disconnect from the peacefulness is the recently added TV room (request a room far away from it, as the noise carries) and the downstairs tavern (formerly a fine-dining restaurant). Open early-May to late-October.

◖ The Inn on the Harbor (Main St., P.O. Box 69, Stonington 04681, 207/367-2420 or 800/942-2420, www.innontheharbor.com, $119–199) is exactly as its name proclaims. Its expansive deck hangs right over the harbor. Although recently updated, the 1880s complex still has an air of unpretentiousness. Most of the 13 rooms and suites, each named after windjammers, have fantastic harbor views and private or shared decks where you can keep an eye on lobsterboats, small ferries, windjammers, and pleasure craft. (Binoculars are provided.) Rooms on the street can be noisy at night. Rates include a continental buffet breakfast. An espresso bar is open 11 A.M.–4:30 P.M. Nearby are antique, gift, and craft shops; guest moorings are available. Open all year, but call ahead off-season, when rates are lower.

In downtown Stonington, just up the hill from the Inn on the Harbor and convenient for walking to everything (even a small sandy beach a mile away) is **Près du Port** (W. Main St. and Highland Ave., P.O. Box 319, Stonington 04681, 207/367-5007, www.presduport.com, $110), a bright B&B run by amiable innkeeper Charlotte Casgrain. After many summers at a Deer Isle French summer camp

and a career as a Connecticut French teacher, she's settled here. Two rooms have detached baths, and one has a private bath; there are vanity sinks in the rooms. Children are welcome; there's even a toy cupboard to entertain them. No credit cards. Open May–October. When Deer Isle beds are scarce at the height of summer, Charlotte is the best resource for dozens of last-minute overnight rooms in local homes. This location is ideal if you're en route to or returning from Isle au Haut.

Eggemoggin Reach is almost on the doorstep at **The Inn at Ferry Landing** (77 Old Ferry Rd., Deer Isle 04627, 207/348-7760, www.ferrylanding.com, $120–175), overlooking the abandoned Sargentville–Deer Isle ferry wharf. The view is wide open from the inn's "great room," where guests gather to read, play games, talk, and watch passing windjammers. Professional musician Gerald Wheeler has installed two grand pianos in the room; it's a treat when he plays. His wife, Jean, is the hospitable innkeeper, managing three water-view guest rooms and a suite. A harpsichord and a great view are big pluses in the suite. The Mooring, an annex that sleeps five, is rented by the week ($1,400, without breakfast). The inn is open all year except Thanksgiving and Christmas.

Motels

Here's a wallet-friendly find. Just after you go over the bridge from Brooksville, immediately on your right and fronting Eggemoggin Reach is **◖ Eggemoggin Landing** (204 Little Deer Isle Rd., P.O. Box 126, Little Deer Isle 04650, 207/348-6115, www.acadia.net/eggland, $67–85). Rooms are clean with fabulous views, and rates include a continental breakfast. Sisters, a takeout restaurant, is also on the property, as are a small playground, picnic area, dock, and beach (brrrr). Sailing cruises, as well as bicycle, sea kayak, and motorboat rentals, are available.

Right in downtown Stonington, just across the street from the harbor, is **Boyces Motel** (44 Main St., P.O. Box 94, Stonington, 207/367-2421 or 800/224-2421, www.boycesmotel.com,

$60–115). Eleven units all have TV, phones, and refrigerators; some have kitchens and living rooms, and one has two bedrooms. Across the street, Boyce's has a private harborfront deck for its guests. Ask for rooms well back from Main Street to lessen the noise of locals cruising the street at night. Open year-round.

Seasonal Rentals

For house and cottage rentals by the week, month, or season, contact **Island Vacation Rentals** (P.O. Box 446, Stonington 04681, 207/367-5095, www.deerisleproperties.com). Plan well ahead, as the best properties get snapped up as much as a year in advance. Another rental agency is **Sargent's Rentals** (P.O. Box 115, Stonington 04681, 207/367-5156, www.sargentsrentalsinc.com).

Campgrounds

Deer Isle has only two campgrounds, both owned by **Old Quarry Ocean Adventures** (130 Settlement Rd., Stonington, 207/367-8977, www.oldquarry.com, www.sunshine-campground.com), so plan ahead if you're thinking about camping. Somewhat dated, **Sunshine Campground** has 15 wooded sites for small RVs (maximum 40 feet, $28 for two plus $14 for each additional person, $5 for children younger than 12, includes water and electricity) and seven tent sites ($24 for two, $12 for each additional person, $5 for children 5–12). Facilities include a laundry, firewood, and a small store. Ocean access is available at Old Quarry. Open Memorial Day weekend to mid-October. From Deer Isle Village, the campground is on the Sunshine Road, 5.7 miles east of Route 15. **Old Quarry Ocean Adventures Campground** has both oceanfront and secluded sites for tents; RVs are allowed only in the off-season, although pop-ups and small RVs are permitted in two sites and the parking lot. Each site has a 12-by-12 platform, picnic table, deck chairs, and fire grill. Sites are $28–34 for two, plus $14–17 for each additional person. An overflow site, without platform, table, or fire ring, is $16 per night.

Campground facilities include swimming pond, hiking trails, laundry, camp store (lobsters available), and kayak launch. Parking is designed so that vehicles are kept away from most campsites, but you can use a garden cart to transport your equipment between your car and your site. The campground is adjacent to Settlement Quarry Park.

FOOD

Stonington is a dry town, so you'll want to plan for beer or wine with dinner (except for the Whale's Rib Tavern, Goose Cove Lodge, and Finest Kind Dining, which have liquor licenses). Burnt Cove Market can fix you up with the regular stuff; buy fine wines at The Clown.

Local Flavors

Craving sweets? Head to **Susie Qu's Sweets and Curiosities** (180 Sunset Crossroad, Deer Isle, 207/348-6013, 10 A.M.–4 P.M. Tues.–Sat.). Susan Scott bakes a fine selection of cookies and pies and also carries gifty items.

Best pizza on the island? Head for **Burnt Cove Market** (Rte. 15, Stonington, 207/367-2681, 6 A.M.–9 P.M., opens at 9 A.M. Sun.). Besides pizza, you can get fried chicken and sandwiches, plus beer and wine.

Creativity defines the menu at ◖ **Lily's Café** (450 Airport Rd. at Rte. 15, Stonington, 207/367-5936, 7 A.M.–5 P.M. Mon.–Fri.), in a cute house at the corner of the Airport Road just over two miles from downtown. It's all very casual; order at the counter and find a table. (Some of the tables have fun windowpane shadowboxes.) Eat here or assemble a *haute gourmet* picnic: veggie and meat sandwiches, Mediterranean salads, cheeses, and homemade soups and breads. BYOL. Upstairs is the Chef's Attic, with a smattering of antiques as well as works by local artists. Out back is an organic produce stand. Alas, it's only open for lunch (although you can pick up the fixings for a fine takeout-and-eat-later dinner) and closed on weekends.

Between May and October, every Friday the Island Community Center (School St.,

Stonington) is the locale for the lively **Island Farmers Market,** selling smoked and organic meats, fresh herbs and flowers, produce, Asian foods, maple syrup, jams and jellies, crafts, and more. Hours are 10 A.M.–noon.

Casual Dining

In 2005, owner Rob DeGennaro waved his magician's cape over the Pilgrim's Inn, a long-established gourmet destination, and reopened the restaurant as the **Whale's Rib Tavern** (20 Main St./Sunset Rd., Deer Isle Village, 207/348-5222, opens daily at 4:50 P.M.). The family friendly restaurant has won over locals with low prices, ample portions, and home-style-plus foods, along with an extensive children's menu. Adult choices range from fried fish to steak scampi, with a Monday night Lotsa Pasta all-you-can-eat special for just $9.95. There' s a full bar.

Family Friendly

In July or August, don't show up at **Finest Kind Dining** (70 Center District Crossroad, Deer Isle, 207/348-7714, www.finestkinden-terprises.com, 5–9 P.M., mid-May–mid-Oct.) without a dinner reservation. This log-cabin family restaurant is no longer a secret. Expect good, homemade all-American food—pizza, pasta, prime rib, seafood—served conscientiously in a come-as-you-are setting. And save room for dessert. Finest Kind provides wheelchair access and has a liquor license. The restaurant, owned by the Perez family, is halfway between Route 15 and Sunset Road (Route 15A). The enterprising Perezes also own the adjacent **Round the Island Mini Golf** (same phone, open the same months) and rent canoes, kayaks, and bicycles.

◖ **Harbor Café** (Main St., Stonington 04681, 207/367-5099, 6 A.M.–8 P.M. Mon.–Thurs., to 9 P.M. Fri. and Sat., and to 2 P.M. Sun.) is *the* place to go for breakfast (you can eavesdrop on the local fisherfolk if you're early enough), but it's also reliable for lunch and dinner (especially on Friday nights for the seafood fry, with free seconds). The food is well prepared, and there's a lot more than fried fish on the menu. Try to snag the front window table and watch the world go by.

In late 2005, **The Fisherman's Friend Restaurant** (Main St., Stonington, 207/367-2442, 11 A.M.–8 P.M. daily, to 9 P.M. in July and August) planned to move from its longtime uptown digs to a harborfront location, complete with great views and outdoor deck seating. The restaurant gets high marks for respectable food, generous portions, fresh seafood, and outstanding desserts. Prices are reasonable—the Friday night fish fry, with free seconds, is $7.99. BYOL. It's open mid-May–October.

Fine Dining

Creative three-course dinners are served to guests and the public, by reservation, in the attractive main lodge restaurant, called The Point, at **Goose Cove Lodge** (Goose Cove Rd., Sunset, 207/348-2508, www.goosecove-lodge.com, 5–9 P.M. Tues.–Sun.). The view is gorgeous. The menu emphasizes foods from local farmers and growers, organic whenever possible. A three-course prix-fixe menu ($28) is served 5–6:30 P.M.; otherwise entrees run $15–22. The inn has a children's program, 5:30–8:30 P.M. nightly in July and August that includes dinner. It's free for lodge guests, $25 per child for visitors. Call well ahead for holiday and weekend reservations: Goose Cove may be remote, but it's no secret. Open mid-May to mid-October.

Setting a new tone for dining in downtown Stonington is **Maritime Café** (27 Main St., Stonington, 207/367-2600, www.maritime-cafe.com, 11:30 A.M.–2:30 P.M. and 5:30–8:30 P.M.). Big windows frame the harbor from the dining room, and there's also seating on the harborside deck. The menu emphasis seafood (no surprise), but there are other choices and always a vegetarian selection. Entrees run $14–24. Every Friday and Saturday evening, weather permitting, there's a fixed-price oceanside lobster bake, complete with mussels, corn-on-the-cob, coleslaw, and live music; BYOL.

Seafood-in-the-Rough

When the weather's perfect, and you want seafood that's a bit different, in a fabulous setting, **[C** Cockatu** (Carter's Seafood, 24 Carter Ln., off Oceanville Rd., Stonington, 207/367-0900, noon–8 P.M. daily, late May–early Sept.) delivers. Fresh, fresh, fresh seafood, right out of the fish store, is cooked to order with some interesting, Portuguese-inspired preparations complementing the usual fried clams and lobster rolls. Most choices are $13–20, although lunch rolls (fish, crabmeat, scallop) begin at $8. It's takeout by definition: order inside, then grab an outside table with serene views over idyllic Webb Cove and by the cockatoo, from which the operation gets its name. You won't find a finer place or better price for lobster, either. Do save room for the homemade but fancy European-style desserts. BYOL. While most folks arrive by car, you can also canoe or kayak here. Be forewarned, when it's busy, it can take a long while to get your dinner.

New owners at **Eaton's Lobster Pool** (Blastow's Cove, Little Deer Isle, 207/348-2383, www.eatonslobsterpool.com, 5–9 P.M. Mon.–Fri., noon–9 P.M. Sat. and Sun., mid-June to mid-Sept., Fri.–Sun. in spring and fall) have gussied up the place a bit, including adding beer and wine service and a lot more than lobster to the menu. You'll find more interesting food and faster service at other island restaurants, but you'd be hard put to find a better view than here on Blastow's Cove—but you'll pay for it. Dramatic sunsets can even subdue the usual din in the rustic dining room. Reservations are advisable, especially on weekends. Look for signs across from the chamber of commerce information booth.

INFORMATION AND SERVICES

The **Deer Isle-Stonington Chamber of Commerce** (P.O. Box 459, Stonington 04681, 207/348-6124, www.deerislemaine.com) has a summer information booth on a grassy triangle on Route 15 in Little Deer Isle, a quarter of a mile after crossing the bridge from Sargentville (Sedgwick). Staffed by volunteers, the office has a rather erratic schedule, even during the summer: allegedly 10 A.M.–4 P.M. weekdays and 11 A.M.–5 P.M. Sunday.

Library

Across from the Pilgrim's Inn is the **Chase Emerson Memorial Library** (Main St., Deer Isle Village, 207/348-2899, 11 A.M.–3 P.M. Mon. and Wed., 9 A.M.–noon Sat.). Those hours complement those of the **Stonington Public Library** (Main St., Stonington, 207/367-5926, 12:30–4:30 P.M. Tues. and Fri., 9 A.M.–noon Sat.).

Public Restrooms

Public restrooms are at the Atlantic Avenue Hardware pier and at the Stonington Town Hall, Main Street; at the Chase Emerson Library in Deer Isle Village; and behind the information booth on Little Deer Isle.

Isle au Haut

Eight miles off Stonington lies 4,700-acre Isle au Haut, roughly half of which belongs to Acadia National Park. Pronounced variously as "I'll-a-HO" or "I'LL-a-ho," the island has nearly 20 miles of hiking trails, excellent birding, and a tiny village.

About 60 souls call 5,800-acre Isle au Haut home year-round, most of them eking out a living from the sea. Each summer, the population temporarily swells with day-trippers, campers, and cottagers—then settles back in fall to the measured pace of life on an offshore island.

Samuel de Champlain, threading his way through this archipelago in 1605 and noting the island's prominent central ridge, came up with the name of Isle au Haut—High Island. Appropriately, the tallest peak (543 feet) is now named Mount Champlain.

More recent fame has come to the island thanks to island-based author Linda Greenlaw,

of *Perfect Storm* fame, who wrote *The Lobster Chronicles*. Although that book piqued interest, Isle au Haut remains uncrowded and well off the beaten tourist track.

Most of the southern half of the six-mile-long island belongs to Acadia National Park, thanks to the wealthy summer visitors who began arriving in the 1880s. It was their heirs who, in the 1940s, donated valuable acreage to the federal government. Today, this offshore division of the national park has a well-managed 18-mile network of trails, a few lean-tos, several miles of unpaved road, and summertime passenger-ferry service to the park entrance.

In the island's northern half are the private residences of fisherfolk and summer folk, a minuscule village (including a market and post office), a five-mile paved road, and a lighthouse inn. The only vehicles on the island are owned by residents.

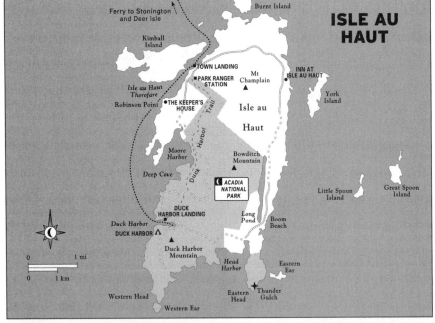

If spending the night on Isle au Haut sounds appealing (it is), you'll need to plan well ahead; it's no place for spur-of-the-moment sleepovers. (Even spontaneous day trips aren't always possible.) The best part about staying overnight on Isle au Haut is that you'll have much more than seven hours to enjoy this idyllic island.

◖ ACADIA NATIONAL PARK

Mention Acadia National Park and most people think of Bar Harbor and Mount Desert Island, where more than three million visitors arrive each year. The Isle au Haut section of the park sees maybe 5,000 visitors a year—partly because only 48 people a day (not counting campers) are allowed to land here. The remoteness of the island and the scarcity of beds and campsites also contribute to the low count, leaving the trails and views for only a few hardy souls.

Near the town landing, where the year-round mailboat and another boat dock, is the **Park Ranger Station** (207/335-5551), where you can pick up trail maps and park information—and use the island's only public facilities. (Do yourself a favor, though: Plan ahead by downloading Isle au Haut maps and information from the Acadia National Park website, www.nps.gov/acad/.)

HIKING

Hiking on Acadia National Park trails is the major recreation on Isle au Haut, and even in the densest fog, you'll see valiant hikers going for it. A loop road circles the whole island; an unpaved section goes through the park, connecting with the mostly paved nonpark section. Walking on that is easy. Beyond the road, none of the park's 18 miles of trails could be labeled "easy"; the footing is rocky, rooty, and often squishy. But the park trails *are* well marked, and the views—of islets, distant hills, and ocean—make the effort worthwhile. Go prepared with proper footwear.

Duck Harbor Trail

- Distance: 4 miles one-way
- Duration: 2 hours one-way

- Elevation Gain: minimal
- Effort: moderate
- Trailhead: Park Ranger Station, north end of the island

The most-used park trail connects the town landing with Duck Harbor. (You can either use this trail or follow the island road—mostly unpaved in this stretch—to get to the campground when the summer ferry ends its Duck Harbor runs.)

Duck Harbor Mountain Trail

- Distance: 2.4 miles round-trip
- Duration: 3–4 hours round-trip
- Elevation Gain: 300 feet
- Effort: strenuous
- Trailhead: Western Head Road

Even though the summit is only 314 feet, this is the island's toughest trail. Still, it's worth the effort for the stunning, 360-degree views from the summit. *Option:* Rather than return via the trail's steep, bouldery sections, cut off at the Goat Trail and return to the trailhead that way.

Western Head and Cliff Trails

- Distance: 2 miles one-way
- Duration: 2 hours
- Elevation Gain: 150 feet
- Effort: moderate
- Trailhead: Western Head Road

For terrific shoreline scenery, take these two trails at the island's southwestern corner that form a nice loop around Western Head. The route follows the coastline, ascending to ridges and cliffs and descending to rocky beaches, with some forested sections. *Options:* Close the loop by returning via the Western Head Road. If the tide is out (and *only* if it's out), you can walk across the tidal flats to the quaintly named Western Ear for views back toward the island. Western Ear is private, so don't linger. The Goat Trail adds another four miles (round-trip) of moderate coastline hiking east of the Cliff Trail; views are fabulous and birding is good, but if you're only here for a day, you'll need to decide whether there's time to catch the return mailboat. If you do have the time and the energy, you can connect from the Goat Trail to the Duck Harbor Mountain Trail.

Long Pond Trail

- Distance: 3 miles round-trip
- Duration: 2 hours
- Elevation Gain: 150 feet
- Effort: strenuous
- Trailhead: main road, western side of the island

Big views are the rewards for this difficult loop hike that crosses from the west to the east side of the island and passes along a ridge parallel-ing Long Pond before climbing to the summit of Bowditch Mountain. *Options:* The trail intersects with the Median Ridge Trail (1.6 miles of moderate terrain to where it intersects with the main road) and the Bowditch Trail.

Bowditch Trail

- Distance: 4 miles round-trip
- Duration: 2 hours round-trip
- Elevation gain: 350 feet
- Effort: moderate
- Trailhead: off Duck Harbor Trail (1.5 mi from the ranger station)

The Bowditch Trail passes through bogs, forests, and wet ledges as it climbs to the mountain's 405-foot summit, where it connects to the Median Ridge Trail. Varied terrain and good views make the effort worthwhile.

Walks and Unmarked Hikes

Befriend a local and ask for directions to **Seal Trap,** an easy trail to a postcard harbor on the island's west side. The unmarked trail crosses private property, so do ask locally whether you can hike it, and practice good trail etiquette. Another unmarked trail that's worth discovering is **Mt. Champlain,** a moderate hike up to the 543-foot summit, which provides few views as it's heavily forested. Access is on the north end of the island.

When the water's rough, **Boom Beach,** on the island's east side, is the place to be. As crashing waves roll in over the round rocks, they rumble, hence the boom. The stormier it is, the wilder this spot becomes. It's an easy five-minute walk to the stone beach along a spruce-lined path edged with moss- and lichen-covered rocks. Bring a picnic, but don't even consider swimming here. Boom Beach is approximately one-quarter mile north of Long Pond beach; look for a grassy pullout, where there might be a few metal lobster traps. Ticks can be a problem here, so be wary.

If you're traveling counterclockwise around the island, just north of Head Harbor, take the first road on the right, when the road turns to tar (you'll see a bright yellow house just down the road), and continue to a red and gray house, then look for a sign for **Thunder Gulch.** Follow the trail through the woods and down the middle of Eastern Head. Tension seems to build as you walk through the woods, then the trail emerges to open ocean views. Waves roll into a cleavage in the rock, before erupting in a tower of spray. One islander describes it as a Zen-like place "where all your questions will be answered."

BIKING

Pedaling is limited to the 12 or so miles of mostly unpaved roads, and while it is a way to get around, frankly, the terrain is neither exciting, fun, nor view-worthy. Mountain bikes are not allowed on the park's hiking trails, and rangers try to discourage park visitors from bringing them to the island. If you're staying at The Keeper's House or Inn at Isle au Haut, you can borrow a bike, which is handy around the "village" and for going swimming in Long Pond. You can also rent a bike ($18–20 per day) on the island from the Isle au Haut Ferry Service or Old Quarry Ocean Adventures. It costs $8 round-trip to bring your own bike aboard the Isle au Haut Ferry. Both boats carry bikes *only* to the town landing, not to Duck Harbor.

SWIMMING

For superb freshwater swimming, head for Long Pond, a skinny, 1.5-mile-long swimming hole running north-south on the east side of the island, abutting national park land. You can bike over there, clockwise along the road, almost five miles, from the town landing. Or bum a ride from an island resident. There's a minuscule beach-like area on the southern end with a picnic table and a float. If you're here only for the day, though, there's not enough time to do this *and* get in a long hike. Opt for the hiking—or do a short hike and then go for a swim (the shallowest part is at the southern tip).

ACCOMMODATIONS AND FOOD

There are no restaurants serving breakfast or lunch on Isle au Haut, so if you're coming for a day trip, bring sufficient food and water. If you're staying overnight, both inns provide all meals. Cottage dwellers can also arrange for dinner at the Inn at Isle au Haut.

The most exotic and priciest overnight option is ◖ **The Keeper's House** (P.O. Box 26, Lighthouse Point, Isle au Haut 04645, off-island 207/460-0257, www.keepershouse.com), Maine's only light-station inn. Attached to Robinson's Point Light (automated) and within night sight of three other lighthouses, this is a must-visit for lighthouse fans and others seeking unusual lodgings. Judi Burke, daughter of a Cape Cod lightkeeper, bought the 1907 National Historic Register building with her husband, Jeff, in 1986, and turned it into an inn. Former Peace Corps volunteers, commune dwellers, and union organizers, the Burkes are avid recyclers and environmentalists. Although it will undoubtedly disappoint past guests, the Burkes have decided to downsize their operation. They now rent only two rooms on an all-inclusive, Monday through Thursday package (the inn is closed Thursday night through Sunday night). The Garret ($1,300) is an expansive room with private bath, built under the eaves on the third floor. The Oil House ($950), a primitive and tiny one-room building sitting on the ocean's edge, has a solar shower and private backhouse with composting toilet. Rates include breakfast, lunch, and candlelight four-course dinners (a lobster bake on Wednesday nights). Even breakfast is fanciful, perhaps smoked salmon Benedict with orange-dill sauce and cranberry scones or fresh haddock cakes and cinnamon rolls. Jeff offers a very informative tour during which he explains the inn's reverse-osmosis water process,

Stay at the Keeper's House on Isle au Haut, and the island's lighthouse is out your front door.

photovoltaic systems, solar hot-water heater, solar cooker, and other innovative programs designed for sustainable living. He ends with a demonstration of the process used to create bio-diesel fuel for the inn's boat. In season, the mailboat drops guests at the inn; off-season, Jeff meets the boat at the town dock. BYOL and pack light. Single-speed bikes are available free for guests. If you're going hiking or biking, the Burkes will pack you a lunch. No electricity, no phones, no smoking, no credit cards, no pets, no stress. Nirvana. Open mid-May–mid November. Also on the Keeper's House premises is a one-bedroom housekeeping cottage, the **Woodshed,** that rents for $2,000 per week late June through early September, $1,750 in the spring and fall. Woodshed guests are invited to the Wednesday night lobster bake.

On the east side of the island is **The Inn at Isle au Haut** (P.O. Box 78, Lighthouse Point, Isle au Haut 04645, off-island 207/335-5141, www.innatisleauhaut.com, $250–315), a mansard-roofed, waterfront Victorian home that Diana Santospago has turned into an inn. An accomplished cook, Diana whips up fabulous breakfasts, lunches, dinners for her guests; others can make reservations for the five-course dinner ($55); bring your own beer or wine. The downstairs room with private bath is most spacious. Three rather small rooms on the second floor share one bath; all but one have water views. Bikes are provided for guests, and it's an easy pedal to Long Pond for swimming or to connect with park trails. Open late May–early October.

Camping

The only camping on Isle au Haut is in lean-tos at the Acadia National Park campground. So you'll need to get your bid in early to reserve one of the five six-person lean-tos at **Duck Harbor Campground,** open May 15–Oct. 15. Before April 1, contact the park for a reservation request form: Acadia National Park (P.O. Box 177, Bar Harbor 04609, 207/288-3338, www.nps.gov/acad). Anytime from April 1 on (not before, or they'll send it back to you), return the completed form, along with a check for $25, covering camping for up to six people

for a maximum of five nights May 15–June 14, three nights June 15–September 15, and five nights again September 16–October 15. Mark the envelope: "Attn: Isle au Haut Reservations." Competition is stiff in the height of summer, so list alternate dates. The park returns the check if there's no space; otherwise, it's nonrefundable and you'll receive a "special-use permit" (*DO NOT* forget to bring it along). There's no additional camping fee.

Unless you don't mind backpacking nearly five miles to reach the campground, try to plan your visit between mid-June and Labor Day, when the mail boat makes a stop in Duck Harbor. It's wise to call the Isle au Haut Company for the current ferry schedule before choosing dates for a lean-to reservation.

Trash policy is carry-in/carry-out, so pack a trash bag or two with your gear. Also bring a container for carting water from the campground pump, since it's 0.3 mile from the lean-tos. It's a longish walk to the general store for food—when you could be off hiking the island's trails—so bring enough to cover your stay.

The three-sided lean-tos are big enough (8 feet by 12 feet, 8 feet high) to hold a small (two-person) tent, so bring one along if you prefer

Isle au Haut Light, built in 1907, is now listed on the National Historic Register.

being fully enclosed. Alternatively, a tarp will do the trick. (Also bring mosquito repellent—some years, the critters show up here en masse.) No camping is permitted outside of the lean-tos, and nothing can be attached to trees.

Food

Isle au Haut is pretty much a BYO place—and that means BYO food. There is no restaurant. Unless you're staying at one of the two inns, the only source of food is the **Isle au Haut General Store,** not far from the town landing. (The Inn at Isle au Haut is open to the public for dinner by reservation, but you need to get there and back. Unless you're staying in a rental cottage with a car, there's no way to do so.) Thanks to the store, you won't starve. The inventory isn't extensive, but it can be intriguing, due to the store manager who travels worldwide and stocks the shop with her finds. On the other hand, food probably won't be your prime interest here—Isle au Haut is as good as it gets.

GETTING THERE

Until recently, unless you had your own vessel, the only access to Isle au Haut's town landing was the mailboat. That's still the only way to get there year-round, but two companies now offer transportation to and from the island. Use Isle au Haut Boat Company if your destination is the park, as it lands right at Duck Harbor twice daily during peak season.

Isle au Haut Boat Company

The **Isle au Haut Boat Company** (Seabreeze Ave., P.O. Box 709, Stonington 04681, 207/367-5193, www.isleauhaut.com) generally operates five daily trips Monday–Saturday, plus an extra trip on Friday evening, and two on Sunday between mid-June and Labor Day. Other months, there are two or three trips Monday–Saturday. Best advice is to request a copy of the current schedule, covering dates, variables, fares, and extras.

April to mid-October round-trips are $32 adults, $16 kids under 12 (two bags per adult, one bag per child). Round-trip surcharges:

bikes ($16), kayaks/canoes ($30 minimum), pets ($8). If you're considering bringing a bike, be sure to inquire about on-island bike rentals ($20 per day). Weather seldom affects the schedule, but be aware that ultraheavy seas could cancel a trip.

From mid-June to Labor Day, there is twice-daily ferry service from Stonington to Duck Harbor, at the edge of Isle au Haut's Acadia National Park campground. For a day trip, the schedule allows you 6.5 hours on the island Mon.–Sat. and 4.5 hours on Sunday. No boats or bikes are allowed on this route, and no dogs are allowed in the campground. A ranger boards the boat at the town landing and goes along to Duck Harbor to answer questions and distribute maps. Before mid-June and after Labor Day, you'll be off-loaded at the Isle au Haut town landing, about five miles from Duck Harbor. The six-mile passage from Stonington to the Isle au Haut town landing takes 45 minutes; the trip to Duck Harbor is 1.25 hours.

Ferries depart from the **Isle au Haut Boat Company Dock** (Seabreeze Ave., off E. Main St. in downtown Stonington). Parking ($9 per day outside, $11 indoors) is available next to the ferry landing. Arrive at least an hour early to get all this settled so you don't miss the boat. Better yet, spend the night on Deer Isle before heading to Isle au Haut.

Old Quarry Ocean Adventures

New kid on the block offering seasonal service to Isle au Haut, **Old Quarry Ocean Adventures** (Stonington, 207/367-8977 or 877/479-8977, mobile 207/266-7778, www.oldquarry.com) transports passengers on the recently renovated *Nigh Duck.* The boat usually leaves Old Quarry at 9 A.M. and arrives at the island's town landing one hour later. It departs from the same point at 5 P.M., arriving back at Old Quarry around 6 P.M. The fee is $32 round-trip for adults, $15 for children under 12. You can add an island bike rental for an additional $18. Old Quarry also offers a private taxi service to Isle au Haut for $125 each way for up to six people, $145 for larger groups.

ELLSWORTH AND TRENTON

The punchline to an old Maine joke is "Ya cahn't get they-ah from he-ah." Truth is, you can't get to Acadia without going through Ellsworth and Trenton. Indeed, when you're crawling along in bumper-to-bumper traffic, it might seem as if all roads lead to downtown Ellsworth. Truth is, many do.

While there are ways to skirt around a few of the worst bottlenecks, the region does have its calling cards. Ellsworth boasts historical homes, a grand theater, a delightful bird sanctuary, an inviting downtown shopping area, and a few choice dining spots. Trenton, linked by a bridge to Mount Desert, is little more than a six- or seven-mile strip of restaurants, lodgings, shops, and activities.

One more plus for the area is the new Bar Harbor Chamber of Commerce Information Center, opening in 2006 in the former Acadia Information Center location on Rte. 3 in Trenton. If you're day-tripping to Mount Desert Island, you can leave your car here and hop aboard the free Island Explorer bus, eliminating driving and parking hassles.

PLANNING YOUR TIME

Route 1, the main thoroughfare along the coast, and Route 1A, which connects to Bangor, meet in downtown Ellsworth. Route 172 leads to the Blue Hill Peninsula and on to Deer Isle, Stonington, and the mailboat to Isle au Haut. Route 1 continues north, providing

© TOM NANGLE

HIGHLIGHTS

◖ **Woodlawn:** This treasure-filled Georgian mansion has gardens, carriage houses, and walking trails (page 216).

◖ **Birdsacre:** Ornithologist Cordelia Stanwood's homestead is now a preserve, with a nature center, walking trails, and a bird rehabilitation center (page 216).

◖ **Aerial Touring:** Get a proper introduction to Mount Desert Island by gliding with the hawks or getting an eagle's eye view from a small plane (page 221).

◖ **The Great Maine Lumberjack Show:** A must with kids, this show demonstrates all the old-time woods skills (page 222).

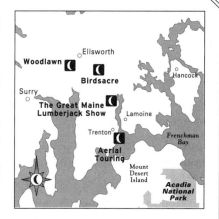

LOOK FOR ◖ TO FIND RECOMMENDED SIGHTS, ACTIVITIES, DINING, AND LODGING.

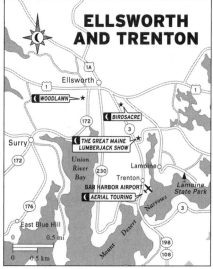

ELLSWORTH AND TRENTON

© AVALON TRAVEL PUBLISHING, INC.

access to the Schoodic Peninsula and a remote section of the park. And the Bar Harbor Road (Route 3) is something of an Achilles heel—often a summertime bottleneck as it funnels all traffic to Mount Desert Island.

This became all too clear in June 2003, when a wealthy island summer resident had a mature apple tree moved from Ellsworth—via Trenton, of course—to his Northeast Harbor home. With no passing room to spare on the narrow two-lane roads, and the need to raise phone, cable, and electric wires along the entire route for the 20-foot-high tree, the traffic backed up halfway to Bangor—a costly 12-hour nightmare. Public works and local government officials learned a hard lesson, residents and commuters earned a public apology in the newspapers, and wags vowed to sneak in and sample those expensive apples if and when the tree bears fruit in its new soil.

Ellsworth

Hancock County's shire town has mushroomed with the popularity of Acadia National Park, but you can still find handsome architectural remnants of the city's 19th-century lumbering heyday (which began shortly after its incorporation in 1800). Brigs, barks, and full-rigged ships—built in Ellsworth and captained by local fellows—loaded lumber here and carried it round the globe. Despite a ruinous 1855 fire that swept through downtown, the lumber trade thrived until late in the 19th century, along with factories and mills turning out shoes, bricks, boxes, and butter.

These days, Ellsworth is the region's shopping mecca. Antique shops and small stores line Main Street, which doubles as Route 1 in the downtown section; supermarkets, strip malls, and big-box stores line Routes 1 and 3 between Ellsworth and Trenton. Amidst all this roadside clutter, there are a few gems worth visiting.

SIGHTS
(Woodlawn

Very little has changed at the Woodlawn (Surry Rd./Rte. 172, Ellsworth, 207/667-8671, www.woodlawnmuseum.com, 10 A.M.–5 P.M. Tues.–Sat. and 1–4 P.M. Sun. June–Sept., 1–4 P.M. Tues.–Sun. May and Oct., $7.50 adults, $3 children 5–12; grounds are free) since George Nixon Black donated his home, also known as the Black Mansion, to the town in 1928. Completed in 1828, the Georgian house is a marvel of preservation—one of Maine's best—filled with Black family antiques and artifacts. Enthusiastic docents lead hourlong tours, beginning on the hour, to point out the circular staircase, rare books and artifacts, canopied beds, a barrel organ, and lots more. Even kids appreciate all the unusual stuff. Afterward, plan to picnic on the manicured grounds, then explore two sleigh-filled barns, the Memorial Garden, and the two miles of mostly level trails in the woods up beyond the house. Restrooms are next to the parking area.

On several Wednesday afternoons in July and August, there are elegant teas in the garden (or in the carriage house if it's raining). China, silver, linens, special-blend tea, sandwiches, pastries, and live music—all for $15 a person; reservations are required. The grounds are accessible all year. In winter, there's cross-country skiing on the trails. On Route 172, 0.25 mile southwest of Route 1, watch for the small sign and turn into the winding uphill driveway.

(Birdsacre

En route to Bar Harbor, watch carefully on the right for the sign that marks Birdsacre (Rte. 3, Bar Harbor Rd., Ellsworth, 207/667-8460), a 185-acre urban sanctuary. Wander the trails in this peaceful preserve—spotting wildflowers, birds, and well-labeled shrubs and trees—and you'll have trouble believing you're surrounded by prime tourist territory. The sanctuary is

Walk the trails at Birdsacre, a 185-acre urban sanctuary.

open all year, sunrise to sunset. At the sanctuary entrance is the 1850 **Stanwood Homestead Museum,** with period furnishings and wildlife exhibits. Once owned by noted ornithologist Cordelia Stanwood, the volunteer-operated museum is open for tours by chance or appointment, mid-May–mid-October. To be sure, call ahead for an appointment. Admission is free to the preserve and the homestead, but donations are needed and greatly appreciated. Birdsacre is also a wildlife rehabilitation center, so expect to see all kinds of winged creatures, especially hawks and owls, in various stages of rescue. Some will be returned to the wild, while others remain here for educational purposes. Stop by the Nature Center for even more exhibits.

The New England Museum of Telephony

What was life like before cell phones or touch-tone dialing? Find out at The New England Museum of Telephony (166 Winkumpaugh Rd., Ellsworth, 207/667-9491, www.ellsworthme.org/ringring, 1–4 P.M. Wed. and Sun. July.–Sept., $4 adult, $2 kids, $10 family), a hands-on museum with the largest collection of old-fashioned switching systems in the East, including many from Maine. Place a call to see how these old systems work. To find the museum, head 10 miles north on Route 1A (toward Bangor), then go left on Winkumpaugh Road for one mile.

RECREATION
Hiking

One of the newest efforts by the young Frenchman Bay Conservancy (207/422-2328, www.frenchmanbay.org) is the 13-acre **Indian Point Preserve.** The reward for following the footpath to the Union River shorefront is a lovely view of the city. Future plans call for a loop trail with wheel chair access. To find the preserve, drive south on Water Street, cross Card Brook, and at the top of the next hill, look for Tinker Farm Way on your right. The road to the preserve's parking lot angles off to the right.

Nature trails lace **Birdsacre** (Rte. 3, Bar Harbor Rd., Ellsworth, 207/667-8460), a 185-acre urban sanctuary with three small ponds. Two miles of mostly level trails can also be found behind the Black House at **Woodlawn** (Surry Rd./Rte. 172, Ellsworth, 207/667-8671, www.woodlawnmuseum.com).

Boat Launches

If you've brought your own boat, you can launch it into the Union River at the **Waterfront Park and Marina** (Water Street). To find it, when heading north on Route 1, take a right at the first light in town. Another launch is on **Graham Lake,** just above the dam, on Route 180. To find it, take Route 1A north from downtown Ellsworth, then Routes 180/179 to the split, then Route 180. Look for the boat launch sign on your right, just after the dam.

Sports Facilities

Ellsworth has public basketball courts on Route 1 A, heading north toward Bangor; a running track on Forest Avenue, off Route 1A; and tennis courts at Ellsworth High School, on Route 1A.

The **James Russell Wiggins Downeast Family YMCA** (238 State St., Ellsworth, 207/667-3086, www.defymca.org) has a gym and indoor pool. It's open 5:30 A.M.–9 P.M. Mon.–Fri., 8 A.M.–5 P.M. Sat. and noon–5 P.M. Sunday. A day pass is $8 per adult, $5 senior or college, $3 youth, or $10 family. It's adjacent to the Skatepark and Ice Rink on Route 1A.

SHOPPING
Antiques and Books

You're unlikely to meet a single soul who has left the **Big Chicken Barn Books and Antiques** (Rte. 1, 1768 Bucksport Rd., Ellsworth, 207/667-7308) without buying *something.* You'll find every kind of collectible on the vast first floor, courtesy of more than four dozen dealers. Climb the stairs for books, magazines, old music, and more. With 21,000 square feet, this place is addictive, offering free coffee, restrooms, and hassle-free browsing. The Big Chicken is 11 miles east of Bucksport, 8.5 miles west of Ellsworth.

The 40-plus-dealer **Old Creamery Antique Mall** (207/667-0522) has two shops: the original, 6,000-square-foot shop (13 Hancock St.) and a smaller shop just around the corner (163 Main St., Rte. 1). Both are fun to poke around.

Eclectic Shops

Don't miss **Rooster Brother** (29 Main St., Rte. 1, Ellsworth, 207/667-8675 or 800/866-0054, www.roosterbrother.com), for gourmet cookware, cards, and books on the main floor; coffee, tea, candy, cheeses, a huge array of exotic condiments, fresh breads, and other gourmet items on the lower level; and discounted merchandise on the second floor, open seasonally. You can easily pick up all the fixings for a fancy picnic here. The shop is in a handsome old riverside building on busy Route 1. Access to the store's parking lot can be tricky at times because of traffic patterns, so be cautious and patient.

It's hard to categorize **J & B Atlantic Co.** (142 Main St., Rte. 1, 207/667-2082). It takes up a good portion of the block, with room after room filled with furniture, home accessories, gifts, books, and antiques.

John Edwards Market (158 Main St., Ellsworth, 207/667-9377) is a two-fold find. Upstairs is a natural foods store. Downstairs is the Wine Cellar Gallery, a terrific space showcasing Maine artists throughout the year.

Sporting Goods and Toys

For an extensive sporting-gear inventory, plus advice on outdoors activities, stop in at **Cadillac Mountain Sports** (34 High St., Rte. 1, Ellsworth, 207/667-7819).

If there are kids on your shopping list, pay a visit to the **Toymaker Gift Shop** (Rte. 1A, Ellsworth, 207/667-3714), run by a guy who happens to look a lot like Santa Claus. All sorts of wooden toys, many made in Maine, as well as other wooden wares are inside. It's seven miles north of the intersection with Route 3.

Discount Shopping

You can certainly find bargains at the **L.L. Bean Factory Store** (150 High St., Rte. 1, Ellsworth, 207/667-7753), but this is an outlet, so scrutinize the goods for flaws and blemishes before buying.

Across the road is **Reny's Department Store** (Ellsworth Shopping Center, High St., Rte. 1, Ellsworth, 207/667-5166), a Maine-based discount operation with a you-never-know-what-you'll-find philosophy. Trust me, you'll find something here.

In an adjacent shopping plaza is **Marden's** (225 High St./Rte. 1A, Ellsworth, 207/669-6036, www.mardenssurplus.com), another Maine bit-of-this, bit-of-that enterprise with the catchy slogan: I shoulda bought it, when I saw it. Good advice.

ENTERTAINMENT

The carefully restored art deco **Grand Auditorium** of Hancock County (100 Main St., Ellsworth, 207/667-9500) is the year-round site of films, concerts, plays, and art exhibits. Most films are at 7:30 P.M. Call for schedule.

First-run films, usually showing twice a night, plus bargain matinees in midsummer, are on the docket at **Hoyts Cinemas Maine Coast Mall** (225 High St., Rte. 1, Ellsworth, 207/667-3251).

A summer highlight is the **Ellsworth Concert Band** concert series, held Wednesday evenings in July and August in the plaza outside Ellsworth City Hall (an imposing building just north of Main Street). If it rains, it's held inside City Hall. Practice begins at 6:30 P.M.; concerts start at 8 P.M. The 50-member community band even welcomes visitors with talent and instruments. Just show up at practice time. The repertoire is mostly marches and show music; a prize goes to the person who correctly identifies a mystery tune.

ACCOMMODATIONS
Motels and B&Bs

National chain (Comfort Inn, Holiday Inn, TraveLodge) and independent motels line High Street (Rtes. 1 and 3), a densely commercial stretch in Ellsworth, and continue southward through Trenton toward Mount Desert Island. Most of the motels and cabin complexes along the Trenton stretch are smaller, family-owned operations—not fancy, but their rates are far lower than what you'd find on Mount Desert. (Bar Harbor is 20 miles from downtown Ellsworth.)

White Birches (Rte. 1, P.O. Box 743, Ellsworth 04605, 207/667-3621 or 800/435-1287, www.birches.com) is a clean, generic, somewhat dated motel with 67 rooms ($70–100 d, in shoulder and peak seasons; kids 16 and younger free). It's popular with tour groups. The resort has a nine-hole par 3 course ($20 per visit). Request a room overlooking the course. The motel's family-oriented **Czy Gil's Restaurant** does a breakfast buffet 8–11 A.M. and dinner (4–9 P.M., entrees $8–16), with an emphasis on seafood. Rooms have phones and cable TV; some have air-conditioning. Open all year.

Simple accommodations are provided at **Mrs. Bancroft's Bed & Breakfast** (6 Wood St., Ellsworth, 207/667-4696, $55), a rambling 1876 home in a quiet, residential neighborhood within walking distance of downtown shops and restaurants.

FOOD
Local Flavors

Order breakfast anytime at **The Riverside Café** (151 Main St., Ellsworth, 207/667-7220, 6 A.M.–3 P.M. Mon.–Fri., opens at 7 A.M. Sat. and Sun., closes at 2 P.M. Sun.), owned and operated by sisters Beth Fendl and Barbara Guida. The fresh-squeezed juices are fabulous, the buckwheat pancakes are outstanding, and there's even a vegetarian menu with vegan choices. Lunch menu includes homemade soups, salads, sandwiches, grilled sandwiches, and high-cal desserts. Sunday brunches are legendary. Breakfast is served all day; lunch service begins at 11 A.M. And the cafe's name? It used to be down the street, overlooking the Union River.

On the Main Street spur heading east from Ellsworth (also called Washington Junction Road), **Larry's Bakery** (241 Main St., Ellsworth, 207/667-2557, 6 A.M.–5 P.M. Mon.–Sat.) may look unassuming, but *everyone* goes there for bread, rolls, pies, and Saturday night's

baked beans. There's good reason it's been in biz for more than 50 years. No preservatives are used and no credit cards are accepted.

Go to **Frankie's Café & Good Stuff** (40 High St., Rte. 1, in the Cadillac Mountain Sports building, 207/667-7701, 8 A.M.–5:30 P.M. Mon.–Fri.), for excellent Mediterranean/vegetarian specialties ($5–6) like veggie-rice pie, spanakopita, brie pasta pie, sesame- and butter-topped bagels. Pâté and meat sandwiches are available. Everything's very casual. There's only a handful of tables, so order food to go if it's crowded (which it often is).

Ice cream doesn't get much finer than that sold at **Morton's Ice Cream** (13 School St., Ellsworth, 207/667-1146, 11 A.M.–7:30 P.M. Tues.–Fri., noon–7:30 P.M. Sun.), a tiny shop with a deservedly giant reputation for homemade Italian gelato, sorbet, and ice cream. It's well worth the slight detour.

The **Ellsworth Farmers Market** gets under way behind 245 East Main Street, next to Larry's Bakery, early June to late October, 2–5:30 P.M. Monday and Thursday and 9:30 A.M.–12:30 P.M. Saturday. It features fresh produce as well as jams, pickles, maple syrup, homemade breads, and homespun yarns.

Ethnic Fare

Relatively new on the scene and earning rave reviews is ◖ **Cleonice Mediterranean Bistro** (112 Main St., Ellsworth, 207/664-7554, 11:30 A.M.–9 P.M. Mon.–Sat. and 5–9 P.M. Sun., but call ahead off-season), named for chef/owner Richard Hanson's mother, Cleonice Renzetti. (It helps if you learn how to pronounce it: "klee-oh-NEESE.") Gleaming woodwork and brass lighting fixtures combine for a golden glow in the long dining room, lined with wooden booths on one side, a 32-foot wooden bar, dating from 1938, on the other. The fare is outstanding. The tapas and meze selection alone is worth the trip—covering the Mediterranean circuit (spanakopita, hummus, Manchego cheese with pear sauce, and even brandade de morue); most are around $5. Dinner entree range is $18–22. Do treat yourself to a carafe of the Tunisian spiced lemonade, made with lemon, rose blossoms, and spices. Cleonice occasionally offers multi-course, fixed-price wine dinners. Definitely make reservations for dinner, as this is one popular place.

Mediterranean seems to be the *cuisine du jour* in Ellsworth. Another fine contender is **Turriglio's Ristorante Italiana** (59 Franklin St., Ellsworth, 207/667-0202, www.turriglios .com, 4 P.M.–close, Tues.–Sun.), owned by Manhattan escapee Matthew Parker (Italian on his mother's side). The Little Italy decor runs to vintage posters, antique radios, and photos of Rome in this storefront place (a few steps off Main Street). The pasta dishes are creative, and the Italian wine list is impressive. Entrees run $12–23; a children's menu is available. Downstairs is **Parker's Bar and Grill** (207/667-8700, parkersbarandgrill.com, 4:30 P.M.–close, Tues.–Sat.), with karaoke on Wednesday nights, live music on Friday nights, and a surprisingly wide-ranging menu (subs and pizzas to prime rib). Pool table and big-screen TVs create a bit of a sports-bar atmosphere.

The Mex (191 Main St., Ellsworth, 207/667-4494, www.themex.com, 11 A.M.–9 P.M. daily, until 10 P.M. Sat. and Sun.) has been a popular local eatery since 1979. The menu is punnily entertaining ("Juan-derful Beginnings"), service is good, and you won't go hungry. Lots of vegetarian choices. Entrees are $10–16. Take home a bottle of the fiery hot sauce.

Ellsworth even has a popular Thai restaurant. **The Bangkok Restaurant** (321 High St., Rte. 3, Ellsworth, 207/667-1324, 11 A.M.–3 P.M. and 4–9 P.M. Mon.–Sat., and 4–9 P.M. Sun. all year) does a creditable job, and the always-popular pad Thai is a winner. Entree range is $7–16. No MSG is used.

Lobster

Of course you can get lobster. Brian and Jane Langley's **Union River Lobster Pot** (8 South St., Ellsworth, 207/667-5077, www.lobster-pot.com, 11:30 A.M.–9 P.M. mid-June–early Sept., then 5–9 P.M. through mid-Sept.) is tucked behind Rooster Brother, right on the banks of the Union River. Lobster's the main

attraction, but the menu delivers everything from burgers, steaks, and ribs to sandwiches, chowder, and fried food. And remember to save room for the pie—especially the blueberry.

INFORMATION AND SERVICES

It can be hard to spot the **Ellsworth Area Chamber of Commerce** (163 High St., P.O. Box 267, Ellsworth 04605, 207/667-5584, www.ellsworthchamber.org) amid the malls and fast-food places lining High Street (Route 1). Watch for a small gray building topped by an Information Center sign (on the right, close to the road, when heading toward Bar Harbor, just before Shaw's Plaza). Open daily during July and August, Mon.–Sat. in late June and early September, and weekdays the rest of the year.

Library

Don't miss a chance to visit one of the state's loveliest libraries, the **Ellsworth Public Library** (46 State St., Ellsworth, 207/667-6363). The National Historic Register Federalist building was donated to the city in 1897 by George Nixon Black, grandson of the builder of the Woodlawn Museum. Services include photocopies, computer and Internet access, lectures, art exhibits, and a popular paperback exchange (take one and leave one). Open 9 A.M.–5 P.M. Monday, Tuesday, and Friday, until 8 P.M. Wednesday and Thursday, until 2 P.M. Saturday.

Newspapers

The respected *Ellsworth American* (207/667-2576), published weekly, has been around since the mid-19th century. The *Ellsworth Weekly,* a newcomer, appears every Thursday (207/667-5514). In summer and fall, the *Ellsworth American* publishes **Out & About in Downeast Maine,** a very helpful free monthly vacation supplement in tabloid format.

Getting There and Around

The Maine Department of Transportation's **Explore Maine** website (www.explore-maine.org) is the best resource for finding every mode of transportation servicing every area of the state, with links for schedules.

Vermont Transit (800/522-8737, www.vermonttransit.com) operates one round-trip daily between Bar Harbor and Bangor, via Ellsworth, and connecting with Portland, Boston, and New York City.

West Bus Service (207/546-2823 or 800/596-2823, www.westbusservice.com) provides daily service between Bangor and Calais, with a scheduled stop in Ellsworth and flag stops in Hancock, Sullivan, and Gouldsboro. Bicycles are taken on a space-available basis for $5.

Downeast Transportation (207/667-5796, www.exploremaine.org/region/downeast.html)

provides intra- and inter-town service throughout the region, with a schedule that varies by the day. It's best to check the website, then call with questions.

Airport & Harbor Car Service (207/667-5995 or 888/814-5995, www.mymainecarservice.com) provides car service without boundaries. Brian and Patti Jones's service has picked up clients in New York City and Boston who prefer not to fly or drive. They also offer Acadia tours, courier service, and pretty much everything else for which you might need a vehicle. Their fleet ranges from sedans to vans, and rates vary widely. Clients pay a mandatory 15 percent gratuity for the driver and all fees and tolls.

Trenton

Unless you're arriving by boat, you can't get to Mount Desert Island without first going through Trenton, straddling Route 3 from Ellsworth southward. Big-box stores, restaurants, motels, amusements, and gift shops line the congested six-mile strip, and some are worth at least a genuflect. If you're traveling with children, count on being begged to stop.

SIGHTS
Acadia Zoo
Acadia Zoo (446 Bar Harbor Rd., Rte. 3, Trenton, 207/667-3244, www.acadiazoo.org, 9:30 A.M.–dusk, Mon.–Sat., until 6 P.M. Sun., $7.50 adults, $6 seniors and kids 3–12), a nonprofit educational facility, has more than 100 exotic and not-so-exotic creatures—reindeer, bison, wolves, moose, and more. Enter the barn and—voilà—you're in a simulated rainforest populated with monkeys, Amazon fishes, and tropical birds and reptiles. Shows featuring the zoo's bears, moose, big cats, primates, and wolves are scheduled throughout the day.

◖ Aerial Touring
It's difficult to envision the Acadia National Park region without getting aloft. Two businesses provide a variety of ways to get an eagle's eye view of the area—allowing you to see that although it takes miles of road to connect the various sections, they're all quite close on the water. Both are based on the Route 3 side of Hancock County/Bar Harbor Airport, just north of Mount Desert Island and 12 miles north of downtown Bar Harbor. Opt for a clear day, if possible.

Scenic Flights of Acadia (Bar Harbor Rd., Rte. 3, Trenton, 207/667-6527) offers low-level flightseeing services in the Mount Desert Island region. Flights range 22–60 minutes and begin at $55 per person, with a two-passenger minimum. Reservations are accepted or you can take your chances and just show up; the wait is seldom longer than 20 minutes. Planes operate daily, weather permitting, mid-May–October (fall foliage flights are fabulous); winter flights can be arranged by appointment.

Island Soaring (Bar Harbor Rd., Rte. 3, Trenton, 207/667-7627, www.islandsoaring.net) lets you soar in silence, with daily glider flights. The one- or two-passenger gliders are towed to at least a 2,500-foot altitude, then released. An FAA-certified pilot guides the glider. Rates begin at $179 for two, $129 for

© TOM NANGLE

Soar in silence above Mount Desert Island with Island Soaring, based at Bar Harbor Airport in Trenton.

one, for a 20-minute flight. Best time to fly is between noon and 3 P.M., when thermal activity is usually at its peak, but if there's a good breeze in the morning, call. Maximum weight is 330 pounds. Island Soaring also offers **biplane rides** (www.biplaneridesoverbarharbor.com) from the same location. A 20-minute ride in an open-cockpit plane is $225 for two, 40 minutes costs $325, and a one-hour flight is $425; subtract $50 for single-passenger rates.

RECREATION
Seacoast Fun Park

Water slides, mini golf, go-carts, an indoor paintball arena, sling shot trampoline, and more can all be found at Seacoast Fun Park (Bar Harbor Rd., Rte. 3, Trenton, 207/667-3573, www.seacoastfunparks.com). A Max Pass ($22 pp) covers all-day golf and water slides and one ride; a Multi Pass ($18 adults, $16 kids under 4'10") covers all-day golf and two rides. Other packages are available, or pay separate fees for individual activities.

Lamoine State Park

Lamoine State Park (23 State Park Rd., Rte. 184, Lamoine 04605, 207/667-4778) features a pebble beach and picnic area with a spectacular view and a children's play area. If you've brought your own boat, the park also provides a boat ramp for launching. Careful though, the currents are strong here. Though the park isn't officially open in winter, it's popular for cross-country skiing and snowshoeing. This is strictly do-it-yourself fun, as there are no marked trails.

Day-use admission is $3 adults, $1 children 5–11. The park is open daily mid-May to mid-October and also offers campsites.

Golf

Try to keep your eye on the ball rather than the views at the challenging 18-hole **Bar Harbor Golf Course** (Junction Rtes. 3 and 204, Trenton, 207/667-7505). Despite the name, it's not in the island community, nor even on the island.

ENTERTAINMENT
The Great Maine Lumberjack Show

Ace lumberjack "Timber" Tina Scheer has been competing around the world since she was seven, and she shows her prowess at The Great Maine Lumberjack Show (Rte. 3, 207/667-0067, www.mainelumberjack.com, 7 P.M. mid-June–late Aug., $8.50 adult, $6.50 ages 4–11). During the 75-minute "Olympics of the Forest," you'll watch two teams compete in 14 events, including ax throwing, cross-cut sawing, log rolling, speed climbing, and more. Some are open to participation. (Kids can learn log rolling by appointment.) Performances are held rain or shine. Seating is under a roof, but dress for the weather if it's inclement. The ticket office opens at 6 P.M.

ACCOMMODATIONS
Campgrounds
Equally convenient (or not) to the Schoodic Region and Mount Desert Island is the 55-acre **Lamoine State Park** (23 State Park Rd., Rte. 184, Lamoine 04605, 207/667-4778), which is just off the shortcut route from Mount Desert Island to Schoodic. In July and August, when every campsite on Mount Desert Island is booked solid, those in the know go to the wooded, no-frills campground at Lamoine. Camping (62 sites) is $20 per site per night for nonresidents ($15 for Maine residents), plus a $2-per-night fee for reservations. A two-night minimum and 14-night maximum stay is enforced and there are no hookups. Leashed pets are allowed, but not on the beach, and cleanup is required. Camping season is mid-May to mid-September. From January 2, reserve online at www.state.me.us/doc/parks/reservations using a credit card, or call 207/287-3824 weekdays.

The waterfront **Narrows Too Camping Resort** (1150 Bar Harbor Rd./Rte. 3, Trenton, 207/667-4300, www.barharborcampgrounds.com) is the sibling of The Narrows Campground on Mount Desert Island. The 110 sites accommodate everything from tents to gigunda RVs requiring full hookups. Rates for two adults and two children younger than 18 range from $28 for tent site to $75 for an oceanfront site with water and electric. Facilities include a heated pool, grocery, laundry, video arcade, exercise room, and even live entertainment. A shuttle bus provides transportation to Bar Harbor. It's open Memorial Day through Columbus Day.

FOOD
Route 3 (Bar Harbor Road) is lined with eateries, including several lobster pounds that deserve a stop. One of the best-known and longest-running (since 1956) is **❮ Trenton Bridge Lobster Pound** (Rte. 3, Bar Harbor Rd., Trenton, 207/667-2977, www.trentonbridgelobster.com, 11 A.M.–7:30 P.M. Mon–Sat. Memorial Day–Columbus Day), on the right next to the bridge leading to Mount Desert Island. Watch for the "smoke signals"—steam billowing from the huge vats; the lobster couldn't be much fresher.

Edging the ocean at Mount Desert Narrows is the **Thompson Island Picnic Area** (Route 3, Thompson Island, Trenton). It has picnic tables, fire grills, a water fountain, and restrooms. At low tide, you might see locals raking the mud flats for clams.

INFORMATION AND SERVICES
The **Thompson Island Visitor Center** (Route 3, Thompson Island, Trenton, P.O. Box 396, Bar Harbor 04609, 207/288-3411) represents the Mount Desert Island Regional Chambers of Commerce, which includes the Trenton Chamber of Commerce. The center opens for the season in mid-May and is open 8 A.M.– 6 P.M. daily until Columbus Day.

The **Ellsworth Area Chamber of Commerce** (163 High St., P.O. Box 267, Ellsworth 04605, 207/667-5584, www.ellsworth-chamber.org) also covers Trenton.

Also, in Trenton, en route from Ellsworth on Route 3, and shortly before you reach Mount Desert, you'll see (on your right) the **Bar Harbor Chamber of Commerce** (Rte. 3, Trenton, P.O. Box 158, Bar Harbor 04609, 207/288-5103 or 888/540-9990, www.barharbormaine.com). You'll find all sorts of info on the island as well as other locations, restrooms, phones, and a helpful staff.

ELLSWORTH AND TRENTON

Getting There and Around

The **Hancock County-Bar Harbor Airport** (BHB) (Rte. 3, Bar Harbor Rd., Trenton, 207/667-7171, www.bhbairport.com), is serviced by USAirways Express/Colgan Air (207/667-7171 or 800/428-4322, www.colganair.com or www.usairways.com) daily in season, with service from Boston on commuter planes.

The **Island Explorer** bus system, which primarily serves Mount Desert Island with its fleet of propane-fueled, fare-free vehicles, has one route linking the Hancock County/Bar Harbor Airport with downtown Bar Harbor. Operated by Downeast Transportation, the Island Explorer runs between late June and Columbus Day (more information is available in the *Acadia on Mount Desert Island* chapter).

If you need van service, check with the airport-terminal desk of **Airport and Harbor Car Service** (207/667-5995 or 888/814-5995, www.mymainecarservice.com), which also will do runs to Bangor International Airport. In the middle of summer, a reservation is essential for trips to and from Bangor.

Before or after visiting Mount Desert Island, if you're headed farther Down East—to Lamoine, the eastern side of Hancock County, and beyond—there's a good shortcut from Trenton. About five miles south of Ellsworth on Route 3, just north of the Acadia Zoo, turn east onto Route 204.

If your destination is the Schoodic region, at the intersection of Route 1A and Main Street/Route 1 in downtown Ellsworth, stay on Main Street and avoid the Route 1 strip. Main Street eventually will become the Washington Junction Road and will reconnect with Route 1 beyond the Route 3 split for Mount Desert Island and the worst congestion.

BACKGROUND

The Land

IN THE BEGINNING...

Maine is an outdoor classroom for Geology 101, a living lesson in what the glaciers did and how they did it. I've told anyone who will listen that I plan to be a geologist in my next life—and the best place for the first course is Acadia National Park.

Geologically, Maine is something of a youngster; the oldest rocks, found in the Chain of Ponds area in the western part of the state, are only 1.6 billion years old—more than two billion years younger than the world's oldest rocks.

But most significant is the great ice sheet that began to spread over Maine about 25,000 years ago, during the late Wisconsin Ice Age. As it moved southward from Canada, this continental glacier scraped, gouged, pulverized, and depressed the bedrock in its path. On it continued, charging up the north faces of mountains, clipping off their tops and moving southward, leaving behind jagged cliffs on the mountains' southern faces and odd deposits of stone and clay. By about 21,000 years ago, glacial ice extended well over the Gulf of Maine, perhaps as far as the Georges Bank fishing grounds.

© TOM NANGLE

But all that began to change with meltdown, beginning about 18,000 years ago. As the glacier melted and receded, ocean water moved in, covering much of the coastal plain and working its way inland up the rivers. By 11,000 years ago, glaciers had pulled back from all but a few minor corners at the top of Maine, revealing the south coast's beaches and the intriguing geologic traits—eskers and erratics, kettleholes and moraines, even a fjord—that make Mount Desert Island and the rest of the state such a fascinating natural laboratory.

Mount Desert's Somes Sound (named after pioneer settler Abraham Somes)—the only fjord on the eastern seaboard—is just one distinctive feature on an island loaded with geologic wonders. There are pocket beaches, pink-granite ledges, sea caves, "pancake" rocks, wild headlands, volcanic "dikes," and a handful of pristine ponds and lakes. And once you've glimpsed The Bubbles—two curvaceous, oversized mounds on the edge of Jordan Pond—you'll know exactly how they earned their name.

CLIMATE

Acadia National Park fits into the National Weather Service's **coastal** category, a 20-mile-wide swath that stretches from Kittery on the New Hampshire border to Eastport on the Canadian border. In the park (and its surrounding communities), the proximity of the Gulf of Maine moderates the climate, making coastal winters generally warmer and summers usually cooler than elsewhere in the state.

Average June temperatures in **Bar Harbor,** adjoining the park, range from 53°F to 76°F; July and August temperatures range 60–82°F. By December, the average range is 20–32°F.

The Seasons

Maine has four distinct seasons: summer, fall, winter, and mud. Lovers of spring weather need to look elsewhere in March, the lowest month on the popularity scale, with mud-caked vehicles, soggy everything, irritable tempera-

ments, tank-trap roads, and occasionally the worst snowstorm of the year.

Summer can be idyllic—with moderate temperatures, clear air, and wispy breezes—but it can also close in with fog, rain, and chills. Prevailing winds are from the southwest. Officially, summer runs from June 21 to September 23, but consider summer June, July, and August. The typical growing season is 148 days long.

A poll of Mainers might well show autumn as the favorite season—days are still warmish, nights are cool, winds are optimum for sailors, and the foliage is brilliant—particularly throughout Acadia. Fall colors usually reach their peak in the park in early October, about a week before Columbus Day. Early autumn, however, is also the height of hurricane season, the only potential flaw this time of year.

Winter, officially December 21 to March 20, means an unpredictable potpourri of weather along the park's coastline. But when the cold and snow hit this region, it's time for cross-country skiing, snowshoeing, and ice-skating.

Spring, officially March 20 to June 21, is the frequent butt of jokes. It's an ill-defined season that arrives much too late and departs all too quickly. Spring planting can't occur until well into May; lilacs explode in late May and disappear by mid-June. And just when you finally can enjoy being outside, black flies stretch their wings and satisfy their hunger pangs. Along the shore, fortunately, steady breezes often keep the pesky creatures to a minimum.

Northeasters and Hurricanes

A northeaster is a counterclockwise, swirling storm that brings wild winds out of—you guessed it—the northeast. These storms can occur any time of year, whenever the conditions brew them up. Depending on the season, the winds are accompanied by rain, sleet, snow, or all of them together.

Hurricane season officially runs from June through November, but it is most active in late August and September. Some years, Maine remains out of harm's way; other years, head-on hurricanes and even glancing blows have eroded beaches, flooded roads, splintered boats, downed trees, knocked out power, and inflicted major residential and commercial damage. Winds—the greatest culprit—average 74–90 mph. A hurricane watch is announced on radio and TV about 36 hours before the hurricane hits, followed by a hurricane warning that indicates that the storm is imminent. Find shelter away from plate-glass windows, and wait it out. If especially high winds are predicted, make every effort to se-cure yourself, your vehicle, and your posses-sions. Resist the urge to head for the shore to watch the show; rogue waves combined with ultrahigh tides have been known to sweep away unwary onlookers. Schoodic Point, the mainland section of Acadia, is a particularly perilous location in such conditions.

Sea Smoke and Fog

Sea smoke and fog, two atmospheric phenomena resulting from opposing conditions, are only distantly related. But both can radically affect visibility and therefore be hazardous. In winter,

ACADIA FACTS

Acadia National Park was established by Congress in 1929, after previous incarnations as Lafayette National Park (1919) and Sieur de Monts National Monument (1916).

- Acadia covers more than 47,000 mainland and island acres, including more than 11,000 acres protected by conservation easements. Its permanent boundaries were established by Congress in 1986.

- Acadia has 26 mountains ranging in height from 284 feet (Flying Mountain) to 1,530 feet (Cadillac). Cadillac is the highest point on the eastern seaboard of the United States.

- Nine "great ponds" (covering more than 10 acres) lie within the park boundaries. Five others abut parkland. Depths of these lakes and ponds range between 7 feet (Aunt Betty Pond) and 150 feet (Jordan Pond). Mount Desert Island's lakes and ponds have restrictions on swimming and personal and motorized watercraft.

- Acadia has about 130 miles of hiking trails. At the height (so to speak) of trail construction, in the early 20th century, there were some 230 miles. Some of the discontinued trails are being rehabilitated via the Acadia Trails Forever program, a joint project of the park and Friends of Acadia.

- Acadia has about 2.5 million visitors each year, most in the months of July, August, and September.

- The "creature counts" in Acadia, on Mount Desert Island, and in the surrounding waters include 273 species of birds, more than 6,500 insect species and subspecies, at least five reptile species, 24 species of fish, at least 11 species of amphibians, and at least 40 mammal species.

- The Park Loop Road is 20 miles, with an additional seven miles for a round-trip to the summit of Cadillac Mountain.

- The park has 45 miles of car-free, broken-stone carriage roads for walking, biking, and horseback riding, as well as cross-country skiing and snowshoeing in winter; 12 miles of privately owned carriage roads south of Jordan Pond are usable by walkers and horses but no bicycles.

- Acadia has three campgrounds—two on Mount Desert Island, one on Isle au Haut. Only one (Blackwoods) is open all year. Backcountry camping is not allowed in Acadia. (A dozen or so commercial campgrounds are located on Mount Desert Island beyond park boundaries.)

- The Schoodic Peninsula is the only park acreage that's on the mainland; all other park properties are on islands. A bridge connects Mount Desert Island to the mainland town of Trenton, but other parcels must be reached by boat.

© TOM NANGLE

Chances are you'll experience at least one or two foggy days during your visit.

when the ocean is at least 40°F warmer than the air, billowy sea smoke rises from the water, creating great photo ops for camera buffs but seriously dangerous conditions for mariners.

In any season, when the ocean (or lake or land) is colder than the air, fog sets in, creating nasty conditions for drivers, mariners, and pilots. Romantics, however, see it otherwise, reveling in the womblike ambience and the muffled moans of foghorns.

Storm Warnings

The National Weather Service's official daytime signal system for wind velocity consists of a series of flags representing specific wind speeds and sea conditions. Beachgoers and anyone planning to venture out in a kayak, canoe, sailboat, or powerboat should heed these signals. The signal flags are posted on all public beaches, and warnings are announced on TV and radio weather broadcasts, as well as on cable TV's Weather Channel and the NOAA broadcast network.

Flora and Fauna

In the course of a single day at Acadia National Park—where more than two dozen mountains meet the sea—the casual visitor can pass through a landscape that lends itself to a surprising diversity of animal and plantlife. On one outing, you can explore the shoreline—barnacles encrust the rocks, and black crowberry, an arctic shrub that finds Maine's coastal climate agreeable, grows close to the ground alongside the trail. On the same outing, you can wander beneath the boughs of the leafy hardwood forest that favors more southern climes, as well as the spruce–fir forest of the north. A little farther up the trail are subalpine plants more typically associated with mountain environments, and neotropical songbirds providing background music.

Acadia's creatures and plants will endlessly intrigue any nature lover; the following is but a sampling of what you might encounter during a visit.

OFFSHORE

Acadia National Park is surrounded by the sea—from the rockbound Schoodic Peninsula jutting from the mainland Down East to the offshore island in Penobscot Bay that Samuel de Champlain named Isle au Haut. While the park's boundaries do not extend out to sea, the life that can be found there draws tourists and scientists alike.

The Maine coastline falls within the Gulf of Maine, a "sea within a sea" that extends from Nova Scotia to Cape Cod and out to the fishing grounds of Brown and Georges Banks. It is one of the most biologically rich environments in the world. Surface water, driven by currents off Nova Scotia, swirls in counterclockwise circles, delivering nutrients and food to the plants and animals that live there. Floating microplants, tiny shrimp-like creatures, and jellyfish benefit from those nutrients and once supported huge populations of ground-fish, now depleted by overfishing.

These highly productive waters lure not only fishing vessels but also **sea mammals.** Whales may rarely swim into the inshore bays and inlets bounded by Acadia, but whale-watch cruises based on Mount Desert Island ferry passengers miles offshore to the locales where whales gather. Whales fall into two groups: toothed and baleen. Toothed whales hunt individual prey, such as squid, fish, and the occasional seabird; they include porpoises and dolphins, killer whales, sperm whales, and pilot whales. Baleen whales have no teeth, so they must sift food through horny plates called baleen; they include finback whales, minke whales, humpback whales, and right whales. Any of these species may be observed in the Gulf of Maine.

Harbor porpoises, which grow to a length of six feet, can be spotted from a boat in the inshore waters around Mount Desert Island, traveling in pods as they hunt schools of herring and mackerel. The most you'll usually see of them are their gray backs and triangular dorsal fins as they perform their graceful ballet through the waves.

Of great delight to wildlife watchers is catching glimpses of **harbor seals.** While the shores of Mount Desert Island are too busy with human activity for seals to linger, they are usually spotted during nature cruises that head out to the well-known "seal ledges." Check the tide chart and book an excursion for low tide. Seals haul themselves out of the ocean at low tide to rest on the rocks and sunbathe. Naps are a necessity for harbor seals, which have less blubber and fur to insulate them from the frigid waters of the Gulf of Maine than other seal species. Hauling out preserves energy otherwise spent heating the body, and it replenishes their blood with oxygen.

At high tide, you might see individual "puppy dog" faces bobbing among the waves as the seals forage for food. Harbor seals, sometimes called "sea dogs," almost disappeared along the coast of Maine in the early 20th century. It was believed they competed with fishermen for the much-prized lobster and other valuable catches, and they were hunted nearly into oblivion. When it became obvious that the absence of seals did not improve fish stocks, the bounty placed on them was lifted. The Marine Mammal Protection Act of 1972 made it illegal to hunt or harm any marine mammal, except by permit—happily, populations of harbor seals now have rebounded all along the coast.

Every now and then, park rangers receive reports of "abandoned" seal pups along Acadia's shore. Usually it's not a stranded youngster, but rather a pup left to rest while its mother hunts for food. If you discover a seal pup on the shore, leave it undisturbed and report the sighting to rangers.

ALONG THE SHORE

Whether walking the shore or cruising on a boat, there is no symbol so closely associated with the coast as the ubiquitous **gull.** Several species of gulls frequent Acadia's skies, but none is more common than the herring gull. Easily dismissed as brassy sandwich thieves (which, of course, they are), herring gulls almost vanished in the 20th century as a result of hunting and egg collecting. Indeed, many seabird populations declined in the early 1900s due to the demand for feathers to adorn ladies' hats. Conservation measures have helped some of these bird species recover, including the large, gray-backed herring gull, an elegant flyer that often lobs sea urchins onto the rocky shore from aloft to crack them open for the morsels within.

Common **eider-duck** females, a mottled brown, and the black-and-white males (nicknamed "floating skunks") congregate in large "rafts" on the icy ocean during the winter to mate. When spring arrives, males and females separate. While the males provide no help in raising the young, the females cooperate with one another, often gathering ducklings together to protect them from predators. Adult eiders may live and breed for 20 years or more, though the morality rate is high among the young. Present along Acadia's shore all year long, they feed on mussels, clams, and dog whelks, their powerful gizzards grinding down shells and all.

A smaller seabird regularly espied around Acadia is the **black guillemot,** also known as the "sea pigeon" and "underwater flyer" because it seems to fly through the water. Guillemots learn to swim before they learn to fly. Black-and-white with bright red feet, guillemots are cousins to puffins. They nest on rock ledges along the shore, laying pear-shaped eggs that won't roll over the edge and into the waves below.

Bald eagles and **ospreys** (also known as fish hawks) take advantage of the fishing available in Acadia's waters. Both of these majestic raptors suffered from the effects of the pesticide DDT, which washed down through waterways and into the ocean, becoming concentrated in the fish the raptors consumed. As a result, they laid thin-shelled eggs that broke easily, preventing the development of young. The banning of DDT in the United States has resulted in a strong comeback for both species and the removal of the bald eagle from the federal endangered species list. Along the coast of Maine, however, the bald eagle's return has been less triumphant than in other parts of the country. Biologists continue to seek explanations for the lag, and the bald eagle remains on state and federal lists as a threatened species.

Boat cruises (some with park rangers aboard) departing from several Mount Desert Island harbors offer good chances for sightings. They allow passengers to approach (but not too closely) nesting islands of eagles and ospreys. Both species create large nests of sticks, from which they can command a wide view of the surrounding area. Some osprey nests have been documented as being 100 years old, and researchers have found everything from fishing tackle to swim trunks entwined in the sticks of the nests.

Look also for eagles and ospreys flying above inland areas of the park. Ospreys hunt over freshwater ponds and lakes, hovering until a fish is sighted, then plummeting from the sky into the water to grab the prey. For aerodynamic reasons, they carry the fish headfirst.

Acadia visitors often ask rangers if there are sea otters in the park. After all, there is an Otter Creek, which flows into Otter Cove, which is bounded by Otter Cliffs. At one time, Gorham Mountain was known as Peak of Otter! With all these place names devoted to the otter, it would be logical to assume that Mount Desert Island teems with them. In fact, though, there are no sea otters along the entire eastern seaboard of the United States—perhaps the earliest European settlers mistook sea minks (now extinct) for sea otters. River otters do reside in the park, though they are reclusive and spend most of their time in freshwater environments. You might observe one during the winter frolicking on a frozen pond.

INTERTIDAL ZONE

Some of the most alien creatures on earth live where the ocean washes the rocky shoreline. The creatures of this **intertidal zone** are at once resilient and fragile, and always fascinating. Some of the creatures and plants live best in the upper reaches of the intertidal zone, which is doused only by the spray of waves and the occasional extra-high tide. Others, which would not survive the upper regions, thrive in the lower portions of the intertidal zone, which is almost always submerged. The rest live in rocky pockets of water in between, and all are influenced by the ebb and flow of the tide. Temperature, salinity, and the strength of crashing waves all determine where a creature will live in the intertidal zone.

As you approach the ocean's edge, the first creatures likely to come underfoot are **barnacles**—vast stretches of rock can be encrusted with them. Step gently, for walking on barnacles crushes them. Their tiny, white, volcano-shaped shells remain closed when exposed to the air, but they open when submerged to feed. Water movement encourages them to sweep the water with feathery "legs" to feed on microscopic plankton.

Despite the tough armor with which barnacles cover themselves, they are preyed upon by dog whelks (snails), which drill through the barnacle shells with their tongues to feed on the creature within. A **dog whelk** can be distinguished from the common periwinkle by the elliptical opening of its shell. Periwinkles have teardrop-shaped openings.

Sea stars find blue mussels yummy. Blue mussels siphon plankton from the water and anchor themselves in place with byssal threads. Sea stars creep up on the mussels, wrap their legs around them, and pry open their shells just enough to insert their stomachs and consume the animal inside. Look for sea stars and mussels in the lower regions of tidepools.

Related to sea stars are **sea urchins**—spiky green balls most often seen as empty, spineless husks littered along the shoreline (they are frequently preyed upon by gulls). If you come upon a live sea urchin, handle it with care. While their spikes are not poisonous, they *are* sharp. Gently roll a sea urchin over to see its mouth and the five white teeth with which it gnaws on seaweeds and animal remains. (While the green sea urchins found in Acadia do not possess poisonous spines, some of their counterparts in other regions do.)

Limpets, with cone-shaped shells, are snails that rely on seaweeds for food. They suction themselves to rocks, which prevents them from drying up when exposed at low

TIDES

Nowhere is the adage "Time and tide wait for no man" more true than along the Maine coastline. The nation's most extreme tidal ranges occur in Maine, and they become even more dramatic as you head "Down East," toward the Canadian Maritime provinces. Every six hours or so, the tide begins either ebbing or flowing, so you'll have countless opportunities for observing tidal phenomena.

Tides govern coastal life, and everyone is a slave to the tide calendar or chart, which coastal-community newspapers diligently publish in every issue. Each issue of the official park visitor guide, the *Beaver Log,* also contains a tide chart (as well as times of sunrise and sunset). In tidal regions, boats tie up with extra-long lines, clammers and worm-diggers schedule their days by the tides, hikers have to plan ahead for shoreline exploring, and kayakers need to plan their routes to avoid getting stuck in the muck.

Average tidal ranges (between low tide and high tide) in the area around Acadia National Park are 10 or 11 feet, and extremes are 12 or 13 feet. Visit www.harbortides.com – it's free to join. Plug in Bar Harbor (or the zip code – 04609), then print out the tide chart for the time you'll be in Acadia. (Moon phases and times of sunrise and sunset are also included.)

Tides, as we all learned in elementary school, are lunar phenomena, created by the gravitational pull of the moon; the tidal range depends on the lunar phase. Tides are most extreme at new and full moons – when the sun, moon, and earth are all aligned. These are **spring tides,** supposedly because the water springs upward (the term has nothing to do with the season). And tides are smallest during the moon's first and third quarters – when the sun, earth, and moon have a right-angle configuration. These are **neap tides** ("neap" comes from an Old English word meaning "scanty"). Other lunar/solar phenomena, such as the equinoxes and solstices, can also affect tidal ranges.

The best time for shoreline exploration is on a new-moon or full-moon day, when low tide exposes mussels, sea urchins, sea cucumbers, sea stars, periwinkles, hermit crabs, rockweed, and assorted nonbiodegradable trash. Rubber boots or waterproof, treaded shoes are essential on the wet, slippery terrain.

Caution is also essential in tidal areas. Unless you've carefully plotted tide times and heights, don't park a car or bike or boat trailer on a beach; make sure your sea kayak is lashed securely to a tree or bollard; don't take a long nap on shoreline granite; and don't cross a low-tide land spit without an eye on your watch.

A perhaps apocryphal but almost believable story goes that one flatlander stormed up to a ranger at a Maine state park one bright summer morning and demanded indignantly to know why they had had the nerve to drain the water from her shorefront campsite during the night. When it comes to tides... you just have to go with the flow.

tide. Do not tear limpets from rocks—doing so hurts the animal.

Many intertidal creatures depend on seaweed for protection and food. **Rockweeds** drape over rocks, floating with the waves, their long fronds buoyed by distinctive air bladders. **Dulse** (edible for people) is common along the shore, as is Irish moss, used as a thickener in ice cream, paint, and other products.

Tidepool Tips

The best way to learn about the fascinating world that exists between the tides is to look for creatures in their own habitat, with a good field guide as a reference.

- Go at low tide—there are two low tides daily, 12 hours apart.
- Tread carefully. Shoreline rocks are slippery.
- Do not remove creatures from their habitats; doing so could harm them.
- Be aware of the ocean at all times. Sudden waves can wash the shore and sweep you to your death.
- Join a ranger-guided shoreline walk to learn more about this unique environment. Check the *Beaver Log,* Acadia's official park newspaper, for the schedule and details.

FRESHWATER LAKES AND PONDS

Known best for its rocky shoreline and mountains, Acadia National Park cradles numerous glistening lakes and ponds in its glacially carved valleys. Several lakes serve as public water supplies for surrounding communities, and swimming is prohibited in most. Echo Lake and the north end of Long Pond are excellent designated swimming areas. Freshwater fishing requires a state license for adults. Please obey posted regulations.

The voice of the northern wilderness belongs to the **common loon,** whose roots are so ancient it is the oldest bird species found in North America. During the summer months, loons are garbed in striking white-and-black plumage, which fades to gray during the winter when loons migrate to the ocean's open waters.

Graceful swimmers, loons are clumsy on land. Their webbed feet are set to the rear of their bodies, making them front-heavy. Land travel is a struggle. Consequently, they nest very close to the water's edge, which makes them vulnerable to such manmade hazards as the wakes of motorized watercraft.

The loon's mysterious ululating call can often be heard echoing across lakes on most any summer evening, an eerie sound not quickly forgotten.

Evening is actually an excellent time to observe wildlife. Creatures that seem shy and reclusive by day tend to be most active at dawn and dusk (crepuscular) or at night (nocturnal). Carriage roads along Eagle Lake, Bubble Pond, and Witch Hole Pond make nighttime walking easy. (Hint: Go at dusk so your eyes adjust with the darkening sky, and keep in mind that flashlight use abruptly ruins night vision.)

Frog choruses form the backdrop to the cries of loons. In Acadia, there are eight **frog and toad species,** which tend to be most vocal during the spring mating season. Close your eyes and listen to see if you can distinguish individual species, such as the "banjo-twanging" croak of the green frog and the "snore" of the leopard frog.

The onset of moonlight may reveal small winged creatures swooping, darting, and careening over lakes and ponds. Acadia is home to several species of **bats,** including the common little brown bat. Don't scream! Bats have no desire to get entangled in your hair. Their echolocation (radar) is so fine-tuned that it can detect a single strand of human hair. Bats are far more interested in the mosquitoes attracted to your body heat. True insect-munching machines, a single pinky-size little brown bat can eat hundreds, if not thousands, of insects in one evening.

Bandit-faced **raccoons** are also creatures of the night, and they sometimes can be found scampering alongside the shore. They are omnivorous, dining on anything from grubs, frogs, and small mammals to fish, berries, and garbage. Rabies is present in Maine, and raccoons are common carriers of the disease. Do not approach sick-acting animals (seeing them during the daytime may indicate illness), and report any strange behavior to a park ranger. When camping or picnicking, stow food items in your vehicle and dispose of scraps properly. Raccoons are opportunistic thieves that have been known to claw their way into tents to find food.

And where are the moose? The question is asked often at Acadia's visitors center, and wildlife watchers are disappointed to learn that moose, the largest member of the deer family, are rarely sighted in the park. Moose are more frequently observed in western and northern Maine, in the Moosehead Lake and Baxter State Park regions. However, individuals are spotted from time to time on Mount Desert Island, and there may even be a small family group residing on the west side. Moose like to dine on aquatic vegetation, such as the tubers of cattails and lily pads, and they frequent marshes and lakes to escape biting flies. Bass Harbor Marsh is inviting habitat for moose, but good luck spotting one.

A prehistoric-looking creature sometimes encountered on carriage roads near ponds is the **snapping turtle.** An average adult may weigh 30 pounds or more. Keep well clear of the snapper's powerful beak, which is lightning-quick when grabbing prey; it can do real damage, such as biting off fingers. Adult snappers have no predators (except people), and they will dine on other turtles, frogs, ducklings, wading birds, and beaver kits.

By midsummer, many of Acadia's ponds are beautifully adorned with yellow water lilies and white pond lilies. Lily pads are a favorite food of beavers. **Beavers** emerge from their lodges—large piles of sticks and mud—at dusk and dawn to feed and make necessary repairs to their dams. Beavers create their own habitat by transforming streams into ponds. They move awkwardly on land, so they adjust the water level close to their source of building materials and other favored foods: aspen and birch trees. Doing so limits their exposure to dry land and predators.

Beavers are large rodents that were trapped excessively for centuries for the fur trade. They have since made a strong comeback in Acadia—to the point that their ponds now threaten roads, trails, and other park structures. Resource man-

agers try to keep ahead of the beavers by inserting "beaver foolers" (PVC pipes) through dams that block road culverts. This moderates pond levels and prevents damage to roads by allowing water to drain through the culvert. Sometimes the beavers, however, get ahead of the resource managers. They have been known to plug the "beaver foolers" with sticks and mud, or chew through them with their strong teeth.

Amazingly adapted for life in the water, beavers are fascinating to watch. A very accessible location along the Park Loop Road, just past Bear Brook Picnic Area, is Beaver Dam Pond, featuring a few lodges, a dam, and an active beaver population. The best viewing times are dawn and dusk. In the fall the beavers are busiest, preparing food stores for the winter to come. The park often presents a beaver-watch program at that time of year, which is a great way to learn more about the habits and adaptations of the beaver.

Beavers act as a catalyst for increasing natural diversity in an area. Their ponds attract ospreys, herons, and owls; salamanders, frogs, and turtles; insects and aquatic plants; foxes,

heron

deer, muskrats, and river otters. Their ponds help maintain the water table, enrich soils, and prevent flooding.

While beavers may bring diversity to a wetland, an invader has been endangering Acadia's ponds and lakes. **Purple loosestrife,** a showy stalked purple flower nonnative to North America, was introduced into gardens as an ornamental. Highly reproductive and adaptive and with no natural predators, purple loosestrife escaped the confines of gardens and has literally choked the life out of some wetlands by crowding out native plants on which many creatures depend and creating a monoculture. Few native species find purple loosestrife useful.

Purple loosestrife has been contained at Acadia, but it's an ongoing process. Uprooting it seems to encourage more to grow, and jostling stalks at certain times of the year disperses vast numbers of seeds, so resource managers have resorted to treating individual plants with an approved herbicide in a way that does not harm the surrounding environment.

WOODLANDS

A dark, statuesque **spruce-fir forest** dominates much of Acadia's woodlands and does well in the cooler, moist environs of Maine's coast. Red spruce trees are tall and polelike and often cohabitate with fragrant balsam fir. The spruce grows needles only at the canopy, sparing little energy for growing needles where the sun cannot reach. Because the sun barely touches the forest floor, little undergrowth emerges from the bump and swale of acidic, rust-colored needles that carpet the ground, except for more tiny, shade-loving spruce, waiting for their chance to grow tall.

The spruce–fir forest can be uncannily quiet, especially in the middle of the day. The density of the woods and the springy, needle-laden floor seem to buffer noise from without. Listen closely, however, and you may hear the cackle of ravens, the squabble of a territorial red squirrel, or the rat-a-tat of a woodpecker.

Red squirrels are energetic denizens of the spruce–fir forest, scolding innocent passersby or sitting on tree stumps scaling spruce cones and stuffing their cheeks full of seeds. Observant wildlife watchers will find their middens (heaps of cone scales) about the forest. Squirrels are especially industrious (even comical) in autumn as they frantically prepare for the winter by stocking up on food stores, tearing about from branch to branch with spruce cones poking out of their mouths like big cigars.

Woodpeckers favor dead, still-standing trees, shredding the bark to get at the insects infesting the trunk. The pileated woodpecker—a large black-and-white bird with a red cap—is relatively shy, so you are more likely to encounter evidence of its passage (rectangular and oval holes in trees) than the bird itself. Other common woodpeckers you might observe are the hairy and the downy.

The face of Acadia's woodlands changed dramatically in 1947. That fall, during a period of extremely dry conditions, a fire began west of the park's present-day visitors center in Hulls Cove. Feeding on tinder-dry woods and grasses, and whipped into an inferno by gale-force winds, the fire roared across the eastern half of Mount Desert Island, miraculously skirting downtown Bar Harbor but destroying numerous year-round and seasonal homes. In all, 17,000 acres burned (10,000 in the park).

Researchers have studied 6,000 years of the park's fire history by pulling core samples from ponds to analyze the layers of pollen and charcoal that have settled in their bottoms over time, the latter indicating periods of fire. The most significant layer of charcoal appeared in the period around 1947, indicating the intensity of the great fire.

The aftermath of the fire—the scorched mountainsides and skeletal, blackened remains of trees—must have been a devastating sight. Loggers salvaged usable timber and removed unsafe snags. Seed was ordered so replanting could begin in earnest. Soils needed to be stabilized and the landscape restored.

Then a curious thing happened the following spring: As the snow melted, green shoots began to poke up out of the soils among the sooty remains. "Pioneer plants," such as lowbush blueberry and Indian paintbrush, took

FALL FOLIAGE

The timing and quality of Maine's fall foliage owes much to the summer weather that precedes it, but the annual spectacle never disappoints. In early September, as deciduous trees ready themselves for winter, they stop producing chlorophyll, and the green begins to disappear from their leaves. Taking its place are the spectacular pigments – brilliant reds, yellows, oranges, and purples – that paint the leaves and warm the hearts of every "leaf-peeper," shopkeeper, innkeeper, and restaurateur.

The colorful display begins slowly, reaches a peak, then fades – starting in Maine's north in early to mid-September and working down to the southwest corner by mid-October. Peak foliage in **Acadia National Park** typically occurs in early October, with the last bits of color hanging on almost to the end of the month.

The fall palette is stunning, especially in Acadia. The leaves of white ash turn purple; sumac and sugar and red maples turn scarlet; mountain ash, beech, basswood, and birch trees turn various shades of yellow.

Trees put on their most magnificent show after a summer of moderate heat and rainfall. A summer of excessive heat and scant rainfall means colors will be less brilliant and disappear more quickly. Throw a September or October northeaster or hurricane into the mix, and estimates are up for grabs.

So predictions are imprecise, and you'll need to allow some schedule flexibility to take advantage of optimum color. From early September to mid-October, check the foliage section on the state Department of Conservation's website (www.mainefoliage.com) for frequently updated maps, panoramic photographs, recommended driving tours, and weekly reports on the foliage status (this is gauged by the percentage of "leaf drop" in every region of the state). Between early September and early October, you can even sign up via the website for weekly email reports (Acadia straddles zones 1 and 2 in the report maps). The state's toll-free fall-foliage hotline is 888/624-6345.

Fall-foliage trips are extremely popular and have become more so in recent years, so lodging can be scarce. Plan ahead and make reservations; sleeping in your car can be mighty chilly at that time of year.

© TOM NANGLE

Eagle Lake

over the job of stabilizing soils. By the time the ordered seeds arrived two years later (demand had been overwhelming, for much of Maine had burned in 1947), nature was already mending the landscape without human intervention. What had been blackened showed promise and renewal in green growing things.

Over the decades since then, a mixed decid-uous forest has grown up from the ashes of the fire, supplanting the dominance of the spruce–fir forest on Mount Desert Island's east side. **Birch, aspen, maple, oak,** and **beech** have embraced wide-open sunny places where shady spruce once thrived. The new growth not only added colorful splendor to the autumn landscape but also diversified the wildlife.

Populations of **white-tailed deer** benefited from all the new browse (and a lack of major predators), and by the 1960s, the island's deer herd soared. Recent studies have shown the population to be healthy and stable—perhaps due to car–deer collisions and predation from the recently arrived eastern coyote.

Coyotes crossed the Trenton Bridge and wandered onto Mount Desert Island in the 1980s. They had been expanding their territory throughout the northeast, handily picking up the slack in the food chain that was vacated when other large predators, such as the northern gray wolf and the lynx, were hunted and trapped out of the state. While coyote sightings do occur, you are more likely to be serenaded by yipping and howling in the night. Their vocalizations warn off other coyotes, or let them keep in touch with the members of their packs.

The **snowshoe hare,** or varying hare, is a main prey of the coyote. The large hind feet of these mammals allow them to stay aloft in the snow and speed away from predators. Camouflage also aids these fleet-footed hares—their fur turns white during the winter and brown during the summer, hence the name varying hare. Not all hares escape their predators. It is not uncommon to encounter coyote scat full of hare fur along a carriage road or trail.

Also along a carriage road or trail, you might encounter a **snake** sunning itself on a rock. Five species of snakes—including the garter snake, milk snake, and green snake—inhabit Acadia. None of these snakes are poisonous, but they will bite if provoked.

While autumn may cloak Acadia's mountainsides in bright beauty, spring and summer bring relief to Mainers weary of ice storms, shoveling, freezing temperatures, and short, dark days. Spring arrives with snowy clusters of star flowers along roadsides, and white mats of **bunchberry** flowers (dwarf members of the dogwood family) on the forest floor. Birdsong provides a musical backdrop. Twenty-one species of wood warblers migrate to Acadia from South America to nest—among them are the **American redstart, ovenbird, yellow warbler,** and **Blackburnian warbler.** At the visitors center, request a bird checklist, which names 273 species of birds that have been identified on Mount Desert Island and adjacent areas. Then join a ranger for an early morning bird walk. Check the *Beaver Log* for details.

The fire of 1947 may have transformed a portion of Acadia's woodlands, but change is always part of a natural system. While the broad-leafed trees that grew up in the wake of the fire continue to grow and shed leaves as the cycle of nature demands, young spruce trees poke up through duff and leaf litter, waiting in the shade for their chance to dominate the landscape once again.

MOUNTAINS

A hike up one of Acadia's granite-domed mountains will allow you to gaze down at the world with a new perspective. Left behind is the confining forest—the woods, in fact, seem to shrink as you climb. On the south-facing slopes of some mountains, you'll encounter squat and gnarled pitch pines. The fire of 1947 not only was beneficial to the growth of deciduous vegetation but it also aided in the regeneration of **pitch pines,** which rely on heat, such as that generated by an intense fire, to open their cones and disperse seeds.

Wreathing rocky outcrops and trailsides are such shrubs as **low-bush blueberry, sheep laurel (lambkill),** and **bayberry.** In the fall, their leaves turn blood-red. In the spring, **shadbush** softens granite mountainsides with white blossoms.

Green and gray lichens plaster exposed rocks in patterns like targets. Composed of algae and fungi, lichens were probably among the first organisms to grow in Acadia as the vast ice sheets retreated 20,000 to 10,000 years ago. Sensitive to air pollution and acid rain, lichens have become barometers of air quality all over the world.

On mountain summits, the trees are stunted. These are not necessarily young trees—some may be nearly 100 years old. The tough, cold, windy climate and exposed conditions of summits force plantlife to adapt to survive.

Growing close to the ground to avoid fierce winds is one way in which trees have adapted to life at the summit.

Other plants huddle in the shallow, gravelly soil behind solitary rocks, such as **three-toothed cinquefoil,** a member of the rose family that produces a tiny white flower in June and July, and **mountain sandwort,** which blooms in clusters June through September.

While adapted to surviving the extreme conditions of mountain summits, plants can be irreparably damaged by feet trampling off-trail, or by removal of rocks to add to cairns (trail markers) or stone "art." One has only to look at the summit area of Cadillac Mountain to see the damage wrought by millions of roving feet: the missing vegetation and the eroded soils. It may take 50 to 100 years for some plantlife, if protected, to recover. Some endangered plant species that grow only at summits may have already disappeared from Cadillac due to trampling.

To protect mountain summits and to preserve the natural scene, follow Leave No Trace principles of staying on the trail and on durable surfaces, such as solid granite. Do not add to cairns or build rock art, a form of graffiti that not only damages plants and soils but also blemishes the scenery for other visitors.

Autumn provides a terrific opportunity to observe **raptors** of all kinds. In the fall, during their southward migration, raptors take advantage of northwest winds flowing over Acadia's mountains. Eagles, red-tailed hawks, sharp-shinned hawks, goshawks, American kestrels, peregrine falcons, and others can be spotted. (The peregrine, a seasonal mountain dweller, has been reintroduced to Acadia after a long absence; see the sidebar *Peregrine Falcons* in the *Acadia on Mount Desert Island* chapter.) From late August to mid-October, join park staff for the annual Hawkwatch atop Cadillac Mountain (weather permitting) for viewing and identifying raptors. Check the *Beaver Log* for details. In 2002, hawkwatchers counted 1,659 raptors from 10 species (down a bit from the annual average of 2,500). The most prevalent species are American kestrels and sharp-shinned hawks.

WILDLIFE-WATCHING TIPS

- Seek out wildlife at dusk and dawn when it is more active. Bring binoculars and a field guide.

- Leave Rover at home—pets are intruders into the natural world, and they will scare off wildlife. If leaving your dog behind is not an option, remember that in the park, pets must be restrained on a leash no longer than six feet. This is for the safety of both the pet and wildlife, and it is courteous to other visitors.

- Never approach wildlife, which could become aggressive if sick or feeling threatened. Enjoy wildlife at a distance.

- Do not feed wildlife, not even gulls. Feeding turns wild animals into aggressive beggars that lose the ability to forage for themselves, and often ends in their demise.

- Join walks, talks, hikes, cruises, and evening programs presented by park rangers to learn more about your national park and its flora and fauna. Programs are listed in the *Beaver Log,* readily available at the Hulls Cove Visitor Center, the Sieur de Monts Nature Center, and park campgrounds, as well as online at **www.nps.gov/acad/.**

- Visit the Nature Center at Sieur de Monts Spring, where exhibits show the diversity of flora and fauna in the park, and the challenges that resource managers face in protecting it.

See *Suggested Reading* for a selection of books (including field guides) on Acadia's natural history.

(The Flora and Fauna *section of this chapter was written by Kristen Britain, former writer/editor for Acadia National Park.)*

Environmental Issues

You've already read about some of Acadia's major environmental issues, but still others exist. Tops among these are air pollution and overcrowding. Of utmost importance is the matter of "zero impact," addressed by the Leave No Trace philosophy actively practiced at Acadia.

AIR QUALITY

In 2002, a study by the private National Parks Conservation Association revealed that Acadia National Park had the fifth-worst air quality of all the national parks; Acadia allegedly has twice as much haze as the Grand Canyon. Most scientists and environmentalists attribute the problem primarily to smoke and haze from power plants in the Midwest and South. New England is "the end of the line," so to speak, for airborne pollutants, and it's estimated that 80 percent of Maine's pollution arrives from other regions. Maine has the highest asthma rate in the nation, rivers and lakes have high concentrations of mercury, and rainfall at Acadia is notably acidic. Maine's four legislators, and others in the region, have been especially active in their efforts to strengthen the Clean Air Act and improve conditions at Acadia and in the rest of New England.

To heighten public awareness of pollution problems, a new government/private joint program has initiated **CAMNET,** an intriguing monitoring system that provides real-time pollution and visibility monitoring. Acadia is one of the nine New England sites with cameras updating images every 15 minutes. Log on to www.hazecam.net for data on current temperature and humidity, wind speed and direction, precipitation totals, visual range, and the air-pollution level (low, medium, or high). The site also includes a selection of photos showing

LEAVE THE ROCKS FOR THE NEXT GLACIER

Acadia's relatively small size among national parks (compared to Yosemite, say, or Yellowstone) and high volume of visitors have necessitated a very active campaign to heighten sensitivity to the park's ecosystem. While you're in Acadia (and, for that matter, anywhere else), do your part to "Keep Acadia Beautiful" by adhering to principles (guidelines, really) developed by the national Leave No Trace (LNT) organization, based in Boulder, Colorado (www.lnt.org):

- Plan ahead and prepare.
- Travel and camp on durable surfaces.
- Dispose of waste properly.
- Leave what you find.
- Minimize campfire impacts.
- Respect wildlife.
- Be considerate of other visitors.

While all seven of these are important, two are especially critical for Acadia:

- **Travel and camp on durable surfaces.** Since there is no backcountry camping in Acadia, and park rangers do their best to monitor the park's three "front-country" campgrounds (two on Mount Desert, one on Isle au Haut), the focus is on hiking – and use of the trails. Stay on existing trails – paying attention to signposts, blazes, and cairns – and don't be seduced by false trails where hikers have begun to stray. Walk single file down the center of a trail to avoid trampling the sensitive vegetation alongside; slow-growing lichens are particularly fragile. Remember, plants grow by the inch and die by the foot. Every footstep can make a difference. If you must step off the trail, step onto a durable surface. Acadia's most fragile sites are the summits and ridges. Especially vulnerable is the summit of Cadillac – it's a matter of

the variations that have occurred in the past at Acadia. In the "clear day" photo, visibility was pegged at 199 miles! Ozone alerts (according to EPA standards) usually occur at Acadia a couple of times each summer. When they do, rangers put out signs to caution visitors—particularly hikers and bikers—to restrict strenuous activity.

While pollution is an Acadia issue—affecting the park, its vegetation and wildlife, and its visitors—the solution must be a national one. Stay tuned.

PARK CAPACITY

With nearly three million visitors each year, Acadia and National Park Service officials are wrestling with the question, How many people are too many people? Other national parks have initiated visitor limitations, but Acadia has so far not done so. The time may come, however.

The establishment of the propane-powered Island Explorer bus service has greatly alleviated traffic (and thus also auto, SUV, and RV emissions) during the months it operates (late June to Columbus Day), and freed up space in Acadia's parking areas, but will it encourage more visitors?

Cruise-vessel visits in Bar Harbor have multiplied exponentially in recent years, and most passengers spend at least some time in the park, but it's minimal time—often just a carriage ride or a visit to Jordan Pond House or the Cadillac summit. (Bar Harbor merchants, of course, welcome the influx.)

Heaviest use of the park occurs in July and August, with marginally less use in September, yet there are still quiet corners of the park. It's a matter of finding them. The best advice, therefore, is to visit in "shoulder" periods—May and June, late September, early October. You take your chances then with weather and temperature, but if you're flexible and adaptable, it could be the best vacation you've ever had.

---

sheer numbers. Yes, walk the summit loop for its great views, but above all, stick to the trail or at least step on solid rock.

- **Leave what you find.** That means *take NO souvenirs.* Save the wildflowers for the next visitors to enjoy, and leave the tidepool creatures where you find them. Above all, don't mess with cairns, the carefully constructed stone trail markers. Resist the urge to build or unbuild or rebuild cairns along the way – in some instances, removal or addition of a single stone can threaten a cairn's stability. It's a safety issue, too – a collapsed cairn becomes a missing link in the trail-marking system. Follow cairns, don't build them. As the slogan has it, "leave the rocks for the next glacier." Imagine if every one of the park's nearly three million visitors each year removed one cobble or rock. (Unfortunately, enough already have. Bar Harbor Airport screeners, under heightened security regulations, have been seeing visitors departing with beach rocks. But what to do with them? Who can say exactly where they came from? Please leave them where you found them.) If you're planning to camp at one of the park campgrounds, bring firewood – you'll see dozens of Firewood for Sale signs along the roads leading to the park. Stop and buy a bundle; it'll set you back only a dollar or two.

Also essential – anywhere, not just in Acadia – is the "carry in, carry out" message. If you're planning a picnic, enjoy it (on a durable surface – there's plenty of granite in Acadia), then remove all evidence of it. Carry trash bags and use them.

To keep wildlife wild, *do not feed* any of the park's wildlife – a problem of increasing concern at Acadia. Animals become dependent on humans and risk being hit by cars or otherwise meeting their end.

We all love the park, but we can't love it to death.

History

NATIVE AMERICANS

As the great continental glacier receded northwestward out of Maine about 11,000 years ago, some prehistoric grapevine must have alerted small bands of hunter-gatherers—fur-clad Paleo-indians—to the scrub sprouting in the tundra, burgeoning mammal populations, and the ocean's bountiful food supply. Because they came to the shore in droves—at first seasonally, then year-round. Anyone who thinks tourism is a recent phenomenon in this part of Maine need only explore the shoreline of Mount Desert Island, where cast-off oyster shells and clamshells document the migration of early Native Americans from woodlands to waterfront. "The shore" has been a summer-time magnet for millennia.

Archaeological evidence from the Archaic period in Maine—roughly 8000–1000 B.C.—is fairly scant, but paleontologists have unearthed stone tools and weapons and small campsites attesting to a nomadic lifestyle supported by fishing and hunting (with fishing becoming more extensive as time went on). Toward the end of the tradition, during the late Archaic period, there emerged a rather anomalous Indian culture known officially as the Moorehead phase but informally called the Red Paint People; the name comes from their curious trait of using a distinctive red ocher (pulverized hematite) in burials. Dark red puddles and stone artifacts have led excavators to burial pits in Ellsworth and Hancock, close to Mount Desert Island. Just as mysteriously as they had arrived, the Red Paint People disappeared abruptly and inexplicably around 1800 B.C.

Following them almost immediately—and almost as suddenly—hunter-gatherers of the Susquehanna Tradition arrived from well to the south, moved across Maine's interior as far as the St. John River, and remained until about 1600 B.C., when they, too, enigmatically vanished. Excavations have turned up relatively sophisticated stone tools and evidence that they cremated their dead. It was nearly 1,000 years before a major new cultural phase appeared.

The next great leap forward was marked by the advent of pottery making, introduced about 700 B.C. The Ceramic period stretched to the 16th century, and cone-shaped pots (initially stamped, later incised with coiled-rope motifs) survived until the introduction of metals from Europe. During this time, at Pemetic (their name for Mount Desert Island) and on some of the offshore islands, Native American fishermen and their families built houses of sorts—seasonal, wigwam-style birch-bark dwellings—and spent the summers fishing, clamming, trapping, and making baskets and functional birch-bark objects.

ARRIVAL OF THE EUROPEANS

The identity of the first Europeans to set foot in Maine is a matter of debate. Historians dispute the romantically popular notion that Norse explorers checked out this part of the New World as early as A.D. 1000. Even an 11th-century Norse coin found in 1961 in Brooklin (near Blue Hill, the next peninsula west of Mount Desert) probably was carried there from farther northeast.

Not until the late 15th century, the onset of the great Age of Discovery, did credible reports of the New World (including what's now Maine) filter back to Europe's courts and universities. Thanks to innovations in naval architecture, shipbuilding, and navigation, astonishingly courageous fellows crossed the Atlantic in search of rumored treasure and new routes for reaching it.

John Cabot, sailing from England aboard the ship *Mathew,* may have been the first European to reach Maine, in 1498, but historians have never confirmed a landing site. There is no question, however, about the account of Giovanni da Verrazzano, a Florentine explorer commanding *La Dauphine* under the French flag, who reached the Maine coast in 1524.

Encountering less-than-friendly Indians, Verrazzano did a minimum of business and sailed onward toward Nova Scotia. (Four years later, he died in the West Indies.) His brother's map of their landing site (probably on the Phippsburg Peninsula, near Bath) labels it "The Land of Bad People." Esteban Gomez, a Portuguese explorer sailing under the Spanish flag, followed in Verrazzano's wake in 1525, but the only outcome of his exploits was an uncounted number of captives whom he sold into slavery in Spain. A map created several years later from Gomez's descriptions seems to indicate he had at least glimpsed Mount Desert Island.

More than half a century passed before the Maine coast turned up again on European explorers' itineraries. This time, interest was fueled by reports of a Brigadoon-like area called Norumbega (or Oranbega, as one map had it), a myth that arose, gathered steam, and took on a life of its own in the decades following Verrazzano's voyage.

By the 17th century, when Europeans began arriving in more than twos and threes and getting serious about colonization, Native American agriculture was already underway, the cod fishery was thriving on offshore islands, Indians far to the north were hot to trade furs for European goodies, and the birch-bark canoe was the transport of choice when the Penobscots headed down Maine's rivers toward their summer sojourns on the coast.

MOUNT DESERT ISLAND "DISCOVERED"

In the early 17th century, English dominance of exploration west of the Penobscot River (roughly from present-day Bucksport down to the New Hampshire border and beyond) coincided roughly with increasing French activity east of the river—including Mount Desert Island and the nearby mainland.

In 1604, French nobleman Pierre du Gua, Sieur de Monts, bearing a vast land grant for *La Cadie* (or Acadia) from King Henry IV, set out with cartographer Samuel de Champlain to map the coastline. They first reached Nova Scotia's Bay of Fundy and then sailed up the

---

PRONOUNCING MOUNT DESERT: THE "SAHARA SCHOOL" VS. THE "ICE CREAM AND CAKE SCHOOL"

Noted maritime author Admiral Samuel Eliot Morison, in *The Story of Mount Desert Island* (published by Little, Brown, 1960) devotes a long footnote to the controversy over the pronunciation of *Desert* in Mount Desert. Here's his wry take on it:

[Explorer Samuel de Champlain's] exact words are: *"Le sommet de la plus part d'icelles est desgarny d'arbres parceque ce ne sont que roches. Je l'ay nommée l'Isle des Monts-déserts."* Right here we may grapple with the problem [of] how to pronounce it in English − whether we should follow what many people call the "Sahara School" and accent the penult, pronouncing it "Mount DEZ-ert," or what opponents call the "Ice Cream and Cake School," pronouncing it "Mount Dez-ERT," with accent on the last syllable. I should say that the spelling "Mount Desart" on *The Atlantic Neptune* and other old maps indicates that, like "clerk," "sergeant," and other words containing "er," it was pronounced "ar," and that the accent was then on the last syllable. Charles Tracy recorded, in his journal of 1855, that the natives called it "Mount Desert."

St. Croix River. Mid-river, just west of present-day Calais, a crew planted gardens and erected buildings on today's St. Croix Island while de Monts and Champlain went off exploring. The two men and their crew sailed up the Penobscot River to present-day Bangor (searching fruitlessly for Norumbega) and next "discovered" the imposing island Champlain named *l'Isle des Monts Déserts,* because of its treeless summits. Here they entered Frenchman Bay, landed at today's Otter Creek in early September, and explored inlets and bays in the vicinity before returning to St. Croix Island to face the elements with their ill-fated compatriots. Scurvy, lack of fuel and water, and a ferocious winter wiped out nearly half of the 79 men in the St. Croix settlement. In spring 1605, de Monts, Champlain, and other survivors headed southwest again, exploring the coastline all the way to Cape Cod before returning northeastward and settling permanently at Nova Scotia's Port Royal (now Annapolis Royal).

Eight years later, French Jesuit missionaries en route to the Kennebec River (or, as some allege, seeking Norumbega) ended up on Mount Desert Island. With a band of about three dozen French laymen, they set about establishing the St. Sauveur mission settlement at present-day Fernald Point. Despite the welcoming presence of amiable Indians (led by Asticou, an eminent Penobscot sagamore), leadership squabbles led to building delays, and English marauder Samuel Argall—assigned to reclaim this territory for England—arrived in his warship *Treasurer* to find them easy prey. The colony was leveled, the settlers were set adrift in small boats, the priests were carted off to the Jamestown Colony in Virginia, and Argall moved on to destroy Port Royal.

Even though England yearned to control the entire Maine coastline, her turf, realistically, remained south and west of the Penobscot River. During the 17th century, the French had expanded from their Canadian colony of Acadia. Unlike the absentee bosses who controlled the English territory, French merchants actually showed up, forming good relationships with the Indians and cornering the market in fishing, lumbering, and fur trading. And French Jesuit priests converted many a Native American to Catholicism. Intermittently, overlapping Anglo-French land claims sparked messy local conflicts.

In the mid-17th century, the strategic heart of French administration and activity in Maine was Fort Pentagoet, a sturdy stone outpost built in 1635 in what is now Castine (on the next peninsula west of Mount Desert). From Pentagoet, the French controlled coastal trade between the St. George River and Mount Desert Island and well up the Penobscot River. In 1654, England captured and occupied Pentagoet and much of French Acadia, but, thanks to the 1667 Treaty of Breda, title returned to the French in 1670, and Pentagoet briefly became Acadia's capital.

A short but nasty Dutch foray against Acadia in 1674 resulted in Pentagoet's destruction ("levell'd with ye ground," by one account) and the raising of yet a third national flag over Castine.

THE REVOLUTION AND STATEHOOD

From the late 17th to the late 18th century, half a dozen skirmishes along the coast—often sparked by conflicts in Europe—preoccupied the Wabanaki (Native American tribes), the French, and the English. In 1759, roughly midway through the Seven Years' War, the British came out on top in Quebec, allowing Massachusetts Governor John Bernard to divvy up the acreage on Mount Desert Island. Two bravehearts—James Richardson and Abraham Somes—arrived with their families in 1760, and today's village of Somesville marks their settlement. Even as the American Revolution consumed the colonies, Mount Desert Island maintained a relatively low profile (politically speaking) into the early 19th century. A steady stream of homesteaders, drawn by the appeal of free land, sustained their families by fishing, farming, lumbering, and shipbuilding. On March 15, 1820, the District of Maine (which included Mount Desert) broke from Massachusetts to become the 23rd state in the Union, with its capital in Portland. (The capital moved to Augusta in 1832.)

ARRIVAL OF THE "RUSTICATORS"

Around the middle of the 18th century, explorers of a different sort arrived on Mount Desert Island. Seeking dramatic landscapes rather than fertile land, painters of the acclaimed Hudson River School found more than enough inspiration for their canvases.

Thomas Cole (1801–48), founder of the group, visited Mount Desert only once, in 1844, but his onetime student Frederic Edwin Church (1826–1900) vacationed here in 1850 and became a summer resident two decades later. Once dubbed "the Michelangelo of landscape art," Church traveled widely in search of exotic settings for his grand landscapes. After his summers on Mount Desert, he spent his final days at Olana, a Persian-inspired mansion overlooking the Hudson.

It's no coincidence that artists formed a large part of the 19th-century vanguard here: The dramatic landscape, with both bare and wooded mountains descending to the sea, still inspires everyone who sees it. Those pioneering artists brilliantly portrayed this area, adding a few romantic touches to landscapes that really need

FREDERIC EDWIN CHURCH: CONSUMMATE ROMANTIC

One of the best-known second-generation members of the Hudson River School – 19th-century painters of vast landscapes, riverscapes, and seascapes – was Frederic Edwin Church. Born in 1826 in Hartford, Connecticut, Church was a contemporary of Winslow Homer, Fitz Hugh Lane, and James McNeill Whistler. By the time he first visited Mount Desert Island in 1850, Church had already studied under Hudson River School founder Thomas Cole and had been admitted to the National Academy of Design in New York. Cole proudly claimed that his one and only protégé had "the finest eye for drawing in the world." Captivated by Mount Desert's bare summits, broad vistas, and rough shoreline, Church produced dramatic, atmospheric paintings of the area.

Among the best known of Church's Mount Desert paintings are *Otter Creek, Mount Desert* (about 1850), *Twilight in the Wilderness* (1860), and *Mount Newport on Mount Desert Island* (ca. 1851-53); the latter fetched $4.2 million at auction in May 2000. (Mount Newport, named for Christopher Newport, captain of the 1607 Jamestown Colony fleet, is now Mount Champlain.)

One reviewer used an apt musical metaphor to describe the range of Church's extraordinary work: "The painter best known nowadays for what might be termed visual symphonies or operas also regularly created concertos, hymns, and smaller works – the equivalents of sonatas, études, and Lieder."

In 1853, Church set out for South America, following the route of German naturalist Alexander von Humboldt through New Granada (now Colombia) and Ecuador, and creating sketches he used for later paintings of the Andean region. Subsequent journeys to South America, the Canadian Maritimes, Mexico, and the Caribbean, as well as extended explorations of Europe and the Middle East in 1867, served as inspirations for Church masterpieces of the Parthenon, Petra, Baalbek, and Jerusalem.

In 1860, Church married Isabel Carnes, with whom he had six children (two died of diphtheria in 1865). Isabel died in 1899.

Debilitated by rheumatism during the last 15 years of his life, Church retreated to Olana, his Persian-inspired mansion on the Hudson River designed by Calvert Vaux (a colleague of noted architect Frederick Law Olmsted). Church died in New York in 1900. In 1966, Olana became a New York State Historic Site, open to the public.

The last major painting from Church's easel was not of Peru or Petra or the Hudson River, nor even of Cadillac Mountain. It was an 1895 portrait of Katahdin, in what is now Maine's Baxter State Park – *Mount Katahdin from Millinocket Camp,* the view from his beloved Camp Rhodora, on Millinocket Lake, which he purchased in 1878.

The best collection of Church paintings – indeed, the best collection of work by the members of the Hudson River School – is at the Wadsworth Atheneum in Hartford, Connecticut (www.wadsworthatheneum.org).

no enhancement. Known collectively as "rusticators," the artists and their coterie seemed content to "live like the locals" and rented basic rooms from island fishermen and boatbuilders. But once the word got out and painterly images began confirming the reports, the surge of visitors began—particularly after the Civil War, which had so totally preoccupied the nation. Tourist boardinghouses appeared first, then sprawling hotels—by the late 1880s, there were nearly 40 hotels on the island, luring vacationers for summer-long stays.

At about the same time, the East Coast's corporate tycoons zeroed in on Mount Desert, arriving by luxurious steam yachts and building over-the-top grand estates (quaintly called "summer cottages") along the shore northward from Bar Harbor. (Before long, demand exceeded acreage, and mansions also began appearing in Northeast and Southwest Harbors.) Their seasonal social circuit was a catalogue of Rich and Famous Families—Rockefeller, Astor, Vanderbilt, Ford, Whitney, Schieffelin, Morgan, Carnegie—just for a start. Also part of the elegant mix were noted academics, doctors, lawyers, and even international diplomats. The "Gay Nineties" earned their name on Mount Desert Island.

BIRTH OF A NATIONAL PARK

Fortunately for Mount Desert—and, let's face it, for all of us—many of the rusticators maintained a strong sense of *noblesse oblige,* engaging regularly in philanthropic activity. Notable among them was George Bucknam Dorr (1853–1944), who spent more than 40 years fighting to preserve land on Mount Desert Island and ultimately earned the title "Father of Acadia."

As Dorr related in his memoir (see *Suggested Reading*), the saga began with the establishment of The Hancock County Trustees of Public Reservations, a nonprofit corporation modeled on the Trustees of Public Reservations in Massachusetts and chartered in early 1903 "to acquire, by devise, gift or purchase, and to own, arrange, hold, maintain or improve for public use lands in Hancock County, Maine

[encompassing Mount Desert Island as well as Schoodic Point], which by reason of scenic beauty, historical interest, sanitary advantage or other like reasons may become available for such purpose." President of the new corporation was Charles W. Eliot, president emeritus of Harvard. Dorr became the vice president and "executive officer" and dedicated the rest of his life to the cause.

Dorr wrote letters, cajoled, spoke at meetings, arrived on potential donors' doorsteps, even resorted to polite ruses as he pursued his mission. He also delved into his own pockets to subsidize land purchases. Dorr was a fundraiser par excellence, a master of "networking" decades before the days of instant communications. Gradually he accumulated parcels—ponds, woodlands, summits, trails—and gradually his enthusiasm caught on. But easy it wasn't. He faced down longtime local residents, potential developers, and other challengers, and he politely but doggedly visited grand salons, corporate offices, and the halls of Congress in his quest.

In 1913, Bar Harbor taxpayers—irked by the increasing acreage being taken off the tax rolls—prevailed upon their state legislator to introduce a bill to annul the corporation's charter. Dorr's effective lobbying doomed the bill, but the corporation saw trouble ahead and devised a plan on a grander scale. Again thanks to Dorr's political and social connections and intense lobbying in Washington, President Woodrow Wilson on July 8, 1916, created the Sieur de Monts National Monument from 5,000 acres given to the government by the Hancock County Trustees of Public Reservations. George B. Dorr acquired the new title of Custodian of the Monument.

After the establishment of the National Park Service in late August 1916, and after Sieur de Monts had received its first congressional appropriation ($10,000), George Dorr forged ahead to try to convince the government to convert "his" national monument into a national park. "No" meant nothing to him. Not only did he schmooze with congressmen, cabinet members, helpful secretaries, and even ex-President Theodore Roosevelt, he also provided the pen (filled with ink) and waited in the president's outer office to be sure Wilson signed the bill. On February 26, 1919, Lafayette National Park became the first national park east of the Mississippi River; George Bucknam Dorr became its first superintendent. (Ten years later, the name was changed to Acadia National Park.)

THE GREAT FIRE OF 1947

Wildfires are no surprise in Maine—where woodlands often stretch to the horizon—but 1947 was unique in the history of the state and of Acadia. A rainy spring led into a dry, hot summer with almost no precipitation… and then an autumn with still no rain. Wells went dry, vegetation drooped, and the inevitable occurred—a record-breaking inferno. Starting on October 17 as a small, smoldering fire at the northern end of the island, it galloped south and east, abetted by winds, and moved toward Bar Harbor and Frenchman Bay before coming under control on October 27. More than 17,000 acres burned (including more than 10,000 in Acadia National Park). Sixty-seven magnificent "cottages" were in-cinerated on "Millionaires' Row," along the shore north of Bar Harbor, with property damage of more than $20 million. Some of the mansions, incredibly, escaped the flames, but most of the estates were never rebuilt. Miraculously, only one man succumbed to the fire. A few other deaths occurred from heart attacks and traffic accidents, as hundreds of residents scrambled frantically to escape the island. Even the fishermen of nearby Lamoine and Winter Harbor pitched in, staging their own mini-Dunkirk to evacuate more than 400 residents by boat.

THE PARK TODAY

If only George Dorr could see today's Acadia, covering more than 46,000 acres on Mount Desert Island, the Schoodic Peninsula mainland, and parts of Isle au Haut, Baker, and Little Cranberry Islands. The fire changed Mount Desert's woodland profile—from the dark greens of spruce and fir to a mix of evergreen and deciduous trees, making the fall foliage even more dramatic than in Dorr's day. If ever proof were needed that one person (enlisting the help of many others) can indeed make a difference, Acadia National Park provides it.

ESSENTIALS

Tips for Travelers

FOREIGN TRAVELERS
Entering the United States

Since 9/11, security has been excruciatingly tight for foreign visitors. It's crucial to plan well ahead, pack diligently, and have all necessary paperwork. It's also wise to make two sets of copies of all paperwork, one to carry separately on your trip and another left with a trusted friend or relative at home.

Citizens from 27 countries can enter the United States for tourism or business for 90 days or fewer without obtaining a visa. These are Andorra, Australia, Austria, Belgium, Brunei, Denmark, Finland, France, Germany, Iceland, Ireland, Italy, Japan, Liechtenstein, Luxembourg, Monaco, the Netherlands, New Zealand, Norway, Portugal, San Marino, Singapore, Slovenia, Spain, Sweden, Switzerland, and the United Kingdom. Travelers on the program must have return tickets and machine-readable passports that are valid for six months beyond intended visit dates. For details, see www.travel.state.gov/visa. Note that according to the site, a visa does not guarantee entry into the United States. A visa allows a foreign citizen to travel to the U.S. port-of-entry, and the Department of Homeland

© TOM NANGLE

Security U.S. immigration inspector authorizes or denies admission to the country.

Citizens of countries other than those in the VWP need to be aware that the United States has become exceedingly security-conscious and has tightened the scrutiny of visa applications and the issuance of visas, making delays inevitable—and frustrating. If you need a visa, *plan well ahead!*

Foreigners visiting Acadia National Park typically arrive in the United States via major ports of entry, such as Boston or New York, and then continue to Maine; a smaller number arrive in Maine by road via Canada (New Brunswick or Quebec) or in Bar Harbor via *The Cat,* a fast catamaran ferry from Yarmouth, Nova Scotia. (The only customs facilities on Mount Desert Island are at The Cat Ferry Terminal in Bar Harbor. See the sidebar *Getting Away to Nova Scotia* in this chapter.)

Most Canadian citizens need no visa but do need valid identification that establishes both identity and citizenship to enter the United States through Maine or any other crossover point. Documents that are acceptable for identifying citizenship are birth certificate, citizenship certificate, and passport. Photo identification may be required. Duty-free limits for Canadians returning home are C$50 after a 24-hour stay, C$200 after 48 hours, and C$750 after seven days (not counting departure day).

There is no limit on the amount of money or travelers checks a nonresident may bring into the United States. If the amount exceeds $10,000, however, it's necessary to fill out an official report form.

No fruit, vegetables, or plant materials can be taken across the border in either direction.

Other banned items—some self-evident, some not—include drugs and drug paraphernalia (except medically authorized), firearms, and most meat and poultry products (including dried meat). For more detailed information, check the website of the Customs and Border Protection division of the Department of Homeland Security (www.cbp.gov).

TIME ZONE

Acadia National Park (as well as the rest of Maine) is in the eastern time zone—the same as New York; Washington, D.C.; Philadelphia, Pennsylvania; and Orlando, Florida. Eastern standard time (EST) runs from the last Sunday in October to the first Sunday in April; eastern daylight time (EDT), one hour later, is in effect otherwise. If your itinerary also includes the Canadian Maritimes, remember that the provinces of New Brunswick and Nova Scotia are on Atlantic time—one hour later than eastern. Surprising to many first-time visitors is how early the sun rises in the morning and how early it sets at night in midsummer.

WHAT TO BRING

No matter when you come, bring a camera and plenty of film or memory cards (you can purchase both here, and many photo shops in larger communities will download images onto a CD for a small fee). Don't forget prescription glasses, prescription medicines, binoculars, perhaps a journal or sketchpad, and any financial cards you plan on using, such as debit, credit, and ATM. If you're planning to venture into Canada, make sure you have appropriate identification (passport required as of Dec. 31, 2005) and any necessary paperwork.

Tent Camping

If you're planning to tent-camp, get out your camping checklist and load up all its items.

Other important gear: flashlight, compass and/or GPS, Swiss Army knife, small first-aid kit, binoculars, sunglasses, lip balm, sunscreen, camera (with an extra battery), whistle, small waterproof carryall, plastic water bottle with a belt hook or strap, health-insurance card, hiking maps and guides, and, perhaps most important of all, bug dope! In fact, if you plan to spend any time outdoors in Maine between early May and late September, insect repellent is critical for keeping at bay the state's winged annoyances—especially black flies, mosquitoes, and midges. Ben's and Cutter's work well,

GETTING AWAY TO NOVA SCOTIA

Bar Harbor is the starting point for the summertime car-and-passenger ferry to **Yarmouth, Nova Scotia,** which shaves more than 600 miles off the driving route. From mid-May to mid-October, the high-speed 900-passenger catamaran called *The Cat,* owned by Bay Ferries, zips to Yarmouth in 165 minutes. Not without controversy when it first went into service, *The Cat* was criticized for creating harbor wakes and even received speeding tickets. But after several years of operation, it's enough of a hit that service between Portland and Yarmouth, N.S., is planned for 2006.

The Cat's fast: It's powered by four 9,500-horsepower marine diesel engines, making it capable of speeds up to 55 mph. If you take it, be sure to make a trip to the back deck and watch the four water jets – they can fill an Olympic swimming pool in 33 seconds. It's also comfortable, with onboard food service, a small casino, a duty-free shop, and two TV/cinema lounges. A couple of caveats: First, the ferry doesn't have a full kitchen aboard, so the menu is somewhat limited. What's available is okay, but you might be happier bringing takeout aboard, especially if you're fussy or have any dietary restrictions. Second, the air-conditioning keeps the boat very cool (which helps prevent seasickness). Even in the midst of summer, it's wise to bring a fleece jacket and perhaps warm-up pants to slip on if you're cold.

In summer, you can even go to Yarmouth for the day, without a car, departing in the morning and returning on an evening ferry. It's a long day. If you're taking the day cruise without your car, consider making arrangements in advance for a day tour of the area. Frankly, you can cover downtown Yarmouth's shops and walkable sights in a few hours, and you'll be in town for much longer than that. The tours get you out and about to other sights, while throwing in a good dose of history and heritage to boot. You can make reservations for a tour when you book the ferry or take your chances and try to sign up on the spot with an operator that might have space available.

Settlers Shore Experience (Rte. 1 Box 50N. Kemptville, NS, Canada, 902/761-3105, www.tocons.com) offers both two-hour and six-hour tours that coordinate with *The Cat's* season (mid-May–mid-October). While both cover the same territory, the six-hour one includes admission to and time in a museum and a meal. As one guide noted, the tour in-

---

and Avon Skin-So-Soft lotion has become an inadvertent favorite recently (supermarkets and convenience stores seldom carry Avon products, but all carry the clone Skintastic, produced by the manufacturer of Off!). A new product getting good results is Buzz-Off, an all-natural repellent concocted by Alison Lewey, a Passamaquoddy/Maliseet Indian. It's widely available in Maine. Home remedies (try at your own risk) include eating garlic, drinking alcohol, or rubbing cider vinegar, tansy leaves, or crushed lemon thyme on your skin.

Not much daunts the black flies of spring and early summer, but you can lower your appeal by not using perfume, aftershave lotion, or scented shampoo and by wearing light-colored clothing.

Other handy items are a small backpack for day trips or light hiking and a small or collapsible cooler for picnics or storing food.

TRAVELING BY RV

Bringing a recreational vehicle (RV) to Mount Desert Island and Acadia National Park creates something of a conundrum. No question, the vehicles are convenient for carting kids and gear, but they're a major source of traffic problems on the island, and especially within the park. All of the island's roads are two lanes, and even though the island offers more designated bike lanes than almost anywhere else in Maine, bikes and RVs often have to share the road. RV parking is very limited, and even banned in some locales (such as downtown Bar

cludes "fact, fiction, and folklore, and it's up to you to figure out what's what." No matter, it's fascinating and fun. Highlights include the story behind the *Titanic* mystery ship, a tour of a lobster-holding facility, a visit to the Old English Settlers Church and cemetery, and time at the Cape Forchu lighthouse. If you take the two-hour (which usually lasts closer to three hours), you'll still have plenty of time left over to visit downtown shops and have dinner. Expect to pay about $60 pp U.S. for the six-hour tour, $20 for the two-hour tour.

If you prefer to explore on your own, make your first stop the information center one block up the hill from the ferry. It's staffed with friendly, knowledgeable folks and is filled with brochures and pamphlets on the region covering topics including a Yarmouth walking tour, regional driving tours, and Nova Scotia birding. Special packages are available if you want to stay longer and explore Nova Scotia, with or without your car.

If you do go, proposed Homeland Security regulations require a passport for all air and sea travel to and from Canada, effective December 31, 2006, and for all land crossings, effective December 31, 2007; so plan accordingly. Pets and dogs may be brought into Canada as long as they have a valid rabies vaccination certificate. For a list of goods that cannot be brought into Canada, visit www.inspection.gc.ca For other questions about Canadian customs, call 506/636-5064 from the U.S. or 800/461-9999 from Canada, or visit www.cbsa-asfc.gc.ca.

Plans call for the ferry to split its runs between Portland and Yarmouth and Bar Harbor and Yarmouth (unfortunately by law, it cannot provide that ideal connection between Portland and Bar Harbor, but you might be able to connect Portland to Yarmouth and then on to Bar Harbor). For a current schedule and fare information, contact **Bay Ferries** (207/288-3395 or 888/249-7245, www.catferry.com).

You can get information and make reservations or pick up reserved tickets (saving time and waiting in line in the morning) at the Bar Harbor ferry terminal (121 Eden St., Rte. 3, Bar Harbor) or at the office in downtown Bar Harbor (65 Main St., corner of Cottage St.), known locally as Cat Corner. In summer, Nova Scotia's **Yarmouth County Tourism Association** (207/288-9432 or 902/742-5355) has staff at both locations to help you plan your trip.

Harbor). Ideally, you should consider bringing an RV to Acadia only between late June and Columbus Day—when you can park the vehicle in one of the island's dozen commercial campgrounds and travel around the island via the Island Explorer shuttle service.

Incidentally, be aware that the maximum trailer (or RV) length in the national park's two campgrounds is 35 feet, maximum width is 12 feet, and only one vehicle is allowed per site. Neither park campground has water or electric hookups. (More details on the two campgrounds appear in the *Acadia on Mount Desert Island* chapter.)

Plans are in the works (but no date has been set) to provide parking facilities and a shuttle stop in Trenton, which promises to be a major plus for day-trippers with RVs. Until then, however, you can park on a space-available basis near the park's Hulls Cove Visitor Center and in a designated area on Lower Main Street (watch for signs) in Bar Harbor.

TRAVELING WITH CHILDREN

Acadia National Park isn't a turn-the-toddlers-loose kind of place (too many cliffs and other potential hazards), but for school-age youngsters and cooperative teenagers, it's a fabulous family-vacation destination. There are family-oriented kayak tours, Park Ranger tours, whale-watching trips, hiking and biking trails, carriage rides, and boat excursions. There's saltwater (literally breathtaking for adults, but not for kids) swimming at Sand Beach and freshwater swimming at several lakes and ponds. Incredibly, McDonald's and Burger King haven't invaded Mount Desert Island (although Subway has), but Bar Harbor and other towns have plenty of pizza and lobster joints, as well as two cinemas (one year-round, one seasonal) and several museums for rainy days.

Be forewarned that in-line skates and skateboards are not allowed anywhere within the park. The island communities surrounding the park are all small and—especially at the height of summer—congested. In-line skates can come in handy, but use them sensibly; skateboards, on the other hand, are a major hazard in these villages. Bikes are *not* allowed on any of the park's hiking trails, but the car-free carriage-trail network is ideal for biking.

How about doing a family volunteer stint? Consider spending a morning on a trail-maintenance crew (8:30 A.M.–12:30 P.M., Tuesday, Thursday, and Saturday, June–Oct.). You'll help cut back vegetation along trails and carriage roads, rebuild walls or drainages, clean up, and other such activities. Bring water, insect repellent, and a bag lunch for a post-work picnic—the camaraderie is contagious. It's advisable to dress in layers, and do wear sturdy shoes. The nonprofit Friends of Acadia organization chalks up more than 8,000 volunteer hours every year. Check the website before you come (www.friendsofacadia.org), or call 207/288-3934 when you get here for the recorded schedule of work projects. (Volunteer crews meet at Park Headquarters on Rte. 233, Eagle Lake Road.)

TRAVELING WITH PETS

If you're used to traveling with your cat or dog, you should be accustomed to playing by the rules. In Acadia National Park, dogs are allowed *only* on leashes, and they are banned from several park locations: Sand and Echo Lake beaches, Duck Harbor Campground (on Isle au Haut), park buildings, and any of the "ladder" hiking trails, which have iron foot- and handholds. (When you see the ladder trails, you'll understand why pets are forbidden.) Don't take pets on the Park Ranger tours,

and do *not* leave your dog unattended (especially in an RV at one of the campgrounds). Be considerate of your pet as well as of other visitors. Of course, guide dogs are exempted from all rules.

To make the best of a visit to Acadia—so you can hike and bike and kayak without worrying about your pet—you might want to reserve kennel space for part of your stay. Mount Desert Island has the **Acadia Woods Kennel** (Crooked Road, Bar Harbor, 207/288-9766, variable rates); on the mainland in nearby Ellsworth is **Downeast Boarding Kennel** (275 High St., Rte. 3, Ellsworth, 207/667-3062, variable rates). In July and August, be sure to call well in advance for a reservation. If you'd prefer to have a dog-sitter come to your hotel or campground, contact Wendy Scott at **Bark Harbor, Inc.** (200 Main St., Bar Harbor, 207/288-0404, www.barkharbor.com). She'll recommend someone who can help. If at all possible, call before you arrive to make arrangements, and when you get here, visit the store—a Toys R Us for pet owners.

SENIORS

Age does have its privileges. U.S. Citizens and permanent residents age 62 or older can purchase a **Golden Age Passport,** valid at more than 300 national parks (including Acadia), historic sites, and monuments for $10, a one-time fee. It also entitles you to half-price camping. Many lodgings and many attractions and sights offer discounts to seniors. It never hurts to ask. Age varies; some begin as young as 55 (egad!). In any case, you'll need proof, such as a driver's license or passport.

Age also often brings achy knees and hips or other such maladies. Many of the accommodations in this area are small inns and B&Bs. If you have mobility problems or difficulty carrying your luggage up a flight of stairs or two, you'll want to make sure that your lodging has either first-floor rooms or elevators.

ACCESSIBILITY

Acadia National Park has been conscientious about providing as much accessibility as possible to people with disabilities. For a start, the Hulls Cove Visitor Center (the park's spring, summer, and fall information center) has a special parking area for easy wheelchair access, bypassing the 52 steps from the main parking area. When you get into the center, request a **Golden Access Passport,** which provides free lifetime entry to any national park (and half-price park campsites) for any citizen or permanent resident who is permanently disabled. (If you've broken your leg or have another temporary disability, you're not eligible.) The passport is also available at the park's two campgrounds, at park headquarters, and at the Sand Beach and Bar Harbor Village Green ticket booths.

Also at the Hulls Cove Visitor Center, pick up a copy of the *Acadia National Park Access Guide,* which provides detailed accessibility information (including parking, entry, restrooms, pay phones, and water fountains) for the park's visitors centers, the two campgrounds, picnic areas, beaches, and gift shops, as well as carriage rides, some boat cruises, and nonpark museums on Mount Desert Island. A few of the Park Ranger programs are wheelchair-accessible, as are all of the evening programs at the park's two campgrounds. Access to the carriage-road network depends on your ability (there are some steep grades); even the easiest trails may require some assistance. Each of the Island Explorer shuttle buses—operating between late June and Columbus Day—has room for at least one wheelchair.

Parking lots at some of the park's most popular locales (such as Thunder Hole, the Cadillac summit, and Jordan Pond House) have designated handicapped spaces.

Wheelchair rentals are handled by **West End Drug Co.** (105 Main St., Bar Harbor 04609, 207/288-3318).

To plan your Acadia trip in advance, order a Golden Access Passport online, then download the accessibility information from the park's website (www.nps.gov/acad/accessibility.htm). If you're reserving a campsite online (reservations.nps.gov/) for the Blackwoods Campground—up to four months before your arrival—you'll need the Golden Access Passport beforehand.

For additional accessibility information, call 207/288-3338 (voice) or 207/288-8800 (TTY). For emergencies in the park or elsewhere on Mount Desert Island, dial 911. (If you call the main park number during working hours regarding an emergency, a recorded message will tell you to hang up and dial 911.)

While newer properties must meet the strict standards of the Americans with Disabilities Act, older and historic lodgings and restaurants often don't have accessible rooms or facilities. It's wise to ask detailed questions pertaining to your needs before booking a room or making a restaurant reservation.

ACCOMMODATIONS, FOOD, AND ALCOHOL
Accommodations

For all accommodations listings, rates are quoted for peak season, which is usually July and August but may extend through foliage (mid-October). Rates drop, often dramatically, in the shoulder and off-season at accommodations that remain open. Especially during peak season, many accommodations require a two- or three-night minimum.

For the best rates, be sure to check Internet specials and to ask about packages. Many accommodations also provide discounts for members of travel clubs such as AAA, to seniors and the military, and other such groups. Unless otherwise noted, accommodations have private baths.

A note about B&Bs: If you've never stayed in a B&B, begin by putting aside any ideas you may have about them. No two are alike, but all are built on the premise that your experiences will be richer if it's easy to meet other travelers. You will find few of the old-style homestay B&Bs—where a number of rooms share one bath as well as the owner's living quarters—in the region, with the notable exception of offshore islands. Almost all B&Bs have private baths for each room and special areas for guests to relax and dine; some have in-room fireplaces or fancy bathrooms with jetted tubs. Many also provide private tables for breakfast—ask before booking, if you're

MAINE FOOD SPECIALTIES

Everyone knows Maine is *the* place for lobster, but there are quite a few other foods that you should sample before you leave.

For a few weeks in May, right around Mother's Day (the second Sunday in May), a wonderful delicacy starts sprouting along Maine woodland streams: **fiddleheads,** the still-furled tops of the ostrich fern *(Matteuccia struthiopteris).* Tasting vaguely like asparagus, fiddleheads have been on May menus ever since Native Americans taught the colonists to forage for the tasty vegetable. Don't go fiddleheading unless you're with a pro, though; the lookalikes are best left to the woods critters. If you find them on a restaurant menu, indulge.

As with fiddleheads, we owe thanks to Native Americans for introducing us to **maple syrup,** one of Maine's major agricultural exports. The syrup comes in four different colors/flavors (from light amber to extra dark amber), and inspectors strictly monitor syrup quality. The best syrup comes from the sugar or rock maple, *Acer saccharum.* On Maine Maple Sunday (usually the fourth Sunday in March), several dozen syrup producers open their rustic sugarhouses to the public for "sugaring-off" parties – to celebrate the sap harvest and share the final phase in the production process. Woodsmoke billows from the sugarhouse chimney while everyone inside gathers around huge kettles used to boil down the watery sap. (A single gallon of syrup starts with 30–40 gallons of sap.) Finally, it's time to sample the syrup every which way – on pancakes and waffles, in tea, on ice cream, in puddings, in muffins, even just drizzled over snow. Most producers also have containers of syrup for sale. For a list of participating sugarhouses, contact the Maine Department of Agriculture (207/287-3491, www.getrealmaine.com).

The best place for Maine maple syrup is atop pancakes made with Maine **wild blueberries.** Packed with antioxidants and all kinds of good-for-you stuff, these flavorful berries are prized by bakers because they retain their form and flavor when cooked. Much smaller than the cultivated versions, wild blueberries are also raked, not picked. Although most of the Down East barren barons harvest their crops for the lucrative wholesale market, a few growers let you pick your own blueberries in mid-August. Contact the Wild Blueberry Commission (207/581-1475) or the state Department of Agriculture (207/287-3491) for locations, recipes, and other wild-blueberry information, or log on to the website of the Wild Blueberry Association of North America, headquartered in Bar Harbor: www.wildblueberries.com.

The best place to simply *appreciate* blueberries is Machias (an easy day trip from most anywhere in the Acadia region), site of the renowned annual Wild Blueberry Festival, held the third weekend in August. While harvesting is under way in the surrounding fields, you can stuff your face with blueberry everything – muffins, jam, pancakes, ice cream, pies. Plus you can collect blueberry-logo napkins, T-shirts, fridge magnets, pottery, and jewelry.

Another don't miss while in Maine is Maine-made **ice cream.** Skip the overpriced Ben & Jerry's outlets. Locally made ice cream is fresher and better, and often comes in an astounding range of flavors. The big name in the state is Gifford's, with regional companies being Shain's and Round Top. All beat the out-of-state competition by a long shot. Even better are some of the one-of-a-kind dairy bars and farm stands. Good bets are Morton's, in Ellsworth, and Ben & Bill's, in Bar Harbor.

Finally, whenever you get a chance, shop at a **farmers market.** Their biggest asset is serendipity – you never know what you'll find. Everything is locally grown and often organic. Herbs, unusual vegetables, seedlings, baked goods, meat, free-range chicken, goat cheese, herb vinegars, berries, exotic condiments, smoked salmon, maple syrup, honey, and jams are just a few of the possibilities. For a list of all the markets (including those in inland areas), contact the Maine Department of Agriculture.

just not up to being sociable first thing in the morning. The shared breakfast table does provide an opportunity to trade experiences with other guests. Some also provide afternoon refreshments, another opportunity to chat. Many B&Bs are quite exquisite and decorated with antiques and fine art, which means they're often inappropriate for young children. Others are equipped with in-room TV, CD player, VCR or DVD player, air-conditioning, phone, and other modern conveniences. A number of Mount Desert Island B&Bs are in grand historical cottages that survived the fire, providing a taste of that lifestyle and a peek into those rambling homes. Most B&Bs are operated by folks who live here year-round (some for generations), so they are able to provide recommendations based on their in-depth knowledge. B&Bs, especially, reflect their owners, so expect any to be different than described if they have new owners.

Food

Days and hours of operation listed for places serving food are for peak season. These do change often, sometimes even within a season, and it's not uncommon for a restaurant to close early on a quiet night. To avoid disappointment, call before making a special trip.

Outside of Ellsworth, do not expect to see much in the way of fast food in this region. There just isn't the year-round population base to support it.

Alcohol

As in the rest of the country, Maine's minimum drinking age is 21 years—and bar owners, bartenders, and serving staff can be held legally accountable for serving underage imbibers. Owners and employees also may be held liable for accidents caused by *legal* drinkers. Stiff anti-drunken-driving efforts in Maine (including random roadblocks, license revocation or suspension, hefty fines, and jail terms) have reduced but by no means halted the fatalities. If your blood alcohol level is .08 percent or higher, you are legally considered to be operating under the influence.

SMOKING

Maine now has laws banning smoking in restaurants, bars, and lounges as well as enclosed areas of public places, such as shopping malls. Only a handful of B&Bs and country inns permit smoking, and more and more motels, hotels, and resorts are limiting the number of rooms where smoking is permitted. Many accommodations have instituted high fines for anyone who smokes in a nonsmoking room.

What's a smoker to do? If you're unable to find a smoking room, your best bet is probably a motel that allows smoking on the premises, although not in the room. Most motels open directly to the outdoors, so all you'll have to do is step outside for a puff. Do ask, however, as some don't permit smoking where it might enter another guest's room through an open window.

Health and Safety

There's too much to do and see in Acadia National Park to spend even a few hours laid low by illness or mishap. Be sensible—get enough sleep, wear sunscreen and appropriate clothing, know your limits and don't take foolhardy risks; heed weather and warning signs, carry water and snacks while hiking, don't overindulge in food or alcohol, always tell someone where you're going, and watch your step. If you're traveling with children, quadruple your caution.

Even though Maine's public transportation network is woefully inadequate, and the crime rate is one of the lowest in the nation, it's still risky to hitchhike or pick up hitchhikers.

MEDICAL CARE
Emergencies
The **Mount Desert Island Hospital** (10 Wayman Ln., Bar Harbor, 207/288-5081, www.mdihospital.org) has round-the-clock emergency-room services with doctors and dentists on duty or on call.

The next nearest hospital, even larger, is **Maine Coast Memorial Hospital** (50 Union St., Ellsworth, 207/664-5311 or 888/645-8829, emergency room 207/664-5340, www.mainehospital.org). Healthcare Express (207/664-5341), at the hospital, handles minor problems daily between noon and 8 P.M. The hospital is 20 miles north of Bar Harbor.

The region's largest hospital is **Eastern Maine Medical Center** (489 State St., Bangor, 207/973-7000 or 877/366-3662, emergency room 207/973-8000, www.emmc.org); Bangor is 50 miles from Bar Harbor. EMMC also is one of two Maine bases for LifeFlight of Maine, operating medical air-rescue helicopters statewide.

MDI Hospital operates the **Community Health Center** (9 Village Green Way, Southwest Harbor, 207/244-5630). It's open Monday, Tuesday, and Wednesday, 8 A.M.–7 P.M., and Thursday and Friday 8 A.M.–5 P.M.

Blue Hill Memorial Hospital (57 Water St.,

Blue Hill, 207/374-2836, www.bhmh.org) has 24-hour emergency- room service.

Alternative Health Care
Nontraditional health-care options are available on Mount Desert Island as well as on the Blue Hill Peninsula and Deer Isle. After some overambitious hiking or biking expeditions, a massage might be in order. Holistic practitioners, as well as certified massage therapists and acupuncturists, are listed in the Yellow Pages of local phone books. Also, check the bulletin boards and talk to the managers at the health-food stores in Bar Harbor, Ellsworth, and Blue Hill. They always know where to find homeopathic doctors.

Pharmacies
The major pharmacy chain in and near Acadia is **Rite-Aid;** Hannaford supermarkets also have pharmacy departments. Mount Desert Island has independent drugstores in each of its towns. All carry prescription and over-the-counter medications. There are no round-the-clock pharmacies. Some independent pharmacists post emergency numbers on their doors and will go out of their way to help, but your best bet for a middle-of-the-night medication crisis is the hospital emergency room.

If you take regular medications, be sure to pack an adequate supply, as well as a new prescription in case you lose your medicine or unexpectedly need a refill.

ALLERGIES
If your medical history includes extreme allergies to shellfish or bee stings, you already know the risks of eating a lobster or wandering around a wildflower meadow. However, if you come from a landlocked area and are new to crustaceans, you might not be aware of the potential hazard. Statistics indicate that only about 2 percent of adults have a severe shellfish allergy, but for those victims, the reaction can set in quickly. Immediate treatment

is needed to keep the airways open. If you have a history of severe allergic reactions to *anything*, be prepared when you come to the Maine coast dreaming of lobster feasts. Ask your doctor for a prescription for an EpiPen (epinephrine), a preloaded, single-use syringe—enough to tide you over until you can get to a hospital.

HYPOTHERMIA AND FROSTBITE

Wind and weather can shift dramatically in Maine, especially at higher elevations, creating prime conditions for contracting hypothermia and frostbite. At risk are hikers, swimmers, canoeists, kayakers, sailors, bicyclists, and cross-country skiers.

When body temperature plummets below the normal 97°F to 98.6°F, hypothermia is likely to set in. Symptoms include disorientation, a flagging pulse rate, prolonged shivering, swelling of the face, and cool skin. Quick action is essential to prevent shock and keep body temperature from dropping into the 80s, where cardiac arrest can occur. Emergency treatment begins with removal of as much wet clothing as possible without causing further exposure. Wrap the victim in anything dry—blankets, sleeping bag, clothing, towels, even large plastic trash bags—to keep body heat from escaping. Be sure the neck and head are covered. Or practice the buddy system—climb into a sleeping bag with the victim and provide skin contact. Do not rub the skin, apply hot water, or elevate the legs. If he or she is conscious, offer high-sugar snacks and nonalcoholic hot drinks (never give alcohol; it dilates blood vessels and disrupts the warming process). As quickly as possible, transport the victim to a hospital emergency room.

When extremities begin turning blue or gray, with red blotches, frostbite may be setting in. As with hypothermia, add warmth slowly but do not rub frostbitten skin. Offer snacks and warm nonalcoholic liquids.

To prevent hypothermia and frostbite, dress in layers and remove or add them as needed. Wool, waterproof nylon (such as Gore-Tex), and synthetic fleece (such as Polartec) are the best fabrics for repelling dampness; cotton does not do the job. Polyester fleece lining wicks excess moisture away from your body. If you plan to buy a down jacket, be sure it has a waterproof shell; down will just suck up the moisture from snow and rain. Especially in winter, always cover your head, since body heat escapes quickly through the head; a ski mask will protect ears and nose. Wear wool- or fleece-lined gloves and wool socks.

Even during the height of summer, be on the alert for mild hypothermia when children stay in the ocean too long. Bouncing in and out of the water, kids become preoccupied, refuse to admit they are cold, and fall prey to wind chill.

HUNTING SEASON

During Maine's fall hunting season (October to Thanksgiving weekend)—and especially during the November deer season—walk or hike only in wooded areas marked No Hunting, No Trespassing, or Posted. Although no hunting is permitted in the park, it is permitted in the Donnell Pond Public Reserved Lands and elsewhere. Even if an area *is* closed to hunters, don't decide to explore the woods during deer or moose season without wearing a "hunter orange" (read: eye-popping fluorescent) jacket or vest. If you take your dog along, be sure it, too, wears an orange vest. Deer hunters are required to wear two items of orange clothing—a hat and usually a vest. Orange gear is available in sporting-goods stores, hardware stores, and some supermarkets and convenience stores. Hunting is illegal on Sundays.

During hunting season, moose and deer are on the move and made understandably skittish by the hunters invading their turf. Moose are primarily found inland, but deer are everywhere, and even the occasional moose strays into coastal Maine. At night, particularly in wooded areas, these huge creatures often end up alongside or in the roads, so ratchet up your defensive-driving skills. Reduce your normal speed, use high beams when there's no oncoming traffic, and remain extra-alert. In a moose-vs.-car encounter, no one wins, and human fatalities are common. An encounter between a deer and a car may be less dangerous to humans (although the deer usually dies), but some damage is inevitable.

LYME DISEASE

A bacterial infection that causes severe arthritis-like symptoms, Lyme disease (named after the Connecticut town where it was first identified, in 1975) has been documented in Maine since 1986. (In Europe, the disease is known as borreliosis, after the *Borrelia burgdorferi* bacterium that causes it.) In 2003, 219 cases of Lyme disease were reported in Maine—a huge increase from the *three* cases reported in 1989. No reliable statistics exist on visitors who have left the state and experienced delayed onset of the disease—a frequent occurrence. Health officials monitor the situation carefully and issue warnings during prime tick season—mid-May into August. Atlanta's Centers for Disease Control and Prevention (www.cdc.gov) has cited the wooded, marshy areas of Maine's southernmost counties as the highest-risk areas, but incidences of Lyme disease have been reported in Acadia National Park.

Lyme disease is spread by bites from tiny deer ticks (not the larger dog ticks; they don't carry it), which feed on the blood of deer, mice, songbirds, and humans. Symptoms include joint pain, extreme fatigue, chills, a stiff neck, headache, and a distinctive ring-like rash. In the past, early-stage treatment has involved a fairly expensive round of antibiotics, but considerable success has been reported from treatment with doxycycline or amoxicillin. Except for the rash, which occurs only in about 80 percent of victims, the symptoms mimic those of other ailments, such as the flu, so the disease is hard to diagnose. The rash, which expands gradually and usually is not painful, may appear one or two weeks after a bite. If left untreated, Lyme disease eventually can cause cardiac and neurological problems and debilitating arthritis. Preventive measures are essential. (LYMErix, a vaccine approved by the FDA in 1998, was withdrawn from the market in 2002.)

The best advice is to take precautions: wear a long-sleeved shirt and long pants, and tuck the pant legs into your socks. Light-colored clothing makes the ticks easier to spot. Buy tick repellent at a supermarket or convenience store and use it liberally on your legs. Spray it around your cuffs and beltline. While you're hiking, stay away from long grasses and keep to the center of trails. (You should do this anyway—part of the Leave No Trace philosophy—to preserve Acadia's fragile ecosystem.) After any hike, check for ticks—especially behind the knees, and in the armpits, navel, and groin. Monitor children carefully. If you find a tick or suspect you have been bitten, head for the nearest hospital emergency room. If you spot a tick on you (or anyone else), try to remove it with tweezers and save it for analysis, since not all deer ticks are infected with the bacterium.

MOSQUITO-BORNE VIRUSES

While neither West Nile nor Eastern equine encephalitis have been reported among people in Maine, that doesn't mean the viruses aren't here. In 2005, a few cases of EEE were reported in New Hampshire and Massachusetts, and in southern Maine, a horse was diagnosed with it. West Nile has been found in a handful of mosquito pools in southern Maine. The danger isn't high, but it's wise to take precautions. Try to stay inside between dusk and dark, when mosquitoes are most active. If you must be outside, wear long pants and long-sleeved shirts. At all times, cover any exposed skin with insect repellent, and reapply if you'll be outside for long periods of time, especially if you might sweat it off.

RABIES

Incidents of rabies—a life-threatening, nerve-attacking disease for which there is no cure unless treated immediately—have increased dramatically in Maine since 1994. The biggest jumps were among rabid skunks and raccoons. Only one human has ever survived a case of rabies, and the disease is horrible, so *do not* approach, or let any child approach, any of the animals known to transmit it: raccoons, skunks, squirrels, bats, and foxes. Domestic dogs are required to have biennial rabies inoculations, thus providing a front line of defense for humans. If you're bitten by any animal, especially one acting suspiciously, head for the nearest hospital emergency room. The virus travels along nerve roots to the brain, so a facial bite is far more critical, relatively speaking, than a leg bite. Treatment (a series of injections) is not as painful as it once was, but it's very expensive—although, I might add, much better than the alternative. For statewide information about rabies, contact the Maine Disease Control Administration in Augusta, 207/287-3591.

SEASICKNESS

Samuel Butler, the 19th-century author of *Erewhon,* wrote, "How holy people look when they are sea-sick." And he wasn't kidding. Seasickness conjures visions of the pearly gates and an overwhelming urge for instant salvation. Fortunately, even though the ailment seems to last forever, it's only temporary—depending on where you are, what remedies you have, and how your system responds. If you're planning to do any boating in the waters around Acadia National Park—particularly sailing or whale-watching—you'll want to be prepared. (Being prepared, in fact, may keep you from succumbing, since fear of seasickness just about guarantees you'll get it.)

Seasickness allegedly stems from an inner-ear imbalance caused by boat motion, but researchers have had difficulty explaining why some people on a vessel become violently ill and others have no problem at all.

To prevent seasickness, try to stay in good shape. Get enough sleep and food, and keep your clothing warm and dry (not easy, of course, on a heeling sailboat). Some veteran sailors swear by salted crackers, sips of water, and bites of fresh ginger. If you start feeling queasy, keep your eyes on the horizon and stay as far away as possible from odors from the engine, the galley, the head, and other seasick passengers. If you become seasick, keep sipping water to prevent dehydration.

Dramamine, Marezine, and Bonine, taken several hours before a boat trip, have long been the preventives of choice. They do cause drowsiness, but anyone who's been seasick will tell you he or she would rather be drowsy. Another popular preventive is the scopolamine patch (available by prescription under the trademark Transderm Scop), which gradually releases medication into the bloodstream for up to three days. Behind an ear or a knee is the best location for the little adhesive disc. Wash your hands after you touch it—the medication can cause temporary blurred vision if you inadvertently rub your eyes. Children, pregnant women, and the elderly should not use scopolamine. Discuss the minor side effects with the physician who gives you the prescription.

Some people swear by the pressure bracelet, which operates somewhat on the principle of acupressure, telling your brain to ignore the fact that you're not on terra firma. Great success has been reported with these prophylactics in the last decade. Before embarking, especially if the weather is at all iffy, go ahead and put on a patch or a bracelet. Any such preventive measure also improves your mental attitude, relieving anxiety.

SUNSTROKE

Since Acadia National Park lies above the 44th parallel, sunstroke is not a major problem, but don't push your luck by spending an entire day frying on Sand Beach or the granite shoreline. Not only do you risk sunstroke and dehydration, but you're also asking for skin cancer down the road. Early in the season, slather yourself, and especially children, with plenty of PABA-free sunblock. (PABA can cause skin rashes and eruptions, even on people not abnormally sensitive.) Depending on your skin tone, use sun protection factor (SPF) 15 or higher. If you're in the water a long time, slather on some more. Start with 15 to 30 minutes of solar exposure and increase gradually each day. When you're hiking, carry water. If you don't get it right, watch for symptoms of sunstroke: fever, profuse sweating, headache, nausea or vomiting, extreme thirst, and sometimes hallucinations. To treat someone for sunstroke, find a breezy spot and place a cold, wet cloth on the victim's forehead. Change the cloth frequently so it stays cold. Offer lots of liquids—strong tea or coffee, fruit juice, water, or soft drinks (no alcohol).

Information and Services

MONEY AND CURRENCY EXCHANGE

Since Maine's Down East (geographically, northeast) coast borders Canada, don't be surprised to see a few Canadian coins mixed in with American ones when you receive change from a purchase. In such cases, Canadian and U.S. quarters are equivalent, although the exchange rate is in fact drastically different. Most services (including banks) will accept a handful of Canadian coins at par, but you'll occasionally spot No Canadian Currency signs.

It's not absolutely necessary to exchange currency when traveling between the United States and Canada, but Canadian dollars are worth far less in the United States (and U.S. dollars are worth more in Canada). Also, the farther south of Canada you roam, the more likely you'll find resistance to Canadian currency in restaurants and shops. It's easier to convert it.

Other foreign currencies are not easily convertible (without losing in the exchange) at the small local banks on Mount Desert Island. Acadia National Park has no ATMs (automated teller machines) within its boundaries, but there are ATMs in Bar Harbor and other communities on Mount Desert Island.

Credit Cards and Traveler's Checks

Bank credit cards have become so preferred and so prevalent that it's nearly impossible to rent a car or check into a hotel without one (the alternative is payment in advance or a hefty cash deposit). MasterCard and Visa (or EuroCard) are most widely accepted in Maine, and Discover and American Express are the next most popular; Carte Blanche, Diners Club, and EnRoute (Canadian) lag far behind. Be aware, however, that small restaurants (including lobster pounds), shops, and B&Bs off the beaten track might not accept credit cards or nonlocal personal checks; you may need to settle your account with cash or travelers checks (preferably $50 or under, for ease of cashing in Maine).

Taxes

Maine charges a 5 percent sales tax on items such as gifts, snacks, books, clothing, and video rentals, and a 7 percent tax on all bar, restaurant, and lodging bills. Bear in mind, especially when making reservations by phone, that restaurants and lodgings usually do *not* include the 7 percent tax when quoting their prices. A whopping 10 percent tax is added to car-rental rates.

Tipping

The longtime restaurant tipping standard—15 percent of the total bill—still prevails in most of Maine in most restaurants, but a big-city 20 percent rate isn't unusual in the upscale restaurants. Of course, the restaurant tip always should depend on the quality of the service. If you've ever worked in a restaurant, you know how much tips are appreciated—but they need to be earned. Don't penalize a waitperson for the kitchen's mistakes or incompetence, but do reduce the tip if the service is sloppy. If for any reason you don't tip, do let a host or hostess know the reason, so you're not just considered chintzy.

Taxi drivers expect a 15 percent tip; airport porters expect at least $1 per bag, depending on the difficulty of the job. If a porter simply unloads a suitcase from a car, 50 cents is plenty; if he has to escort you to a ticket counter—and especially if he arranges for speedier service—a dollar per bag is appropriate.

Usual tip for housekeeping services in accommodations is $1–2 per person, per night, depending upon the level of service. It's not necessary to tip at B&Bs, if the owners do the housekeeping.

Some accommodations add a 10- to 15-percent service fee onto rates; you don't need to tip on top of this.

COMMUNICATIONS AND MEDIA
Postal and Shipping Services

Post offices in Maine cities and towns are open six days a week, Mon.–Saturday, usually 8 A.M.–5 P.M., although Saturday service in small communities typically is 8 A.M.–noon.

Cities and large towns have strategically placed Express Mail, UPS (800/742-5877), and Federal Express (800/463-3339) boxes. Other national/international delivery services available in Maine are Airborne Express (800/247-2676) and DHL (800/225-5345). Ask locally about businesses that provide packing and shipping services.

If you expect to receive mail while visiting Maine, have your correspondents address it to you c/o General Delivery in the town or city where you expect to be and mark it "Hold for arrival on [your estimated arrival date]." Be sure to give them that post office's correct zip code (every post office has a national zip code directory; overseas residents can check with the nearest U.S. embassy or consulate, or log on to www.usps.com).

Telephone Service

Maine still has only one telephone area code, **207.** To call long distance in-state and out-of-state, dial 1 plus the area code before the number. For directory assistance, dial 411. Any

number with an area code of 800, 888, 877, 866, 855, 844, 833, or 822 is toll-free.

Cell phone service is spotty in many areas, so don't count on being able to use yours, even if your provider has coverage in the area.

Internet Access

Internet access is widely available at libraries and coffeehouses. Most hotels and many inns and B&Bs also offer Internet access; many provide data ports or Wi-Fi.

Newspapers

The *Mount Desert Islander* (www.mountdesertislander.com) began publication in 2001 under the respected leadership of the former *Bar Harbor Times* editor. Four times each summer, the *Islander* also co-publishes (with the *Ellsworth American)* a very helpful tabloid-format supplement, *Out & About in Downeast Maine,* which goes well beyond fluffy travel info. You'll find history, trail advice, dining and lodging listings, event info, maps, ferry info, and more (the online version of *Out & About* is at www.acadiavisitor.com). *The Bar Harbor Times* (www.barharbortimes.com), founded in 1914, is published each Thursday, with extensive calendar listings. Also worth picking up are the *Acadia Weekly,* a round-up of activities, sights, events, and more published monthly in spring and fall and weekly in peak season, and the annual *Bar Harbor and Mount Desert Island Menu Guide.* Both are free and published by Acadia Publishing.

In Blue Hill, look for the *Weekly Packet;* in Castine it's the *Castine Patriot;* and on Deer Isle, pick up *Island Ad-Vantages.* All are published on Thursday.

The Bangor Daily News, published Monday through Saturday, is the largest paper in the region. On Sundays, you can pick up a copy of the state's largest paper, the *Maine Sunday Telegram.*

Getting There

ORIENTATION

Acadia National Park lies about three-fifths of the way up the Maine coast. The primary section, on Mount Desert Island, is located about 46 miles south of Bangor and 160 miles northeast of Portland. Here is where you'll find the park's visitors center. Although it's an island, Mount Desert is connected to the mainland by bridges and causeways, so you can arrive by car or bus. Not so with Isle au Haut, the most remote section of the park. Isle au Haut is located off the tip of the Blue Hill/Deer Isle peninsula (southwest of Bangor) and can only be reached by boat. Access is limited, unless you have your own boat, and facilities are few. The Schoodic section of the park tips a mainland peninsula east of Bar Harbor and is easily reachable by car or via passenger ferry from Bar Harbor. There is a small, volunteer-staffed information center here.

There are no direct, commercial flights from overseas to any of Maine's airports. The closest international airport is Boston's Logan (BOS). Bus service to Portland, Bangor, and in season, Bar Harbor, is available from Logan; train service is available from Boston's North Station terminal to Portland. Rental cars are available at Logan.

DRIVING ROUTES

The major highway access to coastal Maine from the south is the **Maine Turnpike,** which links with I-95 at the New Hampshire border. Other busy access points are **Route 1,** also from New Hampshire; **Route 302,** from North Conway, New Hampshire, entering Maine at Fryeburg; **Route 2,** from Gorham, New Hampshire, to Bethel, and a couple of crossing points from New Brunswick into Washington County in northeastern Maine.

Maximum speed on I-95 and the Maine Turnpike is 65 mph, 55 mph on some stretches. In snow, sleet, or dense fog, the limit drops to 45 mph; only rarely does the highway close. On other highways, the speed limit is usually 55

mph in rural areas and posted in built-up areas. Published distances can be deceptive—whereas the Turnpike and the Interstate have 65 and 55 mph limits, you'll never average even 55 mph on the two-lane roads.

The Interstate and the Maine Turnpike

The interstate can be a bit confusing to motorists; it's important to consult a map and pay close attention to the green directional signs to avoid heading off in the wrong direction. Between York and Augusta, I-95 is the same as the Maine Turnpike (a toll highway). I-295 splits from I-95 in Portland and heads up the coast to Brunswick, before veering inland and rejoining I-95 in Gardiner. Between Kittery and Portland, there's one service area with gas and fast food, and that's in Kennebunk. All exit numbers along I-95 reflect distance in miles from the border. Exits on I-295 reflect distance from where it splits from I-95 just south of Portland at Exit 44.

The Maine Turnpike becomes mega-congested on summer weekends, especially summer *holiday* weekends. More than 300,000 vehicles use the turnpike on Memorial Day, Fourth of July, and Labor Day weekends. Worst times on the turnpike are Friday 4 P.M.–8 P.M. (northbound), Saturday 11 A.M.–2 P.M. (southbound; most weekly cottage rentals run from Saturday noon to Saturday noon), and Sunday 3 P.M.–7 P.M. (southbound). On three-day holiday weekends, avoid heading southbound on Monday between 3 and 7 P.M.

Route 1

Two lanes wide from Kittery in the south to Fort Kent at the top, U.S. Route 1 is the state's most congested road, particularly in July and August. Mileage distances can be extremely deceptive, since it will take you much longer than anticipated to get from point A to point B. If you ask anyone about distances, chances are good that you'll receive an answer in hours rather than miles. Plan accordingly. If you're trying to make time, it's best to take I-95; if you want to see Maine, take U.S. 1 and lots of little offshoots.

From Boston

It would be interesting to know the statistics on how many people drive directly from Boston to Acadia National Park without stopping en route. I'd guess not many (perhaps mostly those who have summer homes on Mount Desert Island or nearby). The trip is 268 miles, and not all of that trek is on multilane highway. You can't count on averaging 60 mph, especially in midsummer, when you hit the two-lane roads. Even on the four- and six-lane I-95, traffic can choke up at tollbooths. Also, you'll need bathroom breaks, snack breaks, maybe a gas fill-up—and all of Maine south of Acadia has its own attractions to lure you into detours (L.L. Bean and the Freeport outlet shops are major magnets).

But if you're determined to drive through from Boston, the best route is I-95, through 18 miles of New Hampshire (the Hampton tollbooths often cause major backups), into Maine and directly toward Bangor (the Maine Turnpike and I-95 are the same road for some stretches). Take Exit 182-A for Route 395 and watch for signs for Route 1-A to Ellsworth and then Route 3 to Bar Harbor. (*Do not* take Route 1-A to Hampden, or you'll end up on the wrong side of the Penobscot River.) For the Schoodic Section of the park, when Routes 1 and 3 split in Ellsworth, take Route 1 north to Gouldsboro, then head south on Route 186. For the Blue Hill Peninsula, Deer Isle, and Isle au Haut, from Ellsworth take Route 1 south to Route 172, then in Blue Hill, Route 15 south to reach Stonington and the boat to Isle au Haut.

PUBLIC TRANSPORTATION

To reduce congestion on the roads of Mount Desert Island during the peak summer months, it would be ideal if everyone arrived by some mode of public transport rather than bringing a car or RV. That hasn't happened yet, but maybe someday it will, as more and more possibilities are becoming available.

Using public transport to get to Acadia, of course, requires more scheduling than just hopping into the car and driving, and in the end it will take more time without a car. But once you get to Mount Desert, you can leave your vehicle at your lodging and explore virtually the entire island with the Island Explorer bus system (available between late June and Columbus Day).

If, for example, you want to reach Acadia from Boston, you can fly to Hancock County/Bar Harbor Airport and pick up the Island Explorer at the airport to go into downtown Bar Harbor. Or you can take the **Amtrak** "Downeaster" train from Boston to Portland, where you can pick up a bus (Concord Trailways, in the same complex as the train station, or Vermont Transit, a short cab or free bus ride away) for Bangor. From Bangor, you can take the bus (Vermont Transit) to Bar Harbor.

BANGOR
Airport

Bangor International Airport (BGR) (299 Godfrey Boulevard, 207/947-0384 or 866/359-2264, www.flybangor.com) is northern and eastern coastal Maine's hub for flights arriving from Boston and points beyond. Bangor is the closest large airport for getting to Bar Harbor, Acadia National Park on Mount Desert Island, and the park's other outposts. About half a million passengers annually move through Bangor International, a user-friendly facility on the outskirts of the city. Although flights tend to be pricier to Bangor than to Portland or especially Boston, there's a big convenience factor when flying in here.

Despite the "International" in the airport's name, passenger service from international destinations to Bangor tends to be limited to charter airlines, which sometimes arrive here to clear customs (and refuel) and then continue on to points south and west, and terror alerts, in which badly behaving passengers are removed from international flights here. More typically, international visitors arrive in Bangor via New York or Boston gateways. Bad weather in Portland or Boston also can create unexpected domestic and international arrivals at Bangor's less-foggy airfield.

The airport's lower level has an interactive information kiosk, where you can contact local hotels and motels for rooms and airport shuttle service.

Suggested Driving Routes

Drive Route 1-A to Ellsworth and then Route 3 to Bar Harbor. (*Do not* take Route 1-A to Hampden, or you'll end up on the wrong side of the Penobscot River.) For the Schoodic Section of the park, when Routes 1 and 3 split in Ellsworth, take Route 1 north to Gouldsboro, then head south on Route 186. For the Blue Hill peninsula, Deer Isle, and Isle au Haut, from Ellsworth take Route 1 south to Route 172, then in Blue Hill, Route 15 south to reach Stonington and the boat to Isle au Haut.

Car Rentals

In July, August, and September, it's essential to reserve a car a week or two before your arrival. Bangor is slightly less than 50 miles from Bar Harbor, but you'll be traveling almost entirely on two-lane roads; in summer, figure on an hour at the very least.

On-airport car rental companies are: Avis (207/947-8383 or 800/831-2847, www.avis.com), Budget (207/945-9429 or 800/527-0700, www.drivebudget.com), Hertz (207/942-5519 or 800/654-3131, www.hertz.com), and National (207/947-0158 or 800/227-7368, www.nationalcar.com).

Bus and Taxi Services

Concord Trailways (1039 Union St., Route 222, Bangor, 800/639-3317 or 945-4000, www.concordtrailways.com) provides daily bus service year-round from Logan Airport in Boston to Bangor via Portland. No reservations are accepted, but you can purchase tickets online. The Concord Trailways station in Bangor is less than a mile from the airport, but plan to take a taxi for that short distance.

Vermont Transit (800/552-8737, www.grey-hound.com), a division of Greyhound, operates a once-a-day seasonal bus service between Bangor (Bangor Bus Terminal, 158 Main St.) and downtown Bar Harbor. You can buy tickets online for Vermont Transit. The run coordinates with continuing service to/from Boston via Portland.

Round-the-clock **taxi service** is provided by Airport/River City Taxi, 207/947-8294 or 800/997-8294, and Town Taxi, 207/945-5671 or 800/750-9935. There are many other companies listed on the airport's website.

Accommodations

Bangor International Airport is approximately 45 miles from Bar Harbor. Depending upon when your flight arrives, you may wish to spend the night here and begin your journey refreshed. Most of the mid-rate chains have properties here. Your choice of a hotel or motel near the Bangor Mall or the Bangor Airport may depend on your frequent-flyer memberships or where you get the best auto club deal. There are lots of options, and most offer free shuttle service to and from the airport.

Many properties book far in advance for the fourth weekend in August, when the American Folk Festival is in town and traffic can be a bear. Avoid it, unless you're planning on attending—not a bad idea, actually; it's a free and fabulous event.

Linked to the terminal by a skyway, the **Four Points Sheraton Hotel** (308 Godfrey Blvd., Bangor, 207/947-6721 or 800/228-4609, www.bangorsheraton.com, $159 d) has 103 rooms, a restaurant, and an outdoor pool. Next closest (two miles) to the airport are Marriott's 153-room **Fairfield Inn** (300 Odlin Rd., Bangor, 207/990-0001 or 800/228-2800, www.marriotthotelreservations.com, $69–$109), with an indoor pool, sauna, whirlpool, and exercise room, free Wi-Fi and continental breakfast, and guest laundry, and the 207-room **Holiday Inn-Bangor** (404 Odlin Rd., Bangor, 207/947-0101 or 800/914-0101, www.holidayinn.com, $109), with a fitness center, coin laundry, and pools indoors and out.

Next to the Bangor Mall, with restaurants

and food court, are the 119-room **Hampton Inn** (10 Bangor Mall Blvd., Bangor, 207/990-4400 or 800/998-7829, www.bangorhamptoninn.com, $109–129), with free movies, local calls, and continental breakfast as well as a Kids Stay Free program, and the 96-room **Country Inn at the Mall** (936 Stillwater Ave., Bangor, 207/941-0200 or 800/244-396, www.maineguide.com/bangor/countryinn/, $79) including continental breakfast, free lodging for kids rooming with parents, free local calls, and free HBO.

Twelve miles southeast of Bangor (and about 40 miles northwest of Bar Harbor) is **The Lucerne Inn** (Bar Harbor Rd., Rte. 1A, Dedham/R.R. 3, Box 540, Holden 04429, 207/843-5123 or 800/325-5123, www.lucerne-inn.com, $99–199), a retrofitted early 19th-century stagecoach hostelry on a 10-acre hilltop overlooking Phillips Lake and the hills beyond. The fall panorama is spectacular. Despite the highway out front, noise is no problem in the antiques-filled, rear-facing rooms, all with lake view, gas fireplace, and whirlpool tub. Outside there's a pool. The Sunday brunch buffet (9 A.M.–1 P.M.) in the inn's dining room (where moderately priced dinners are served 5–9 P.M. nightly) is a big draw, as is the adjacent golf course. One-night packages, including dinner, are a good idea, as you're in the middle of nowhere and not likely to head out again once you get here.

Campgrounds

On Bangor's western perimeter are two clean, well-managed campgrounds convenient to I-95 and Bangor. The emphasis is on RVs, but tent sites are available. Closest to the city is the 52-site **Paul Bunyan Campground** (1862 Union St., Rte. 222, Bangor, 207/941-1177, www.paulbunyancampground.com), about three miles northwest of I-95 on Route 222 west. Facilities at this attractive campground include a recreation hall and huge outdoor heated pool; activities are offered most weekends in midsummer. Leashed pets are welcome (cleanup is required) and noise rules are strictly enforced. Sites (for two adults, two children)

are $18 with no hookup, $31 with full hookup. Open mid-April–October.

About two miles farther out on Route 222, **Pleasant Hill Campground** (Rte. 222, 45 Mansell Rd., Hermon, 207/848-5127, www.pleasanthillcampground.com), also a Good Sampark, has 105 sites on 60 acres. Facilities include mini-golf, laundry, play areas, rec room, heated pool, free showers, and a small store. Pets are welcome. Rates are $20–34 (the latter for full hookups), and the campground is open May–mid-October.

Food

You'll find lots of fast food and family-friendly chains between the airport and the mall. Across from the airport, **Captain Nick's** (1165 Union St., Rte. 222, Bangor, 207/942-6444) is well known for seafood, including a triple-lobster special, but it also serves up steak, chicken, and pasta. Nothing fancy here, but the fish is definitely fresh. There's live entertainment at 7 P.M. Saturday in the lounge. Reservations are a good idea on summer weekends. It's open 11 A.M.–9:30 P.M. Mon.–Thurs., 11 A.M.–10 P.M. Friday and Saturday, and 11 A.M.–9 P.M. Sunday; open until 10 P.M. in summer.

If you want something with more local flavor, **Sea Dog Brewing Co.** (26 Front St., Bangor, 207/947-8004) is a downtown, riverfront brewpub with a wide-ranging menu and seating indoors and out. It's open 11:30–1 A.M.

PORTLAND

For anyone planning to go *just* to Acadia National Park, the primary gateway typically is Bangor. But if you're visiting Acadia as part of a Maine vacation, you might well choose Portland—160–180 miles south of Bar Harbor, depending on your route—as a springboard for getting to Acadia. Portland is about a six-hour drive from New York City, about two hours from Boston.

Airport

Although it keeps expanding, **Portland International Jetport** (207/774-7301, www.portlandjetport.org, PWM) is a small, easily navigable airport, where all flights leave and arrive from the same building. Don't be fooled by the International in the airport's name; you can't even get a direct flight to Canada from here. Note: Being on the coast, the Portland airport is more subject to fog shutdowns than Bangor.

Portland's amenities include a newsstand/gift shop, coffee shop, restaurant/lounge, restrooms, large waiting area, ATM, and plenty of coin- and card-operated telephones. There's a business center in the gate area with Internet access. Visitor information is dispensed from a desk (not always staffed, unfortunately) between the gates and the baggage-claim area. No need to rush out to grab your luggage, though—Portland has one of the slowest baggage-claim operations in the country. Plan to stop at the restrooms, browse through the gift shop, and pick up tourism information after you arrive—and even then you may still have to wait for your luggage. Complaints to management elicit the response that Portland is the terminus of many airline routes, and the airline companies (who provide the baggage handlers and unloading equipment) give low priority to locations that don't require fast turnaround. As a result, carry-on luggage is a plus here. Baggage-handling offices surround the luggage carousels. Airlines are responsible for luggage, so if you have a problem, contact a representative from your airline. If you have an emergency, contact the airport manager at 207/773-8462.

Train

Amtrak's Downeaster (800/872-7245, www.thedowneaster.com) makes four daily round-trip runs between Boston's North Station and Portland's Transportation Center, with stops in Wells, Saco, and seasonally in Old Orchard Beach (May 1–Oct. 31). Call or check the website for discounted fares and special rates for children and seniors. From the station, Portland's Metro municipal bus service will take you gratis to downtown Portland; just show your Amtrak ticket stub.

Amtrak trains from Washington via New York arrive in Boston at South Station (not North Station). Believe it or not, there's no direct link between the two. While you can connect via the T (Boston's subway), it's a real hassle with baggage. Instead, splurge on a taxi.

Train service terminates in Portland. There are no train connections to the Acadia region.

Suggested Driving Routes

There are several routes for driving from Portland to Mount Desert Island. Route A follows the four-lane Interstate for most of the way, then finishes up on two-lane roads. Route B is fifty-fifty: half Interstate, half two-lane roads. Route C is almost all on two-lane roads—it's also the most scenic and the slowest route. As with most other Maine auto explorations, it's particularly helpful to use the DeLorme *Maine Atlas and Gazetteer* ($19.95, www.delorme.com).

For **Route A,** depart Portland northward on I-295 and continue to just south of Augusta, where it merges with I-95. Continue on I-95 to Bangor, where you pick up I-395 eastbound toward Holden and Ellsworth (and Acadia). At the end of 395, you're also at the end of four-lane highways. It's two lanes for the rest of the way. Continue on Route 1A to Ellsworth, then Route 3 through Trenton to Mount Desert Island.

For Blue Hill, Deer Isle, and Isle au Haut, from Ellsworth, head south on Route 1/Main Street, through town, then take Route 172 south to Blue Hill, then Route 15 south to reach Stonington and the boat to Isle au Haut.

For the Schoodic Peninsula, in Ellsworth, take Route 1 north to Gouldsboro, then take Route 186 south to the park.

For **Route B,** start out the same way from Portland, on I-295 to I-95, then just north of Augusta, exit for Route 3 East. (You'll now be on two-lane roads for the rest of the way.) Route 1 doubles as Route 3 from Belfast to the southern end of Ellsworth.

For the Blue Hill Peninsula, Deer Isle, and Isle au Haut, take Route 15 south from Orland. If your destination is Castine, take Route 175 south from Bucksport.

For the Schoodic peninsula, stay on Route 1 to Gouldsboro, then Route 186.

Route C is the coastal route, where you'll be winding through and skirting small communities the whole way. This route lends itself to (no, requires!) stops—for photos, for exploring, for shopping, for overnights. Stopping only for lunch and restrooms, you'll still need to allow five or six hours from Portland to Bar Harbor. And all bets are off on Friday afternoon in summer, when towns such as Wiscasset and Camden can be major bottlenecks. (They're lovely towns, though—definitely worth a stop.)

To take Route C from Portland, you can start right off on two-lane Route 1, or you can go north on I-295 and I-95 (four lanes) to Brunswick, then cut over when you see the Coastal Route 1 sign. Follow Route 1 the rest of the way—through Bath, Wiscasset, Newcastle, Waldoboro, Thomaston, Rockland, Rockport, Camden, Belfast, Searsport, Bucksport, Orland and the turn-offs for the Blue Hill peninsula, and on to Ellsworth, where you'll split off onto Route 3 and head for Mount Desert Island or stay on Route 1 to Gouldsboro and the Schoodic Peninsula.

Between Brunswick and Rockland, down each of the "fingers" east of Route 1, are even more towns and villages—Harpswell, Phippsburg, Georgetown, Boothbay Harbor, Damariscotta, Friendship, and Cushing.

Which brings us to the bottom line: You could spend *weeks* visiting Portland and making your way from there to Acadia!

Car Rentals

Five major rental agencies are located at the airport complex (Alamo's office is at the edge, but connected via shuttle). If you're arriving by bus or train, either take the free Explorer bus to the airport or a taxi.

Your choices are Alamo (207/775-0855 or 800/462-5266, www.goalamo.com), Avis (207/874-7500 or 800/230-4898, www.avis.com), Budget (207/772-6789 or 800/527-0700, www.drivebudget.com), Hertz (207/774-4544 or 800/654-3131, www.hertz.com), and National (207/773-0036 or 800/227-7368, www.nationalcar.com).

Bus

Concord Trailways (800/639-3317, www.concordtrailways.com) departs downtown Boston (South Station Transportation Center) and Logan Airport for the 100-mile trip to Portland about 10 times daily, making pickups at all Logan airline terminals (lower level). Portland's bright, modern Trailways terminal is at the Portland Transportation Center on Thompson Point Road, just west of I-295 (Exit 5 northbound, Exit 5A southbound; it's well signposted). The terminal is not particularly convenient to downtown Portland for pedestrians, but as with Amtrak, if you show your Trailways ticket stub to the Metro bus driver (buses stop regularly outside the terminal), you'll have a free ride downtown. If you need to leave a car at the Transportation Center, there's a large lot, with unlimited parking for $2 a day.

Once-a-day buses to and from Calais coordinate with the Bangor bus schedules. The Calais line, stopping in Ellsworth and Gouldsboro, is operated by **West's Bus Service,** in Steuben, 207/546-2823 or 800/596-2823. Flag stops along the route are permitted.

Vermont Transit Lines (950 Congress St., Portland, 207/772-6587 or 800/552-8737 or 800/451-3292, www.vermonttransit.com), a division of Greyhound Bus Lines, serves Maine, the rest of New England, and beyond, connecting with Greyhound routes. The schedule is slightly less convenient than that of Concord Trailways, but rates are slightly lower and you can buy tickets online.

You can connect to Bar Harbor via Vermont Transit. There's one four-hour trip a day in each direction between Portland and Bar Harbor via Bangor (departing Portland in early afternoon, departing Bar Harbor very early in the morning).

Local Transportation

Portland airport's small size and practically downtown location are big pluses for many travelers. It's simple to get on I-95 headed north if you're heading right out. If you're planning on spending the night, you can be in downtown Portland within 10 to 15 minutes.

Expect the fare to be about $16 in a metered taxi from the Jetport to the Portland waterfront, $10 to the Portland Transportation Center (Concord Trailways buses and Amtrak), and $11 to the Vermont Transit (Greyhound) terminal at 950 Congress Street. Flat rate to Bar Harbor is about $336. The airport website has a useful **Ground Transportation Guide** with a list of taxi fares and other relevant local information.

The **Portland Explorer bus service** (207/774-4457 www.portlandexplorer.org, $2, kids under 12 free) connects all of Portland's transportation sites—the Jetport, Portland Transportation Center, Vermont Transit (on demand), and Casco Bay Ferry Lines—following a route that begins at the Jetport. It also stops at the Maine Mall and a handful of hotels. It operates noon–7 P.M., making the loop about once an hour on an erratic schedule.

Accommodations and Food

You'll find most of the major chain hotels in the Greater Portland area. Also here are some lovely B&Bs and excellent independent hotels and inns (see www.visitportland.com). Some offer an airport shuttle service, but the **Explorer** bus circulates to many in the downtown area. The accommodations below are all either near the airport or bus terminals. Fast food and family friendly chains are clustered near the Maine Mall, which is just a mile or two from the airport. If you're willing to venture into downtown Portland, the choices are abundant, with most restaurants concentrated in the Old Port and Arts District sections of the city.

Railroad tycoon John Deering built **The Inn at St. John** (939 Congress St., Portland 207/773-6481 or 800/636-9127, www.innatstjohn.com, $55–180) in 1897. The clean, comfortable, moderately priced 37-room hostelry welcomes children and pets and even has bicycle storage. Cable TV, air-conditioning, free local calls, free parking, free airport pickup, and continental breakfast are provided. It's across the street from the Vermont Transit bus terminal and a short taxi ride from Portland's Transportation Center. Just a couple doors

down is tiny **Dogfish Cafe** (953 Congress St., 207/253-5400, 11:30 A.M.–10 P.M. Mon.–Sat.), which packs 'em in for salads and sandwiches and grilled goodies, with heartier dinner specials served Wednesday–Saturday evenings.

Close by the Portland Transportation Center, where both Concord Trailways and Amtrak arrive, is the **Doubletree Hotel** (1230 Congress St., 207/774-5611, $129–239), with an indoor pool, restaurant, lounge, and free airport shuttle.

Right at the airport, with free shuttles, are: **Embassy Suites Hotel** (1050 Westbrook St., Portland, 207/774-2200, $169–229), with an indoor heated pool, restaurant, free full breakfast, and coin laundry, and the **Hilton Garden Inn** (145 Jetport Blvd., Portland, 207/7828-1117, $149–219), with indoor heated pool and coin laundry.

Near the Maine Mall and providing a free shuttle is the **Comfort Inn** (990 Maine Mall Rd., South Portland, 207/7775-0409, $80–199), with free continental breakfast.

TRENTON
Airport

The most convenient air access to Acadia is **Hancock County-Bar Harbor Airport** (207/667-7329, www.bhbairport.com, BHB). It's located 12 miles from downtown Bar Harbor, but this isn't a big-jet airport—in case you're squeamish about small planes. (Despite its name, the airport is located in Trenton, just north of Mount Desert Island.) USAirways Express/Colgan Air (207/667-7171 or 800/428-4322, www.colganair.com or www.usairways.com) operates daily commuter-plane service from Boston to Bar Harbor Airport, sometimes with a stop in Owls Head, near Rockland (Knox County Municipal Airport). Flight time from Boston to Trenton is about 70 minutes direct. (Driving time from Boston to Trenton would be a minimum of six hours, usually longer.)

Suggested Driving Routes

Lucky you; this one's quick and easy. Take Route 3 west for Mount Desert Island and

Bar Harbor (just take a left when exiting the airport). For the Schoodic Section of the park, head east on Route 3 to the junction with Route 1 in Ellsworth, then north on Route 1 to Gouldsboro, then south on Route 186. For the Blue Hill Peninsula, Deer Isle, and Isle au Haut, take Route 3 east through Ellsworth to Route 172, then in Blue Hill, Route 15 south to reach Stonington and the boat to Isle au Haut.

Rental Cars

Hertz (207/667-5017 or 800/654-3131, www.hertz.com) provides on-site rental cars.

Budget (207/667-1200 or 800/527-0700, www.budget.com, May–Oct.) and Enterprise (207/664-2662 or 800/325-8007, May–Oct.) also have rental-car offices at the Bar Harbor Airport; in summer, be sure to reserve a car well in advance.

Bus

The free **Island Explorer** (207/667-5796, www.exploreacadia.com) stops at the airport between late June and Columbus Day. Connections service most of Mount Desert Island, including Bar Harbor, Southwest Harbor, and Acadia National Park.

Getting Around

How will you get around once you get here? Europeans are always shocked at Maine's minimal public transport. The few larger cities have bus systems, but there's almost nothing in small towns. The national Amtrak system enters Maine only at its southern tip. Fortunately, buses link the major urban centers, such as Portland and Bangor—with stops in small towns when they happen to be along the way.

Among less-populated areas, Mount Desert Island stands out, thanks to its fare-free, propane-fueled **Island Explorer** bus system, subsidized by your park fees, Friends of Acadia, L. L. Bean, and local businesses. It services most of the island, as well as Bar Harbor Regional Airport in Trenton. The good news is that it's a very efficient network; the bad news is that it runs only between late June and mid-October. So try to come during the Explorer's season, when you can rubberneck all you want from the comfort of a bus seat. No missed turns, no near-misses. Less pollution, less frazzle. If you've arrived by car, leave it at your lodging and hop on the bus.

The Island Explorer also circulates around the southern end of the Schoodic Peninsula, from Winter Harbor to Prospect Harbor, with a loop through the park. It meets the passen-

ger ferry that connects Bar Harbor to Winter Harbor, so you can visit the Schoodic section of the park from Mount Desert Island without needing a car.

The outer islands are also accessible from Mount Desert Island, although there are no public transportation systems on any of these. Most can be explored on foot or bicycle (rentals are available in Bar Harbor and Southwest Harbor). Passenger ferries from Southwest Harbor and Northeast Harbor cruise to the Cranberry Isles. A state car-ferry services Swan's Island and Frenchboro. From Stonington, a passenger ferry connects Deer Isle to Isle au Haut.

You'll need a car to explore the other regions covered in this book: Blue Hill Peninsula, Deer Isle, the Schoodic region beyond the Island Explorer's reaches, and Ellsworth.

DRIVING

Almost all gas stations in Maine are self-serve (pumps are marked Self; at those marked Full, you'll pay more to have an attendant pump the gas for you), and many now allow you to pay at the pump with a credit card. (Many also have ATMs, but you'll usually have to pay a bank surcharge.) Note: Irving stations have extremely clean restrooms and usually have a good selection of teas and coffees in addition to fast foods.

Important Driving Regulations

Seat belts are mandatory in Maine. You cannot be stopped for not wearing one, but if you're stopped for any other reason, you can be fined if you're not buckled in. Maine allows right turns at red lights, after you stop and check for oncoming traffic. In rare cases, you'll see a No Turn on Red sign—in which case, heed it. *Never* pass a stopped school bus in either direction. Wait until the bus's red lights have stopped flashing and all children are well off the road. Maine law also requires drivers to turn on their car's headlights any time the windshield wipers are operating. Keep right on multi-lane roads except to pass.

Roadside Assistance and Road Conditions

Since Maine is enslaved to the automobile, it's not a bad idea for vacationers to carry membership in AAA in case of breakdowns, flat tires, and other car crises. Contact your nearest AAA office or AAA Northern New England (425 Marginal Way, Portland, 207/780-6800 or 800/482-7497, www.aaanne.com). The emergency road service number is 800/222-4357.

For real-time information on road conditions, weather, construction, and major delays, dial 511 in Maine, 866/282-7578 from out of state, or visit www.511maine.gov. Information is available in both English and French.

State Visitor Information Centers

If you're arriving by car, the Maine Tourism Association operates state visitor information centers in Calais, Fryeburg (May–October), Hampden, Houlton, Kittery, and Yarmouth. These are excellent places to visit to stock up on brochures, pick up a map, ask advice, and utilize restrooms.

TOURISM INFORMATION AND MAPS
Maine Tourism Association

The Maine Tourism Association (325 Water St.,

Hallowell 04347, 207/623-0363, www.maine-tourism.com) publishes the free, annual magazine-style guidebook *Maine Invites You,* which details sights throughout the state and provides listings of chambers of commerce and other info helpful for travelers. It also publishes a free state map. Call, write, or visit the website to request a copy and a state map.

Maine Office of Tourism

The Maine Office of Tourism has established an award-winning website, www.visit-maine.com. You'll find chamber of commerce addresses, articles, photos, information on lodgings, and access to a variety of Maine tourism businesses. You can use the website to request a free state map and copy of *Maine Invites You.* The state's toll-free information hotline is 888/MAINE-45 (888/624-6345).

Local Chambers of Commerce and Tourism Offices

Tourism is Maine's largest source of revenue, so almost every community of any size has some kind of information office. Information on these is listed in the destination chapters.

Maps

Peek in any Mainer's car, and you're likely to see a copy of *The Maine Atlas and Gazetteer,* published by DeLorme Mapping Company, in Yarmouth. Despite an oversize format inconvenient for hiking and kayaking, this 96-page paperbound book just about guarantees that you won't get lost (and if you're good at map reading, it can get you out of a lot of traffic jams). Scaled at one-half inch to the mile, it's meticulously compiled from aerial photographs, satellite images, U.S. Geological Survey maps, GPS readings, and timber-company maps, and it's revised annually. It details back roads and dirt roads and shows elevation, boat ramps, public lands, campgrounds and picnic areas, even trailheads. DeLorme products are available nationwide in book and map stores, but you can also order direct (800/452-5931, www.delorme.com). The atlas is $19.95 and shipping is $4 (Maine residents need to add 5 percent sales tax).

RESOURCES
Suggested Reading

CARRIAGE ROADS

Abrell, D. *A Pocket Guide to the Carriage Roads of Acadia National Park.* Camden, ME: Down East Books, 1985, 1995. A dozen excellent carriage-road loops (ranging from 1.2 to 11.1 miles) for hiking, biking, or horseback riding—presented in a portable format.

Roberts, A. R. *Mr. Rockefeller's Roads.* Camden, ME: Down East Books, 1990. The fascinating story behind Acadia's scenic carriage roads, written by the granddaughter of John D. Rockefeller Jr. (who created them).

HISTORY

Brechlin, E. *Bygone Bar Harbor: A Postcard Tour of Mount Desert Island and Acadia National Park.* Camden, ME: Down East Books, 2002. A charming little book with reproductions of 100 historic postcards.

Collier, S. F. *Mount Desert Island and Acadia National Park: An Informal History,* rev. ed. Camden, ME: Down East Books, 1978. An oft-cited source for island and park history.

Dorr, G. *The Story of Acadia National Park.* 3rd ed. Bar Harbor: Acadia Publishing, 1997 (reprinted, combining 1942 and 1948 originals). How Acadia began—and the roller-coaster struggles involved—related by George Dorr, "the Father of Acadia."

Duncan, R. F., E. G. Barlow, K. Bray, and C. Hanks. *Coastal Maine: A Maritime History.* Woodstock, VT: Countrymen Press, 2002. Updated version of the classic work.

Helfrich, G. W., and G. O'Neil. *Lost Bar Harbor.* Camden, ME: Down East Books, 1982. Fascinating collection of historic photographs of classic, turn-of-the-century "cottages," most obliterated by Bar Harbor's Great Fire of 1947.

Isaacson, D., ed. *Maine: A Guide "Down East."* 2nd ed. Maine League of Historical Societies and Museums, 1970. Out of print. Revised version of the Depression-era WPA guidebook. Still interesting for background reading.

Judd, R. W., E. A. Churchill, and J. W. Eastman, eds. *Maine: The Pine Tree State from Prehistory to the Present.* Orono: University of Maine Press, 1995. The best available Maine history, with excellent historical maps.

Morison, Adm. S. E. *The Story of Mount Desert Island.* Boston: Little, Brown, 1960. A quirky, entertaining little history—from Native Americans to 20th-century Americans—by the late maritime historian, a longtime Mount Desert summer resident.

Paine, L. P. *Down East: A Maritime History of Maine.* Gardiner, ME: Tilbury House, 2000. A noted maritime historian provides an enlightening introduction to the state's seafaring tradition.

LOBSTERS AND LIGHTHOUSES

Caldwell, W., *Lighthouses of Maine.* Camden, ME: Down East Books, 1986. A historical tour of Maine's lighthouses, with the emphasis on history, legends, and lore.

Corson, T. *The Secret Life of Lobsters.* New York: HarperCollins, 2004. Everything you wanted—or perhaps didn't want—to know about lobster.

Hartnett, R., and P. D. Bachelder *Maine Lighthouse Map & Guide.* Hartnett House Map Publishing, 2000. An illustrated map and guide providing directions on how to locate all Maine beacons as well as brief histories.

Woodward, C., *The Lobster Coast: Rebels, Rusticators, and the Struggle for a Forgotten Frontier.* New York: Viking, 2004. A veteran journalist's take on the history of the Maine Coast.

NATURAL HISTORY AND NATURE GUIDES

Bennett, D. *Maine's Natural Heritage: Rare Species and Unique Natural Features.* Camden, ME: Down East Books, 1988.

Butcher, Russell D. *Field Guide to Acadia National Park, Maine.* Lanham, MD: Taylor Trade Publishing, 2005. A detailed, illustrated guide to Acadia's flora, fauna, and geology, including some trail descriptions with what to look for along the way.

Conkling, P. W. *Islands in Time: A Natural and Cultural History of the Islands of the Gulf of Maine.* 2nd ed. Camden, ME: Down East Books, and Rockland, ME: Island Institute, 1999. A thoughtful overview by the president of Maine's Island Institute.

Edwardsen, E. *Longstreet Highroad Guide to the Maine Coast.* Atlanta: Longstreet Press, 1999. Attractively presented general guide, with especially helpful natural-history information; more than 50 pages devoted to Mount Desert Island, Isle au Haut, and the Schoodic Peninsula.

Grierson, R. G. *Acadia National Park: Wildlife Watcher's Guide.* Minocqua, WI: NorthWord Press, 1995. You're not likely to see any creature in the park that isn't mentioned in this handy guide.

Kendall, D. L. *Glaciers & Granite: A Guide to Maine's Landscape and Geology.* Unity, ME: North Country Press, 1993. Explains knowledgeably why Maine looks the way it does.

Newlin, William V. P. *Lakes & Ponds of Mount Desert.* Camden, ME: Down East Books, 1989. Covers more than the title reveals—includes great picnicking, hiking, biking advice, from a longtime summer resident. Out of print, but try used bookstores.

Perrin, S. *Acadia's Native Flowers, Fruits, and Wildlife.* Fort Washington, PA: Eastern National, 2001. This handy reference to the park's flora and fauna runs chronologically through three seasons (spring through fall). It's not a complete field guide, but rather a selective collection of photos in a portable square format.

Pierson, E. C., J. E. Pierson, and P. D. Vickery. *A Birder's Guide to Maine.* Camden, ME: Down East Books, 1996. An expanded version of *A Birder's Guide to the Coast of Maine.* A valuable resource for any ornithologist, novice or expert, for exploring Acadia (and the rest of Maine).

Scheid, M. *Discovering Acadia: A Guide for Young Naturalists.* Mount Desert, ME: Acadia Publishing, 1990. A delightful book for children—as well as the adults who accompany them.

OFFSHORE ISLANDS
General

Conkling, P. W. *Islands in Time: A Natural and Cultural History of the Islands of the Gulf of Maine.* 2nd ed. Camden, ME: Down East Books, and Rockland, ME: Island Institute, 1999. A thoughtful overview, including cultural and natural history, by the president of Maine's Island Institute.

Cranberry Isles

Eliot, C. W. *John Gilley: One of the Forgotten Millions.* Bar Harbor: Acadia Press, 1989 (reprint of 1904 book). Poignant story of 19th-century life in the Cranberries, as told by the

Harvard president who was instrumental in the establishment of Acadia.

PICTORAL

Blagden, T., Jr., and C. R. Tyson, Jr. *First Light: Acadia National Park and Maine's Mount Desert Island.* Englewood, CO: Westcliffe Publishers, and Bar Harbor: Friends of Acadia, 2003. A gorgeous, large-format book with spectacular photographs.

Thompson, C. *Maine Lighthouses: A Pictorial Guide.* 3rd ed. Mount Desert, ME: CatNap Publications, 2001. What they look like, how to find them (sometimes only by boat), with some historical and contemporary background.

Wilmerding, J. *The Artist's Mount Desert: American Painters on the Maine Coast.* Princeton, N.J.: Princeton University Press, 1995. A respected art historian's perspective on Mount Desert's magnetic attraction to such American artists as Thomas Cole, Frederic Church, and Fitz Hugh Lane.

Frenchboro (Long Island)

Lunt, D. L. *Hauling by Hand: The Life and Times of a Maine Island.* Frenchboro, ME: Islandport Press, 1999. A sensitive history of Frenchboro (a.k.a. Long Island), eight miles offshore, written by an eighth-generation islander, now a journalist.

Isle au Haut

Greenlaw, L. *The Lobster Chronicles.* New York: Hyperion, 2002. Essays on island life, warts and all, by the talented writer and lobsterwoman who first gained fame as a swordfishing skipper in *The Perfect Storm.*

Pratt, C. *Here on the Island.* New York: Harper & Row, 1974. An appealing, realistic portrait of life on Isle au Haut several decades ago.

RECREATION GUIDES
General

Evans, Lisa Gollin. *An Outdoor Family Guide to Acadia National Park.* Seattle: The Mountain-

eers, 1997. An excellent resource for hiking, biking, and paddling with kids in Acadia.

Monkman, J. and M. *Discover Acadia National Park: A Guide to Hiking, Biking, and Paddling.* Boston: Appalachian Mountain Club Books, 2nd ed., 2005. Well-planned and well-written guide, in the Appalachian Mountain Club tradition, including foldout AMC map.

Bicycling

Hale S. and D. Gibbs, *Mountain Bike Maine: A Guide to the Classic Trails.* Birmingham, Ala., 1998. Good detail on five Acadia region rides: the loop around Isle au Haut, two Carriage Roads on Mount Desert, Schoodic Mountain, and Donnell Pond.

Minutolo, A. *A Pocket Guide to Biking on Mount Desert Island.* Camden, ME: Down East Books, 1996. A third-generation islander's expert advice; this book covers the whole island, not just the park.

Stone, H. *25 Bicycle Tours in Maine: Coastal and Inland Rides from Kittery to Caribou.* 3rd ed. Woodstock, VT: Backcountry Publications, 1998. Includes half a dozen Acadia routes.

Cruising Guide

Taft, H., J. Taft, and C. Rindlaub. *A Cruising Guide to the Maine Coast.* 4th ed. Peaks Island: Diamond Pass Publishing, 2002. Don't even consider cruising the coast around Acadia without this thoroughly researched volume.

Hiking

Gillmore, R. *Great Walks of Acadia National Park & Mount Desert Island.* rev. ed. Goffstown, NH: Great Walks (P.O. Box 410, Goffs-town, NH 03045), 1994. Two dozen trails in Acadia—some stretch the limits of their definition of "walks."

Kong, D., and D. Ring. *Hiking Acadia National Park.* Guilford, CT: Globe Pequot/Falcon

Guide, 2001. Excellent hiking guide, with useful, accurate descriptions of 94 trails on Mount Desert Island, Isle au Haut, and the Schoodic Peninsula. The authors include a list of their 25 favorites and advocate the Leave No Trace philosophy.

St. Germain, T. A., Jr. *A Walk in the Park: Acadia's Hiking Guide.* 10th ed. Bar Harbor: Parkman Publications, 2004. Arguably the best Acadia hiking guide, in a handy Michelin-style vertical format. Bar Harbor resident St. Germain hikes a thousand miles a year in Acadia, so he's the expert. The book includes plenty of historical tidbits about the trails, the park, and the island. Part of the proceeds go to the Acadia Trails Forever campaign to maintain and rehabilitate the park's trails. It's updated regularly; ask for the most recent edition.

Seymour, T. *Hiking Maine.* 2nd ed. Guilford, CT: Globe Pequot Press, 2002. Covers the state, but has good detail on more than 20 hikes in the region spanning Bucksport to Milbridge.

Kayaking and Canoeing

Brechlin, E. D. *A Pocket Guide to Paddling the Waters of Mount Desert Island.* Camden, ME: Down East Books, 1996. Registered Maine Guide Brechlin recommends 17 places to paddle your kayak or canoe—in saltwater as well as freshwater ponds and lakes. This little handbook (64 pages) includes locations for parking and launching areas, as well as route maps.

Bumsted, L. *Hot Showers! Maine Coast Lodgings for Kayakers and Sailors.* 2nd ed. Brunswick, ME: Audenreed Press, 2000. Excellent, well-researched resource for anyone paddling or cruising the shoreline and yearning for alternatives to a sleeping bag.

The Maine Island Trail Guidebook. Rockland, ME: Maine Island Trail Association, updated annually. Available only with MITA membership (annual dues $45, www.mita.org), providing access to dozens of islands along the watery trail, including many in the Acadia region between Schoodic Point and Deer Isle.

Miller, D. S. *Kayaking the Maine Coast.* Woodstock, VT Countryman Press/Backcountry Guides, 2000. Thoroughly researched guide by a veteran kayaker; good maps and particularly helpful information. With this book and a copy of *Hot Showers!* you're all set.

Wilson, A., and J. Hayes. *Quiet Water Canoe Guide, Maine: Best Paddling Lakes and Ponds for All Ages.* 2nd ed. Boston: Appalachian Mountain Club Books, 2005. Comprehensive handbook, with helpful maps, for inland paddling.

Rock Climbing

Butterfield, J. *Acadia: A Climber's Guide.* The most up-to-date and thorough climbing guide for the park.

REFERENCE

The Maine Atlas and Gazetteer. Yarmouth, ME: DeLorme, updated annually. You'll be hard put to get lost on the roads in this region or anywhere else in Maine if you're carrying this essential volume; it contains 70 full-page (oversize format) topographical maps with GPS grids.

Internet Resources

ACADIA NATIONAL PARK INFORMATION

Acadia National Park
www.nps.gov/acad/

A comprehensive site with extensive detailed information about Maine's only national park. Download natural and cultural history articles, accessibility charts, list of hiking trails, FAQ, maps of the park and its outlying sections (Isle au Haut and Schoodic Peninsula), and the latest issues of the *Beaver Log,* the park's summer newspaper. Also included is a link for online reservations at Blackwoods Campground, as well as info for making Isle au Haut camping reservations.

Friends of Acadia
www.friendsofacadia.org

A very active nonprofit organization that acts as a financial safety net for the park and also organizes frequent volunteer work parties for various maintenance projects in the park. Its newsletters are posted on the website, as is information about where and when you can volunteer.

Island Explorer Bus System
www.exploreacadia.com

Everything you need to know about using the propane-fueled, fare-free Island Explorer buses (operating late June–Columbus Day on Mount Desert, late June–Labor Day on the Schoodic Peninsula). Included are suggestions for getting to Mount Desert without a car, as well as for exploring the park with the bus.

ARTS AND ENTERTAINMENT

Maine Archives and Museums
www.mainemuseums.org

The Maine Arts and Heritage Tourism Partnership has produced this useful site (a printed guide is also available) with links to dozens of major and minor museums, archives, historical societies, and historic sites. Opening hours and admission fees are provided, although some fees listed are out of date.

Maine Arts Commission Directory
www.mainearts.com/directory/dir_adv_search.shtml

Find artists and artisans by name, location, or specialty.

Maine Fiber Arts
www.mainefiberarts.org

Everything you wanted to know about fiber artists, farms producing fiber, fiber-related events and festivals, fiber-arts teachers, fiber-arts exhibitions and more. (Fiber arts include rugs, sculpture, sewing, basketry, quilting, weaving, spinning, and beadwork.)

Maine Maritime Heritage Trail
www.maritimemaine.org

Information about and links to maritime museums, boatbuilding schools, lighthouses, historic homes, fishing, naval history, forts, historic sites, and much more.

Music
www.mainemusic.org

Comprehensive site covering almost everything having to do with music in the state, from performances and festivals to musicians, composers, and instrument makers.

FOOD AND DRINK

Maine Brewers' Guild
www.drinkmainebeer.com

Find breweries and brewpubs statewide.

Maine Department of Agriculture
www.getrealmaine.com

Information on all things agricultural, including fairs, farmers markets, farm vacations, places to buy Maine foods, berry- and apple-picking sites, and more.

Maine Lobster Promotion Council
www.mainelobsterpromo.com
All lobster, all the time, with links for ordering Maine lobster and organizing your own lobster bake, plus recipes for preparing lobster in more ways than you ever thought possible.

Maine Restaurant Association
www.mainerestaurant.com
Statewide trade organization site provides searchable listings of member restaurants by name or location.

Wild Blueberry Association of North America
www.wildblueberries.com
Information on blueberries as well as numerous recipes.

GENERAL INFORMATION

Maine Emergency Management Association
www.state.me.us/mema/weather/weather.htm
Five-day weather forecasts broken down by 32 zones.

Maine Information
www.maine.info
A privately operated site with a mother lode of links handy for vacation planners.

Maine Office of Tourism
www.visitmaine.com
The state's official tourism site is the biggest and most useful and comprehensive of all Maine-related tourism sites, with sections for where to visit, where to stay, things to do, trip planning, packages, calendar of events, and search capabilities. Also lodging specials and a comprehensive calendar of events. See links to the Downeast and Acadia Region.

Maine Tourism Association
www.mainetourism.com
A private organization funded by the state that serves as an information clearinghouse. Find lodging, camping, restaurants, attractions, services, and more as well as links for weather, foliage, transportation planning, and chambers of commerce.

Island Institute
www.islandinstitute.org
The institute serves as a clearinghouse/advocate for Maine's islands; the website provides links to the major year-round islands.

State of Maine
www.maine.gov
Everything you wanted to know about Maine and then some, with links to all government departments and Maine-related sites. Buy a fishing license online, reserve a campsite at Lamoine State Park (near Acadia), or check the fall-foliage conditions via the site's Leaf-Cam. (You can also access foliage info at www.mainefoliage.com, where you can sign up for weekly email foliage reports in September and early October.) Also listed is information on accessible arts and recreation.

PARKS AND RECREATION

Bicycle Coalition of Maine
www.bikemaine.org
Tons of information for bicyclists including routes, shops, events, organized rides, and much more.

Department of Conservation, Maine Bureau of Parks and Lands
www.maine.gov/doc/parks
Information on state parks, public reserved lands, and state historic sites, details on facilities such as campsites, picnic areas, and boat launches. Make state campground reservations online.

Golf Maine
www.golfme.com
Lists member courses, stay-and-play packages, and golf links statewide.

Healthy Maine Walks
www.healthymainewalks.com
Lists places for walking statewide.

Maine Association of Sea Kayaking
Guides & Instructors
www.maineseakayakguides.com
Information and links to about two dozen members who meet state requirements to lead commercial trips.

Maine Audubon
www.maineaudubon.org
Information about Maine Audubon's environmental centers statewide. Activity and program schedules are included.

Maine Birding
www.mainebirding.net
A must-visit site for anyone interested in learning more about birding in Maine, includes news, checklists, events, forums, trips, and more.

Maine Island Trail Association
www.mita.org
The mission and activities of MITA, as well as information on becoming a member and receiving the annual guidebook to the island trail.

Maine Land Trust Network
www.mltn.org
Maine has dozens of land trusts statewide managing lands that provide opportunities for hiking, walking, canoeing, kayaking, and other such activities.

Maine Professional Guides
Association
www.maineguides.org
Find licensed and Registered Maine Guides for sporting adventures, including sea kayaking, hunting, fishing, and recreation (such as canoeing trips and wildlife safaris).

The Nature Conservancy
www.nature.org/wherewework/
northamerica/states/maine/
Information about Maine preserves, field trips, and events.

REGIONAL INFORMATION

Bar Harbor Chamber of Commerce
www.BarHarborMaine.com
Access to information about Mount Desert Island's major town. In addition to its helpful website, with lodging links, its annual visitor booklet is published earlier than most, allowing trip planning to begin in January.

Deer Isle – Stonington
Chamber of Commerce
www.deerislemaine.com
Where to sleep and eat on Deer Isle, en route to Acadia National Park on Isle au Haut.

DownEast & Acadia Regional Tourism
www.downeastacadia.com
Information about the region from Bucksport through Calais.

Schoodic Peninsula
Chamber of Commerce
www.acadia-schoodic.org
Where to sleep and eat in Eastern Hancock County near Acadia National Park's Schoodic Peninsula section.

Southwest Harbor/Tremont
Chamber of Commerce
www.acadiachamber.com
Visitor information (including accommodations, restaurants, activities, shops) for the southwest corner of Mount Desert Island. The chamber's visitor booklet is especially informative, and the chamber has a free map of hiking trails on the west side of Mount Desert.

SHOPPING

Maine Antiquarian Booksellers Association
www.mainebooksellers.org
Lists independent shops that specialize in used, antiquarian, and rare books.

Maine Antiques Dealers Association
www.maineantiques.org
Lists member dealers statewide by location and specialty and provides information on upcoming antiques events.

TRANSPORTATION

Bay Ferries
www.catferry.com
Schedule and fare information for the passenger-and-car high-speed catamaran ferry operating daily mid-May–mid-October between Bar Harbor and Yarmouth, Nova Scotia (and Portland and Yarmouth, Nova Scotia).

Downeast Windjammers
www.downeastwindjammer.com
More (and less) than what the name sounds like, this site has information on the windjammer schooner *Margaret Todd,* sailing out of Bar Harbor, as well as ferry services to the Schoodic Peninsula (also www.barharborferry.com) and the Cranberry Isles.

Explore Maine
www.exploremaine.org
Explore Maine is an invaluable site for trip planning, with information on and links to airports, rail service, bus service, automobile travel, and ferries, as well as links to other key travel-planning sites.

Isle au Haut Ferry
www.isleauhaut.com
Schedule and fare information for year-round ferry service from Stonington (on Deer Isle) to Isle au Haut.

Maine Department of Transportation
www.511maine.gov
Site provides real-time information about major delays, accidents, road construction, and weather conditions. You can get the same info and more by dialing 511 in-state.

Maine State Ferry Service
www.state.me.us/mdot/opt/ferry/ferry.htm
Schedule and fare information for ferries to offshore islands, including Swan's and Frenchboro; regular updates for cancellations and changes.

Glossary

alewives herring
ayuh yes
barrens as in "blueberry barrens"; fields where wild blueberries grow
beamy wide (as in a boat or a person)
beans shorthand for the traditional Saturday-night meal, which always includes baked beans
blowdown a forest area leveled by wind
blowing a gale very windy
camp a vacation house (small or large), usually on freshwater and/or in the woods

chance serendipity or luck (as in "open by appointment or by chance")
chicken dressing chicken manure
chowder (pronounced "chowdah") soup made with lobster, clams, or fish, or a combination thereof; lobster version sometimes called lobster stew
chowderhead mischief- or troublemakers, usually interchangeable with idiot
coneheads tourists (because of their presumed penchant for ice cream)
cottage a vacation house (anything from a

bungalow to a mansion), usually on saltwater

culch (also cultch) "stuff"; the contents of attics, basements, and some flea markets

cull a discount lobster, usually minus a claw

cunnin' cute (usually describing a baby or small child)

dinner (pronounced "dinnah") the noon meal

dinner pail lunchbox

dite a very small amount

dooryard the yard near a house's main entrance

downcellar in the basement

Down East with the prevailing wind; the old coastal sailing route from Boston to Nova Scotia

dry-ki driftwood, usually remnants from the logging industry

ell a residential structural section that links a house and a barn; formerly a popular location for the "summer kitchen," to spare the house from woodstove heat

exercised upset; angry

fiddleheads unopened ostrich-fern fronds, a spring delicacy

finest kind top quality; good news; an expression of general approval; also, a term of appreciation

flatlander a person not from Maine, often but not exclusively someone from the Midwest

floatplane a small plane equipped with pontoons for landing on water; the same aircraft often becomes a skiplane in winter

flowage a water body created by damming, usually beaver handiwork (also called "beaver flowage")

frappe a thick drink containing milk, ice cream, and flavored syrup, as opposed to a milk shake, which does not include ice cream (but beware: a frappe offered in other parts of the United States is an ice-cream sundae topped with whipped cream!)

from away not native to Maine

galamander a wheeled contraption formerly used to transport quarry granite to building sites or to boats for onward shipment

gore a sliver of land left over from inaccurate boundary surveys. Maine has several gores; Hibberts Gore, for instance, has a population of one.

got done quit a job; was let go

harbormaster local official who monitors water traffic and assigns moorings; often a very political job

hardshell lobster that hasn't molted yet (more scarce, thus more pricey in summer)

hod wooden "basket" used for carrying clams

ice-out the departure of winter ice from ponds, lakes, rivers, and streams; many communities have ice-out contests, awarding prizes for guessing the exact time of ice-out, in April or May

Italian long soft bread roll sliced on top and filled with peppers, onions, tomatoes, sliced meat, black olives, and sprinkled with olive oil, salt, and pepper; veggie versions available

jimmies chocolate sprinkles, like those on an ice cream cone

lobster car a large floating crate for storing lobsters

Maine Guide a member of the Maine Professional Guides Association, trained and tested for outdoor and survival skills; also called Registered Maine Guide

market price restaurant menu term for "the going rate," usually referring to the price of lobster or clams

molt what a lobster does when it sheds its shell for a larger one; the act of molting is called ecdysis (as a stripper is an ecdysiast)

money tree a collection device for a monetary gift

mud season mid-March to mid-April, when back roads and unpaved driveways become virtual tank traps

nasty neat extremely meticulous

near stingy

notional stubborn, determined

off island the mainland, to an islander

place another word for a house (as in "Herb Pendleton's place")

pot trap, as in "lobster pot"

public landing see "town landing"

rake hand tool used for harvesting blueberries

rusticator a summer visitor, particularly in bygone days

scooch (or scootch) to squat; to move sideways

sea smoke heavy mist rising off the water when the air temperature suddenly becomes much colder than the ocean temperature

select a lobster with claws intact

Selectmen the elected men and women who handle local affairs in small communities; the First Selectman chairs meetings. In some towns, "people from away" have tried to propose substituting a gender-neutral term, but in most cases the effort has failed.

shedder a lobster with a new (soft) shell; generally occurs in July and August (more common then, thus less expensive than hardshells)

shire town county seat

shore dinner the works: chowder, clams, lobster, and sometimes corn-on-the-cob, too; usually the most expensive item on a menu

short a small, illegal-size lobster

slumgullion tasteless food; a mess

snapper an undersize, illegal lobster

soda cola, root beer, etc. (often referred to as "pop" in other parts of the country

softshell see "shedder"

some very (as in "some hot")

spleeny overly sensitive

steamers clams (before or after they are steamed)

sternman a lobsterman's helper (male or female)

summer complaint a tourist

supper (pronounced "suppah") evening meal, eaten by Mainers around 5 or 6 P.M. (as opposed to flatlanders and summer people, who eat dinner between 7 and 9 P.M.)

tad slightly; a little bit

thick-o'-fog zero-visibility fog

to home at home

tomalley a lobster's green insides; considered a delicacy by some

town landing shore access; often a park or a parking lot, next to a wharf or boat-launch ramp

upattic in the attic

Whoopie! Pie the trademarked name for a high-fat, calorie-laden, cakelike snack that only kids and dentists could love

wicked cold! frigid

wicked good! excellent

williwaws uncomfortable feeling

Index

CRUISES AND BOAT EXCURSIONS

GARDENS, PARKS, AND PRESERVES

HIKING

LIGHTHOUSES

MUSEUMS AND HISTORIC HOUSES

Acknowledgments

For Tom

The only way to compile all the tidbits of information required for a guidebook is to be everywhere at once, which is physically impossible. While I spent the better part of my spring, summer, and fall in the Acadia region researching every aspect of this book, it seemed no sooner did I leave the Blue Hill peninsula for Mount Desert Island, than something changed. Restaurants open and close. Outfitters change their offerings. B&Bs are sold. New trails are cut; old ones rerouted. Museums expand. Hotels renovate. And on it goes. Which all goes to say, I couldn't have done this without the help of many people who served as additional eyes and ears.

I'll start with Kathleen Brandes, who wrote the first edition of this book and whose friendship I valued and whose work and dedication I respected long before I began working on this edition. My appreciation for her extensive research, her ability to capture a place or a person with a quick turn of phrase, or her dead-on accuracy has no bounds.

Big thank-yous, too, to those who sat down with me and shared local info, sheltered me along the way, fed me, helped with arrangements, verified information, called me with updates, or simply encouraged me: Wanda Moran, Fred Cook, Risteen Masters, Anne Beerits, Barbara Maurer, Jeff and Judi Burke, Bill Baker, Sally and Jim Littlefield, Dom and Joanne Parisi, Costas Christ, Gena Farnsworth, Sharon Broom, Tom Minutolo, Michael Good, Jeff and Terri Anderholm, Megan Moshier, Ben and Sonja Walter-Sundaram, Roy Kasindorf and Helene Harton, Anne Bradford, Stephanie Seacord, Mary and Don Hartley, Jack Burke, Julie Van de Graaf, Charlene Williams, Rose Whitehorse, and the rest of the gang at Nancy Marshall Communications. I couldn't have done this without all your help and support.

More thank-yous are due to the folks at Avalon Travel Publishing who shepherded me through the process: Bill Newlin, Rebecca Browning, Kevin McLain, Jane Musser, Elizabeth Jang, Amber Pirker, Kemi Oyesiku, and especially my editor, Sabrina Young. Also, thank you to the many other behind-the-scenes Avalon staffers who worked on this book, and more thanks to those who are promoting it, especially Leslie Walters and Hannah Cox.

I save my biggest thanks for my husband, Tom, who drove me everywhere and didn't complain (too much) when I made him backtrack two or three times along the same stretch of road, while seeking an elusive address; who waited patiently while I visited practically every restaurant, inn, and B&B in the Acadia region; who let me order for him in restaurants; who tackled research projects; and who supported me in every way possible throughout the entire process—all while shooting photographs for the book. I couldn't have done it without him.

And to you, dear reader, thank you for using this book to plan your visit to Acadia National Park.

www.moon.com

For helpful advice on planning a trip, visit www.moon.com for the **TRAVEL PLANNER** and get access to useful travel strategies and valuable information about great places to visit. When you travel with Moon, expect an experience that is uncommon and truly unique.

MAP SYMBOLS

▦▦▦ Expressway	【 Highlight	✗ Airfield	⚲ Golf Course
▦▦▦ Primary Road	○ City/Town	✗ Airport	ℙ Parking Area
▦▦▦ Secondary Road	◉ State Capital	▲ Mountain	▰ Archaeological Site
▪ ▪ ▪ Unpaved Road	⊛ National Capital	✛ Unique Natural Feature	♦ Church
- - - - Trail	★ Point of Interest		⛽ Gas Station
⋯⋯ Ferry	● Accommodation	⑂ Waterfall	◉ Glacier
┼─┼─ Railroad	▼ Restaurant/Bar	▲ Park	Mangrove
▨▨ Pedestrian Walkway	■ Other Location	▣ Trailhead	Reef
▢▢▢ Stairs	Λ Campground	⛷ Skiing Area	Swamp

CONVERSION TABLES

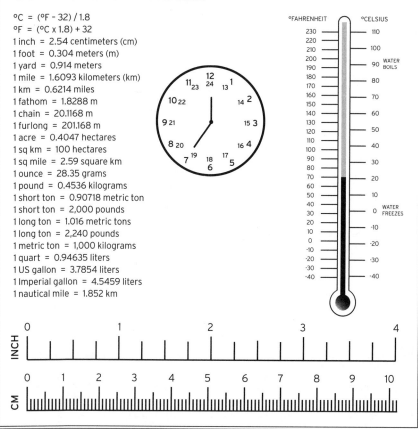

°C = (°F - 32) / 1.8
°F = (°C x 1.8) + 32
1 inch = 2.54 centimeters (cm)
1 foot = 0.304 meters (m)
1 yard = 0.914 meters
1 mile = 1.6093 kilometers (km)
1 km = 0.6214 miles
1 fathom = 1.8288 m
1 chain = 20.1168 m
1 furlong = 201.168 m
1 acre = 0.4047 hectares
1 sq km = 100 hectares
1 sq mile = 2.59 square km
1 ounce = 28.35 grams
1 pound = 0.4536 kilograms
1 short ton = 0.90718 metric ton
1 short ton = 2,000 pounds
1 long ton = 1.016 metric tons
1 long ton = 2,240 pounds
1 metric ton = 1,000 kilograms
1 quart = 0.94635 liters
1 US gallon = 3.7854 liters
1 Imperial gallon = 4.5459 liters
1 nautical mile = 1.852 km

MOON ACADIA NATIONAL PARK

AVALON
publishing group incorporated

Avalon Travel Publishing
An Imprint of
Avalon Publishing Group, Inc.

1400 65th Street, Suite 250
Emeryville, CA 94608, USA
www.moon.com

Editors: Sabrina Young, Cinnamon Hearst
Series Manager: Kathryn Ettinger
Acquisitions Manager: Rebecca K. Browning
Copy Editor: Valerie Sellers Blanton
Graphics Coordinator: Elizabeth Jang
Production Coordinator: Elizabeth Jang
Cover & Interior Designer: Gerilyn Attebery
Map Editor: Kat Smith
Cartographers: Landis Bennett, Kat Bennett
Cartography Manager: Mike Morgenfeld
Indexer: Greg Jewett

ISBN-10: 1-56691-925-8
ISBN-13: 978-1-56691-925-8
ISSN: 1546-8062

Printing History
1st Edition – 2004
2nd Edition – May 2006
5 4 3 2 1

KEEPING CURRENT

If you have a favorite gem you'd like to see included in the next edition, or see anything that needs updating, clarification, or correction, please drop us a line. Send your comments via email to feedback@moon.com, or use the address above.